Senior Care and Services

Senior Care and Services

Essays and Case Studies on Practices, Innovations and Challenges

Edited by JOAQUIN JAY GONZALEZ III,
ROGER L. KEMP *and* WILLIE LEE BRITT

McFarland & Company, Inc., Publishers
Jefferson, North Carolina

ALSO OF INTEREST AND FROM MCFARLAND

Veteran Care and Services: Essays and Case Studies on Practices, Innovations and Challenges, edited by Joaquin Jay Gonzalez III, Mickey P. McGee and Roger L. Kemp (2020) • *Cities and Homelessness: Essays and Case Studies on Practices, Innovations and Challenges,* edited by Joaquin Jay Gonzalez III and Mickey P. McGee (2020) • *Legal Marijuana: Perspectives on Public Benefits, Risks and Policy Approaches,* edited by Joaquin Jay Gonzalez III and Mickey P. McGee (2019) • *Cybersecurity: Current Writings on Threats and Protection,* edited by Joaquin Jay Gonzalez III and Roger L. Kemp (2019) • *Eminent Domain and Economic Growth: Perspectives on Benefits, Harms and New Trends,* edited by Joaquin Jay Gonzalez III, Roger L. Kemp and Jonathan Rosenthal (2018) • *Small Town Economic Development: Reports on Growth Strategies in Practice,* edited by Joaquin Jay Gonzalez III, Roger L. Kemp and Jonathan Rosenthal (2017) • *Privatization in Practice: Reports on Trends, Cases and Debates in Public Service by Business and Nonprofits,* edited by Joaquin Jay Gonzalez III and Roger L. Kemp (2016) • *Immigration and America's Cities: A Handbook on Evolving Services,* edited by Joaquin Jay Gonzalez III and Roger L. Kemp (2016) • *Corruption and American Cities: Essays and Case Studies in Ethical Accountability,* edited by Joaquin Jay Gonzalez III and Roger L. Kemp (2016)

LIBRARY OF CONGRESS CATALOGUING-IN-PUBLICATION DATA

Names: Gonzalez, Joaquin Jay, III, editor. | Kemp, Roger L., editor. | Britt, Willie Lee, 1953– editor.
Title: Senior care and services : essays and case studies on practices, innovations and challenges / edited by Joaquin Jay Gonzalez III, Roger L. Kemp and Willie Lee Britt.
Description: Jefferson : McFarland & Company, Inc., Publishers, 2020. | Includes bibliographical references and index.
Identifiers: LCCN 2020012183 | ISBN 9781476673271 (paperback : acid free paper) ∞
ISBN 9781476638829 (ebook)
Subjects: LCSH: Older people—Care—United States. | Older people—Services for—United States. | Social work with older sexual minorities—United States.
Classification: LCC HV1461 .S456 2020 | DDC 362.60973—dc23
LC record available at https://lccn.loc.gov/2020012183

BRITISH LIBRARY CATALOGUING DATA ARE AVAILABLE

ISBN (print) 978-1-4766-7327-1
ISBN (ebook) 978-1-4766-3882-9

Front cover images © 2020 Shutterstock

Printed in the United States of America

McFarland & Company, Inc., Publishers
Box 611, Jefferson, North Carolina 28640
www.mcfarlandpub.com

Jay dedicates this book to the Pilipino Senior Resource Center,
San Francisco, California

—— ✦✦✦ ——

Roger dedicates this book to his granddaughter, Anika,
the best and the brightest

—— ✦✦✦ ——

Willie dedicates this book to Gilma, Brian, and Michael

—— ✦✦✦ ——

Jay, Roger, and Willie also dedicate this book
to the late Dr. Paul Mico

Acknowledgments

We are grateful for the support of the Mayor George Christopher Professorship at Golden Gate University and GGU's Pi Alpha Alpha Chapter. We appreciate the encouragement from Dean Gordon Swartz and our wonderful colleagues at the Edward S. Ageno School of Business, the Department of Public Administration, and the Executive MPA Program.

Our heartfelt "Thanks!" goes to the contributors listed in the back section and the individuals, organizations, and publishers below for granting permission to reprint the material in this volume and the research assistance. They all expressed support for practical research and information sharing that benefits our citizens, communities, and cities.

AARP Public Policy Institute
Administration for Community Living
Alan R. Roper
American Society for Public Administration
Benefits.gov
Claire M. Rygg
Coral H. Gonzalez
DeKalb County (Georgia) Office of Aging
Elisha Harig-Blaine
Flora G. Becket
Gabby V. Moraleda
Golden Gate University Library
Idelfonso "Tatang Floro" Bagasala
International City/County Management Association
Irina Reykhel
Jeanine R. Kelada
Kaiser Health News
Karen Garrett
Lichao Zhang
Makati Chiropractic Center
Medicare.gov
Michelle Hong-Gonzalez

Mickey P. McGee
National Institute on Aging
National Institute on Health
National League of Cities
National Science Technology Council's Committee on Technology
PA Times
Pilipino Senior Resource Center
PM Magazine
Rachel L. Fontenot
Ruth Astle Samas
San Francisco Department of Aging and Adult Services
San Francisco Human Services Agency
State of Washington
theconversation.com
U.S. Census Bureau
U.S. Consumer Financial Protection Bureau
U.S. Department of Veteran Affairs
University of San Francisco Library
White House Conference on Aging
Yueqing (Queenie) Lin

Table of Contents

Acknowledgments   vi

Preface   1

Part I. Introduction
A. *Our Seniors and Our Cities*

1. Who Knew? Life Begins (Again) at 65
   BRUCE HOROVITZ   7

2. Three Ways Cities Can Navigate the "Silver Tsunami"
   ELISHA HARIG-BLAINE   10

3. Aging in Place and Smart Growth
   INTERNATIONAL CITY/COUNTY MANAGEMENT ASSOCIATION   13

4. DeKalb County, Georgia, Senior Services
   DEKALB COUNTY OFFICE OF AGING   19

5. City and County of San Francisco's Aging and Adult Services
   SAN FRANCISCO DEPARTMENT OF AGING AND ADULT SERVICES   29

6. Empowerment of the Aging: Policies and Programs in Local
   California Communities
   FLORA G. BECKET *and* WILLIE LEE BRITT   33

B. *Seniors and the U.S. Government*

7. Older Americans Act and Timeline of Programs for Older Americans
   ADMINISTRATION FOR COMMUNITY LIVING   39

8. U.S. Healthcare: From the 19th Century to the Affordable Care Act
   WILLIE LEE BRITT   45

9. Navigating Benefits.gov User Series: Senior Citizens
   BENEFITS.GOV   51

10. The White House Conference on Aging
    WHITE HOUSE CONFERENCE ON AGING   54

11. The Elder Justice Act
    ADMINISTRATION FOR COMMUNITY LIVING   57

Part II. Services, Innovations and Challenges

A. Health and Wellness

12. Seniors and Health Care and Service: My Administrator's Perspective
    WILLIE LEE BRITT   63

13. Breaking Through the Noise: The Facts About the Medicaid Program
    BRENDAN FLINN *and* JEAN ACCIUS   70

14. Getting Started with Medicare
    MEDICARE.GOV   74

15. Why Older Adults Should Eat More Protein (And Not Overdo
    Protein Shakes)
    JUDITH GRAHAM   77

16. Before the Fall: How Oldsters Can Avoid One of Old Age's Most
    Dangerous Events
    MATTHEW LEE SMITH, ELLEN SCHNEIDER, MARCIA G. ORY
    and TIFFANY SHUBERT   80

17. Making Smarter Decisions About Where to Recover After
    Hospitalization
    JUDITH GRAHAM   83

18. End-of-Life Planning
    JEANINE R. KELADA *and* WILLIE LEE BRITT   87

19. No Cure for Alzheimer's Disease in My Lifetime
    NORMAN A. PARADIS   96

20. Guidelines Proposed for Newly Defined Alzheimer's-Like
    Brain Disorder
    NATIONAL INSTITUTE ON AGING   99

B. Longevity

21. As Life Expectancies Rise, So Are Expectations for Healthy Aging
    MARCIA G. ORY, BASIA BELZA *and* MATTHEW LEE SMITH   102

22. Research Shows Old Age Is Getting Younger All the Time
    WARREN SANDERSON *and* SERGEI SCHERBOV   105

23. It's Time to Measure 21st Century Aging with 21st Century Tools
    WARREN SANDERSON *and* SERGEI SCHERBOV   108

24. Patients Experiment with Prescription Drugs to Fight Aging
    MARISA TAYLOR   111

25. A "Fountain of Youth" Pill? Sure, if You're a Mouse
    MARISA TAYLOR   114

C. Caregiving

26. Strengthening the National Family Caregiver Support Program:
    The Time Has Come
    LYNN FRISS FEINBERG   120

27. Frail Seniors Find Ways to Live Independently
    JUDITH GRAHAM   123

28. Seniors Helping Seniors: Maximizing Potentials
    SUNDAY AKIN OLUKOJU   126

29. A Critical Examination of Long-Term Care in the San Francisco
    Bay Area
    IRINA REYKHEL *and* WILLIE LEE BRITT   128

30. Without Safety Net of Kids or Spouse, "Elder Orphans" Need Fearless
    Fallback Plan
    JUDITH GRAHAM   132

31. Understanding Loneliness in Older Adults—And Tailoring a Solution
    JUDITH GRAHAM   135

32. Social Isolation, Loneliness in Older People Pose Health Risks
    NATIONAL INSTITUTE ON AGING   139

D. Housing and Accommodations

33. Housing Policy Solutions to Support Aging with Options
    SHANNON GUZMAN, JANET VIVEIROS *and* EMILY SALOMON   144

34. The Need for Safe and Healthy Homes in Order to Age in Place
    RACHEL L. FONTENOT *and* WILLIE LEE BRITT   152

35. Engaging Nonprofit Sector Institutions for Housing Seniors
    JOSHUA ODETUNDE   158

36. Advancing Independence, Integration and Inclusion Throughout Life
    ADMINISTRATION FOR COMMUNITY LIVING   161

37. Accessibility Solutions for Colton Hall
    CLAIRE M. RYGG *and* WILLIE LEE BRITT   164

38. Township Taps Former Mayor for Age-Friendly Initiative
    INTERNATIONAL CITY/COUNTY MANAGEMENT ASSOCIATION   169

39. Seniors and the California Courts
    RUTH ASTLE SAMAS   172

E. Social Security and Finance

40. Social Security: Who's Counting on It?
    ALISON SHELTON   180

41. Five Things to Consider Before You Collect Your Social Security Benefits
    STACY CANAN *and* HECTOR ORTIZ   184

42. Top 11 Elder Scams
   U.S. Consumer Financial Protection Bureau   186

43. Guaranteed Returns in Retirement Savings Plans: Are They Worth
   the Cost?
   William G. Gale   190

44. Seven Ways to Keep Medical Debt in Check
   Gail Hillebrand   194

45. Consumer Advisory: Don't Be Misled by Reverse Mortgage Advertising
   Nora Dowd Eisenhower   196

46. Four Things Older Americans Can Do About Debt Collection Problems
   Nora Dowd Eisenhower   198

F. Immigrants, Minorities and LGBTQ+

47. Kimochi: Japanese Self-Help for the Elderly
   Paul Mico and Willie Lee Britt   200

48. The Pilipino Senior Resource Center, a Glimpse of Our Very Essence
   Gabby V. Moraleda   204

49. Advocacy for Aging World War II Immigrant Veterans
   Joaquin Jay Gonzalez III   208

50. San Francisco and Older Adult LGBTQ Population
   San Francisco Human Services Agency   215

G. Intergenerational Lifelong Learning and Technology

51. The Intergenerational Imperative
   Irv Katz   218

52. Intergenerational Outreach
   Yueqing (Queenie) Lin   223

53. Belichick Versus McVay: An Age-Old Question of Leadership
   Megan Gerhardt   226

54. Seniors and Lifelong Learning
   Alan R. Roper   229

55. Participating in the Arts Creates Paths to Healthy Aging
   National Institute on Aging   234

56. Public Service Delivery for Aging Populations: Using Social Media
   to Support Seniors
   Jeffrey Zimmerman   238

57. The Use of Social Media Platforms to Support Seniors
   Andrew Vaz   240

58. Emerging Technologies to Support an Aging Population
    TASK FORCE ON RESEARCH AND DEVELOPMENT FOR TECHNOLOGY
    TO SUPPORT AGING ADULTS 242

Part III. The Future

59. Keep Age Out of It: Ageism Has No Place in Hiring Practices
    ROBERT SHAPIRO 249

60. Seniors Increasingly Getting High, Study Shows
    CARMEN HEREDIA RODRIGUEZ 253

61. Day-Tripping to the Dispensary: Seniors in Pain Hop Aboard
    the Canna-Bus
    STEPHANIE O'NEILL 255

62. Lethal Plans: When Seniors Turn to Suicide in Long-Term Care
    MELISSA BAILEY *and* JONEL ALECCIA 258

63. Does a Year in Space Make You Older or Younger?
    SUSAN BAILEY 265

64. NASA Twins Study Reveals Health Effects of Space Flight
    NATIONAL INSTITUTE ON AGING 268

65. State Revenues and the Aging Population
    KATHERINE BARRETT *and* RICHARD GREENE 271

Appendices

Appendix A: Glossary of Senior Care and Services
    ALAN R. ROPER 275

Appendix B: Older Americans Month: Profile America Facts for Features
    U.S. CENSUS BUREAU 284

Appendix C: Senior Citizens Services Act
    STATE OF WASHINGTON: CHAPTER 74.38 RCW 288

About the Contributors 295

Index 299

Preface

There is no turning back time. Healthier lifestyles and improving urban living conditions continue to increase life expectancies. Hence, the number of seniors is surging at an unprecedented rate. By 2030, all members of the baby boomer generation will be older than age 65. This will expand the size of the older population so that one in every five Americans will be retirement age. By 2035, there will be 78.0 million people 65 years and older compared to 76.7 million under the age of 18. Seniors will outnumber the youth.

How have citizens and cities been preparing for this "silver tsunami"? Are preparations sufficient? What are the challenges of caring for our aging Depression era and baby boomer generations? Are our urban streets, residences, businesses, transportation system, public facilities and infrastructure designed and built with their mobility, safety, comfort, and accessibility in mind? How are Generations X, Y (Millennials) and Z stepping up to care for the generations that raised and nurtured them? What about elderly minorities and aging LGBTQ+ community members?

These questions and many more are the subject of this cutting-edge compilation of essays detailing current practices, innovations, and challenges. We underscore the fact that many of the innovative best practices are driven not just by governments but also nonprofit and for-profit organizations. Government budgets are not always sufficient, so creative collaborative partnerships between and among them is the norm. Cities and municipalities are also more cost-effective and responsive when they contract out to experienced service delivery providers. And with less of their direct involvement required, federal, state, and regional governments have shifted to sharing lessons learned, guidance, coordination, and financing from their "big picture" vantage point.

Senior Care and Services brings together the thoughts and experiences of a mix of experts—academics, researchers, advocates, journalists, social workers, healthcare professionals, urban planners, city officials, and federal agencies. Their contributions are sharp and substantive but easy to read so citizens will be able to use the practical knowledge they gain to immediately engage their leaders and make smart suggestions.

The book is divided into four parts.

Part I: Introduction

Part I is an essential overview of senior care and services. Section A, "Our Seniors and Our Cities," is a cluster of six chapters that: revisit the definition of "senior citizen"; detail the services to our senior citizens under the program titled Silver Tsunami; demonstrate how Smart Growth has helped the aging population; elaborate on aging services in DeKalb County, Georgia; and elucidate on how a couple of San Francisco Bay Area cities are dealing with this issue.

Section B, "Seniors and the U. S. Government," is comprised of five chapters that describe how our national government agencies mandate senior programs and services to our nation's aging population. In 1965, the Older Americans Act was passed in response to concerns about the lack of community social services for older persons. Thereafter, the various healthcare policies are reviewed all the way to the Affordable Care Act. This chapter is followed by a description of the roles of the various national agencies from the Social Security Administration to the Department of Treasury. The final two chapters examine the White House Conference on Aging and the 2010 Elder Justice Act—the first comprehensive federal legislation to address the abuse, neglect, and exploitation of older adults.

Part II: Services, Innovations and Challenges

The 47 chapters in Part II are the centerpieces of this volume. They are stacked as essential sections on health and wellness; longevity; caregiving; housing and accommodations; social security and finance; immigrants, minorities, and LGBTQ+; and lastly, intergenerational lifelong learning and technology.

The first section, "Health and Wellness," offers nine chapters dealing with senior citizens and available healthcare services, including such services as provided by Medicaid and Medicare programs. Also examined are senior citizen dietary guidelines and suggestions and information on how senior citizens can quickly recover after a hospital visit. This section also includes information on end-of-life planning and what services senior citizens throughout our nation can use to combat Alzheimer's disease.

"Longevity," Section B, provides examples of health care and medical services that are provided to our nation's senior citizens. Such topics as increasing life expectancy, fighting aging, and a review of innovative healthcare services and drugs that senior citizens should be aware of to help them maintain a good quality-of-life in their old age are highlighted.

Section C, "Caregiving," elaborates on the characteristics of national family caregiver health care support programs, highlights ways that senior citizens can help other senior citizens in their aging and examines long-term health care options for senior citizens. Various social-service related programs, such as understanding loneliness, aging issues, social isolation, and other common issues, are also reviewed.

The next section, "Housing and Accommodations," shows housing, residential care and service options that are available. It also includes discussions on how to create age-friendly cities which increase accessibility, mobility, inclusion, independence, and accommodate the needs of the elderly even in the courts.

"Social Security and Finance," Section E, contributes insights into such topics as the healthcare services provided to senior citizens by our Social Security program, ways to reduce senior citizen healthcare costs, how to deal with senior scams, and how to reduce outstanding medical expenses for our aging population. Also discussed are financial, retirement, and legal options to help our aging populations better manage their outstanding healthcare and living expenses, mortgage, and debt.

"Immigrants, Minorities and LGBTQ+," Section F, is about the challenges and innovative practices of aging care and services for new immigrants and people of color as well as LGBTQ+ community members.

Section G, "Intergenerational Lifelong Learning and Technology," demonstrates contemporary issues relating to the provision of aging care and services to our senior citizen population, important legal decisions on healthcare services, and even discusses the possibilities of using the arts, social media, lifelong learning, and technology applications for our aging population.

Part III: The Future

In closing the main body of the book, Part III predicts some emerging trends and challenges relating to their care and needs including: age-discrimination as more and more seniors continue to work and seek employment beyond the normal retirement age; increasing use of marijuana and other substances to alleviate mental and physical concerns; turning to suicide; effects of space flight; and the continuing financial support needed from state governments.

Appendices

The three appendices offer essential definitions and documents related to the field of senior care and services. Since the study of aging citizens is a very specialized field, an extensive glossary is provided on various terms and acronyms significant for the readers. A U.S. Census Older Americans Month fact sheet tracks the demographic facts and figures of our nation's senior citizen population. The last appendix is a review of the State of Washington's Senior Citizens Services Act.

We hope that you have a "good read" on these important and timely topics. We also hope that you will use the knowledge contained in *Senior Care and Services* to help improve the quality of care, services, and support that are being provided to our senior citizens and their caregivers in cities and states throughout our nation.

We appreciate the opportunity to gather a wealth of voices and experiences in this field and present the best practices for senior citizens by various public and nonprofit organizations throughout our nation to the providers and users of these services. It is an honor for us to serve our nation's senior citizen population, as well as the public officials and citizens that work in nonprofit and public and private organizations that provide these services to our growing senior citizen population, as well as to their families and caregivers.

PART I

Introduction

1. Who Knew?*

Life Begins (Again) at 65

BRUCE HOROVITZ

I was convinced I would become an adult when I turned 21. But now, I'm certain that turning 65 was the watershed moment that finally grew me up.

I'm pleased as pomegranate punch to be 65—and alive. Not just alive and breathing, but actively engaged in making the right choices about this next chapter.

"We enter this phase of life without a playbook or anything equivalent to institutions like elementary school and college that prepare youth for adulthood," said James Firman, CEO of the National Council on Aging, who turned 65 two years ago. "There's really nothing to prepare us for the transition to this next phase of life."

My playbook on preparing for life after 65:

- Consider enrolling in Medicare Part A, to cover hospitalization expenses. It works for me because my family is still covered under my wife's healthcare plan.
- Double up on checkups. My annual visit to my primary care doctor evolved into a biannual visit. "Age 65 is a time to proactively visit a geriatric physician instead of just going when you're in trouble," said Dr. Ardeshir Hashmi, director of the Center for Geriatric Medicine at Cleveland Clinic. "Don't wait until things get to a point where you're in a cycle of being in and out of the hospital all the time." Starting at age 65, he said, these visits should last longer than the standard 20 minutes—so older patients have time to discuss what's on their minds. Older patients who do this regularly tend to require "minor tweaks" instead of major repairs, said Hashmi.
- Schedule annual visits to the dermatologist, ophthalmologist—and visits every five years to the gastroenterologist. "Establishing a coordinated care team becomes more important at 65," said Jean Setzfand, senior vice president of programs at AARP.

*Originally published as Bruce Horovitz, "Who Knew? Life Begins (Again) at 65," *Kaiser Health News*, https://khn.org/news/who-knew-life-begins-again-at-65/ (October 15, 2018). *Kaiser Health News* is a nonprofit news service covering health issues. It is an editorially independent program of the Kaiser Family Foundation that is not affiliated with Kaiser Permanente. KHN's coverage of these topics is supported by the John A. Hartford Foundation, the SCAN Foundation and the Silver Century Foundation.

- Take the leap and sign up for long-term health insurance. My wife and I finally did after putting it off for years. Remember, it's a lot easier—and cheaper—to get when you're younger than 65.
- Stick to a vaccine regimen. Vaccines are important again. I've since received my first pneumonia vaccine. My doctor also told me to get the new shingles vaccine, Shingrix, because I developed shingles about five years ago.
- Evaluate your diet. I have mostly stopped eating red meat, except for the very occasional burger. I now opt for meals mostly composed of fruit, veggies and my new diet staple that I used to gag on as a kid: salmon.
- Bone up on Social Security. I attended a free county-funded seminar at the local library. Then, to discuss my personal needs, I met (for free) with the same volunteer who led the seminar.
- Challenge your financial plan. I changed financial advisers—based on recommendations from trusted friends—because my portfolio really matters now.
- Serve your community. I bumped-up my volunteer schedule to once a week instead of once a month at a local food pantry. I also volunteer every other week at a local homeless shelter on the 5 p.m.-to-midnight shift. I've most recently started to volunteer at an equestrian therapy center for kids with mental or physical handicaps. Each of my volunteer gigs reflect my personal interests.
- Stay active. I extended my daily exercise routine from five days to seven. I now swim at least five days a week; take our dog, Shadow, for 45-minute walks twice daily; and hit the weight room at least twice weekly. I also play Wallyball (a fast-moving form of indoor volleyball where the walls are considered inbounds) every week with friends who are equally motivated to stay in shape.
- Stay flexible. I learned to stretch my back muscles an extra long time before beginning any strenuous exercise. When I forget, I inevitably pay for it.
- Look to the future. I initiated "adult," end-of-life conversations with my kids that I wish my parents had had with me.
- Get your paperwork in order. I not only updated my will but I filled out a "Five Wishes" end-of-life pamphlet created by the Aging with Dignity nonprofit group; and I got very specific, in writing, about where I want my ashes to be scattered.
- Stay connected—and not solely to devices. I stopped taking my friends for granted, banished past grudges and re-established contact with a best buddy from college whose friendship I'd foolishly let slip away.

Age 65 is when many of us realize that we're mortal. "This is when we start thinking about our next 20 to 30 years," said Hashmi. "It's when we ask: How can I be smart about investing my remaining decades wisely?"

Eric Tyson, author of *Personal Finance After 50 for Dummies*, theorizes that one of the most powerful undercurrents of turning 65 is how it affects the working lives of so many Americans. It's when the majority go from working full time to working less—or not working at all, he said. "The best scenario is when this change can unfold over many years instead of all at once."

It has for me. Things started changing at age 62, when I took a buyout from *USA*

Today, where I'd worked for 20-plus years as a marketing reporter. I'm now a freelance writer and media training consultant.

So, at 65, the one thing I've opted to put off for at least a few years is retiring. While 65 still remains the most common retirement age, more and more folks are breaking that tradition, said AARP's Setzfand.

Call it living with purpose.

Turning 65 is not just an extension of middle age. It's a new life chapter that's waiting to be written. "It's a new stage of life that reminds us we don't have forever," said Firman. About a decade ago, at age 56, Firman had a quintuple bypass operation. His father, grandfather and uncle all died of heart disease in their 40s and 50s.

Firman isn't distraught over the family genes he inherited. Instead, he's celebrating his survival. When he turned 65 two years ago, he said, he had a realization that the real purpose of aging is to make the world a better place. "Life is a gift," he said. "Success in old age starts with an attitude of gratitude."

It seems Firman and I share one common trait: We both grew up at 65.

2. Three Ways Cities Can Navigate the "Silver Tsunami"*

Elisha Harig-Blaine

The so-called "silver tsunami" has become a relatively well-known form of shorthand for the demographic fact that roughly 10,000 baby boomers turn 65 years old every day. This reality began in 2011 and will continue until 2030. For key lessons from an area with a large population of senior citizens, let's look at the area around Miami, Florida.

In the City of Miami Gardens, Navy veteran Gary Brown illustrates the need facing seniors and their communities. Mr. Brown served in the Navy during the Vietnam War as an engineer. Trained as an air-conditioning technician and electrician, he worked as a handyman and carpenter until he was forced to retire due to numerous disabilities including hip and knee problems that led to replacements, limited vision in his right eye and complete blindness in his left.

Brown's disabilities left him unable to maintain his home, resulting in substantive safety hazards. Most notably, the home's roof had been leaking since 1992, causing extensive interior damage. Thanks to the support and partnership of Rebuilding Together with the Home Depot Foundation and the Team Depot from a nearby store, Brown's home received a new roof, kitchen and bathroom renovations, plumbing repairs, new flooring, doors and drywall, as well as painting and landscaping.

With many seniors facing circumstances like Brown, how can cities more systematically ensure services are delivered in a coordinated and collaborative manner?

Use Data to Identify Gaps in Service

The primary funding that supports seniors comes due to the Older Americans Act through Area Agencies on Aging (AAAs). In Miami–Dade County, the AAA is the Alliance for Aging. Their work provides a "no wrong door" approach for seniors. To better understand what seniors needed, the Alliance not only held public hearings, but they surveyed front-line staff and looked at client assessments. It was recognized that a

---

*Originally published as Elisha Harig-Blaine, "Three Ways Cities Can Navigate the 'Silver Tsunami,'" https://citiesspeak.org/2016/07/21/3-ways-cities-can-navigate-the-silver-tsunami/#_ga=2.191197033. 29049585.1553888189-259213687.1553888189 (July 21, 2016).

quarter of elders reported "problems" with their home, and like Brown, more than half of these seniors identified issues related to major or minor repairs, including roofing or plumbing issues.

At the core of ensuring we meet the needs of seniors is access to safe and stable housing. Cities must be able to provide seniors with the ability to not just "age in place," but to "age in community." The installation of wheelchair ramps, grab-bars, the lowering of counters and cabinets, widening doorways and modifying bathrooms with roll-under sinks can help seniors stay in their homes, remain as independent as possible and avoid costly long-term care facilities.

Build and Support Partnerships That Reflect Your Community

To most effectively meet these housing needs of seniors, the area's leaders recognized the need to strategically cultivate relationships based on key population characteristics. For example, local leaders recognized that a significant number of veterans lived in the area, so they connected with the Veterans Affairs Medical Center around the VA's Veteran Directed Home and Community Based Services program. In addition, it was recognized that low-income seniors were over-represented in specific geographic areas.

To help reach these individuals, connections were made with community action agencies to help leverage resources such as the Low Income Home Energy Assistance Program, the Emergency Home Energy Assistance for the Elderly Program and the Supplemental Nutrition Assistance Program. Finally, the diversity of the community was reflected through partnerships with immigrant organizations and faith-based groups such as Catholic Charities and Jewish Community Services of South Florida. Through these partnerships, the AAA identified three groups to provide home modifications and/or repairs. The experience and histories of United Home Care, Little Havana Activities and Nutrition Centers, and 1st Quality Home Care uniquely reflect the area's population.

Understand and Document the Cost-Savings

In the ever-present reality of limited resources, it is critical for communities to work together so they can document the cost implications of their service coordination. Not only can this information be used to show the fiscal implications of program investments as a means of educating state and federal officials, the data can also be used as a way of exploring the potential of innovative financing mechanisms. Through its services alone, the Alliance for Aging reports the prevention of 50,359 months of nursing home care at a savings of about $201,435,168 and a rate of nursing home use per Medicaid eligible elder that is 33 percent lower than the state average.

By working with AAA to document these impacts, cities can better target their resources to ensure they are being as effectively used as possible. In April 2016, the Older Americans Act was re-authorized. Importantly though, a key section for services has received level funding ever since overall cuts that were implemented as part of the Budget Control Act of 2011. This is particularly concerning in the face of the rising number of seniors in communities.

If funding is not administered through your city, it is essential that local leaders connect with the administrating entity so area residents can be directed to the existing systems in place to meet their needs. To learn what organization is the Area Agency on Aging for your community, visit www.eldercare.gov.

3. Aging in Place and Smart Growth*

INTERNATIONAL CITY/COUNTY MANAGEMENT ASSOCIATION

Many have noted that a community that works well for children and for seniors is livable for everyone. Smart growth strategies provide significant advantages for older adults-transportation choices, healthy environments, affordable housing opportunities, access to services, social interaction, and more. Advocates for older adults have traditionally focused on critical individual needs for enhancing quality of life, such as home modification strategies and affordable prescription drugs. As the retirement age for the baby boom generation edges nearer, however, community-wide livability is increasingly being recognized as a more sustainable way to enhance quality of life for more people over time.

Sweeping demographic shifts over the next 25 years will entail dramatic changes at the community level. The percentage of older people in our society will climb sharply over the next 25 years. After the baby-boom generation has fully entered what is traditionally considered retirement age, the number of adults over the age of 65 will double in size to make up about 20 percent of our nation's population. The frailer 85-and-over age cohort—the fastest growing segment—will then make up 5 percent of the nation's population.[1] These older people have overwhelmingly and consistently indicated a desire to remain in their own homes as long as they can, in as independent a manner as possible.[2] This phenomenon is known as "aging in place."

Conventional urban design characteristics present significant obstacles to older peoples' independence and social integration. Much of the "graying" trend will be felt in communities that were designed for young families and for people who can drive. According to the Administration on Aging, in 2002 half the population aged 65 and older lived in the suburbs, with about another 27.4 percent in central cities, and 22.6 living in nonmetropolitan areas.[3] These statistics reflect, in part, that the parents of baby boomers remain in the same suburban neighborhoods where they raised their children.

The physical and psychological changes experienced during the process of aging can affect individuals' daily choices and priorities. As people age, their mobility can

---

*Reprinted with permission from "Aging in Place and Smart Growth" by ICMA, November 2005. https://icma.org/documents/smart-growth-issue-summary-aging-place-and-smart-growth.

decline. Disability is not unusual: in 2002, 14 percent of men and 23 percent of women over the age of 65 were unable to walk 2–3 blocks.[4] Although a big yard might once have been their preference, people who now have only limited strength and agility find it difficult to do routine outdoor maintenance, such as mowing the lawn. While a large, single-family house provides valuable privacy and space to a family, it can be a financial and physical burden for older people who are living alone on a limited income. Likewise, large, residential subdivisions that shield families from other uses can also isolate people from their daily needs.

Transportation is a sensitive issue for older people. Many older Americans associate the decision to stop driving with social isolation and a loss of independence. Even if people might not feel perfectly comfortable behind the wheel, they may be reluctant to stop driving if they live in neighborhoods that do not provide other options for getting around. One-fifth of adults aged 65 and older in this country do not drive, and of those, more than half stay home each day, in part because of limited transportation choices.[5] In 2001, nondrivers aged 65 or over experienced 15 percent fewer trips to the doctor, 59 percent fewer trips for shopping and eating out, and 69 percent fewer trips for social, family, and religious reasons than their counterparts who drove.[6] Finally, while seniors use public transit when it is available, only half of Americans aged 65 or older have access to public transportation for their daily use.[7] As older adults stop driving, their ability to meet their critical daily needs is significantly reduced, placing more pressure on public services to meet the need, particularly for lower-income seniors.

Financial security is an important concern. At the present time, a majority of older adults enjoys personal and financial security, social and civic connectedness, and adequate housing, but a smaller number are significantly lacking in these areas. For example, one-third of people aged 65 and older currently lack confidence that their housing will remain affordable as they age.[8] For those who own their own homes, rising property taxes and maintenance costs can be a significant financial burden if they are on a fixed income. The challenge is increased because, as they age, many individuals require home modifications, which can be costly.

Older adults need to remain actively engaged in society. Adults aged 65 and older are already active supporters of community and stakeholder collaboration in a range of decisions, with the vast majority (85 percent) actively voting in local elections as well as expressing their needs to elected officials and to the police.[9] Often holding positions of leadership, they may also serve the community as volunteers in civic or social organizations, through social activism, by contributing to charity, or through their place of employment. Nineteen percent of seniors provide informal caregiving. Where opportunities for social engagement are lacking or inaccessible, however, individual health and quality of life can suffer. Social isolation can easily result in depression and general health decline among older adults.

Communities need to critically assess their readiness for the "age boom." Today's decisions about the built environment will impact the quality of life of older adults for years to come. Without adequate preparation and foresight, unexpected needs can challenge communities' abilities to maintain quality of life for all residents. Local government and non-profit partners need to engage in proactive and creative problem solving to address future community challenges and to identify win-win solutions.

Smart growth approaches answer many seniors' needs. A recent survey identified several transportation-related issues as perceived neighborhood-level problems that can detract from elder-livability. Examples include heavy traffic, limited access to public transportation, and too few and/or too fast traffic lights.[10] Other concerns include: a lack of affordable housing, distance from shopping, and distance from parks. Many smart growth strategies, such as traffic calming, public transit and walkable neighborhoods, as well as mixed land use, compact building design, infill and housing choices, address these problems.

Ideas to Consider

Planning and Coordination. The Atlanta Regional Commission (ARC) and Cobb County, Georgia, a suburban community just outside Atlanta, have partnered to develop a comprehensive aging-in-place strategy that will help prepare the county for its rapidly growing older adult population. The team is educating the community about the needs of older residents. At the same time, ARC and Cobb County are analyzing the impact of cur-rent county policies on older adults.

Using ARC's Aging in Place toolkit, they will examine transportation, housing, in-home services, zoning, infrastructure, and recreational services to develop a set of rec-ommendations on how best to address the primary needs of older adults in Cobb County.[11] The findings will inform ARC's work in other Atlanta-area communities.

Community Involvement and Visioning. Futures Festival is a model for a local intergenerational event aimed at identifying and answering a community's needs. Geared toward youth and older adults, a Futures Festival event provides an opportunity for residents and public officials to share ideas about community development through a variety of media such as murals, models, photographs, theater, games, and other activities. They can focus on specific sites or address community wide concerns.[12]

Policy and Public Education. The City of New Westminster, British Columbia applies a Smart Growth Checklist to any project seeking a zoning amendment or development permit. Developed by staff in consultation with local architects and developers, the Checklist suggests ways to include smart growth concepts and reach stated community goals, including livability for all ages.

The Checklist includes important senior-friendly qualities such as: public transportation; housing adaptability, accessibility, and affordability; pedestrian environment and safety; and proximity to health services, shopping, and parks.[13]

Smart Growth Communities

Promote a range of housing choices to reflect their residents' varied abilities, independence, and income. For those who cannot find attractive, affordable housing choices nearby, or who are already in housing that stretches their budgets, moving to a more affordable home may mean leaving a community altogether. The unvaried housing stock and single-use zoning that are common in many communities limit choices for older people who want to remain close to family and friends but who need less living space.

To address this concern, communities should critically evaluate zoning codes and subdivision covenants in order to address any unintended barriers that they may place in the way of older people seeking appropriate housing. Existing restrictions can be amended to permit accessory dwelling units or "granny flats" and the subdivision of larger suburban houses into duplexes.[14]

Codes can be changed to allow smaller lot sizes, home sharing, construction of additional structures on existing lots, and temporary elder cottages that can increase density while providing additional options for affordable shelter. Finally, adaptive reuse of existing structures can create additional affordable senior housing in urban centers, where services are close by. Besides providing for older residents, these and related smart growth strategies ensure that communities provide a variety of housing options for the entire life cycle, so that people are not forced to leave their communities as they age.

Facilitate access. Older adults benefit from a range of neighborhood amenities that enable them to meet their needs, such as: walkable sidewalks and neighborhoods, reliable public transit, and traffic-calmed streets, among others. In fact, as people age, they may shift mode—from driving to transit or walking—or they may vary their behavior to compensate for limitations. Smart growth communities provide that freedom. Compared to the long distances and low densities in many communities, the attributes of smart growth communities—such as mixed uses, compact building design, walkability, and downtown revitalization—facilitate access to a wide variety of daily needs with a minimal amount of driving. It is not surprising, therefore, that denser communities see nearly five times as many older nondrivers out walking on any given day than do areas with more dispersed land use.[15]

The qualities of smart growth contribute to an enjoyable walk in the park or a spontaneous visit with neighbors, enable a trip to the store to be combined with several other errands, and may even provide opportunities for affordable housing close to shopping or other needs.

Encourage walking as a means of transportation, social interaction, and individual health.[16] Walking is a vital transportation option for those who do not drive. Whether it is walking to a transit stop or to a final destination, this easy, free activity enables individuals to age independently. It also contributes to better overall health and psychological well-being and prevents falls and mobility-reducing illnesses such as osteoporosis.[17]

Many groups organize group walks as an opportunity for social interaction, so walking can clearly achieve several benefits at the same time. Walkable communities are also safer places for children and families. Walkability requires good street design, sidewalks, and crosswalks.

Provide a quality environment for caregivers. Those who care for older people, including professionals and family members, need communities where they can live in close proximity to these older adults and still meet their own needs. A 2001 survey found that 44 percent of adults of the baby-boom generation are taking care of their own families, older family members, and, increasingly, other older adults.[18]

Nearly one-third of the adults in this situation—particularly Asian Americans, African Americans, and Hispanic Americans, especially those with low incomes—feel heavily burdened and may be experiencing stress. Being able to live near the older adults whom they help enables caregivers to run errands for elders or help them with housework with a minimal commute and more time available for their other activities.

Assist in the provision of cost-effective services. The cost of local government and nonprofit services are affected by land use, housing, and transportation systems. As seniors age and experience changing needs, they may need help to orient themselves among service providers. They may require frequent or infrequent home assistance, including healthcare, property maintenance, help with shopping, and other kinds of support. Service provision to a broadly dispersed population is expensive and can force a community to reduce levels of service or even drop services altogether. Denser residential areas can enable service providers to answer several people's needs with less driving. NORCs (naturally occurring retirement communities) provide particularly good opportunities for service providers—from meals on wheels to paratransit services (or on-demand bus service)—to deliver assistance to numerous people at one time. Because of economies of scale, service providers that are located close to both shopping and residences can provide a broader range of services to more people on a regular basis. Mixed land uses also allow older residents to address several needs in a single trip and can facilitate social interactions in daily activities.

Provide flexible options for a diverse aging population. To maintain older residents' dignity, avoid costly overprovision of local services, and ensure that communities are livable for everyone, it is critical that communities recognize that people experience aging in different ways. Inclusive and elder-friendly communities enable people to stay independent as long as possible and provide a series of supportive services that can be combined to meet changing individual needs in housing, transportation, services, and shopping, as they are needed.

Conclusion

Smart growth communities enable older adults to enjoy independent, healthy lives. As older adults make up an increasing share of this nation's population, and communities begin to experience shifts in priorities, smart growth provides a holistic framework for meeting those evolving needs while also providing a community that is livable for all ages. Advocates for older adults and smart growth proponents should therefore work together to craft lasting solutions on the community level. Certainly, their goals are aligned. Hopefully, a common set of assumptions can assist diverse community groups and local government staff to better provide for older people's needs, and will encourage caregivers and advocates for older adults to reach out to supporters of smart growth strategies.

NOTES

1. Federal Interagency Forum on Aging-Related Statistics, Older Americans 2004: Key Indicators of Well-Being (Washington, D.C.: U.S. Government Printing Office. November 2004), www.agingstats.gov/chartbook2004/default.htm.

2. Penny H. Feldman et al., "A Tale of Two Older Americas: Community Opportunities and Challenges" (New York: Visiting Nurse Service of New York, Center for Home Care Policy and Research, April 2004), www.vnsny.org/advantage/AI_NationalSurveyReport.pdf.

3. Administration on Aging, A Profile of Older Americans: 2003 (Washington, D.C.: Department of Health and Human Services, Administration on Aging, 2003), http://research.aarp.org/general/profile_2003.pdf.

4. Federal Interagency Forum on Aging-Related Statistics, Older Americans 2004: Key Indicators of Well-Being (Washington, D.C.: U.S. Government Printing Office. November 2004), www.agingstats.gov/chartbook2004/default.htm.

5. Linda Bailey, Aging Americans: Stranded Without Options (Washington, D.C.: Surface Transportation Policy Project, April 2004), www.transact.org/report.asp?id=232.

6. *Ibid.* This statistic disproportionately affects seniors living in low-density areas including small towns and rural communities.

7. *Ibid.*

8. Penny H. Feldman et al., "A Tale of Two Older Americas," 27.

9. Elisabeth Simantov and Mia R. Oberlink, "When Older Adults Are Involved in a Community, the Benefits Are Mutual" (New York: Visiting Nurse Service of New York, Center for Home Care Policy and Research, March 2004), www.vnsny.org/advantage/fact/AI_FS_Involvement.pdf.

10. Penny H. Feldman et al., "A Tale of Two Older Americas," 7.

11. M. Scott Ball, Aging in Place: A Toolkit for Local Governments (Atlanta: Atlanta Regional Commission and Community Housing Resource Center, n.d.). www.atlantaregional.com/qualitygrowth/Aging_In_Place_Tool.pdf. Also see www.atlantaregional.com/qualitygrowth/toolkit.html#aging.

12. For more information about conducting a Futures Festival, see facilitator's guide at http://intergenerational.cas.psu.edu/Futures.pdf.

13. See: http://www.city.new-westminster.bc.ca/cityhall/planning/ 06publications/zoning_dev.html.

14. For more discussion of these issues see Deborah Howe, Aging and Smart Growth: Building Aging-Sensitive Communities, Translation Paper no. 7 (Miami: Funders Network for Smart Growth and Livable Communities, December 2001). www.fundersnetwork.org/usr_doc/aging_paper.pdf.

15. Bailey, Aging Americans.

16. See Eric Feldman, Active Living for Older Adults: Management Strategies for Healthy and Livable Communities (Washington, D.C.: International City/County Management Association, 2003). http://icma.org/activeliving.

17. Physical Activity and Health: A Report of the Surgeon General (Atlanta: U.S. Department of Health and Human Services, Center for Disease Control and Prevention, National Center for Chronic Disease Prevention and Health Promotion, 1996).

18. AARP, In the Middle: A Report on Multicultural Boomers Coping with Family and Aging Issues (Washington, D.C.: Belden, Russonello, & Stewart; Great Falls, Va.: Research/Strategy/Management, July 2001), http://research.aarp.org/il/in_the_middle.pdf.

4. DeKalb County, Georgia, Senior Services*

DeKalb County Office of Aging

DeKalb County is home to more than 100,000 older adults and they are the roots from which our community grows. Senior Services is dedicated to providing opportunities that enrich their lives and encourage them to engage in healthy activities, manage their wellness, have access to resources, and become socially involved. Providing adequate resources ensures community members can benefit from the contributions and experiences of older adults. With an emphasis on home and community-based services that support independent living, DeKalb County is committed to raising awareness about issues facing older adults, and helping all individuals thrive in communities of their choice for as long as possible.

DeKalb County Office of Aging's motto is: Engage! Enhance! Embrace Active Aging! Its mission:

- To connect DeKalb County's senior citizens and caregivers to services and resources to keep seniors healthy and safe in their environments.
- To combat social isolation and food insecurity through innovation, collaboration, coordination and communication.

The DeKalb County Office of Aging (OOA) is committed to providing exceptional resources and information to DeKalb County Seniors. OOA serves as the designated County-Based Aging Program/Nutrition Services Provider. The DeKalb County Office of Aging (formerly the Office of Senior Affairs) has a renewed commitment to providing great services to DeKalb County seniors and communities.

A.I.-Line (Aging Information Line)

DeKalb County's A.I.-Line (Aging Information Line) is a free Information and referral for older adults, their families, caregivers and community and is a "gateway to senior services." The A.I.-Line connects seniors to resources to allow seniors to remain in their homes to "age in place" through referrals that are serviced with Information and Assistance

---

*Originally published as DeKalb County Office of Aging, "DeKalb County, Georgia Senior Services," https://www.dekalbcountyga.gov/senior-services/senior-services-1 (2019).

specialists. Seniors or their caregivers can speak to a specialist Monday through Friday from 8:30 a.m. to 5 p.m. The community and seniors can receive information on the following:

- Neighborhood-based Senior Center Operations to include Congregate Meals
- Case Management
- Information & Referral Assistance
- Home-Delivered Meals
- In-Home Services (Personal Care, Homemaker [light housekeeping], Respite)
- Non-Emergency Medical Transportation, Medical Appointments, Dialysis

The services listed are designed to help those with the greatest economic and social need.

In Home Services

A.I.-Line (Aging Information Line) provides referrals for Homemaker Services, which include light housekeeping, meal preparation, grocery shopping and escorts to appointments. Personal Care Services provide help with personal grooming, bathing and hygiene. These In-home services are available through DeKalb County contracts with local agencies in accordance with provisions of the Older Americans Act–In-Home Services for frail seniors.

To apply for Homemaker Services, Home Delivered Meals, and Personal Care Services, seniors or their caregivers must first call the A.I. Line (Aging Information Line). The two contracted In-Home Services providers are Rem Kiks Homecare and Jojo Healthcare.

Multi-Purpose Senior Centers

DeKalb County has two Multi-Purpose Active Centers:

The Lou Walker Senior Center is DeKalb's first multi-purpose and county-funded senior center for active seniors age 55 and older. Named after DeKalb County's 7th District Commissioner, Lou Walker, the 40,000 square foot facility offers spaces and amenities to meet the needs of active seniors as well as the community. Lou Walker offers its active seniors a variety of activities and amenities such as a swimming pool, a gym, an on-site hair salon and barber shop, vegetable gardens, cooking classes and so much more.

The Central DeKalb Senior Center is a county-funded multi-purpose senior center located in the heart of DeKalb County and a block away from Toco Hill–Avis G. Williams Library. The center was built in 2014 and had its Grand Opening on February 2, 2015. The center is designed for DeKalb County residents 62 and older who are active and independent. Central DeKalb offers its senior participants a variety of activities such as arts and crafts classes, exercise classes, computer classes, line dancing, yoga, hootenanny, and health and wellness classes.

Neighborhood Senior Centers

DeKalb County has four neighborhood senior centers:

DeKalb-Atlanta Senior Center is a federally funded neighborhood senior center located within the Kirkwood Community in Atlanta. The center is designed for DeKalb County residents 60 and older. DeKalb-Atlanta offers its senior participants a variety of activities such as arts and crafts classes, exercise classes, computer classes, line dancing, inspirational dancing, group trips and health and wellness classes.

Lithonia/East DeKalb Senior Center is a federally funded neighborhood senior center located minutes away from downtown Lithonia. This center is designed for DeKalb County residents 60 and older. Lithonia/East DeKalb offers a variety of activities for seniors such as sewing, arts and crafts, line dancing, chair aerobics, tai chi, group trips and health and wellness classes.

The North DeKalb Senior Center is a federally funded neighborhood senior center located within walking distance of the Chamblee MARTA station in Chamblee. This center is designed for DeKalb County residents 60 and older. The North DeKalb Senior Center offers a variety of activities for seniors such as chair aerobics, tai chi, dance classes, group trips and health and wellness classes.

The South DeKalb Senior Center is a federally funded neighborhood senior center located next door to the Scottdale/Candler County library in Decatur. The center is designed for DeKalb County residents 60 and older. DeKalb-Atlanta offers its senior participants a variety of activities such as arts and crafts classes, exercise classes, computer classes, line dancing, inspirational dancing, group trips and health and wellness classes.

Atlanta Senior Housing 101

Everyone deserves a place to live and thrive. For many older persons, finding accessible and affordable housing is a primary concern. Maybe you have trouble maintaining your current residence, need some modifications to stay safely in your home, desire to move closer to family members (or to a sunny climate!), or require more help around the house. Regardless of your situation, there is a solution.

Whether you would simply like to downsize, need repairs or modifications to your current home, or are homeless, metro Atlanta has housing options for your situation.

The right living situation is the foundation for a stress-free life. And your family members can relax knowing that you are in a safe environment, with access to the services you may need.

Get to know your options for senior living in Atlanta.

You may consider adapting your own home, moving to an independent living apartment, or perhaps you need the additional hands-on services provided by personal care homes, assisted living, or nursing homes. Once you understand all of your options in depth, you can figure out which is right for you.

Does my home need modifications or repairs? If your mobility needs are changing, you may need modifications—like adding grab bars and ramps—to help make your home a safer and more accessible place. If you own your home, empowerline can help link you to trusted partners who can adapt your home at full, reduced or no cost to you, depending on your circumstances.

If you rent your home, empowerline can help link you to services that can protect your rights as a tenant. As a tenant, you have rights to have your landlord make certain repairs and to a reasonable accommodation of your disability to make your home accessible to you.

Is independent living right for me?

Independent living means you either stay in the home you have owned or rented for years or live in a downsized home or apartment. It is important to realize that independent living options means that hands-on services (sometimes called "personal care") or nursing services are not provided as a service.

If moving from your current home is the option you are considering, there are a variety of independent senior living arrangements that offer services ranging from minimal to comprehensive in metro Atlanta. Some offer hot meals and housekeeping only. Others offer lots of options: dining rooms, housekeeping and laundry services, social and leisure activities, libraries, beauty salons and barber shops, pools, gardens, movie theaters and fitness facilities.

Either way—whether you stay where you currently live or move to a complex designed for independent living—this is a great option for people who do not need hands-on care. Or, if you have care needs, you will need to access personal care or nursing services from a family member or paid service, but not from your landlord or other housing provider. Independent living options are not licensed by the State of Georgia and have no regular inspections to ensure that the setting is meeting minimum service standards.

Paying for Independent Senior Housing

If you can afford to pay the full amount for your housing and plan to move into a complex designed for independent living, you'll find many options available: These residences may be apartments, townhomes, villas, cottages, suites, and for-purchase-condominiums. These options vary widely in cost depending primarily on services offered, amenities, and type of home. Many of these communities have a minimum age criteria for admission.

If you cannot afford to pay the full amount for your housing, there are several "subsidized independent senior living" options available. In these settings (typically apartments), residents pay a reduced rent rate. In many subsidized housing units, social service staff are available on site to offer social activities. Often, these housing options require that residents meet age, physical disability, or income criteria to qualify for the subsidy.

Paying for Services in Your Current or New Home

If you need to bring in professional services to assist you in your home, empowerline can help you find options, including for finding ways to help you access home and community-based services even if you have limited income.

To access in-home personal care or nursing, there are a couple of options of licensed providers agencies in Georgia:

- Private home care provider—an entity that provides direct care services provided at an individual's residence, including nursing services, personal care tasks and companion or sitter tasks.
- Home health agency—an entity that provides home health services according to a written treatment plan signed by the patient's physician in the individual's

residence. Home health services include part-time or intermittent skilled nursing care and at least one of the following: physical, occupational or speech therapy; medical and social services; or home health aide services.

To search for in-home personal care providers, including their inspection histories, visit GaMap2Care.

Is a Personal Care Home or Assisted Living Community Right?

Personal care homes and assisted living communities are options for individuals who'd like some help with day-to-day living. These services are provided directly (or arranged for) by the housing provider. In both cases, individuals receive help with personal services, including individual assistance with or supervision of self-administered medication, as well as other essential daily activities such as eating, bathing, grooming, dressing, and toileting, but do not receive round-the-clock nursing services.

- Personal care home—a residential setting which provides or arranges for housing, meals, and personal services for two or more adults unrelated to the home's owner or administrator. Download our factsheet on personal care homes to learn more, or use our personal care home checklist during your search for the best living situation.
- Assisted living community—a residential setting which provides personal services and medication administration by a certified medication aide for 25 residents or more.

Paying for Personal Care Homes and Assisted Living Communities

Residents of personal care homes and assisted living communities usually pay the rent and other fees with their own private resources. Depending on the type of home and amenities, fees can cost several thousand dollars per month.

Individuals who qualify for Medicaid-funded home and community-based services, including the Community Care Services Program, have the choice of living in a specially enrolled personal care home called "alternative living services." These individuals receive 24-hour supervision, medically oriented personal care, periodic nursing supervision, and health-related support services.

Personal care homes and assisted living communities are licensed by the State of Georgia. You can search for these options and learn about their inspection history. Plus, residents in these options have access to person-centered advocates, called the Long-Term Care Ombudsman Program, to help them resolve any concerns.

Is a nursing home right for me?

The first thing to know about a nursing home is that most nursing homes actually provide two separate categories of service:

- Post-acute—sometimes called short-term rehabilitation or skilled nursing; only available after a qualifying hospital stay and only for a limited time.

- Long-term care—nursing, medical, social and personal services to support individuals who have chronic conditions and need assistance with daily activities.

Paying for a Nursing Home

Nursing home payment options depend on what category of service you are receiving:

- Post-acute services are typically covered by Medicare Part A for a limited time. Almost all nursing homes in Georgia are certified to accept Medicare.
- Long-term care is not covered by Medicare and typical health insurance. This is an important (and often misunderstood) point. Payment options include private pay, private long-term care insurance, and—for those who qualify—Medicaid and Veterans Administration benefits.

An important note about Medicaid: Most nursing home residents in Georgia receive Medicaid to help pay the part of their stay that they cannot afford. Even if they came into facility paying privately, they often end up qualifying for Medicaid due to spending down all of their savings. These individuals provide all of their monthly income (minus a small personal needs allowance) to the nursing home, then Medicaid pays the rest of the bill. Almost all nursing homes in Georgia are certified to accept Medicaid.

Additional Nursing Home Resources

Nursing homes are regulated by the federal government and licensed by the State of Georgia. Plus, residents have access to person-centered advocates, called the Long-Term Care Ombudsman Program, to help them resolve any concerns.

It is important to know that some nursing homes do not have the name "nursing home" in their name. They may be called "health and rehab" or "care center," for example. The best way to know for sure whether a particular facility is a nursing home is to go to Medicare's page to compare nursing homes and search by facility name. By the way, the term "nursing home" has the same meaning as "nursing facility."

What is a Life Plan Community? All of these options—independent living, assisted living, and nursing home—can be found on the same campus in some parts of metro Atlanta. Sometimes they are arranged as part of a "life plan community" (also known as a "continuing care retirement community" or "CCRC"). These are a special category of residential communities designed for people age 62 and older. They require a large upfront fee, which ensures that you will receive a variety of living options and services, all on the same campus, designed to address your changing needs.

Meal Options

Meal options for older persons and individuals with disabilities in the Atlanta region Need to know what's for lunch? Have you been skipping meals or eating too much cheap, but unhealthy, food since you retired? If the answer is yes, you're not alone. In Georgia, lots of older adults leave their best culinary years behind them as incomes tighten and abilities change. Why? Many no longer have the energy needed to plan, shop for, and prepare meals. Some may not be able to afford fresh fruits and vegetables. Many are unfamiliar with the types of foods that support their dietary needs now that they are living with a chronic condition (like diabetes or high blood pressure). Many prefer dining with a friendly face but are living alone. Some may have never learned to cook or no longer feel steady enough to pick up a cutting knife. Transportation to the grocery store may be a challenge.

You should never need to worry about having good nutrition as you age. Whether you're looking to share a meal with friends, to get meals delivered to your home, or to find healthy, low-cost ingredients, we have a menu of options for you to choose from.

Food Service for Older Persons

These regular meal options could be just the right solution:

Community meals: Many senior and community centers offer regular meals to enjoy in the company of friends and neighbors at little or no cost to you. These lunches, sometimes called congregate meals, offer a chance to socialize over a full plate of nutritionally balanced food. The portions are designed to keep your diet balanced, providing at least a third of the nutrition you need every day.

Depending on your situation, the meal at a center may be free or at a low cost. You may be asked for a voluntary contribution to help offset the cost of the meal.

By joining a center for lunch, you can also learn more about improving your health through good nutrition, even if you have special dietary needs. Some centers will even provide transportation to help you get there. Center staff can even work with your doctor to support your health. A regular meal at a center can serve as the cornerstone to your healthy lifestyle—ask any of the staff how you can connect to resources like shopping assistance, health, fitness and educational programs, and recreational activities.

Home delivered meals: If you have trouble getting out of the house on your own, you can arrange for the food to come to you. Many grocery stores offer delivery service and you can now order meal kits that come right to your door.

You've probably heard the phrase meals on wheels, but did you know every community in the Atlanta region has a food delivery option that can bring good nutrition right to your door? Depending on your income, if you are over age 60, you can enjoy regularly delivered meals at little to no cost. Younger adults with disabilities can get free home-delivered meals too, as part of a Medicaid-funded home and community-based service. Some of home-delivered meals partners in the Atlanta region also provide you the option to fully pay for your home-delivered meals.

Plus, with every plate comes a friendly face—if you're living alone, a daily food delivery can be the perfect chance to tell someone about your day and hear about theirs. In addition to food-delivery, these visitors can check on you to make sure you are safe, share nutrition information and help connect you with other supports you may need for your day-to-day life.

Fresh, locally grown produce for free: The Georgia Senior Farmers' Market Nutrition Program (SFMNP) provides income eligible people ages 60 years and older with checks that can be exchanged for fresh, unprepared fruits, vegetables, and herbs from authorized farmers at designated market sites. The checks are issued on a first-come, first-served basis until all are issued.

SFMNP promotes Georgia grown produce and individual local farmers. The Georgia SFMNP's goal is to increase consumption of produce by promoting the expansion of market sites. The Georgia SFMNP season runs annually from June 1 through September 30. SFMNP benefits are not available in all metro Atlanta counties.

Transportation for Seniors and Individuals with Disabilities

Don't drive? Let empowerline help you explore ways to get there.

It's common for many people to outlive their ability to drive or to seek alternate transportation options based on their abilities. But what if the bus line doesn't go past the senior center? What if it's too expensive to take a taxi to the grocery store? What if you're not sure whether public transportation can get you to the doctor's office in time for your appointment?

Whether you're going about your daily routine or looking for opportunities to engage in your community, there are a number of roads to get you there.

What Are My Transportation Options as an Older Person or an Individual with a Disability?

There are many organizations in Georgia that transport older persons and individuals with disabilities to everyday destinations for little or no charge. Ride options include:

- Round-trip from your home to your destination
- Shuttles that follow a regular route to needed community places
- Group trips to social and cultural activities

Riders can expect to travel in vans or buses, subway trains, volunteers' personal vehicles, rideshare vehicles, or private shuttle services.

Let's take a closer look at metro Atlanta's transportation options for older persons and individuals with disabilities.

Specialized Transportation services are popular with active seniors, especially those enrolled in community programs (such as senior centers, senior group lunches, volunteering, and adult day services). Most specialized transportation services provide free and low-cost rides to community program meetings and events. Many services offer on-demand or scheduled transport to medical appointments, shopping centers, and senior centers—some even sponsor group trips to recreational areas and special events. It is important to note that most specialized transportation requires you to be registered in a community program and often there are service limits.

For eligible Medicaid recipients, there are specialized transportation services to medical appointments available. For more information or to book a ride, you can look into LogistiCare or Southeastrans.

Volunteer Driver Programs work well for older adults and individuals with disabilities who prefer door-to-door driver service. Run by local organizations and powered by volunteer drivers, these programs deliver you to medical appointments and daily errands safely and with ease. Metro Atlanta residents have several volunteer driver programs to choose from—such as Lifespan, ICARE (which serves DeKalb County), and the American Cancer Society Road to Recovery (for cancer-specific transportation needs).

Public Transit can also be a convenient and cost-effective method for commuters of all ages and abilities. Depending on your location and abilities, you can choose between buses, ADA compliant paratransit options (including MARTA mobility), MARTA trains, or the Atlanta streetcar to get to your destinations. All public transit services follow regular route-schedules and most are accessible to individuals with disabilities. In the Greater Atlanta region, your transport options include: MARTA (serves Fulton County, DeKalb County, and Clayton County), Cobb County Transit, Gwinnett County Transit, Cherokee County Transit, and the Atlanta Streetcar.

Transportation vouchers are great options for older adults and persons with disabilities that have low-incomes or are otherwise unable to use public transit. Participating transportation providers use the vouchers for ride payment. Additionally, most voucher programs offer arm-through-arm and door-to-door assistance—as well as the option to hand-pick your pre-vetted driver. While these programs vary from county to county, you can find yours by conducting an internet search for your county and the phrase "transportation voucher program." Or, if you need assistance finding a voucher program in your area, contact empowerline. Many transportation voucher programs have financial, physical, or geographic eligibility criteria.

With the proper research, you can be on the road in no time! Solutions exist for every budget, schedule, and ability. We're here to help you find them. To discover which transportation service is right for you, visit SimplyGetThere.org to search for specialized rides and public transportation routes, including for individuals who have trouble getting around. The site can help you compare prices and plan trips based on your personal abilities and preferences.

Not feeling comfortable organizing transportation yet? In the Atlanta area, there are travel training programs for older adults and persons with disabilities. With programs like MARTA Travel Training Program and training from our partners at disAbility Link, you can discover the information and gain the confidence you need to access transportation options in your region.

Booking a ride for the first time?

There are some questions you may want to ask:

- What transportation choices are available?
- What are the costs?
- How is payment handled?
- Is fare assistance available?
- Are there age or income requirements? Is there an application?
- What is the service area?
- How far in advance do I need to schedule a ride?
- Is there evening and weekend service?
- Are there restrictions on the purpose of the ride?
- Can a companion travel too?
- Is it a shared ride? If so, how long can I expect to be in the vehicle?
- What is the pick-up window time frame?

- Are there any additional costs, such as going over a certain number of miles, waiting while I shop, or assisting with bags?

If you need more help, contact one of our trained empowerline counselors who will listen to your transportation needs and advise you on how to best meet them. The horizon is waiting! Chart your course today.

5. City and County of San Francisco's Aging and Adult Services[*]

SAN FRANCISCO DEPARTMENT OF AGING AND ADULT SERVICES

Part of the San Francisco Human Services Agency, the San Francisco Department of Aging and Adult Services (DAAS) coordinates services for older adults, veterans, people with disabilities, and their families to maximize safety, health, and independence.

Providing oversight to the DAAS is the San Francisco Aging and Adult Services Commission, a charter commission of the City and County of San Francisco. The Commission's purpose is to formulate, evaluate, and approve goals, objectives, plans, and programs and to set policies consistent with the overall objectives of the City and County that are established by the Mayor and the Board of Supervisors.

DAAS Benefits and Resources Hub

The DAAS Benefits and Resources Hub (formerly Integrated Intake and Referral) was established in 2008 to streamline access to social services and maximize service connections. Through a single call or visit, seniors and adults with disabilities are able to learn about available services throughout the city and also apply for several DAAS services.

In its role as the "central door" for DAAS services, the unit serves as the hotline for Adult Protective Services reports and completes intake applications for several services, including the Community Living Fund, In-Home Supportive Services (IHSS) (including Care Transitions for those IHSS referrals discharging from the hospital), our Home Delivered Meals Program, and the Office on Aging Case Management Program.

Service is provided in multiple languages, including English, Cantonese, Mandarin, Spanish, Vietnamese, Japanese, and Tagalog.

---

*Originally published as San Francisco Department of Aging and Adult Services, "City and County of San Francisco's Aging and Adult Services," https://www.sfhsa.org/about/departments/department-aging-and-adult-services-daas.

Community Living Fund

The Community Living Fund helps seniors and adults with disabilities evaluate all the funding sources and service options available to them so they can live safely at home.

Are you a senior or an adult with a disability who is living in Laguna Honda Hospital or another care facility? Are you still living at home, but at risk of facility placement because of safety issues? Or are you the advocate for such a person? If so, the Community Living Fund may be able to help you.

Community Living Fund case managers help clients evaluate all the possible funding sources and service options available to them. The Community Living Fund works to fill in the gaps so that seniors and adults with disabilities can live safely at home.

Who is eligible? Any San Francisco adult with a functional impairment or medical condition that requires care and who needs assistance to either avoid moving to an institution or to leave one, and whose annual income is up to 300 percent of the federal poverty level ($35,640 in 2016).

What support is provided? Case managers help clients obtain services from a variety of sources. When Community Living Funding is appropriate, it may support items ranging from the purchase of equipment to modifications to the residence or payment for needed support services. Because every individual is unique, there is no set list of items that may be purchased with Community Living Funds.

In-Home Supportive Services (IHSS)

IHSS helps support older adults and persons with disabilities so they can remain safely in their homes. Those who are eligible can hire someone (a "Provider") to help them with certain activities around their home. Social workers help determine what support services each IHSS Recipient is eligible for based on their functional abilities and needs in the home. IHSS is an alternative to out-of-home care, such as nursing homes or board-and-care facilities. Eligibility criteria:

- Live at home or in a shelter, but not in a board and care facility, nursing home, or hospital.
- Receive Medi-Cal or be eligible for Medi-Cal.
- Demonstrate a need for help with activities of daily living.

Home Delivered Meals Program

If you are unable to shop for or prepare your own meals due to a physical or mental condition, and are homebound, you may be eligible to have meals delivered to your home. A small suggested donation is requested for the meal. Eligible participants will be given an opportunity to donate. No eligible participant will be denied a meal because of inability to contribute.

- Food Pantry Programs. Food pantry programs offer weekly or bi-monthly supplemental groceries to low-income seniors and adults with disabilities for pick-up at numerous sites in San Francisco.

- Congregate Meals Program. The Community Dining Program (Congregate Meals Program) offers nutritious, low-cost meals to seniors aged 60 and older at numerous sites throughout the city.
- CHAMPSS Program. The CHAMPSS Program provides seniors aged 60 and older with a dietitian-approved menu, giving them the ability to sit down and enjoy a complete meal together.

LGBT Care Senior Isolation Prevention Program

This program serves LGBTQ+ older adults who are isolated and may be reluctant to seek traditional health and social services due to a history of discrimination and marginalization.

The DAAS LGBT Care Senior Isolation Prevention program helps lesbian, gay, bisexual, and/or transgender (LGBT) older adults and people with disabilities get connected to useful services and supports. In particular, the program is intended to serve those who are isolated or lonely and who may be reluctant to seek traditional health and social services due to a history of discrimination and marginalization.

Clients served by this program are connected to Care Navigators who conduct assessments and coordinate care, a network of Peer Support volunteers, and supportive programming, including individual emotional and behavioral support, peer support groups, and outreach. This program was created in response to a finding from the LGBT Aging Policy Task Force that there were limited support services for LGBT older adults, and that specialized services were needed to address the emotional, practical, and behavioral health needs of the older LGBT population.

Aging and Disability Resource Centers

The Aging and Disability Resource Centers (ADRC) are centralized sources for free information and assistance on issues affecting seniors and people with disabilities. ADRCs offer the general public a single source for connecting to free information and assistance on issues affecting older people and people with disabilities, regardless of their income. [Note: Aging and Disability Resource Centers do not and shall not discriminate on the basis of race, color, religion (creed), gender, gender expression, age, national origin (ancestry), disability, marital status, sexual orientation, or military status, in any of its activities or operations. These activities include, but are not limited to, hiring and firing of staff, selection of volunteers and vendors, and provision of services. We are committed to providing an inclusive and welcoming environment for all members of our staff, clients, volunteers, subcontractors, vendors, and clients.] These resource centers are welcoming and convenient locations for you and your family to get objective and accurate information, advice, and have access to a wide variety of services.

With hubs throughout San Francisco, the ADRC Information and Assistance Specialists provide a wide range of services in multiple languages. There is a list provided for specific languages spoken at each site.

The ADRC can support individuals with information, referral, and/or assistance in the following areas:

- Caregiver assistance and support
- Case management services
- Employment and training opportunities
- Financial assistance and planning
- Food and nutrition
- Health and wellness
- Housing and shelter
- In home care
- Legal assistance
- Lesbian, gay, bisexual and transgender (LGBT) programs and services
- Medical and dental care
- Mental health and counseling services
- Paperwork and application assistance
- Prescription drug coverage
- Senior centers
- Translation services
- Transportation
- Other community resources

Legal Services

Legal Services provides seniors and adults with disabilities with legal assistance, such as counseling on rights, representation before courts, and drafting of legal documents.

The Legal Services program providers help eligible consumers with, but not limited to, benefit appeals, eviction prevention, consumer fraud/issues, elder abuse prevention, simple will preparation, disability planning and advance directives, debt collection issues, and immigration matters.

Legal services are available to San Francisco residents who are aged 60 and above, or who are aged 18 and above and have a disability. Services provided include:

- Research, advice, and counseling regarding legal rights
- Representation before courts, administrative agencies, and other government bodies
- Assistance in dispute resolution, including negotiation
- Drafting of legal documents
- Assistance in securing alternative legal assistance or other appropriate services
- Technical assistance to advocates on legal questions regarding legal rights of older persons or person with disabilities

6. Empowerment of the Aging

*Policies and Programs in Local California Communities**

FLORA G. BECKET *and* WILLIE LEE BRITT

The senior population in America and in the Santa Clara Valley in California is rapidly growing as a percentage of the total population. The City of San Jose, California, estimated in 1994 that the number of people over 60 in the city would double. The baby boom generation would begin reaching age 60 in the year 2005 and would form a large part of the over-60 age group.

The baby boomers (born 1945–1965) were headed for retirement. Also, some of the World War II and pre–World War II babies were working longer and were healthier and more physically able. As the population ages, it will probably become generally more conservative politically and fiscally.

These older adults will vary widely in physical abilities, cultural and ethnic backgrounds, in gender, in political affiliation, in wealth and in recreational interests. It will not be a simple task to adequately plan for their demands and needs. Some elders will need or want to continue working, some will live with multigenerational families and some will be alone. A study in 2001 sought to determine specific priority areas of action for the local governments of Santa Clara County and San Jose, as well as local communities in California in general.

The central issue examined was the change in government policy and practice to be brought about by the general aging of the U.S. population and its effect in the state. If senior-related services received a greater emphasis in funding and attention, what would the effect be on general government policies relating to immigration, education, law enforcement, and other broad public policies? What plans and adjustments had some communities made already? The study focused on the factors most affecting daily life in cities and counties and the corresponding adjustments in state and local policy issues and programs. It also addressed as much as possible budgetary re-allocation due to a possibly changing tax base due to sales and property taxes.

The research methodology employed a review of a diverse body of relevant research reports, studies, governmental budgets and plans and professional literature. A survey questionnaire was distributed to 41 adults over the age of 50 and the data analyzed.

---

*Published with permission of the authors.

Findings

Common issues identified were transportation, housing, public education, recreation and healthcare along with the funding for these programs. Funds and personnel are not unlimited and a shift in emphasis towards more senior-oriented services would necessarily impact general services; funds directed toward more senior centers may well reduce the ability to provide recreation and other opportunities presently targeted toward youth. These programs become interlinked; however, with the realization that youth programs result in reduction in crime and seniors also demand better protection from crime. Thus, the communities' visions and plans seek to encompass a balance that can achieve a high quality of life overall. At a minimum, transportation services will have to be more accessible by the mobility-impaired. Housing issues in California communities are critical for all groups.

The recreation, leisure and community services at the local level are the agencies that provide parks, leisure facilities, some educational opportunities, youth services and senior meal and recreational programs. As the number of older residents increases, the facilities and personnel dedicated to just the senior programs must grow.

One scenario is very likely: seniors may well mandate the shape of the community's services with their votes. The effect of federal legislation and budgeting cannot be ignored. Of principal concern are the programs such as Social Security and Medicare/Medicaid. In the year 2030, Medicare is projected to exceed Social Security in cost. According to the survey conducted for this research study, if there is a problem with Social Security funding and Medicare, citizens favor covering a shortage with general tax fund dollars. In that case, local communities face some challenges: (1) poorer citizens and (2) greater local health needs. Both of these could draw heavily on local governmental budgets, diverting funds from other programs, and they could draw heavily on community-based organizations.

When planning for the future, most communities failed to take into consideration the shift in the available labor pool. Over the period from 1997 to 2040 the pool of working-age adults (ages 20–64) is projected to drop from about 59 percent of the population to about 56 percent, while the over–65 age group will increase from just over 12 percent to almost 21 percent. Output per capita, savings rates and living standards will be reduced more than if the share of workers remained stable. Offsetting this somewhat would be an increase between 2001 and 2021 of older women in the labor force and the greater experience associated with an older labor force would raise average earnings and productivity per worker. Also, the younger labor cohorts are generally better educated than the older generations.

The baby boomers have fueled the boom in the economy over the past years, but in retirement, they will be removing their funds from the investment market and that capital will no longer be available. The local communities will have to plan around the possible drop in income and sales tax revenues, and in California, pay close attention to demographic shifts as they affect property tax revenues because of Proposition 13. If retirees sell and move, there could be a boom in property tax revenues. However, if they stay put and take advantage of the property tax postponement programs there could be a ten-to-twenty-year leveling off of revenues.

Local governments will find that they must enhance their current organizations with an increase in public-private partnerships so they can leverage their personnel resources and funds to the greatest extent. Some local planners are recommending renovations of older schools, shared facilities by schools, local governments and businesses, and providing for lifelong educational opportunities in cooperation with local colleges and universities.

While cities remain the main focus of local government, there will be a growth in regionalism for many areas of government: land use, transportation, utilities, economic development and environmental quality will be better served in most areas when approached as regional issues. Another consideration for land use is the stimulation of the economic growth of the local community. Natural resources are a shrinking commodity and citizens have an expectation that local governments, states and the federal governments will provide environmental protections.

Different communities will have different experiences with their transportation needs and need to ask these questions:

1. How much provision of special transportation is required for the increased older population?

2. Is the total population of the community likely to increase?

3. What is the correct amount and type of public transportation required by the population density and economy of the community?

4. What requirements are there for special access vehicles for the mobility-impaired?

Education is an area for which communities must plan carefully in light of the following:

1. Older people are more transient and may be more disconnected from their communities resulting in less interest in education below the college level (for example, the Oak Grove School District in San Jose refunds the school tax amount to seniors—$65 per annum);

2. More children are being diagnosed with special needs and federal and local funding are insufficient for those needing special education;

3. Shifts of resources to elderly programs will reduce monies available for all education funding; and,

4. Education for adults is very popular with the over-50 age group.

When seeking to create "elder-friendly" communities, cities and counties are finding some common tangible factors for local communities to include in their planning and legislative measures:

1. Access to opportunities for housing alternatives, jobs, volunteer work or recreation;

2. In-home services for seniors to assist them in remaining in independent living situations as long as possible. In-Home Supportive Services (a federal program administered through the states and counties social service departments) is already available for house and personal care as is Meals on Wheels; communities, either through governmental or non-profits or partnerships of both, are beginning to provide other services as well—such as house and yard maintenance programs, in-home therapy and recreational services, providing life-alert devices, transportation to senior day care or recreational programs and volunteers who simply call seniors daily to see that they are well.

3. Land use plans that provide a local grocery and pharmacy.

4. Transportation to get seniors to the medical facilities.

5. Physical facilities such as large-print signs, wide and unobstructed store aisles, longer walk signals at intersections, and sturdy benches along the sidewalks.

The intangible factors cannot be legislated but they can be taught, and those in the local governments aging programs will need to educate the community at large on maintaining a community where seniors feel safe, liked, needed, respected and can continue to be socially integrated. The local government can take the lead in promoting volunteerism among able seniors, thus benefiting the total community.

The main effects common to all general governmental policies fall into three major categories that are dictated both by voter demands and the realities:

1. The federal government must alter its methods for insuring retirement income and medical care for the elderly. During the time of transition, it must determine how to fund those already retired if there is a shortage of funds. There is certainly a demand for increased benefits already. For future retirees, the most probable course seems to be the greater use of private investment accounts [similar to the IRAs, SEPs, 401(k), 403 (b) plans and the like.] Included in this new method of retirement funding is Medicare as it now is and the increased demand for prescription coverage by Medicare.

2. As the majority of voters age and conservatism increases, it will be more difficult to pass tax increases. Even at the present revenue levels, when resources are of necessity shifted towards the issues associated with aging (Social Security, senior welfare programs, Medicare, housing and transportation), then funds are scarce for budget items such as defense, education, youth programs, transportation infrastructures and non-senior-oriented welfare programs.

3. Governments must make better and more creative uses of technology and partnerships with private enterprises, both for-profit and non-profit, to enable them to meet the increase in service demand with the same or smaller budgets and a shrinking labor pool.

Conclusions and Areas for Research

Local communities seeking to maintain a good quality of life for all citizens and to meet the specific needs of their growing aging population over 65 must begin immediately making long-range plans (at least 10 years out) and begin laying the foundation of organizations and funding to implement their plans.

One of the most important things cities and counties must build into their long-range planning is the actual structure of their bureaucracy. Flexibility, creative innovation, interagency cooperation and a combination of both generalists in management and specialists in the specific service areas are needed. In addition, private/public partnerships and volunteerism are factors of which these local governments should take advantage. They also must creatively use opportunities for regional cooperation among neighboring cities and counties. One appropriate office or analysis which, hopefully, exists should have responsibility to constantly monitor the overall plans for the county or city, note where target goals are not being achieved and report directly to the county or city executive and elected governing board with recommendations for corrective action.

Because older citizens vote more regularly, governments must be prepared for voters approving those programs which directly benefit them and not with the general welfare of the locality. Maintaining a balance of services for all age groups will be more difficult. Older people, however, are more available as volunteers and innovative volunteer programs could assist with program deliveries to both elder and non-elder populations. Meals on Wheels is an excellent example of such a program, but use of retired healthcare, recreation, counselors, business people and other personnel should be considered as a way to offset some costs of services to all ages. Another area for research would be to perform another study regarding the fact that survey respondents indicated their greatest local areas of concern for city planners are housing, health and transportation while at the same time identifying education, morality and crime as the greatest problems in America over the next 10 years.

Programs and services deliveries directly to the aging population will require employing some new methods for most agencies as noted in the following discussions. Findings indicate that the major concerns of the elderly for themselves are healthcare, housing and transportation. They will demand a high level of quality and quantity in these areas.

Using existing facilities, counties and cities can cooperate in providing some clinical services at community centers, hospitals and other locations for those things, which are better done at facility, rather than in the home.

Conclusions Revisited and 2019 Update

For the first time, millennials have surpassed baby boomers as the largest population age group. However, the demand for services to seniors is high. Services offered in many communities include senior centers with programs offering recreation, classes and a nutrition program of hot meals at noon for a nominal charge and cooperation with the food bank to distribute bags of food monthly to seniors.

Housing: More seniors than anticipated are leaving California and the San Francisco Bay Area in particular because the high cost of living has had two effects:

1. Seniors who own homes find they can sell these and move to less expensive states and have a better home and/or money for a good retirement. Some want to be near children in other states. The purchases of homes made available by these sales result in a much higher property tax revenue for communities in California as the assessed value of the homes and resulting property tax amounts are much higher than the assessed value of the former owners, protected by Proposition 13.

2. Seniors who are renters are finding themselves priced out of the area in spite of cities' efforts to promote affordable housing. Santa Clara County Valley Transportation Authority is proposing to use some of the parking lots at its light rail facilities to put in multi-use housing—apartments plus shops and services.

Contrasting the San Francisco Bay Area and the Dallas-Fort Worth area, independent and assisted living facilities cost about double the cost of comparable facilities. Home health aide agencies are also less expensive.

Transportation: While the same county programs are still available, use is made of Uber, Lyft and the like. Seniors who can afford these services find them easier to use than the county accessible transportation system and less expensive than taxis. Medicare covers some limited use of these as an alternative to an ambulance or other special transport. Medicaid covers some forms of transport needs to doctor visits. Transportation options are more available.

Medical: Larger health organizations such as Kaiser Permanente have begun to offer ways to communicate with nurses and doctors that don't require a physical visit: video conferencing, emails, home visits and the like. Also, there are devices available that monitor vital signs and medications and communicate automatically with the doctor's office.

Additional conclusions: The large number of younger people and immigrants replacing the baby boomers (who are dying or leaving) are likely to vote differently on matters of services, housing and transportation because of age and culture. They will likely be less conservative. It will be five to ten years before these shifts become very apparent, but they can be expected.

REFERENCE

Becket, Flora. "Empowerment of the Aging: Analysis of the Policies and Programs That Address Their Needs in Local California Communities." San Francisco: Golden Gate University, 2001.

7. Older Americans Act and Timeline of Programs for Older Americans*

ADMINISTRATION FOR COMMUNITY LIVING

Congress passed the Older Americans Act (OAA) in 1965 in response to concern by policymakers about a lack of community social services for older persons. The original legislation established authority for grants to states for community planning and social services, research and development projects, and personnel training in the field of aging. The law also established the Administration on Aging (AoA) to administer the newly created grant programs and to serve as the federal focal point on matters concerning older persons.

Although older individuals may receive services under many other federal programs, today the OAA is considered to be a major vehicle for the organization and delivery of social and nutrition services to this group and their caregivers. It authorizes a wide array of service programs through a national network of 56 state agencies on aging, 629 area agencies on aging, nearly 20,000 service providers, 244 Tribal organizations, and two Native Hawaiian organizations representing 400 Tribes. The OAA also includes community service employment for low-income older Americans; training, research, and demonstration activities in the field of aging; and vulnerable elder rights protection activities.

2016 Reauthorization of the OAA

The 2016 OAA Act reauthorizes programs for FY 2017 through FY 2019. It includes provisions that aim to protect vulnerable elders by strengthening the Long-Term Care Ombudsman program and elder abuse screening and prevention efforts. It also promotes the delivery of evidence-based programs, such as falls prevention and chronic disease self-management programs.

---

*Originally published as Administration for Community Living, "Older Americans Act and Timeline of Programs for Older Americans," https://acl.gov/about-acl/authorizing-statutes/older-americans-act.

Highlights

Aging and Disability Resource Centers: The 2006 Reauthorization provides the Assistant Secretary for Aging the authority to "implement in all States Aging and Disability Resource Centers." In what ways can States begin planning and directing resources for this implementation?

The Administration on Aging continues to seek and direct resources to assist States in the development and expansion of ADRCs. In addition, many States have creatively used other Federal resources to advance ADRCs. Many ADRC grantee States are seeking increased Federal Financial Participation (FFP) through Medicaid to support their ADRC efforts.

ADRC grantees are also utilizing State and other funding support, for example:

Six States have passed ADRC/single point of entry legislation. Seventeen States have received State funding to support ADRC pilot sites Twenty-four ADRC grantee States report pursuing, or have already received, private grants to support their efforts at the State or local level.

National Family Caregiver Support program: AoA, in partnership with CMS, designed the Aging and Disability Resource Centers (ADRCs), now operational in 43 States and territories, to provide consumers and caregivers information on home and community-based long-term care services. ADRCs provide consumers information, options counseling, referral, assessment, educational and assistance in planning for future needs. AoA is emphasizing the importance of integration of proven evidence-based health promotion interventions, which can lessen disability related to chronic illnesses, prevent falls, and reduce the burden experienced by family caregivers of individuals who are older and/or disabled.

For individuals with a high-risk for nursing home placement, funds can be used by States to target these low and moderate income individuals and their caregivers who may be better served through home and community-based services. Through a variety of consumer-directed options, such consumers may select their own providers and direct how their services will be delivered.

What eligibility changes were made to the National Family Caregiver Support program as a result of the Reauthorization of the Older Americans Act in 2006?
The eligibility changes in the NFCSP are:

—Family caregivers of a person with Alzheimer's disease or a related dementia may be served regardless of the age of the person with dementia.

—Grandparents and other relative caregivers providing care to children (under age 18 years) may receive services at 55 years of age and older;

—Grandparent or relative caregivers, providing care for adult children with a disability, who are between 19 and 59 years of age, can now be served under the NFCSP as follows:

- Caregivers must be age 55 years and older;
- Priority is given to caregivers providing care for an adult child with severe disabilities; and
- Services provided to these caregivers are not counted against the 10% ceiling for grandparents and other caregivers providing care to children under the age of 18 years.

Religious activities: The Older Americans Act does not forbid older adults from praying before a meal at a senior center or some other location that provides a meal with funding from the OAA. The AoA recommends that each nutrition program adopt a policy that ensures that each individual participant has a free choice whether to pray either silently or audibly, and that the prayer is not officially sponsored, led or organized by persons administering the Nutrition Program or the meal site.

Are bible studies and other religious activities allowed at Title III funded program sites? Title III funded programs may not use OAA funds (or local matching funds) to support inherently religious activities, such as worship, religious instruction, or prose-lytization. If the organization engages in such activities, it must offer them separately, in time or location, from the programs or services funded with OAA funds, and participation must be voluntary.

This restriction does not mean that an organization that sponsors the Title III program (i.e., the contractor or grantee) may not engage in inherently religious activities, but only that the organization may not use OAA funds for such purposes.

Transportation: In recognition of the importance of the role of the Aging Services Network, AoA entered into a memorandum of understanding with the Federal Transit Administration in January 2003. As a result of this collaboration, AoA has become a key partner at the federal level in promoting the coordination of transportation across programs and agencies.

The 2006 Reauthorization contains specific requirements for States and area agencies to develop and implement comprehensive and coordinated systems for home and community-based services, including transportation. These requirements afford the Aging Services Network with significant opportunities to strengthen coordination of transportation services and/or ensure its inclusion in the planning and delivery of transportation services. States and communities are encouraged to use the resources available at the National Aging and Disability Transportation Center, to assist in developing and enhancing coordinated transportation services.

Timeline of Programs for Older Americans

1920: The Civil Service Retirement Act provided a retirement system for many governmental employees.

1935: The Social Security Act passed; provides for Old Age Assistance and Old Age Survivors Insurance.

1937: Railroad Retirement Act provided pensions for retired railroad employees and spouses.

1950: President Truman initiated the first National Conference on Aging, sponsored by the Federal Security Agency.

1952: First federal funds appropriated for social service programs for older persons under the Social Security Act.

1956: Special Staff on Aging established within the Office of the Secretary of Health, Education and Welfare, to coordinate responsibilities for aging. Federal Council on Aging created by President Eisenhower.

1958: Legislation introduced in Congress, calling for a White House Conference on Aging.

1959: Housing act authorized a direct loan program for non-profit rental projects, for the elderly at low interest rates, and lowered eligibility ages for public-low-rent housing, for low-income women to age 62.

1960: Social Security Administration eliminated age 50 as minimum for qualifying for disability benefits, and liberalized the retirement test and the requirement for fully insured status.

1961: First White House Conference on Aging held in Washington, D.C.

Social Security Amendments lowered the retirement age for men from 65 to 62, liberalized the retirement test, and increased minimum benefits and benefits to aged widows.

1962: Legislation introduced in Congress, to establish an independent and permanent Commission on Aging.

1965: Older Americans Act signed into law on July 14 1965. It established the Administration on Aging within the Department of Health, Education and Welfare, and called for the creation of State Units on Aging. William Bechill named first Commissioner on Aging. Medicare, Title XVIII, a health insurance program for the elderly was established as part of the Social Security Act. Medicaid, Title XIX, a health insurance program for low-income persons, was added to the Social Security Act.

1967: Older Americans Act extended for two years, and provisions made for the Administration on Aging to study the personnel needs in the aging field. Age Discrimination Act signed into law.

Administration on Aging moved from the Office of the Secretary of HEW and placed in the newly created Social and Rehabilitative Service Agency within the Department.

1968: John Martin named Commissioner on Aging.

1969: Older Americans Act Amendments provided grants for model demonstration projects, Foster Grandparents, and Retired Senior Volunteer Programs.

1971: Second White House Conference on Aging held in Washington, D.C.

1972: A new Title VII is created under the Older Americans Act authorizing funds for a national nutrition program for the elderly.

1973: Older Americans Act Comprehensive Services Amendments established Area Agencies on Aging. The amendments added a new Title V, which authorized grants to local community agencies for multi-purpose senior centers, and created the Community Service Employment grant program for low-income persons age 55 and older, administered by the Department of Labor. Arthur S. Flemming named Commissioner on Aging. Comprehensive Employment and Training Act was enacted; included older persons.

1974: Title XX of the Social Security Amendments authorized grants to states for social services. These programs included protective services, homemaker services, transportation services, adult day care services, training for employment, information and referral, nutrition assistance, and health support. Older Americans Act amendments added transportation under Title III model projects. Housing and Community Development Act enacted; provided for low-income housing for the elderly and handicapped, pursuant to the Housing Act of 1937. National Institute on Aging created to conduct research and training related to the aging process, and the diseases and problems of an aging population. Title V of the Farm and Rural Housing Program of 1949 expanded to include the rural elderly as a target group.

1975: Older Americans Act Amendments authorized grants under Title III to Indian tribal organizations. Transportation, home care, legal services, and home renovation/repair were mandated as priority services.

1977: Older Americans Act Amendments required changes in Title VII nutrition program, primarily related to the availability of surplus commodities through the Department of Agriculture.

1978: Older Americans Act Amendments consolidated the Title III Area Agency on Aging administration and social services, the Title VII nutrition services, and the Title V multi-purpose senior centers, into a new Title III and added a new Title VI for grants to Indian Tribal Organizations. The old Title V became the Community Service Employment grant program for low-income persons, age 55 and older (created under the 1978 amendments as Title IX). Robert G. Benedict named Commissioner on Aging. Congregate Housing Services Act authorized contracts with local public housing agencies and non-profit corporations, to provide congregate independent living service programs. OAA amendments required each state to establish a long-term care ombudsman program to cover nursing homes.

1981: Third White House Conference on Aging held in Washington, D.C. Lennie-Marie Tolliver named Commissioner on Aging. Older Americans Act reauthorized; emphasized supportive services to help older persons remain independent in the community. Act expanded ombudsman coverage to board and care homes.

1984: Reauthorization of the Older Americans Act clarified and reaffirmed the roles of State and Area Agencies on Aging in coordinating community-based services, and in maintaining accountability for the funding of national priority services (legal, access, & in-home). Carol Fraser Fisk named Commissioner on Aging.

1987: Omnibus Budget Reconciliation Act provides for nursing home reform in the areas of nurse aide training, survey and certification procedures, pre-admission screening an annual reviews for persons with mental illness. Reauthorization of the Older Americans Act added six additional distinct authorization of appropriations for services: in-home services for the frail elderly; long-term care ombudsman; assistance for special needs; health education and promotion; prevention of elder abuse, neglect, and exploitation; and outreach activities for persons who may be eligible for benefits under supplemental security income (SSI), Medicaid, and food stamps. Additional emphasis was given to serving those in the greatest economic and social need, including low-income minorities. The Nursing Home Reform Act (Omnibus Budget Reconciliation Act) mandated that nursing facility residents have "direct and immediate access to ombudspersons when protection and advocacy services become necessary." Simultaneously, the OAA reauthorization charged states to guarantee ombudsman access to facilities and patient records, provided important legal protections, authorized state ombudsmen to designate local ombudsman programs and required that ombudsman programs have adequate legal counsel.

1989: Joyce Berry named Commissioner on Aging.

1990: Americans with Disabilities Act extended protection from discrimination in employment and public accommodations to persons with disabilities. Cranston-Gonzalez National Affordable Housing Act reauthorized the HUD Section, 202 Elderly Housing program, and provided for supportive service demonstration programs. Age Discrimination in Employment Act made it illegal, in most circumstances, for companies to discriminate against older workers in employee benefits.

1992: Reauthorization of the Older Americans Act places increased focus on caregivers, intergenerational programs, protection of elder rights and calls for a 1995 White House Conference on Aging. The elevation of Commissioner on Aging to Assistant Secretary for Aging.

OAA amendments added a new Title VII "Vulnerable Elder Rights Activities" which included the long-term care ombudsman; prevention of elder abuse, neglect and exploitation; elder rights and legal assistance development; and benefits outreach, counseling and assistance programs. The legislation emphasized the value of the four programs coordinating their efforts. The amendments highlighted the role of local ombudsman programs and the state ombudsman's role as leader of the statewide program and advocate and agent for systemwide change.

1993: Fernando M. Torres-Gil was sworn in as the first Assistant Secretary for Aging in the Department of Health and Human Services on May 6, 1993.

1995: White House Conference on Aging convened May 2–5, 1995 in Washington, D.C.

Thirtieth anniversaries of Older Americans Act, Medicare, Medicaid & the Foster Grandparent Program. Sixtieth anniversary of Social Security. Operation Restore Trust Initiated.

1997: Jeanette C. Takamura, Ph.D., was sworn in as Assistant Secretary for Aging in the U.S. Department of Health and Human Services on December 8, 1997.

1999: International Year of Older Persons: A Society for All Ages

2000: Older Americans Act Amendments of 2000 signed into law (P.L. 106–501), establishing the new National Family Caregiver Support Program, and reauthorizing the OAA for five years on November 13, 2000.

2001: HHS Secretary Tommy G. Thompson released $113 million for first National Family Caregiver Support Programs grants to states on February 15, 2001. Josefina G. Carbonell sworn in as Assistant Secretary for Aging on August 8, 2001.

2002: Kick off of 30th Anniversary of the Older Americans Act Nutrition Program in March.

2003: Enactment of the Medicare Prescription Drug, Improvement and Modernization Act (MMA).

2005: 5th White House Conference on Aging was held in Washington, D.C.

2006: Medicare Part D Prescription Drug program (part of MMA) went into effect. Enactment of the Lifespan Respite Care Act (administered by AoA). Older Americans Act Amendments of 2006 signed into law (P.L. 109–365), embedding the principles of consumer information for long-term care planning, evidence based prevention programs, and self-directed community based services to older individuals at risk of institutionalization. OAA was reauthorized for five years on October 17, 2006.

2009: Kathy Greenlee appointed by President Obama as 4th Assistant Secretary for Aging.

2010: Enactment of the Affordable Care Act.

2011: First of the nation's baby boomers turn 65.

2012: Administration for Community Living established on April 18, 2012, bringing together the Administration on Aging, the Office on Disability and the Administration on Developmental Disabilities.

8. U.S. Healthcare*

From the 19th Century to the Affordable Care Act

Willie Lee Britt

This overview of significant events in healthcare history is to provide factual information, not a biased account based on any political ideology. The reader can employ critical thinking and focus on the approaches of Republican and Democratic administrations at the federal and state levels. The outcome sought is for you to use this overview to understand, analyze and evaluate the development of healthcare delivery and services or lack thereof in the United States.

19th Century

1854: The Bill for the Benefit of the Indigent Insane (also called the Land-Grant Bill for Indigent Insane Persons, formally the bill "Making a grant of public lands to the several States for the benefit of indigent insane persons") was proposed legislation that would have established asylums for the indigent insane, and also the blind, deaf, and dumb, via federal land grants to the states. The bill was the signature initiative of activist Dorothea Dix and passed both houses of Congress in 1854. However, it was vetoed on May 3, 1854, by President Franklin Pierce. Pierce argued that the federal government should not commit itself to social welfare, which he believed was properly the responsibility of the states.

20th Century

1900–1920: In Theodore Roosevelt's unsuccessful bid for president in 1912, progressive healthcare reformers supported him and universal coverage. The attempt was for sickness insurance guaranteed by the states. The American Medical Association (AMA) opposed what it termed "socialized medicine."
1930–1950: In 1933, Franklin D. Roosevelt wanted to include a publicly funded healthcare program as part of the Social Security legislation. The AMA again opposed it, and

---

*Published with permission of the author.

in 1935 President Roosevelt dropped this reform idea to ensure passage of the Social Security Act.

Individual hospitals began offering their own insurance programs. One of the first was Blue Cross.

In 1945, President Harry Truman proposed a "universal" national health insurance program. He included five components:

The first was to address the number and disparity of physicians, nurses and other health professionals, especially in low-income and rural communities where there were "no adequate facilities for the practice of medicine" and "the earning capacity of the people in some communities makes it difficult if not impossible for doctors who practice there to make a living." To begin to correct this problem, Truman wanted the federal government to construct modern, quality hospitals across the nation—especially where they did not yet exist.

The second issue was the need to develop and bolster public health services (both to control the spread of infectious diseases and improve sanitary conditions across the nation) and maternal and child healthcare. With respect to the latter, Truman reminded Congress, "the health of American children, like their education, should be recognized as a definite public responsibility."

Third, he sought to increase the nation's investment in medical research and medical education.

The fourth problem addressed the high cost of individual medical care. "The principal reason why people do not receive the care they need," Truman noted, "is that they cannot afford to pay for it on an individual basis at the time they need it. This is true not only for needy persons, it is also true for a large proportion of normally self-supporting persons."

Fifth, he focused on the lost earnings that inevitably occur when serious illness strikes. "Sickness," Truman cogently explained, "not only brings doctor bills; it also cuts off income."

Once again, this proposal was opposed by the AMA and termed "socialized medicine."

October 10, 1952: So how did President Dwight Eisenhower reconcile his opposition to "socialized medicine" with his recognition of medical needs? According to *The Heart of Power*, by David Blumenthal and James Morone, Eisenhower reconciled these two goals by pushing for federal subsidies of private insurance plans. Here is what the president said in Salt Lake City that day: "Legislation which compels you to join in a federal health insurance plan is wrong. It is also wrong—morally and economically wrong—to ignore the health problems of those who cannot pay the cost of adequate medical care. Federal aid to local health plans that helps make medical care available to those who need it is right."

1965: On July 30, 1965, President Lyndon Johnson signed into law Medicare and Medicaid. The location of the signing was Independence, Missouri, as former President Harry Truman and his wife, Bess, looked on with pride. As LBJ handed "Give 'Em Hell Harry" and Bess the pens he used to affix his signature to the document, Johnson proclaimed Truman as "the real daddy of Medicare."

1991: First Lady Hillary Clinton proposes universal healthcare or a public option. The proposal was defeated.

21st Century

2006: Massachusetts Governor Mitt Romney signs into law what is later to be referred to as "Romney Care" and part of the basis for the Patient Protection and Affordable Care Act (ACA or "Obamacare").

The Commonwealth of Massachusetts passed a healthcare reform law with the aim of providing health insurance to nearly all of its residents. The law mandated that nearly every resident obtain a minimum level of insurance coverage, provided free healthcare insurance for residents earning less than 150 percent of the federal poverty level, and mandated employers with more than 10 full-time employees to provide healthcare insurance. The law was amended significantly in 2008 and twice in 2010 to make it consistent with the federal Affordable Care Act. Major revisions related to healthcare industry price controls were passed in August 2012, and the employer mandate was repealed in 2013 in favor of the federal mandate (even though enforcement of the federal mandate was delayed until January 2015).

2007: Heritage Foundation Proposal for Patient Responsibility. Robert E. Moffit, director of the Center for Health Policy Studies at the Heritage Foundation, in 2007 offered the following commentary on healthcare reform:

Much of the current debate on health-care policy centers on "mandates." Namely, should government require people to have health insurance? But this question ignores an important fact: Today, there already is a mandate on individual taxpayers.

Under federal law, hospitals must treat each and every person who comes to their emergency rooms, regardless of ability to pay. More than three-quarters of this uncompensated care, tens of billions of dollars annually, is financed, in some way, by taxpayers. So today we have, in effect, a taxpayers' mandate for health care—and no member of Congress has signaled a willingness to change that policy and enable hospitals to deny care to anyone unable to pay.

No one's arguing destitute people should be denied reasonable care. But we need to admit the status quo is financially untenable. We also need to admit that many people who can take precautions and protect themselves—and us—are failing to do so.

That's why my colleagues at the Heritage Foundation support the "personal responsibility principle." All persons have a responsibility to buy their own health insurance, pay their own health-care bills, and not shift those costs to others. Coupled with a restructuring of the health-care market so persons can own and control the health policy of their choice, there are a number of options.

First, people who can reasonably afford it have a responsibility to buy health insurance to protect themselves and their families against the financial devastation of catastrophic illness. Most Americans are able to do that.

Second, if an individual is poor and unable to afford private health insurance, then he or she should be able to get help buying that coverage, either in the form of a refundable health-care tax credit or a voucher.

Finally, if one believes insurance is a bad value for the money, or entertains some ideological hostility to even catastrophic coverage, then one can and should have the right to self-insure. This is an exercise in personal liberty. Persons who do not wish to buy health insurance should be free to do so. But they must also demonstrate in some tangible way that they are really going to pay their hospital bills, either by putting several thousand dollars into an escrow account for that purpose or making some other verifiable arrangement that they are prepared to make good on their promises.

If someone does not wish to pursue any of these options, that's fine. But they should no longer be able to claim a personal tax exemption. Whatever revenues are collected could be used to offset, to some degree at least, a portion of the rising costs of the uncompensated care.

The option not on the table is to charge the cost of one's personal irresponsibility to others (taxpayers). No one has a right to increase the existing burdens of the mandate on individual taxpayers.

So, to be clear, persons should have the personal right to self-insure, but they also have the personal responsibility to pay their own medical bills. Rights and responsibility are inseparable.

2010: The Patient Protection and Affordable Care Act (PPACA), often shortened to the Affordable Care Act (ACA) or nicknamed Obamacare, is a federal statute enacted by the 111th United States Congress with Speaker Nancy Pelosi and signed into law by President Barack Obama on March 23, 2010. Together with the Health Care and Education Reconciliation Act of 2010 amendment, it represents the U.S. healthcare system's most significant regulatory overhaul and expansion of coverage since the passage of Medicare and Medicaid in 1965.

The ACA's major provisions came into force in 2014. By 2016, the uninsured share of the population had roughly halved, with estimates ranging from 20 million to 24 million additional people covered during 2016. The increased coverage was due, roughly equally, to an expansion of Medicaid eligibility and to major changes to individual insurance markets. Both involved new spending, funded through a combination of new taxes and cuts to Medicare provider rates and Medicare Advantage. Several Congressional Budget Office reports said that overall these provisions reduced the budget deficit, that repealing the ACA would increase the deficit, and that the law reduced income inequality by taxing primarily the top 1 percent to fund roughly $600 in benefits on average to families in the bottom 40 percent of the income distribution. The law also enacted a host of delivery system reforms intended to constrain healthcare costs and improve quality. After the law went into effect, increases in overall healthcare spending slowed, including premiums for employer-based insurance plans.

The act largely retains the existing structure of Medicare, Medicaid, and the employer market, but individual markets were radically overhauled around a three-legged scheme. Insurers in these markets are made to accept all applicants and charge the same rates regardless of pre-existing conditions or sex. To combat resultant adverse selection, the act mandates that individuals buy insurance and insurers cover a list of "essential health benefits." However, a repeal of the tax mandate, passed as part of the Tax Cuts and Jobs Act of 2017, became effective on January 1, 2019. To help households between 100 and 400 percent of the Federal Poverty Line afford these compulsory policies, the law provides insurance premium subsidies. Other individual market changes include health marketplaces and risk adjustment programs.

Health Care Choices 2018: According to the opinion authored, unlike Obamacare, the Consensus Group's Health Care Choices plan devotes resources to help finance care for those with expensive healthcare needs, including those with pre-existing conditions. The ACA put these patients in the same pools with everyone else without extra subsidies and that drove up premiums to the point that healthy people are being driven out of the market.

The Consensus Group summarized its Health Care Choices recommendations as follows:

The proposal would repeal the individual entitlement to premium and cost-sharing reduction subsidies and Medicaid expansion. Instead, states would receive block grants from the federal government, which they would use to stabilize their markets and provide assistance to those with low incomes and to the sick and needy.

To assure that people have choices and that the vulnerable are protected, states must make sure that:

- At least 50 percent of the block grant goes toward supporting people's purchase of private health coverage.
- At least 50 percent goes to provide coverage for low-income people (the two categories will overlap).
- A portion of the grant goes to offset the costs of high-risk patients to make sure they get the care they need and that they don't drive up premiums for everyone else in the market.
- Anyone eligible for financial assistance under the block grant, Children's Health Insurance Program (CHIP), or Medicaid can take the value of their premium assistance to purchase the private plan of their choice.
- Life is protected. The grant would be distributed through the CHIP which provides protections against taxpayer money being used to fund abortions.

Obamacare requirements on essential health benefits, single risk pools, minimum loss ratio requirements, and the 3:1 age ratio would not apply in states receiving federal allotments. Nullifying these mandates along with new flexibility to the states would reduce premiums, allow fairer premium variation and, in combination with risk mitigation, assure that the sick get the coverage they need without charging the healthy unfairly high premiums.

Funds to finance the block grants would be based upon spending, as of a fixed date, on ACA subsidies (both tax credits and CSR payments) and Medicaid expansion.

At the end of 2018, this was only a proposal and had not been introduced in Congress to become legislation. When compared to the ACA, it appears that more funding is shifted to the states to provide essential services which are guaranteed by federal law under ACA. Will this reduce rising costs, guarantee the eight categories of essential services under the ACA and provide greater choices?

It should be noted that during 2019, politics continued to be pivotal in determining future outcomes. Lawsuits are progressing to determine whether the ACA will remain legal, given that the individual mandate has been ruled unconstitutional. The Trump Administration and 18 state attorneys general are asking the courts to strike down the entire Affordable Care Act (ACA) as unconstitutional. If the lawsuit were to succeed, approximately 20 million people would lose health insurance, and millions more would face higher costs for health insurance or healthcare. Can this provision which initially upheld the law now be severed to allow the law to still remain in effect, given the impact of this upon those who are covered by the law, and would it provide future protections such as not allowing insurance companies to impose "pre-existing conditions" that disqualify or increase premium payments? At the end of 2019, the U.S. House of Representatives, the State of California and 19 other states filed a lawsuit to protect the ACA. This coalition of Democratic-led states is asking the Supreme Court to immediately take up a challenge to the ACA (Obamacare), calling on the justices to decide the law's fate well ahead of the November 2020 elections. Attorneys general from the 20 states in a legal brief argued the high court needed to quickly take up the case, contending that prolonged uncertainty over the ACA would damage the nation's healthcare system. The U.S. House of Representatives, which is also defending the ACA in court, filed a similar petition on January 3, 2020, asking for immediate Supreme Court review.

Based on research by Bodenheimer and Grumbach (2012) healthcare costs in the United States far exceed per capita cost when compared to other developed nations such as Germany, Canada, Japan and the United Kingdom.

Some may question the access, timeliness and delivery systems of programs and services in other countries, but by any objective measures, U.S. costs are too expensive for the outcomes produced. The free market has not guaranteed reduced costs but has continually caused costs to soar. There has to be some government intervention that counter market forces that are strictly profit driven. The public option is one approach that may significantly bring about more competition, thereby reducing some costs. Bulk purchases of pharmaceuticals, shared use of equipment and technology, more research, and cooperative public-private sector partnerships can advance our effort to greater access, affordability/reduce costs, patient satisfaction, and improved patient outcomes. The public has been conditioned to view any government intervention as a negative. For example, the term "socialized medicine" was coined to oppose government intervention and create a fear that government would somehow take away part of your freedoms. If a person is burdened by medical costs that they cannot afford, then this robs that person of economic freedoms.

What do the Veterans Administration, Medicare and Medicaid have in common? They are government programs that may be considered socialism. Some may question the efficiency and effectiveness, but we can develop high performing organizations that are guided by more than net profits and shareholder dividends. After all, in addition to reducing overall costs, there is a moral obligation we have to our seniors, veterans, disabled, and those who are in need of care but unable to afford it at any given time. As the Heritage Foundation commentary so eloquently pointed out, we pay for healthcare as part of an organized policy for individual responsibility or as a taxpayer for more expensive emergency room mandatory care.

REFERENCES

Blumberg, Linda J., et al. "State-by-State Estimates of the Coverage and Funding Consequences of Full Repeal of the ACA." Urban Institute, March 26, 2019, https://www.urban.org/research/publication/state-state-estimates-coverage-and-funding-consequences-full-repeal-aca.

Bodenheimer, Thomas, and Grumbach, Kevin (2012). *Understanding Health Policy—A Clinical Approach*, 6th ed.

Commonwealth of Massachusetts Health Care (2019). Retrieved from https://en.wikipedia.org/wiki/Massachusetts_health_care_reform.

History of Health Care Reform in the United States (2019). Retrieved from https://en.wikipedia.org/wiki/History_of_health_care_reform_in_the_United_States.

Luthi, Susannah. "Democratic States Ask Supreme Court to Rule on Obamacare Before Election," Politico, January 3, 2020. https://www.politico.com/news/2020/01/03/supreme-court-obamacare-093384.

Moffitt, Robert E. (2007). "Individual Taxpayers Already Under a Mandate." The Heritage Foundation, March 3, 2007.

Patient Protection and Affordable Care Act (2019). Retrieved from https://en.wikipedia.org/wiki/Patient_Protection_and_Affordable_Care_Act.

"69 Years Ago, a President Pitches His Idea for National Health Care." *PBS News Hour,* Health, November 19, 2014.

Turner, Grace Marie (2018). "Health Care Choices Proposal: A New Generation of Health Care Reform." *Forbes*, June 22, 2018.

Ubel, Peter (2014). "A Surprising Early Supporter of Obamacare: Eisenhower?" *Forbes Pharma and Healthcare*, January 21, 2014.

9. Navigating Benefits.gov User Series[*]

Senior Citizens

BENEFITS.GOV

As a senior citizen, you may qualify for assistance programs that can help with healthcare costs, nutrition, increase access to community volunteer activities and offer employment opportunities, among other benefits. Benefits.gov is home to a range of information on senior related resources offered by our Federal Partners.

Our Partner, the Social Security Administration (SSA), is responsible for many programs focusing on the health and financial stability of senior citizens. The Social Security Medicare Program is our country's health insurance program for citizens age 65 or older, or those with a qualifying disability. The Medicare Savings Programs help eligible recipients with limited income and resources to pay for some or all of their Medicare premiums, deductibles, copayments, and coinsurance. Last, Social Security Retirement Insurance Benefits are available for individuals who have earned enough credits and are at least age 62. Visit the Benefits.gov "Social Security Retirement" category to learn more about retirement options. If you would like to find out if you're eligible for any of the Social Security benefits, take the Benefit Eligibility Screening Tool questionnaire.

The Senior Farmers' Market Nutrition Program (SFMNP), managed by the Department of Agriculture (USDA), provides low-income seniors with coupons to access eligible fresh foods at farmers' markets, roadside stands, and community supported agriculture (CSA) programs. Also, the Department of Health and Human Services' (HHS) Administration on Aging offers an overview of topics, programs, and services related to aging, including Disaster Resources for Older Americans.

Seniors can access employment opportunities through the Department of Labor (DOL) Senior Community Service Employment Program (SCSEP). The program provides part-time community service training positions to low-income people age 55 or older. Participants work an average of 20 hours per week in a variety of community service activities and are paid at least the federal minimum wage. Also, the Tax Counseling for

---

[*]Originally published as Benefits.gov, "Navigating Benefits.gov User Series: Senior Citizens," https://www.benefits.gov/news/article/349 (August 23, 2018).

the Elderly (TCE) Program, managed by the Department of Treasury (TREAS), offers free tax assistance from IRS-certified volunteers to people age 60 and older.

Benefits.gov is dedicated to connecting senior citizens to available benefit programs like the ones listed above. With information on over 1,200 programs, the program you're looking for could be just a few simple steps away. We encourage you to visit our Benefit Finder to begin answering questions about your current situation, and instantly view a list of benefits that you may be eligible for.

Highlights of Selected Senior Citizen Services

Social Security Medicare Program is a federally funded program administered by the Centers for Medicare & Medicaid Services (CMS). Medicare is our country's health insurance program. The Social Security Administration (SSA) can provide you general information about the Medicare program.

To qualify for this benefit program you must meet the following requirements:

- Are age 65 or older,
- Receive Social Security Disability benefits, or
- Have certain disabilities or permanent kidney failure (even if under age 65).

Medicare Savings Programs (MSP) are federally funded program administered by each individual state. These programs are for people with limited income and resources and help pay some or all of their Medicare premiums, deductibles, copayments and coin-surance.

There are four Medicare Savings Programs:

- Qualified Medicare Beneficiary (QMB);
- Specified Low-Income Medicare Beneficiary (SLMB);
- Qualifying Individual (QI or QI-1); and
- Qualified Disabled & Working Individuals (QDWI).

Below are general requirements for the MSP:

- Reside in a state or the District of Columbia,
- Are age 65 or older,
- Receive Social Security Disability benefits, or
- People with certain disabilities or permanent kidney failure (even if under age 65)
- Meet standard income and resource requirements.

The Senior Farmers' Market Nutrition Program (SFMNP) under the U.S. Department of Agriculture (USDA) provides low-income seniors with coupons that can be exchanged for eligible foods (fruits, vegetables, honey, and fresh-cut herbs) at farmers' markets, roadside stands, and community supported agriculture (CSA) programs.

The SFMNP is administered by state agencies such as State Department of Agriculture or Aging, and federally recognized Indian Tribal governments. Not all states operate the SFMNP statewide.

The SFMNP serves low-income seniors, generally defined as individuals who are at least 60 years old and who have household incomes of not more than 185 percent of the

U.S. Poverty Guidelines (published each year by the Department of Health and Human Services). Some State agencies accept proof of participation or enrollment in another means-tested program, such as the Commodity Supplemental Food Program (CSFP) or Supplemental Nutrition Assistance Program (SNAP), for SFMNP eligibility.

Disaster Resources for Older Americans at the U.S. Department of Health and Human Services' (HHS) Administration on Aging (AoA) offers a website that provides a comprehensive overview of a wide variety of topics, programs and services related to aging. The AoA website provides a Disaster Preparedness Manual for the Aging Network, which provides valuable safety information in time of a disaster. The emergency preparedness resource page is targeted to older Americans and is available to the public. Whether you are an older individual, a caregiver, a community service provider, a researcher, or a student, you will find valuable user-friendly information.

The **Senior Community Service Employment Program** (SCSEP) under the U.S. Department of Labor (DOL) provides part-time community service training positions to low-income persons age 55 and older. Program participants work an average of 20 hours per week, are paid at least the federal minimum wage, and are employed in a wide variety of community service activities.

In order to qualify for this program, you must be 55 years of age or older, unemployed, and your household's pretax annual income must be 125 percent of the Federal poverty level or less.

The **Tax Counseling for the Elderly (TCE) Program** under the U.S. Department of Treasury provides free tax assistance to people who are age 60 and older. IRS-certified volunteers provide free assistance and basic income tax return preparation with electronic filing to qualified individuals at community locations across the nation. The IRS enters into agreements with private or non-governmental public non-profit agencies and organizations, which will provide training and technical assistance to volunteers who provide free tax counseling services.

You are able to use this program if you are an individual age 60 or older who is in need of either counseling or return preparation services.

10. The White House Conference on Aging[*]

WHITE HOUSE CONFERENCE ON AGING

The White House has held a Conference on Aging every decade, beginning in 1961, to identify and advance actions to improve the quality of life of older Americans. In 2015, the United States marked the 50th anniversaries of Medicare, Medicaid, and the Older Americans Act, as well as the 80th anniversary of Social Security. The 2015 White House Conference on Aging (WHCOA) provided an opportunity to recognize the importance of these key programs as well as to look ahead to the next decade.

On July 13, 2015, President Obama hosted the sixth White House Conference on Aging, joining older Americans and their families, caregivers, and advocates at the White House and virtually through hundreds of watch parties across the country. The July event built on a year-long dialogue; the White House Conference on Aging launched a website to share regular updates on our work and solicit public input; engaged with stakeholders in Washington, D.C., and listening sessions throughout the country; developed policy briefs on the emerging themes for the conference and invited public comment and input on them; and hosted regional forums with community leaders and older Americans in Tampa, Florida; Phoenix, Arizona; Seattle, Washington; Cleveland, Ohio; and Boston, Massachusetts.

These forums and engagements provided the opportunity for older Americans and their families to highlight the issues most important to them, in order to help inform the changing aging landscape in America for the coming decade. The 2015 White House Conference on Aging was truly a national conversation. In addition to the older adults, caregivers, and leaders in the aging field who were in attendance at the White House, this year's conference took advantage of communication channels that were not available for past conferences. Individuals and groups participated via live webcast in watch parties held in every State and were able to ask questions of panelists and others via Twitter and Facebook.

The conference was informed by a year of pre-conference activities and conversations that allowed a broad range of stakeholders to provide substantial input. Additional feedback from the general public and policy experts was received on the conference web-

---

[*]Originally published as White House Conference on Aging, "The 2015 White House Conference on Aging," https://whitehouseconferenceonaging.gov/2015-whcoa-final-report.pdf.

site. As input was gathered, four common themes emerged as particularly important to older Americans: Retirement Security, Healthy Aging, Long-Term Services and Supports, and Elder Justice. These themes provided the focus for discussions at the July conference.

At the conference, the Administration announced an extraordinary number of new public actions and initiatives across the government and across the country to help ensure that Americans have increased opportunity and ability to live in retirement with dignity; that older adults can enjoy full physical, mental, and social well-being; that older adults can maximize their independence and ability to age in place; and that elder abuse and financial exploitation are more fully recognized as a serious public health challenge and addressed accordingly and effectively. Key Federal announcements included the release of a new Centers for Medicare & Medicaid Services proposed rule to thoroughly update, for the first time in nearly 25 years, the quality and safety requirements for more than 15,000 nursing homes and skilled nursing facilities.

These updates will improve quality of life, enhance person-centered care and services for residents in nursing homes, improve resident safety, and bring these regulatory requirements into closer alignment with current professional standards; the Department of Labor's initiative to facilitate State creation of retirement savings programs; a new proposed rule from the U.S. Department of Agriculture to increase accessibility to critical nutrition for homebound, older Americans and people with disabilities by enabling Supplemental Nutrition Assistance Program (SNAP) benefits to be used for services that purchase and deliver food to these households; and U.S. Department of Housing and Urban Development (HUD) guidance confirming that its Equal Access rule applies to all HUD-assisted and HUD-insured multifamily housing, including Section 202 Supportive Housing for the Elderly, and that such housing be made available without regard to actual or perceived sexual orientation, gender identity, or marital status.

Beginning in February 2015, WHCOA held a series of regional forums to engage with older Americans, their families, caregivers, leaders in the aging field, and others on the key issues affecting older Americans.

The forums were co-sponsored by AARP and planned in coordination with AARP and the Leadership Council of Aging Organizations, a coalition of more than 70 of the nation's leading organizations that serve older Americans. Each forum included 200 invited guests—older Americans, family and professional caregivers, aging experts—and featured lively breakout sessions; panels on the conference's four topic areas; and remarks and keynotes by White House Cabinet secretaries and other senior Administration officials, as well as elected officials. Each forum was webcast, so communities could host local viewing sessions, facilitate discussion, and submit feedback.

The Conference also organized five high-profile forums at the White House on the following topics: healthy aging, elder justice, caregiving, older women, and retirement security. Comments were generated at listening sessions and presentations with aging groups to stakeholder organizations in Washington, D.C., and across the country, as well as from more than 700 watch parties held throughout the country on the day of the White House Conference on Aging. While the public submitted ideas and concerns on a variety of topics, some of the most common themes included the need to support caregivers; ways to increase healthy aging; and the importance of Social Security.

Looking to the Future

As most Americans continue to live longer, healthier lives, there needs to be greater collaboration between the public and private sectors, at the national, State, and local levels to ensure older Americans have the opportunity to live with dignity and participate fully in life. Key themes from the conference listening sessions and dialogue with older Americans and their caregivers across the country include the following:

First, we must acknowledge our demographic reality. The United States continues to experience incredible demographic transformation. Over 10,000 baby boomers are turning 65 every day, and the fastest growing demographic in the U.S. is women over age 85. The proportion of older adults representing racial and ethnic minorities is also increasing rapidly.

This age wave will continue into the next decade and beyond. To help every American enjoy a longer, better, more active and independent life, our society needs to be able to effectively engage the challenges and fully embrace the possibilities inherent in an aging population.

The second theme of topics to address over the next decade is support for caregivers, both paid and unpaid. The majority of assistance for older Americans is generally provided at home by informal caregivers, especially family and friends. Informal caregivers are the most familiar face of caregiving, and are often the primary lifeline, safety net, and support system for older adults. Although rewarding, caregiving can be demanding, and informal caregivers need to be supported and sustained with appropriate resources. With family structures changing as Americans are having fewer children and increasingly moving away from families of origin, the availability of family members to provide care is diminishing.

Due to this and other factors, a growing demand for professional caregivers is expected, which raises issues of recruiting and retaining the direct-care workforce. Direct care is a demanding profession with low wages, long hours, and limited benefits. It is critical for there to be efforts to recruit and retain a sufficient number of direct-care workers to keep pace with the growing need.

The third universal theme is the importance of collaboration across sectors. Participants at White House Conference on Aging events focused on the need to break down the silos between housing, transportation, healthcare, and long-term services and supports in order to support healthy aging.

We must also take advantage of technology. Since the last White House Conference on Aging, held 10 years ago, technology has transformed what it means to age in America. An increasing array of web-based technologies, robotics, and mobile devices help older adults access the services they need, stay connected to family and friends, and remain active and independent.

Everywhere WHCOA traveled in 2015 and regardless of which group it engaged with, everyone agreed that it is time to shift the conversation about aging from one that assumes the coming age wave will overwhelm us, to one that recognizes that it can help lift everyone by tapping the power of experience to improve our families, our communities, and our society. Contributing to our society and communities in a meaningful way will be the new definition of aging in America as we go forward.

11. The Elder Justice Act*

Administration for Community Living

Passed in 2010, the Elder Justice Act is the first comprehensive legislation to address the abuse, neglect, and exploitation of older adults. The law authorized a variety of programs and initiatives to better coordinate federal responses to elder abuse, promote elder justice research and innovation, support Adult Protective Services systems, and provide additional protections for residents of long-term care facilities.

The Elder Justice Act established the Elder Justice Coordinating Committee to coordinate activities related to elder abuse, neglect, and exploitation across the federal government.

The Elder Abuse Prevention Interventions Program

The Elder Abuse Prevention Interventions Program provides $5.5 million to states and tribes to test interventions designed to prevent elder abuse, neglect, and exploitation. The funds support five projects and awards range from $625,000 to $1,020,000 for three-year projects. Grantees are developing, testing, and evaluating interventions in partnership with state adult protective services agencies, state units on aging, and appropriate justice system entities. The projects are also participating in a national evaluation.

These initiatives help to implement the Elder Justice Act, enacted in 2010 as part of the Affordable Care Act. The pilots are designed to test community-based elder abuse prevention practices. Identifying the strengths and weaknesses of the pilot projects and assessing overall project performance will determine the success of their replications.

Elder Justice Innovation Grants

Research in the area of elder abuse, neglect, and exploitation is still in its infancy. There is relatively little known about risk and protective factors for being a victim or perpetrator, or about effective and evidence-based prevention, intervention, and remediation practices. Further research around the impacts of elder abuse on health and long-

---

*Originally published as Administration for Community Living, "The Elder Justice Act," https://acl.gov/about-acl/elder-justice-act.

term care systems and costs of care is also needed. This fundamental research is required to develop credible benchmarks for elder abuse, neglect, and exploitation prevention or control.

In FY 2016, ACL established the Elder Justice Innovation Grants program to support the development and advancement of emerging practices to prevent and respond to the abuse of older adults and adults with disabilities. These two-year grants seek to improve the well-being of abuse survivors, study outcomes of Adult Protective Services (APS) interventions, and test promising practices related to APS work. A rigorous evaluation component is built into every grant. ACL awarded eight grants in FY2016 and five grants in FY2017.

State Grants to Enhance Adult Protective Services

To help address gaps and challenges in state adult protective services (APS) systems, ACL received an appropriation for demonstration grants to fund states so they can enhance APS systems statewide and include innovations and improvements in practice, services, data collection, and reporting.

Voluntary Consensus Guidelines for State APS Systems

As the federal home for Adult Protective Services (APS), ACL is committed to supporting efforts to ensure adults are afforded similar protections and services, regardless of their state or jurisdiction. In 2017, ACL facilitated the development of the Voluntary Consensus Guidelines for State APS Systems to assist states in developing efficient, effective APS systems. Overall, the Guidelines are designed to provide APS Administrators with recommendations from the field about quality practice. There are several ways that states may choose to utilize the guidelines: as a model of comparison to existing APS systems offered, to identify new areas of interest, or to identify areas for improvement in current state statutes or policies. The guidelines further inform ACL on many priority APS issues that it can then focus on through other programs, including the National APS Technical Assistance Resource Center and the National Adult Maltreatment Reporting System.

As a field-developed, consensus-driven document, the guidelines do not constitute any standard or regulation, and do not create any new legal obligations, nor impose any mandates or requirements. They will not create nor confer any rights for, or on, any person.

Updating the Guidelines

ACL proposed in 2016 to revisit and update the guidelines every two years, incorporating new research and evidence-based practices as available. In 2018, as part of that revision process, ACL contracted with New Editions Consulting, Inc. (a woman-owned small business) to manage updating the Consensus Guidelines, to include updating the literature review, engaging stakeholders to revise the guidelines as determined by the field, and produce a research agenda to build a stronger evidence-base of best practices for APS.

National Adult Maltreatment Reporting System (NAMRS)

The National Adult Maltreatment Reporting System (NAMRS) is the first comprehensive, national reporting system for adult protective services (APS) programs. It collects quantitative and qualitative data on APS practices and policies, and the outcomes of investigations into the maltreatment of older adults and adults with disabilities. The goal of NAMRS is to provide consistent, accurate national data on the exploitation and abuse of older adults and adults with disabilities, as reported to APS agencies.

While NAMRS is still in its infancy, the information it will provide in the years to come will directly inform prevention and intervention practices at all levels of the adult maltreatment field. It will provide a better understanding of the characteristics of those experiencing and perpetrating abuse, as well as identify system gaps for responding to maltreatment and preventing repeat maltreatment. As states, the District of Columbia, and territories (referred to collectively as "states" for brevity) continue to improve information systems, add data elements, train staff on new data collection methods, and report additional data, NAMRS data will become an extremely valuable tool.

NAMRS is an annual, voluntary system that collects both summary and de-identified case-level data on APS investigations submitted by states. NAMRS consists of three components (please see the NAMRS Definitions of Code Values for a description of the terms used in the three component documents):

1. Agency Component—submitted by all agencies on their policies and practices.

2. Case Component—data on client characteristics, services, and perpetrator characteristics, provided by agencies that have report-level tracking systems.

3. Key Indicators Component—aggregated data on key statistics of investigations and victims, provided by agencies that do not have report-level tracking systems or are unable to provide case-level data.

All states are asked to provide the Agency Component data. States then decide to submit either Key Indicators data, or Case Component data (but not both). For FFY 2016, the first year of data reporting, 54 of 56 states submitted data to NAMRS. In FFY 2017, 55 of 56 states submitted information. This high level of voluntary participation reflects the value that leaders in the field of adult maltreatment see in this data.

PART II

Services, Innovations and Challenges

• *A. Health and Wellness* •

12. Seniors and Health Care and Service[*]

My Administrator's Perspective

WILLIE LEE BRITT

One of my first significant interactions with senior citizens and city services occurred in early 1978 in the city and county of San Francisco. After being honorably discharged from active duty military service, I applied for and obtained a job with the City and County of San Francisco Housing Authority. The title of the job, as I recall, was "new tenant worker." I was assigned to the senior living facility at 1750 McAllister Street. My daily responsibilities included coordination with residents to ensure their social services needs were being fulfilled. I contacted medical providers and ensured prescription drug issues were resolved. I coordinated for the weekly visits from food vendors for fresh vegetables and fruits to those who wanted to solicit products or services. Services were brought to the seniors rather than having them individually obtain these services outside of the facility.

What I quickly learned was that this was a vibrant community with many seniors from varied backgrounds with countless years of experience in the private, public and nonprofit sectors. It readily became apparent that some took leadership roles by serving on committees and providing assistance to those who were less equipped to meet the challenges. I also became aware that this was "home," community and a place for those who may not have the benefits of being kept at home with their biological families. This was their extended family and as with any family, there was not always total agreement, but they shared a common bond of being part of that community. I was convinced that this extended many lives that would have otherwise ended earlier.

This structure appeared to be practical, efficient, effective and equitable. Rather than going to several households at different addresses throughout the city, those services could be brought to one location. Many of the questions addressed stimulated discussion of other questions that all could benefit from in that setting.

Those humble beginnings in 1978 provided a basis for an understanding and commitment that I still share. I serve as vice president of the Pilipino Senior Resource Center. This further begs an examination and codification of what are the best practices to provide

---

*Published with permission of the author.

services to senior citizens in cities. How are the needs different? How can we best serve those needs? What models work particularly well and what others have not met with as much success? How do we distinguish between basic services (needs) and quality of life (desires) that are in demand?

The State of Senior Citizen Health Care Services in Cities

An exhaustive review of literature was completed for the 50 states and U.S. territories that have varying demographics, geographical factors, and represent a cross section of American life, to include political implications that may impact program designs and philosophies. The basic services to be addressed in this analysis and summary are health-care and medicine. The two major programs applicable for seniors are Medicare and Medicaid (Medi-Cal in California).

Medicare is the federal health insurance program for people who are 65 or older. Medicare is a system that working Americans have paid into and are eligible to receive benefits from at age 65. Although Medicare taxes were withheld from earned income of the recipient, the recipient is still required to pay a fixed amount each month to receive Medicare benefits. Disability benefits may be awarded before age 65 for work related compensation. Certain younger people with disabilities may qualify. One example is an individual with end-stage renal disease (permanent kidney failure requiring dialysis or a transplant, sometimes called ESRD). Medicare consists of four parts:

Medicare Part A covers your hospital expenses. This includes hospital stays, skilled nursing care (as long as custodial care isn't the only care you need), hospice, and home health-care services.

Part B is health insurance coverage for outpatient medical services.

Part A coverage	*Part B coverage*
	• Doctor visits both to primary care doctor and specialists
• Your hospital room and hospital meals	• Some vaccines, including the flu shot
• General nursing	• Mental health services
• Prescription drugs received in the hospital	• Annual physical exam
• Skilled nursing facility care	• Durable medical equipment including wheelchairs and walkers
• Hospice care	• Emergency ambulance transportation
• Home health care	• Physical, occupational, and speech therapy
	• Some preventive exams, tests, and screenings

Medicare Part C is often called "Medicare Advantage" plans or "MA Plans." Part C helps pay for hospital and medical costs, plus more. Part C plans are only available through private health insurance companies. They're called and often referred to as Medicare Advantage plans. They cover everything Parts A and B cover, plus more. They usually cover more of the costs you'd have to pay for out of pocket with Medicare Parts A and B. Part C plans put a limit on what you pay out of pocket in a given year, too. Some of these plans cover preventive dental, vision and hearing costs. Original Medicare does not.

Medicare Part D is often called "Prescription Drug Coverage." Part D helps pay for prescription drugs. Part D plans are only available through private health insurance companies. They're called prescription drug plans. They cover commonly used brand-name and generic drugs. Some plans cover more drugs than others.

Medicare usually pays up to 80 percent. Therefore, there are many supplemental insurance policies sold to cover the 20 percent that is not covered. If a person's income is below a qualifying level, then that person may also qualify for Medicaid (Medi-Cal in California).

Medicaid is a program that offers free or low-cost health coverage for children and adults with limited income and resources. If you qualify, you can enroll in Medicaid year-round.

Practices and Possibilities

Any examination of healthcare for seniors needs to integrate the values, philosophies, the roles of actors inside and outside of government, triggering mechanisms, and windows of opportunity. We must also remember the four types of policies: regulatory, distributive, redistributive, and constituent.

These programs must be analyzed and evaluated using performance measures (not just process measures) to determine overall effectiveness in specific categories of services provided. As part of such an examination, we can compare services in other developed countries as presented by Thomas Bodenheimer and Kevin Grumbach's *Understanding Health Policy: A Clinical Approach,* 6th ed. Bodenheimer and Grumbach measured quality of care through four indices: access to care, cost of care, patient satisfaction, and, compared to other countries' providers (Germany, Canada, the United Kingdom, and Japan).

Be aware of symbolic versus substantive approaches to issues and attempts to improve healthcare and pharmaceutical benefits. It is usually much more difficult to pass substantive legislation than symbolic because of the amount of strong feelings and beliefs associated with the four factors that contribute to triggering mechanisms. Those four factors are scope, intensity, time and resources. After legislation is passed or an initiative approved by the voters, the important task of implementation has to occur. At some point we will have to determine the success or failure of legislation based on the implementation or lack thereof of policies and practices associated with programs to implement the laws created. This program evaluation component will force us to explore, examine and analyze. Some evaluations known as SWOT (Strengths, Weaknesses, Opportunities and Threats) can be done prior to program implementation. However, a greater number of evaluations are done after program implementation. It will be critical to differentiate between outputs and outcomes. Many evaluations are "process evaluations" to determine if "standard operating procedures" were followed. To become a high performing organization, we have to conduct performance measurement evaluations to determine outcomes (valuation = output × quality). It is also important to consider and utilize "metaevaluations" to determine if we are measuring what we should be measuring (the right thing as opposed to just process evaluation).

Health care reform has been a subject of debate during the 20th and 21st centuries as the brief overview highlighted. Over the past 15 years the debate has intensified. Should we have universal healthcare? In 2019 the debate centered on whether there should be a Medicare-for-all type program. Is healthcare too expensive and will only a few of us be paying for it, thereby redistributing wealth involuntarily? Should elected and retired (some with as little as eight years of service) officials (politicians) have free or low-cost health benefits and not offer the same benefits to children, the disabled, elderly and others considered incapable of paying? Should we leave it to the market forces in a capitalistic structure? As part of the economic meltdown of 2008, it is recognized that employee benefits are one of the greatest costs for an employer.

Ford, General Motors and other organizations whose employees have collective bargaining units have to spend a significant portion of their budgets for retirees and their family members' health benefits. Organized labor negotiated this over the years as part of collective bargaining agreements. Less pay was sometimes included if the overall compensation included generous health benefits. Most local municipalities, particularly relative to police and fire departments, are similarly affected to provide benefits for current and retired employees. Many argue that preventative care is much more cost effective than emergency room care. It appeared that there were windows of opportunity to reach agreement on healthcare reform since the economic crisis we experienced in 2008 and there are still lingering effects. Some corporations previously allowed their employees to apply for state and federal benefits to reduce corporate contributions to healthcare costs. Has this been a form of socialism for corporations?

The Patient Protection and Affordable Care Act (commonly referred to as the "Affordable Care Act," "ACA," or "Obamacare") has been in effect since 2010. However, the U.S. House of Representatives voted more than 60 times to repeal it with no evidence of a specific plan how to address increasing healthcare costs and simultaneously reduce the number of uninsured. The Democrats passed this legislation without any Republican support. The legislation was not perfect, and changes were needed to improve it, but the two parties could not reach agreement. It is significant to further note that within the legislation were included "risk corridors" which would be extra money from the government to insurance companies to offset their losses and not have these costs passed on to consumers in the form of higher premiums, deductibles and co-pays.

However, the Republican Congress would not approve annual funding to address the losses. Part of the initial legislation also required each state to set up and participate in Medicaid expansion. This would have increased the number of people covered by health insurance. However, Republicans argued that this was an assault on states' rights and took this to the U.S. Supreme Court. The Supreme Court ruled in favor of the Republicans, and states were given an option of enrolling but it was no longer mandated.

During the eight years of the Obama Administration the opposition party that voted 60+ times to repeal "Obamacare" argued that costs could be reduced by selling insurance across state lines and through malpractice reform and privatization measures that have not been formalized in proposed legislation. It should be noted that there is no federal restriction against states allowing insurance companies to sell policies across state lines. The challenge is in the complexity to allow such sales and not to have this negatively impact another given state. States have not taken the lead. (The McCarran-Ferguson Act does not itself regulate insurance, nor does it mandate that states regulate insurance. It provides that "Acts of Congress" which do not expressly purport to regulate the "business of insurance" will not preempt state laws or regulations that regulate the "business of insurance.")

Specifically, with respect to federal antitrust laws, it exempts the "business of insurance" as long as the state regulates in that area, with the proviso that cases of boycott, coercion, and intimidation remain prohibited regardless of state regulation. By contrast, most other federal laws will not apply to insurance whether the states regulate in that area or not.)

Any savings from malpractice reform are not significant enough to impact overall legislation.

The American Health Care Act of 2017 was an attempt to repeal the ACA. However, in 2016, President Obama vetoed the bill. Of the many provisions, there was considerable discussion about what to do with lottery winners who were covered as opposed to malpractice reform that was supposed to yield significant savings.

If we were to adopt a voucher system or health (medical) savings accounts for seniors instead of Medicare, what would be the challenges for older Americans to negotiate premiums and to pay for catastrophic care? Would preexisting conditions be covered or a higher premium be charged because it would be near to impossible for a senior not to have a preexisting condition? Given the medical conditions of some, would this be a burden and would their cognitive skills be such to ensure what is in their best interest? It would appear more reasonable for elected officials to protect these interests rather than make proposals that are counter.

Where are we now? With the 2016 election of Donald Trump as president, the opposition party had control of the House and Senate until the 2018 midterm elections. The American Health Care Act was recently presented to the people in 2018 as the "Repeal and Replacement for Obamacare" that would allow people to have "access to the coverage," implying that purchasing insurance coverage will be less costly, everyone will have access to coverage, and it will be better coverage. On March 13, 2017, the Congressional Budget Office (CBO), which is supposed to be nonpartisan, scored the newly proposed American Health Care Act. The CBO estimated that at least 14 million people who had coverage under Obamacare would lose it by 2018 and as many as 24 million would lose coverage by 2026. The counter argument was that many would not lose health coverage but elect not to have it. To me this is semantics.

If you are not fully covered or not covered at all, then you do not have coverage. The party which introduced it and was advocating for passage of this legislation immediately tried to discredit the CBO's findings. I found this ironic because the head of the CBO was appointed by the opposition (Republican) party during the Obama Administration and findings were then accepted that were presented as being negative toward Obamacare. It should also be mentioned that the new health secretary (who later resigned), who was part of those trying to discredit the head of the CBO, appointed him. Further, this person was previously aligned with lobbyists who were very anti–Obamacare because they felt provisions of Obamacare were not economically friendly to their business interests. Yet, the party in power was trying to discredit this individual who was trying to present an objective analysis.

Caveats and the Future

It appears that the ACA did not offer a "public option" and other "liberal proposals" because President Obama and others working on finding a solution to insure and provide healthcare coverage wanted to blend ideas from both the Republicans and Democrats. The individual mandate was taken from the Heritage Foundation's (Republican conservatives) earlier recommendation that healthcare requires personal responsibility and all individuals must be subject as such. The ACA was further modeled after the Massachusetts Plan ("Romney Care," passed by Republican Governor Mitt Romney). Proponents of the ACA saw a need to include the healthy and unhealthy in the insurance pool to allow a greater capacity to pay for it. It would further appear that it becomes more difficult for the Republicans to design a significantly practical plan that differs from the ACA because many of the ideas already implemented in the ACA are Republican ideas.

Findings and Recommendations

This takes us to one of my original questions, should healthcare be a right or a privilege? We do have to examine if the arguments that are being made are sincere or are they being made to mask other intentions? Do some want no or limited government participation and do some really want to see government be effective in providing services, thereby substantiating a critical role for government as opposed to just leaving it to the marketplace? Where in the world can we point to an example of the marketplace having a successful model of healthcare without any government intervention? There are those who constantly argue that it should be similar to any other product (i.e., auto or home insurance) that we purchase and let competition from the marketplace set the prices, and thereby competition makes prices lower.

My response is that you have a choice to purchase a car or home. When you make that purchase, you are also agreeing to purchase insurance against liability and loss. You do not have a choice to make a purchase of healthcare or not. You will get sick and you will need to get treated. You cannot anticipate the timing or the severity. Unlike a blue book for cars and listings for homes, you do not have a published rate for all medical procedures that you will need based on your individual needs, which practically could include various procedures with varying levels of difficulty and associated costs. The insurance companies have reimbursement tables, but you do not know in advance what you will need or if there is time to compare or negotiate the costs, and if the least expensive services that you need are accessible to you within your geographical area. When you need treatment, it could literally be a life and death matter. Will a health savings account with a few thousand dollars be enough? I seriously doubt it.

Any worldwide standard applied to other developed countries such as Germany, Canada, the United Kingdom, Japan or the United States has four criteria that can be assessed: (1) Do its citizens have access? (2) Is it affordable? (3) What is the satisfaction level with that care? (4) How does the service provided compare to other countries (access, costs, services, and satisfaction)? Much of the talk during 2016 and 2017 was about access only. This to me is disingenuous. I can have access to prime real estate, cars, amenities and other services, but the question is can I afford it? If I cannot afford it, what good is access?

There is still one significant omission from the healthcare debate. This is probably the case because there is a separate appropriation for veterans. Nevertheless, it adds to our overall budget expenditures. Policy should leverage the clout that the VA can wield combined with Medicare and Medicaid. It is important to discuss the impact of spending for military veterans from the wars in Vietnam, Iraq, Afghanistan and survivors from other conflicts. With advances in emergency care on the battlefield and medical care in the first days after injury, many veterans have survived and will survive what would have been fatal casualties. Some veterans will require healthcare for life. This significantly increases costs, but we must uphold our contract and obligations to veterans who risked their lives serving in the armed forces. We can discuss hard power and going into combat, that this will inevitably increase healthcare costs. Although it may not appear interconnected, soft power through the U.S. Department of State can help to negotiate peaceful settlements which will lessen the need for hard power and thereby reduce anticipated healthcare costs for veterans.

Computer Applications (Future Consideration)

Future computer applications for senior citizens must be designed to integrate information from various sources locally, nationally and internationally. Through the literature review, it became abundantly clear that there are volumes of information on senior citizen services and efforts to provide these services in efficient, effective and equitable approaches. For the individual who is seeking information on a specific service in a specific location, it became apparent that a filter is one means to make this search easier. Therefore, the designed application should make readily available concise information in response to a specific request. An additional filter would be to identify criteria such as city resident, U.S. citizen or permanent resident or non-citizen status to qualify for programs. For example, if the request is for affordable healthcare and housing or safe senior citizen housing in Norfolk, Virginia, the parameters must include access to healthcare, public transportation, public services, quality of life activities, and overall cost of living. A greater amount of information would be included for low- and middle-income seniors as opposed to upper-income seniors who most likely have more options available for consideration.

REFERENCES

Bodenheimer, Thomas, and Grumbach, Kevin (2012). *Understanding Health Policy–A Clinical Approach*, 6th ed.

Britt, Willie L. New tenant worker, San Francisco Housing Authority, 1750 McAllister Street, San Francisco, California, 1978.

Britt, Willie L. Distinguished Adjunct Professor, Golden Gate University, EMPA 302, Public Policy Analysis and Program Evaluation (2014–2017).

History of Health Care Reform in the United States (2019). Retrieved from https://en.wikipedia.org/wiki/History_of_health_care_reform_in_the_United_States.

https://www.cms.gov/Medicare/Medicare

https://www.medicare.gov/index

https://www.medicaid.gov/

Mather, Dr. John H., M.D., and Abel, Robert W. (1986). "Medical Care of Veterans: A Brief History." *Journal of the American Geriatrics Society.* Retrieved from https://dol.org/10.1111/j.1532-5415,1986.tb04307.x

Moffitt, Robert E. (2007). "Individual Taxpayers Already Under a Mandate." The Heritage Foundation, March 3, 2007.

Patient-Centered Community Care (PC3). VHA Office of Community. May 11, 2017. https://www.va.gov/COMMUNITYCARE/programs/veterans/pccc/index.asp.

Patient Protection and Affordable Care Act (2019). Retrieved from https://en.wikipedia.org/wiki/Patient_Protection_and_Affordable_Care_Act.

Veterans Choice Program (VCP). VHA Office of Community Care. March 15, 2018. https://www.va.gov/opa/choiceact/.

13. Breaking Through the Noise[*]

The Facts About the Medicaid Program

Brendan Flinn *and* Jean Accius

Medicaid is a lifeline for millions of children, adults with low incomes, individuals with disabilities and older adults who depend on Medicaid for healthcare services and assistance with long-term services and supports (LTSS) such as eating, bathing, and dressing.

This Fact Sheet highlights several key facts that are important to know about Medicaid and the millions of people who depend on this program to address their daily needs.

Medicaid plays a significant role in the nation's healthcare system: In 2016, total Medicaid spending (federal and state) accounted for 17 percent of all U.S. healthcare spending.[1]

Nearly 70 million Americans received health and LTSS coverage through Medicaid. Medicaid is the largest public source of coverage relative to Medicare[2] (45 million), and TRICARE[3] (9 million). By comparison, more than 150 million Americans received health coverage through employer-sponsored insurance or other private coverage.

Medicaid coverage increased by more than 16 million since the enactment of the Affordable Care Act.[4] In the absence of Medicaid, the number of uninsured would be significantly higher. Medicaid is a counter-cyclical program. The number of persons who qualify for Medicaid goes up during times of economic downturn as unemployment rises, individuals and families lose employer-sponsored coverage and incomes decline.

For example, during the Great Recession Medicaid enrollment increased by eight million people.[5]

Medicaid is an efficient program: Medicaid is an efficient program with lower administrative costs in comparison to private insurance. At the aggregate level, Medicaid spending growth is slower than the growth seen in private health insurance. From 2015 to 2016, total Medicaid spending grew by 3.9 percent whereas private insurance spending grew by 5.1 percent.

Spending at the person level follows a similar trend. From 2010 to 2016, annual per

*Originally published as Brendan Flinn and Jean Accius, "Breaking Through the Noise: The Facts About the Medicaid Program," AARP Policy Institute, https://www.aarp.org/ppi/info-2018/breaking-through-the-noise-the-facts-about-the-medicaid-program.html (October 2018). Reprinted with permission of the publisher.

person spending growth was also slower in Medicaid (1.3 percent) than in private insurance (3.5 percent) from 2010 to 2016.[6]

Medicaid provides critical support for children, people with disabilities, and older adults: Children make up the largest group of Medicaid enrollees (41 percent). Medicaid pays for about half of all births in the United States and covers more than three in four children in low-income families. In addition, the program covers close to half (48 percent) of children with special healthcare needs, including disabilities.[7]

Older Americans also rely on Medicaid. Close to one in four (23 percent) enrollees are adults aged 50+, including about 8.7 million adults are between the ages of 50–64 and 6.7 million adults ages 65+. The program also covers close to half of adults ages 18–64 with disabilities (48 percent) and provides critical LTSS that individuals and families are not otherwise able to afford.

While the majority of Medicaid enrollees are children and adults, most of the spending is for older adults and individuals with disabilities because of their high need and high cost for LTSS. Any structural changes to Medicaid financing would disproportionately impact these populations.

Medicaid provides extra help to low-income medicare beneficiaries: Medicaid also provides support to nearly 11 million Medicare beneficiaries (also known as dual eligibles). These individuals are a high need, high cost population and represent some of the poorest and sickest beneficiaries in the Medicare program. Medicaid plays a critical role in their care by covering services for which Medicare does not pay (and low-income older adults cannot cover themselves). It provides access to LTSS and, depending on the state, dental and vision services, among others. In addition, Medicaid can cover monthly Medicare Part B premiums (currently $134 for lower income earners) and Medicare's cost sharing charges for eligible enrollees.[8]

Medicaid is the largest public payer of long-term services and supports: In 2016, Medicaid spent $167 billion on LTSS. Over the last five years, the percentage of LTSS spending going to home and community-based services (HCBS) increased for all populations. However, these figures, mask substantial spending variations, both by state and by demographic group. In FY 2016, more than half (55 percent) of Medicaid LTSS dollars serving older adults and people with physical disabilities went towards institutional settings, such as nursing homes.[9] Nursing home care is about three times the cost of home and community-based services and often out of line with the strong desire among older adults and individuals with disabilities to receive services in their homes and communities.[10]

From a state perspective, the percentage of LTSS spending for older people and adults with disabilities going to HCBS ranged from 13 percent in Kentucky to 73 percent in New Mexico. Furthermore, at least 10 states have actually decreased the share of Medicaid LTSS dollars going toward home and community-based care according to new analysis from AARP Public Policy Institute.[11]

Medicaid is an important support for low-wage workers and their families: The vast majority of adults enrolled in Medicaid are either working (60 percent) or in a family with at least one worker (78 percent). These workers are often employed in industries (e.g., food service) where health coverage is not typically offered. In addition, close to half (42 percent) work for small businesses (fewer than 50 workers) exempt from the employer mandate. Medicaid helps support low-income working families by ensuring that they have access to healthcare coverage when their jobs don't offer this as a benefit.

Of Medicaid-enrolled adults who don't work, more than one-third (36 percent) are ill or disabled, another 30 percent are caregiving or raising families, and 15 percent are students.[12]

Medicaid work requirements and other coverage restrictions threaten access to vital healthcare services: States have considerable leeway when it comes to administering their Medicaid program. Over the last year, states have submitted proposals to the federal government to enact policies that could reduce Medicaid coverage.

This includes work requirements, in which states could eliminate Medicaid coverage for adult enrollees who don't have a job and aren't completing related activities (e.g., education). One state estimate shows that these policies could reduce coverage by 15 percent,[13] and national estimates project that work requirement policies could cause up to four million Americans to lose coverage.[14] Adults ages 50–64 are at particular risk in states where they are or may become subject to work requirements, as they often spend longer seeking employment and experience long-term unemployment at rates higher than their younger counterparts.[15]

Work requirements are often enforced by requiring people to report their work status via a complex, web-based portal. However, a large share of Medicaid enrollees do not have internet access and therefore would experience significant difficulty reporting their compliance. In Arkansas, for example, some estimate that more than 4,000 people lost coverage due to noncompliance.[16]

Medicaid plays a critical role in addressing the opioid crisis: More than two million adults in the U.S. have some type of opioid addiction. By financing treatment and recovery, Medicaid is critical in addressing the opioid epidemic. In 2016, Medicaid covered more than half (55 percent) of low-income adults ages 19–64 with an opioid addiction. Of this same group, just 13 percent had private coverage and nearly a quarter (24 percent) were uninsured. Medicaid-enrolled people with opioid addictions are more likely to seek both inpatient and outpatient treatment than those with other or no health insurance.[17]

Medicaid is a popular program: Medicaid enjoys broad, bipartisan support from the public. Close to three in four (74 percent) Americans have a favorable view of Medicaid, and more than half of Democrats, Republicans and independents say that Medicaid is working well at both the national and state levels. About 6 in 10 people say that Medicaid is important to them and their family, and most (87 percent) want Medicaid funding to be maintained or increased.[18]

NOTES

1. Centers for Medicare and Medicaid Services. "National Health Expenditures." Centers for Medicare and Medicaid Services, April 2018. http://www.cms.gov/Research-Statistics-Data-and-Systems/Statistics-Trends-and-Reports/NationalHealthExpendData/NHE-Fact-Sheet.html.

2. Kaiser Family Foundation. "Health Insurance Coverage of the Total Population." Washington, DC: Kaiser Family Foundation. https://www.kff.org/other/state-indicator/total-population/?dataView=1&current Timeframe=0&sortModel=%7B%22colId%22:%22Location%22,%22sort%22:%22asc%22%7D.

3. Defense Health Agency. Evaluation of the TRICARE Program: Fiscal Year 2018 Report to Congress. Washington, DC: Defense Health Agency. https://health.mil/Reference-Center/Reports/2018/05/09/Evalua tion-of-the-TRICARE-Program-Fiscal-Year-2018-Report-to-Congress.

4. Kaiser Family Foundation. "Total Monthly Medicaid and CHIP Enrollment." Washington, DC: Kaiser Family Foundation. https://www.kff.org/health-reform/state-indicator/total-monthly-medicaid-and-chip-enrollment/.

5. Kaiser Family Foundation. "Medicaid Enrollment: June 2011 Data Snapshot." Washington, DC: Kaiser Family Foundation. https://www.kff.org/medicaid/issue-brief/medicaid-enrollment-june-2011-data-snapshot/.

6. Centers for Medicare and Medicaid Services. National Health Expenditure 2016 Highlights. Balti-

more, MD: Centers for Medicare and Medicaid Services, January 2018. https://www.cms.gov/Research-Statistics-Data-and-Systems/Statistics-Trends-and-Reports/NationalHealth ExpendData/NationalHealthAc countsHistorical.html.

7. Kaiser Family Foundation. "10 Things to Know about Medicaid: Setting the Facts Straight." Washington, DC: Kaiser Family Foundation, 2018. https://www.kff.org/ medicaid/issue-brief/10-things-to-know-about-medicaid-setting-the-facts-straight/.

8. Jean Accius, Lynda Flowers, and Brendan Flinn. "Low-Income Medicare Beneficiaries Rely on Medicaid for Critical Help." Washington, DC: AARP Public Policy Institute, 2018. https://www.aarp.org/ppi/info-2017/low-income-medicare-benefciaries-rely-on-medicaid-for-critical-help.html.

9. Steve Eiken, Kate Sredl, Brian Burwell, and Angie Amos. Medicaid Expenditures for Long-Term Services and Supports in FY 2016. Bethesda, MD: IBM Watson Health. https://w w w.medicaid.gov/medicaid/ltss/downloads/reports-and-evaluations/ltssexpenditures2016.pdf.

10. Joanne Binette and Kerri Vasold. "2018 Home and Community Preferences: A National Survey of Adults Age 18-Plus." Washington, DC: AARP Research, 2018. https://www.aarp. org/research/topics/community/info-2018/2018-home-community-preference.html.

11. Ari Houser, Wendy Fox-Grage, and Kathleen Ujvari. Across the States 2018: Profiles of Long-Term Services and Supports. Washington, DC: AARP Public Policy Institute. http://w w w.aarp.org/acrossthestates.

12. Rachel Garfeld and Robin Rudowitz. "Understanding the Intersection of Medicaid and Work." Washington, DC: Kaiser Family Foundation. https://www.kff.org/medicaid/issue-brief/understanding-the-intersection-of-medicaid-and-work/.

13. Aviva Aron-Dine. Eligibility Restrictions in Recent Medicaid Waivers Would Cause Many Thousands of People to Become Uninsured. Washington, DC: Center on Budget and Policy Priorities. https://www.cbpp.org/research/health/ eligibility-restrictions-in-recent-medicaid-waivers-would-cause-many-thousands-of.

14. Rachel Garfeld, Robin Rudowitz, and MaryBeth Musumeci. "Implications of a Medicaid Work Requirement: National Estimates of Potential Coverage Losses." Washington, DC: Kaiser Family Foundation. https://www.kff.org/medicaid/ issue-brief/implications-of-a-medicaid-work-requirement-national-estimates-of-potential-coverage-losses/.

15. Jennifer Schramm. "An Aging Labor Force and the Challenges of 65+ Jobseekers." Washington, DC: AARP Public Policy Institute, 2018. https://www.aarp.org/ppi/ info-2018/an-aging-labor-force.html.

16. Robin Rudowitz and MaryBeth Musumeci. An Early Look at State Data for Medicaid Work Requirements in Arkansas. Washington, DC: Kaiser Family Foundation, 2018. https://www.kff.org/medicaid/issue-brief/an-early-look-at-state-data-for-medicaid-work-requirements-in-arkansas/.

17. Julia Zur and Jennifer Tolbert. "The Opioid Epidemic and Medicaid's Role in Facilitating Access to Treatment." Washington, DC: Kaiser Family Foundation, 2018. https://www.kff.org/medicaid/issue-brief/the-opioid-epidemic-and-medicaids-role-in-facilitating-access-to-treatment/.

18. Kaiser Family Foundation. "Data Note: 10 Charts About Public Opinion on Medicaid." Washington, DC: Kaiser Family Foundation, 2017. https://www.kff.org/medicaid/ poll-fnding/data-note-10-charts-about-public-opinion-on-medicaid/.

14. Getting Started with Medicare*

MEDICARE.GOV

Whether you're new to Medicare, getting ready to turn 65, or preparing to retire, you'll need to make several important decisions about your health coverage. If you wait to enroll, you may have to pay a penalty, and you may have a gap in coverage.

Medicare is managed by the Centers for Medicare & Medicaid Services (CMS). Social Security works with CMS by enrolling people in Medicare. You don't need to sign up for Medicare each year. However, each year you'll have a chance to review your coverage and change plans.

Use these steps to gather information so you can make informed decisions about your Medicare:

Step 1: Learn about the different parts of Medicare: The different parts of Medicare help cover specific services. Medicare Part A (Hospital Insurance) covers inpatient hospital stays, care in a skilled nursing facility, hospice care, and some home health care. Medicare Part B (Medical Insurance) covers certain doctors' services, outpatient care, medical supplies, and preventive services.

Step 2: Find out when you can get Medicare: There are only certain times when people can enroll in Medicare. Depending on the situation, some people may get Medicare automatically, and others need to apply for Medicare. The first time you can enroll is called your Initial Enrollment Period. Your 7-month Initial Enrollment Period usually:

- Begins three months before the month you turn 65
- Includes the month you turn 65
- Ends three months after the month you turn 65

If you don't enroll when you're first eligible, you may have to pay a Part B late enrollment penalty, and you may have a gap in coverage if you decide you want Part B later.

Step 3: Decide if you want Part A and Part B: Most people should enroll in Part A when they turn 65, even if they have health insurance from an employer. This is because most people paid Medicare taxes while they worked so they don't pay a monthly premium for Part A. Certain people may choose to delay Part B. In most cases, it depends on the type of health coverage you may have. Everyone pays a monthly premium for Part B. The premium varies depending on your income and when you enroll in Part B. Most people

---

*Originally published as Medicare.gov, "Getting Started with Medicare," https://www.medicare.gov/sign-up-change-plans/getting-started-with-medicare.

will pay the standard premium amount of $135.50 in 2019. You must pay your Part B premium every month for as long as you have Part B (even if you don't use it).

Most people should enroll in Medicare Part A (Hospital Insurance) when they're first eligible, but certain people may choose to delay Medicare Part B (Medical Insurance). In most cases, it depends on the type of health coverage you may have, including the following situations:

- I'm currently working, and I have coverage through my job.
- I have coverage through my spouse who is currently working.
- I have retiree coverage (from my former employer or my spouse's former employer) or COBRA coverage.
- I have TRICARE, and I'm a retired service member.
- I have TRICARE, and I'm an active-duty service member.
- I have Veterans' benefits.
- I have CHAMPVA.
- I have End-Stage Renal Disease (ESRD).
- I have Marketplace or other private insurance.

Step 4: Choose your coverage: If you decide you want Part A and Part B, there are two main ways to get your Medicare coverage—Original Medicare or a Medicare Advantage Plan (like an HMO or PPO). Some people get additional coverage, like Medicare prescription drug coverage or Medicare Supplement Insurance (Medigap). Most people who are still working and have employer coverage don't need additional coverage. Learn about these coverage choices.

Step 5: Sign up for Medicare (unless you'll get it automatically): Some people get Medicare Part A (Hospital Insurance) and Medicare Part B (Medical Insurance) automatically and other people have to sign up for it. In most cases, it depends on whether you're getting Social Security benefits. If you're automatically enrolled, you'll get your red, white, and blue Medicare card in the mail three months before your 65th birthday or your 25th month of disability. If you don't get Medicare automatically, you'll need to apply for Medicare online.

Medicare Part C is another name for Medicare Advantage or Medicare Health plans. Medicare Part C is administered by private insurance companies contracted with Medicare. Medicare Part C covers everything that Original Medicare (Part A and Part B) cover and may cover extra benefits as well. Before enrolling in a Part C plan, you must first enroll in Original Medicare—both Part A and Part B. If you decide to use Medicare Advantage, you choose the plan yourself and sign up directly with the private insurer. By law, Part C plans must pay for at least the same healthcare services as Original Medicare. But they sometimes pay for things that are not covered by Original Medicare, such as vision and dental care. Most, but not all, Medicare Advantage plans also provide some prescription drug coverage.

Medicare Part D covers prescription drugs. Part D is optional and available to people who are enrolled in Original Medicare (Parts A and B) and most Medicare Advantage plans. Part D plans are offered by private insurance companies that are approved by Medicare. You sign up for them directly with the private insurer. If you are enrolled in a Part D plan, you will pay a monthly premium and sometimes a deductible, as well as copayments for your drugs.

Step 6: Six things to look for when choosing Medicare drug coverage: Prescription drug coverage can vary by cost, coverage, convenience, and quality. Here are six common situations to consider before making a decision about Medicare drug coverage:

- I take specific drugs.
- I want extra protection from high prescription drug costs.
- I want my drug expenses to be balanced throughout the year.
- I take a lot of generic prescriptions.
- I don't have many drug costs now, but I want coverage for peace of mind and to avoid future penalties.
- I like the extra benefits and lower costs available by getting my healthcare and prescription drug coverage from one plan, and I'm willing to accept the plan's restrictions on what doctors, hospitals, and other healthcare providers I can use.

Step 7: Five tasks for your first year with Medicare:

1. Fill out an Authorization Form if you want your family or friends to call Medicare on your behalf. Medicare can't give personal health information about you to anyone unless you give permission in writing first.

2. Make a "Welcome to Medicare" Preventive Visit appointment during the first 12 months you have Medicare. This free, one-time comprehensive preventive visit puts you in control of your health and your Medicare from the start.

3. Sign up for MyMedicare.gov to access your personal Medicare information 24 hours a day, every day. Through this secure online service, you can:
- Track your healthcare claims
- View your "Medicare Summary Notices" (MSNs)
- Order a replacement Medicare card
- Check your Medicare Part B deductible status
- View your eligibility information
- Track your preventive services
- Find information about your Medicare health plan or Medicare Prescription Drug Plan (Part D) or search for a new one
- Keep your Medicare information in one convenient place

4. Learn what Medicare covers. You'll get a list of tests, items, and services that are covered no matter where you live. If your test, item, or service isn't listed, talk to your doctor or other healthcare provider about why you need it. And, ask if Medicare will cover it.

5. Decide if you want to go paperless and get your next free copy of "Medicare & You" electronically. Next October, you'll get an email linking you to "Medicare & You" instead of a paper copy in your mailbox.

15. Why Older Adults Should Eat More Protein (And Not Overdo Protein Shakes)*

JUDITH GRAHAM

Older adults need to eat more protein-rich foods when losing weight, dealing with a chronic or acute illness, or facing a hospitalization, according to a growing consensus among scientists.

During these stressful periods, aging bodies process protein less efficiently and need more of it to maintain muscle mass and strength, bone health and other essential physiological functions.

Even healthy seniors need more protein than when they were younger to help preserve muscle mass, experts suggest. Yet up to one-third of older adults don't eat an adequate amount due to reduced appetite, dental issues, impaired taste, swallowing problems and limited financial resources. Combined with a tendency to become more sedentary, this puts them at risk of deteriorating muscles, compromised mobility, slower recovery from bouts of illness and the loss of independence.

Impact on functioning: Recent research suggests that older adults who consume more protein are less likely to lose "functioning": the ability to dress themselves, get out of bed, walk up a flight of stairs and more. In a 2018 study that followed more than 2,900 seniors over 23 years, researchers found that those who ate the most protein were 30 percent less likely to become functionally impaired than those who ate the least amount.

While not conclusive (older adults who eat more protein may be healthier to begin with), "our work suggests that older adults who consume more protein have better outcomes," said Paul Jacques, co-author of the study and director of the nutritional epidemiology program at Tufts University's Jean Mayer USDA Human Nutrition Research Center on Aging.

In another study, which was published in 2017 and followed nearly 2,000 older adults over six years, people who consumed the least amount of protein were almost twice as

*Originally published as Judith Graham, "Why Older Adults Should Eat More Protein (And Not Overdo Protein Shakes)," *Kaiser Health News*, https://khn.org/news/why-older-adults-should-eat-more-protein-and-not-overdo-protein-shakes/ (January 17, 2019). *Kaiser Health News* is a nonprofit news service covering health issues. It is an editorially independent program of the Kaiser Family Foundation that is not affiliated with Kaiser Permanente.

likely to have difficulty walking or climbing steps as those who ate the most, after adjusting for health behaviors, chronic conditions and other factors.

"While eating an adequate amount of protein is not going to prevent age-associated loss of muscle altogether, not eating enough protein can be an exacerbating factor that causes older adults to lose muscle faster," said Wayne Campbell, a professor of nutrition science at Purdue University.

Recommended intake: So, how much protein should seniors eat? The most commonly cited standard is the Recommended Dietary Allowance (RDA): 0.8 grams of protein per kilogram (2.2 pounds) of body weight per day.

For a 150-pound woman, that translates into eating 55 grams of protein a day; for a 180-pound man, it calls for eating 65 grams.

To put that into perspective, a 6-ounce serving of Greek yogurt has 18 grams; a half-cup of cottage cheese, 14 grams; a 3-ounce serving of skinless chicken, 28 grams; a half-cup of lentils, 9 grams; and a cup of milk, 8 grams.

Older adults were rarely included in studies used to establish the RDAs, however, and experts caution that this standard might not adequately address health needs in the older population.

After reviewing additional evidence, an international group of physicians and nutrition experts in 2013 recommended that healthy older adults consume 1 to 1.2 grams of protein per kilogram of body weight daily—a 25 percent to 50 percent increase over the RDA. (That's 69 to 81 grams for a 150-pound woman, and 81 to 98 grams for a 180-pound man.) Its recommendations were subsequently embraced by the European Society for Clinical Nutrition and Metabolism.

When illness is an issue: For seniors with acute or chronic diseases, the group suggested protein intake of 1.2 to 1.5 grams per kilogram of body weight while noting that the precise amount needed "depends on the disease, its severity" and other factors. (At the 1.5 grams-per-kilogram level, a 150-pound woman would need to eat 102 grams of protein daily, while a 180-pound man would need to eat 123 grams.) Even higher levels, up to two grams per kilogram of body weight, could be needed, it noted, for older adults who are severely ill or malnourished.

(These recommendations don't apply to seniors with kidney disease, who should not increase their protein intake unless they're on dialysis, experts said.)

"Protein becomes much more important during events in an older adult's life that force them into a situation of muscle disuse—a hip or knee replacement, for instance," said Stuart Phillips, director of McMaster University's Centre for Nutrition, Exercise and Health Research in Canada.

"Higher amounts of protein have value when something in an older adult's body is changing," Campbell agreed. He co-authored a new study in JAMA Internal Medicine that did not find benefits from raising protein intake for older men. This could be because the intervention period, six months, wasn't long enough. Or it could have been because the study's participants had adjusted to their diets and weren't exposed to additional stress from illness, exercise or weight loss, Campbell said.

Per-meal amounts: Another recommendation calls for older adults to spread protein consumption evenly throughout the day. This arises from research showing that seniors are less efficient at processing protein in their diet and may need a larger "per-meal dose."

"The total dose that you eat may not matter as much as the dose you eat at a given meal," said Dr. Elena Volpi, a professor of geriatrics and cell biology at the University of

Texas Medical Branch in Galveston, Texas. "If I eat too little protein during a meal, I may not adequately stimulate the uptake of amino acids into skeletal muscle. If I eat too much, say from a large T-bone steak, I won't be able to store all of it away."

Based on her research, Volpi suggests that older adults eat 25 to 30 grams of protein per meal. Practically, that means rethinking what people eat at breakfast, when protein intake tends to be lowest. "Oatmeal or cereal with milk isn't enough; people should think of adding a Greek yogurt, an egg or a turkey sausage," Volpi said.

Protein in all forms is fine: Animal protein contains all nine essential amino acids that our bodies need; plant protein doesn't. If you're a vegetarian, "it just takes more work to balance all the amino acids in your diet" by eating a variety of foods, said Denise Houston, associate professor of gerontology and geriatric medicine at Wake Forest School of Medicine in North Carolina. Otherwise, "I would typically recommend having some animal protein in your diet." As long as red meat is lean and you don't eat it too often, "that's OK," Houston said.

Supplements: What about powdered or liquid protein supplements? "There's generally no need for supplements unless someone is malnourished, sick or hospitalized," Volpi said.

In a new study, not yet published, she examined the feasibility of supplementing the diets of older adults discharged from the hospital with extra protein for a month. Preliminary data, yet to be confirmed in a larger clinical trial, shows that "this can improve recovery from a hospitalization," Volpi said.

"The first line of defense should always be real food," said Samantha Gallo, assistant director of clinical nutrition at Mount Sinai Hospital in New York. "But if someone isn't able to consume a turkey sandwich and would rather sip a protein shake during the day, we'll try that."

However, older adults should not routinely drink protein shakes instead of meals, Gallo cautioned, adding: "That's a bad idea that can actually result in reduced protein and calorie intake over the long term."

16. Before the Fall*

How Oldsters Can Avoid One of Old Age's Most Dangerous Events

MATTHEW LEE SMITH, ELLEN SCHNEIDER,
MARCIA G. ORY *and* TIFFANY SHUBERT

Baby boomers, who once viewed themselves as the coolest generation in history, are now turning their thoughts away from such things as partying and touring alongside rock bands to how to they can stay healthy as they age. And, one of the most important parts of healthy aging is avoiding a fall, the number one cause of accidental death among people 65 and older.

The issue is growing more pressing each day. More adults than ever—46 million—are 65 and older, and their numbers are increasing rapidly.

The Centers for Disease Control and Prevention estimates that one in four older adults will fall each year. Falls are the leading cause of injury and injury deaths among older adults. And, they are costly. Falls are responsible for an estimated $31 billion in annual Medicare costs. This estimate does not account for non-direct medical or societal costs.

People who fall can lose their physical mobility for life, go into a hospital never to be discharged, require skilled nursing or other caregiver support, or become so fearful about falling again that they dramatically limit their daily activities.

The good news is that most falls are preventable, research has identified many modifiable risk factors for falls, and older adults can empower themselves to reduce their falls risks. This means there are opportunities to intervene in clinical and community settings to promote protective behaviors and improve safety.

A Life-changing Event

Falls can cause fractures, traumatic brain injuries and other conditions that require an emergency room visit or hospitalization. An older adult dies from a fall every 19 min-

*Originally published as Matthew Lee Smith, Ellen Schneider, Marcia G. Ory, and Tiffany Shubert, "Before the Fall: How Oldsters Can Avoid One of Old Age's Most Dangerous Events," *The Conversation*, https://theconversation.com/before-the-fall-how-oldsters-can-avoid-one-of-old-ages-most-dangerous-events-102091 (September 21, 2018). Reprinted with permission of the publisher.

utes, and every 11 seconds an older adult is treated in an emergency room for a fall-related injury. About one in four falls results in needed medical attention, and falls are responsible for about 95 percent of all hip fractures. In addition to the physical and mental trauma associated with the fall itself, falls often result in fear of falling, reduced quality of life, loss of independence and social isolation.

There is no single cause for falling. Falls can result from issues related to biological aging, such as balance problems, loss of muscle strength, changes in vision, arthritis or diabetes. Taking a combination of several prescription drugs can also contribute to falls. Lifestyle behaviors such as physical inactivity, poor nutrition and poor sleep quality can also increase the risk for falling. Environmental hazards inside the home, such as poor lighting and throw rugs, and outside, such as bad weather, standing water and uneven sidewalks, can create situations where falls are more likely to occur.

It Takes a Careful Village

Because falls can be caused by many things, the solutions must also include a diverse set of systems, organizations and professionals. Toward that end, 42 active or developing state fall prevention coalitions, which coordinate initiatives and serve as advocates for policy development and community action, are in place. Their activities foster collaboration across the aging services network, public health and healthcare system. They do such things as host health fairs and fall risk screening events, fall prevention programs, and awareness-raising events to inform decision-makers and legislators about ways to make communities safer for older adults.

Following are some of the key objectives that the coalitions are working on to reduce hazards from falling:

Enhance clinical-community collaboration for programming: There are many fall prevention programs offered in communities to promote healthful behaviors and to reinforce positive mental perspectives about falls being preventable.

People concerned about falling should contact their local Area Agency on Aging to find out where these programs are offered and which can be most beneficial. Also, seniors should ask their doctors about fall-related risk factors and what they can do to reduce risk. Communicate your concerns about falls with your healthcare team and social network, tell them about what you learn during your fall prevention programs, and report back about how they are making a difference in your life.

Manage chronic conditions: About 70 percent of older adults have one or more chronic conditions, many of which can increase the risk for falling. For example, people with diabetes may have vision problems and problems with sensation in their feet. Also, the medications used to treat these conditions can increase fall risk. And, taking five or more medications has been identified with increased frailty and higher risk for falling. Being physically active can help seniors have better balance and reduce the risk of falls.

While healthcare access and utilization are important for chronic disease diagnosis and management, 90 percent of healthcare happens outside the healthcare setting. Therefore, older adults need to manage their diseases better. To do this, however, they often need help. For starters, they should discuss the side effects of all medications with their doctors and also how best to adhere to prescribed treatment regimens, such as when to take medications, whether to take with food and whether there are possible interactions of one medication with another. Seniors also can consider enrolling in evidence-based disease self-management programs to improve their knowledge and confidence to manage their conditions as well as enhance lasting skills for goal setting and action planning, such as being physically active for 30 minutes a day for five days a week.

Alter the physical environment: About 44 percent of falls occur inside the home. In-home risk factors for falls can include dim lighting, clutter on floors, throw rugs and ottomans, missing railings, uncovered wires and extension cords, children and pets underfoot and unsafe bathrooms. An unsafe bathroom is one with an inappropriate toilet height, high shower or bathtub walls and no grab rails.

To identify possible risks in the home, the CDC created a user-friendly safety checklist that can safeguard older adults by eliminating environmental hazards.

Maintain healthful behaviors: Daily lifestyle behaviors such as physical activity, nutrition and sleep quality can influence fall risk, and these are never too late to change. Interventions can be successful for people of all ages. Among the most important is physical activity, namely safely performing lower-body exercises to increase strength, balance and flexibility. Additionally, seniors should work with their healthcare team to have medications reviewed and eyes checked regularly. Also, they should ask about their vitamin D levels and possible nutritional supplementation.

17. Making Smarter Decisions About Where to Recover After Hospitalization*

JUDITH GRAHAM

Every year, nearly two million people on Medicare—most of them older adults—go to a skilled nursing facility to recover after a hospitalization. But choosing the facility can be daunting, according to an emerging body of research.

Typically, a nurse or a social worker hands out a list of facilities a day or two—sometimes hours—before a patient is due to leave. The list generally lacks such essential information as the services offered or how the facilities perform on various measures of care quality.

Families scramble to make calls and, if they can find the time, visit a few places. Usually they're not sure what the plan of care is (what will recovery entail? how long will that take?) or what to expect (will nurses and doctors be readily available? how much therapy will there be?).

If asked for a recommendation, hospital staffers typically refuse, citing government regulations that prohibit hospitals from steering patients to particular facilities and that guarantee patients free choice of medical providers. (This is true only for older adults with traditional Medicare; private Medicare Advantage plans can direct members to providers in their networks.)

"The reality is that we leave patients and families without good guidance at a really vulnerable point in their care trajectory," said Dr. Robert Burke, an assistant professor of medicine at the University of Pennsylvania's Perelman School of Medicine.

Amid stress and confusion, older adults and their families frequently make less than optimal choices. According to a 2018 report from the Medicare Payment Advisory Commission (MedPAC), an independent agency that advises Congress on Medicare, nearly 84 percent of Medicare beneficiaries who go to a skilled nursing facility (SNF) after a hospital stay could have selected a higher-rated provider within a 15-mile radius. On

*Originally published as Judith Graham, "Making Smarter Decisions About Where to Recover After Hospitalization," *Kaiser Health News*, https://khn.org/news/making-smarter-decisions-about-where-to-recover-after-hospitalization/ (April 11, 2019). *Kaiser Health News* is a nonprofit news service covering health issues. It is an editorially independent program of the Kaiser Family Foundation that is not affiliated with Kaiser Permanente.

average, MedPAC noted, hospitals refer patients needing short-term rehabilitation to 34 facilities. (Fewer options are available in rural areas.)

Where older adults go is important "because the quality of care varies widely among providers," MedPAC's report notes, and this affects how fully people recover from surgeries or illnesses, whether they experience complications such as infections or medication mix-ups, and whether they end up going home or to a nursing home for long-term care, among other factors.

A recently completed series of reports from the United Hospital Fund in New York City highlights how poorly older adults are served during this decision-making process. In focus groups, families described feeling excluded from decisions about post-hospital care and reported that websites such as Medicare's Nursing Home Compare, which rates facilities by quality of care and other performance criteria, weren't recommended, easy to use or especially helpful.

What do older adults and family members need to know before selecting a rehab facility after a hospital stay? Recent academic research, policy reports and interviews with experts elucidate several themes.

The Basics

Who needs post-hospital care in a rehabilitation center? Surprisingly, there are no definitive guidelines for physicians or discharge planners. But older adults who have difficulty walking or taking care of themselves, have complex medical conditions and complicated medication regimens, need close monitoring or don't have caregiver support are often considered candidates for this kind of care, according to Kathryn Bowles, professor of nursing at the University of Pennsylvania School of Nursing.

Medicare will pay for short-term rehabilitation at SNFs under two conditions: (1) if an older adult has had an inpatient hospital stay of at least three days; and (2) if an older adult needs physical, occupational or speech/language therapy at least five days a week or skilled nursing care seven days a week.

Be sure to check your status, because not all the time you spend in a hospital counts as an inpatient stay; sometimes, patients are classified as being in "observation care," which doesn't count toward this three-day requirement.

Traditional Medicare pays the full cost of a semiprivate room and therapy at a skilled nursing facility for up to 20 days. Between 21 and 100 days, patients pay a coinsurance rate of $170.50 per day. After 100 days, a patient becomes responsible for the full daily charge—an average $400 a day. Private Medicare Advantage plans may have different cost-sharing requirements.

Nationally, the average stay for rehabilitation is about 25 days, according to a recent editorial on choosing post-hospital care in the Journal of the American Geriatrics Society.

Quality Varies Widely

In its 2018 report, MedPAC documented large variations in the quality of care provided by SNFs. Notably, facilities with the worst performance were twice as likely to read-mit patients to the hospital as those with the best performance. (Readmissions put patients at risk of a host of complications. This measure applied only to readmissions deemed potentially avoidable.) Patients at the best-performing facilities were much more likely to be discharged back home and to regain the ability to move around than those at the worst-performing facilities.

In April 2018, for the first time, Medicare's Nursing Home Compare website is separating out performance measures for short-term stays in SNFs, for people who are recovering after a hospitalization, and long-term stays, for people with severe, chronic, debilitating conditions.

Seven measures for short-term stays will be included: the portion of patients who experience an improvement in their functioning (such as the ability to walk), return home to the community, are readmitted to the hospital, visit the emergency room, get new prescriptions for antipsychotic medications, have pain well controlled, and are adequately treated for bedsores, according to Dr. David Gifford, senior vice president for quality and regulatory affairs at the American Health Care Association, which represents nursing homes and assisted living centers. There will also be a separate "star rating" for short-term stays—an overall indicator of quality.

Questions to Ask

Before making a decision on post-hospital care, older adults and family members should address the following issues:

Your post-hospital needs: Bowles, who has studied what kind of information patients and families find valuable, suggests people ask: What are my needs going to be during the post-hospital period? What kind of help will be needed, and for approximately how long?

Dr. Lena Chen, an associate professor of internal medicine at the University of Michigan who has published research examining wide variations in spending on post-acute care after a hospitalization, suggests asking: What is my anticipated recovery, and what do you think the most difficult parts of it might be?

What the SNF provides: Bowles also suggests people ask why the SNF is being recommended instead of home health care. How will the SNF meet my needs, specifically? What kind of medical care and therapy will I get there? From whom and how often?

Carol Levine, who directs the United Hospital Fund's Families and Health Care Project, suggests that patients and families seek out details about facilities. Is a doctor readily available? (New research suggests 10 percent of patients in skilled nursing facilities are never seen by a physician, nurse practitioner or physician assistant.) What kind of equipment and specialized services are on-site? Can the facility accommodate people with cognitive issues or who need dialysis, for instance?

Getting information early: Dr. Vincent Mor, professor of health services, policy and practice at Brown University's School of Public Health, said patients and families should insist on seeing a discharge planner soon after entering the hospital and start the planning process early. When a planner comes by, "say, 'I don't care about choices: Tell me, what do you think will be best for me?' Be insistent," he advised.

Burke warns that doctors don't typically know which SNF is likely to be the best fit for a particular patient—a topic he has written about. He suggests that older adults or their families insist they be given time to contact facilities if they feel rushed. While there's considerable pressure to discharge patients quickly, there's also a requirement that hospital discharges be safe, Burke noted. "If we're waiting for a family to tell us which facility they want a patient to go to, we can't make a referral or discharge the patient," he said.

18. End-of-Life Planning*

JEANINE R. KELADA *and* WILLIE LEE BRITT

Today, end-of-life planning is not on the forefront of the minds of many patients and their families. A crisis can leave that family unprepared and unsure of the options available. For many people who put off making decisions about end-of-life planning, thinking and talking about these issues can be difficult and documentation can be daunting.

If patients are educated about options available, they may be more prepared. Patients will be more mindful of their choices such as the ability to die at home and to know it is less stressful on the patient and their family. Another benefit is it can reduce healthcare expenses. However, a major problem is that end-of-life planning is not standard on medical questionnaires. Further, physicians find it difficult to talk about it during a routine health examination.

Introduction

Communication about end-of-life planning may involve difficult conversations for patients, loved ones and healthcare professionals. However, a lack of understanding about a person's wishes in regard to his/her future care may result in a loss of dignity for the person and additional stress for the families and health professionals, as well as burden the healthcare system. It is helpful to everyone to start these conversations early so decisions do not have to be made in the absence of adequate information about end-of-life services that are available to patients and their families.

End-of-life care encompasses all healthcare provided to someone in the days or years before death, whether the cause of death is sudden or a result of a terminal illness that runs a much longer course. For people ages 65 and over, the most common causes of death include cancer, cardiovascular disease, and chronic respiratory disease (KFF.org, 2015).

Advance care planning involves multiple steps designed to help individuals: (a) learn about the healthcare options that are available for end-of-life care; (b) determine which types of care best fit their personal wishes; and (c) share their wishes with family, friends, and their physicians (KFF.org, 2015).

---

*Published with permission of the authors.

In some cases, patients have already considered their options and need only one advance care planning conversation with their physician. When considering these options, a patient will put in written instructions intended to reflect the wishes for healthcare to guide medical decision-making in the event that a patient is unable to speak for her/himself. Advance directives typically result from advance care planning and often take the form of a living will which defines the medical treatment that patients prefer if they are incapacitated, or designation of a certain person as a medical power of attorney. There has been a lot of research on end-of-life planning for cancer patients and other terminally ill patients. However, there is minimal research on end-of-life planning for healthy patients.

The topic under these circumstances is just as important because none of us knows what tomorrow will bring, such as a car accident or a serious fall, and subsequently, we are suddenly in the care of another human being who has no idea what our healthcare needs and medical are. That is what makes end-of-life planning for all patients so crucial. Currently, there is no policy on when or how a physician should discuss end-of-life planning with a patient. End-of-life discussions usually happen when a patient is terminally ill and the physician is forced to have the conversation with that patient.

End-of-life planning reviewed by the physician and patient during the patient's routine yearly examination will be beneficial because decisions for end-of-life planning take time and consideration and it is something the physician and patient can plan together on a yearly basis. End-of-life planning conversations should start right away in a patient's healthcare plan, the same way the physician focuses on exercising and healthy eating. The prime age is 18 to start talking to patients because at that age they are becoming responsible for their own healthcare goals. The objective is for patients to be more prepared for end-of-life. Their physician will have a structured conversation with the patient, and thus, the patient will in turn be more educated and empowered and want to document an end-of-life plan accordingly. End-of-life planning is not a one-time decision and done; planning should look different at different stages of life.

The research presented herein looked at the benefits to educating patients before they become Medicare age or terminally ill to determine if it will help increase the rate of end-of-life planning for all patients. Physicians and patients were surveyed on their attitudes and knowledge toward end-of-life planning. The research looked at the physicians' and patients' attitudes and beliefs about end-of-life planning, and this can help develop long term goals for end-of-life planning for patients of all ages.

This research proposed that providing education and resources to the patients during routine examinations early on in a patient's healthcare increase the preparedness for end-of-life decisions. There is a vast amount of education that the patient would need to make any type of end-of-life care decisions. This is where patients need guidance from their physicians to provide them with the proper education and resources. Patients need to decide their wishes such as, dying at home or at the hospital. Will the patient want hospice or palliative care? Does the patient want CPR or fluids given in their final stage of life?

Review of Literature

Advanced care planning has had an abundance of research done over the past decade. Advance care planning is a process of reflection and communication. It is a time for a person to reflect on her/his values and wishes and to let people know what kind of health and personal care that person would want in the future if unable to speak for her/his self. It means having discussions with family and friends, especially the substitute decision maker who is the person who will speak on your behalf if you cannot speak for yourself. It may also include writing your wishes and talking with healthcare providers and financial or legal professionals.

There is a lot to take into account when setting up one's own advanced care. It is not much different than setting up any other goals that need to be achieved in one's lifetime, such as college, marriage or family planning. With advance directives people are less likely to talk about their end-of-life wishes and set up their advanced care plans. Advanced care planning is vital for several reasons: (1) baby boomers are aging, (2) it increases communications among patients, families and physicians, and (3) it is a financial cost saving ("Dying in America," 2015).

Also, planning (1) gives patients peace of mind and understanding of what will happen in their final days, (2) keeps family members from guessing to what measures of life saving methods should be acted upon in the event of a tragic accident, (3) reduces family arguments and hospital distress, and (4) reduces healthcare cost when unnecessary life-saving measures and tests are not performed (National Institute on Aging, 2016).

Advanced Care Planning with Young People

It is important to understand that the approach to advanced care planning for young adults is handled differently than when dealing with elderly patients. The study "End-of-Life Health Care Planning Among Young-Old Adults: An Assessment of Psychosocial Influences" investigated whether end-of-life planning among healthy older adults may protect them from unwanted medical treatments in later life in the event that they become incapable of making healthcare decisions for themselves. The study explored two formal and one informal component of end-of-life planning (living will, durable power of attorney for healthcare, and discussions) and assessed whether one's health and healthcare encounters, personal beliefs, and experience with others' deaths affect these practices.

Some of the findings showed recent hospitalizations, personal beliefs, recent experience with the painful death of a loved one, education, gender, marital status, and religious affiliation all affect end-of-life planning. Healthcare providers may encourage end-of-life preparations by assuaging patients' death anxiety and fostering decision-making autonomy. Initiating discussions about recent deaths of loved ones may be an effective way to trigger patients' own end-of-life preparations (Carr & Khodyakov, 2016). Research shows that current end-of-life planning practices have several limitations. Despite widespread professional support for the use of living wills studies reveal that fewer than 50 percent of older adults have them in their medical files (Hahn, 2003).

Discussing advanced care planning with younger people requires a different type of communication strategy. There are studies that research how to approach the topic with the young terminally ill patients. These studies have merit to this research because healthcare providers will need to approach the younger generation in a different communication manner. Weiner and Ballard's study "How I Wish to Be Remembered: The Use of an Advance Care Planning Document in Adolescent and Young Adult Populations" is particularly relevant. The study was done to create an advance care plan using a base called the five "wishes" that concern different parts of the end-of-life care process:

- The Person I Want to Make Care Decisions for Me When I Can't
- The Kind of Medical Treatment I Want or Don't Want
- How Comfortable I Want to Be
- How I Want People to Treat Me
- What I Want My Loved Ones to Know

The study had a favorable turnout, showing that 95 percent of the participants found filling it out to be less stressful (Weiner & Ballard, 2015). A developmentally appropriate advance care planning document may play an important role in the care of seriously ill adolescents and young adults. It may also be necessary in non-terminally ill adults.

Multiple studies have documented that the older one's age, the more likely one is to have an advanced care plan (Pollack et al., 2010). The most frequent reason older adults give for not having advanced care plans is that they are "too healthy," and the most common reason they give for having an advanced care plan is failing medical conditions (Pollack et al., 2010; Schickedanz et al., 2009).

Studies have shown that the actual use of advance directives is low (Molloy, Russo, Pedlar, & Bedard, 2000; Teno, et al., 1997). Use of advance directives has been associated with a number of factors, including attitude about decision-making in advance (Blackhall, Murphy, Frank, Michel, & Azen, 1995), preferences for life-sustaining treatment, and, race and ethnicity (Caralis, Davis, Wright, & Marcial, 1993). Reasons cited as barriers to completion of advance directives include: (1) lack of time, interest, and commitment; (2) deference to family members or physicians; (3) lack of knowledge; (4) personal discomfort with the topic; (5) lack of a surrogate; (6) religious preferences; and (7) feelings of invincibility. These are the barriers that need to come down to help the younger generation communicate and plan for the advance care directives (Morrison, Zayas, & Mulvihill, 1998). This study shows a great number of reasons why young people do not engage in preparing advanced directives. What shows interest is the lack of knowledge.

Advanced Care Planning for the Elderly

People 65 and older may think of their end-of-life options but that does not mean they take the necessary end-of-life planning steps to have their decisions in place. One study shows whether models of health behavior change can help to inform interventions for advance care planning. That study by Terri R. Fried, M.D., et al., is "Understanding Advance Care Planning as a Process of Health Behavior Change." The study included 63 community-dwelling persons 65 and older and 30 caregivers with experience as decisionmakers. The study was done as focus groups divided up by sections.

One aspect of the study is that even the aging population is not comfortable about the process of making end-of-life decisions (Fried, Bullock, Lannone, & O'Leary, 2009).

What are some reasons why physicians fail to communicate with patients?

- The patient and/or the physician may be in denial of the patient's approaching death and may not want to discuss issues related to end-of-life care. Even though the physicians have identified the patients in the study as having less than six months to live, some of the physicians may not want to acknowledge this in their discussions. A physician may experience a sense of discomfort or failure when discussing approaching death with terminally ill patients and their families and may therefore avoid discussions or handle them poorly. It is also clear from the support studies that many seriously ill patients do not wish to discuss their preferences for end-of-life care.

- Some physicians may lack knowledge of the existence of end-of-life resources in the community and therefore may not bring up such options. Only a small proportion (42 percent) of the patients reported that their physicians discussed hospice care. Some physicians may be reluctant to discuss hospice options because of their limited understanding of the Medicare hospice benefits.
- Some physicians may believe that the available end of-life care options will be unacceptable to some of their patients, in terms of what they believe about these patients' perceptions and preferences. They may, therefore, decide not to discuss these care options.
- Physicians may feel that they do not have time for these types of discussions (Desharnais, Carter, Hennessey, Kurent, & Carter, 2007). Studies have consistently found that patients who talk about their preferences for end-of-life care with their physicians and family members feel less anxiety, feel more involved in their medical decision-making, and perceive their physicians as having a better understanding of their needs (Kass-Bartelmes & Hughes, 2004).

End-of-life conversations have been examined and there is a need for evolution in preemptive conversations. An article titled "End-of-Life Conversations Evolving Practice and Theory" examined the evolution of and need for such conversations. Barriers to end-of-life discussions that have been identified in patients and families, healthcare professionals, and healthcare systems can seriously interfere with the quality of remaining life for terminally ill patients.

Strategies for enhancing end-of-life discussions are most productively linked to: (1) physicians' interpersonal communication skills, (2) a patient-centered model of care, (3) a focus on quality of remaining life, and (4) innovative clinical models for implementing these discussions earlier in the care process (Larson & Tobin, 2000). Physicians might avoid end-of-life conversations because they (1) fear causing pain and bearing bad news, (2) lack knowledge of advance directive laws and training in delivering bad news, (3) view death as an enemy to be defeated, (4) anticipate disagreement with the patient or family, (5) have medical-legal concerns, and (6) feel threatened by such discussions (Larson & Tobin, 2000).

One approach to advanced care planning is characterized by mutual-participation relationships that encourage informed choice and patient autonomy. At the heart of the patient-centered approach is the need to understand the meaning of the illness for the patient, a central goal of any whole-person approach to end-of-life care. This approach recognizes that it is the patient who must ultimately make the decisions that will determine the outcomes in his or her life. It seeks to empower the patient to make the best choices, given his or her values and needs. Key to a patient-centered clinical method is responding in such a way that patients sense that their ideas, feelings, expectations, and fears are understood essential elements of all end-of-life conversations (Larson & Tobin, 2000).

Another study, "Physician Factors Associated with Discussions about End-of-Life Care," by Keating and Associates, dealt with physician/patient communications with terminally ill cancer patients.

Significant Findings

Physicians would like to engage in conversations with their patients about advanced care planning. At the time of the research, physicians indicated they speak to 90 percent of their patients about advanced care plans. It is a difficult topic to bring up with patients who are not ill. So they primarily speak with the Medicare-age patient about advanced care plans. Fifty-eight percent (58 percent) of the physicians felt that patients could use more education. Fifty-five percent (55 percent) of the physicians surveyed felt it was important to discuss advanced care planning.

New Generation and New Ways to Communicate with Health Care Professionals

Technology and communication go hand-in-hand with the new generation as discussed in the literature review. The younger generation wants information faster and less face to face interaction. Social media is the new source of information. The majority of the medical practices are on electronic medical records. Large healthcare systems have patient portals where they can access their own medical records and communicate with their healthcare team via email. The research question proposed was baby boomers think it is very important to talk face to face about end-of-life planning while the other generations are divided on their responses.

The healthcare workforce has grown with the addition of a new group of physicians, nurses, allied health professionals, administrators, and support staff who belong to America's youngest generation now in the workforce—Generation Y, or the millennials. This generation consists of more than 70 million people, the oldest of whom are now in their late 20s and early 30s. They have traits and workplace expectations that differ from those observed in other generations. Technology is different. How patients receive information is different. Healthcare has a growing demand to keep up with the ways to communicate to the young, the elderly, the sick and the terminally ill patients. Each of these literature reviews identified the importance of the discussion of advance care planning and the difficulties the patients and physicians have opening up the dialogue. The question proposed in this research was what is the significance of providing early education during the patient's routine physical exams and if this helps patient to become aware and more prepared to make end-of-life decisions.

Conclusion

Most physicians reported they would not discuss end-of-life options with terminally ill patients who are feeling well, instead waiting for symptoms or until there are no more treatments to offer. More research is needed to understand physicians' reasons for timing of discussions and how their propensity to aggressively treat metastatic disease influences timing, as well as how the timing of discussions influences patient and family experiences at the end of life (Keating et al., 2010). These are interesting findings even in the event when the patient is terminally ill.

Most expect their physician to initiate such dialogue. End-of-life discussions, however, must go beyond the narrow focus of resuscitation. Instead, such discussions should address the broad array of concerns shared by most dying patients and families: fears about dying, understanding prognosis, achieving important end-of-life goals, and attending to physical needs. Good communication can facilitate the development of a comprehensive treatment plan that is medically sound and concordant with the patient's wishes and values. Physicians are trained to maintain health and fight illness, but typically receive little guidance on how to communicate with dying patients and their families. Thus, in our death-averse society, it is not surprising that many physicians find it difficult to engage in end-of-life discussions.

"A Physician's Guide to Talking About End-of-Life Care" addresses how the patient believes it is the physician's responsibility to bring up end-of-life discussions, which may be true. Poor communication leads to suboptimal care. Physicians must therefore accept responsibility to initiate timely dialogue, as many patients will wait for their physician to raise the subject.

Physicians and other healthcare professionals need to acknowledge and develop their own skills in relation to communication with patients about care planning. The findings in the research show that opportunity of communication is always a problem with the physician-patient relationship. There is a strong divide between physicians in the role of responsibility of educating patients in end-of-life planning. Almost half thought it was not their responsibility to educate the patients who were not elderly or terminally ill. Although they understand the importance of end-of-life planning, they find it difficult to start the conversation. The research further found that patients can benefit from learning about end-of-life planning through other modes of technology. Millennials would benefit from more web-based learning about healthcare topics such as end-of-life planning. During the literature review it was discovered that many of the studies were done in other countries several years ago and are not current.

Recommendations

1. Have more public awareness on the importance of end-of-life planning and helping make the public aware where they can go to get information and help. There needs to be more media advertisement that would help people understand the importance of end-of-life planning as they do the importance of saving for their next vacation or savings account. It would be a great public service by an organizational or a government sponsorship. The Veterans Administration has such a program.

2. Establish a physician alliance group for end-of-life planning to help educate doctors how to communicate with patients and create tools that would help the younger patients learn about end-of-life planning and help patients to begin to put advanced care directives in place. The physician alliance group can be the leaders in end-of-life planning with the new advancement and cutting-edge technology to roll

out to patients. It would be a good public initiative that could give the physicians continuing medical education credits or reimbursements credit for attending the courses.

3. Implement better healthcare reimbursement for end-of-life planning to help enable the time for physician-patient time to discuss end-of-life planning at any stage of patient care. This will require policy changes for healthcare insurance reimbursement.

4. Implement healthcare software technology to support end-of-life education on patient portals. This will help the younger generations to be more proactive in doing their own research on end-of-life planning. There can be online forms to fill out that would automatically populate (incorporate) into a patient's chart. This could possibly increase the number of advanced directives on file for patients in the future.

5. Complete more end-of-life research in the United States.

REFERENCES

Blackenhall, L.J., Murphy, S.T., Frank, G., Michel, V., and Azen, S. (2014, September 12). "Ethnicity and Attitudes toward Patient Autonomy." *Journal of the American Medical Association*, 274, 820–825. http://dx.doi.org/10.1001/jama.1995.03530100060035-References-Scientific Research Publish. Retrieved from http://www.scirp.org/reference/ReferencesPapers.aspx?ReferenceID=1284075.

Britt, Willie L. Distinguished Adjunct Professor, Golden Gate University, EMPA 300, "Theory, Ethics and Practice in Public Service," 2018.

Caralis, P.V., Davis, B., Wright, K., and Marcial, E. (1993, July 22). "The Influence of Ethnicity and Race on Attitudes toward Advance Directives, Life-Prolonging Treatments, and Euthanasia." Retrieved from https://repository.library.georgetown.edu/handle/10822/739506.

Carr, D., and Khodyakov, D. (2016, August 18). "End-of-Life Health Care Planning Among Young-Old Adults: An Assessment of Psychosocial Influences." Retrieved from http://psychsocgerontology.oxfordjournals.org/content/62/2/S135.full

Desharnais, S., Carter, R., Hennessey, W., Kurent, J., and Carter, C. (2007, November 3). "Lack of Concordance between Physician and Patient: Reports on End-of-Life Care Discussions." Retrieved from http://online.liebertpub.com/doi/pdf/10.1089/jpm.2006.2543.

"Dying in America." (2015, August 19). "Clinician-Patient Communication and Advance Care Planning–Dying in America—NCBI Bookshelf." Retrieved from https://www.ncbi.nlm.nih.gov/books/NBK285677.

Fried, T., Bullock, K., Lannone, L., and O'Leary, J. (2009, August 4). "Understanding Advance Care Planning as a Process of Health Behavior Change." *Journal of the American Geriatrics Society.* http://onlinelibrary.wiley.com/doi/10.1111/j.1532-5415.2009.02396.x/full.

Hahn, M.E. (2003, January 1). "Advance Directives and Patient-Physician Communication." The JAMA Network. Retrieved from http://jamanetwork.com/journals/jama/fullarticle/195699.

Kass-Bartelmes, B.L., and Hughes, R. (2004, August 5). "Advance Care Planning: Preferences for Care at the End of Life." PubMed, NCBI. Retrieved from https://www.ncbi.nlm.nih.gov/pubmed/15148012.

Keating, N., Landrum, M., Selywn, R., Baum, S., Virnig, B., Huskamp, H., Earle, C., and Kahn, K. (2010, January 10). "Physician Factors Associated with Discussions About End-Of-Life Care." *Cancer.* Retrieved from http://onlinelibrary.wiley.com/doi/10.1002/cncr.24761/full.

Kelada, Janine S. "End of Life Planning." San Francisco, CA: Golden Gate University, 2016.

KFF.org. (2015, June). "10 FAQs: Medicare's Role in End-of-Life Care." Henry J. Kaiser Family Foundation. Retrieved from http://kff.org/medicare/factsheet/10-faqs medicares-role-in-end-of-life-care.

Molloy, D., Russo, R., Pedlar, D., abd Bedard, M. (1999, December 8). "Implementation of Advance Directives Among Community-Dwelling Veterans." Retrieved from http://gerontologist.oxfordjournals.org/content/40/2/213?related urls=yes&legid=geront;40/2/213.

Larson, D., and Tobin, D. (2000, September 27). "The Patient-Physician Relationship, End-of-Life Conversations Evolving Practice and Theory." *JAMA* 2000; 284(12): 1573–1578. doi:10.1001/jama.284.12.1573.

Morrison, S., Zayas, L., and Mulvihill, M. (1998, December 7). "Barriers to Completion of Health Care Proxies." The JAMA Network. Retrieved from http://jamanetwork.com/journals/jamainternalmedicine/fullarticle/1105613.

National Institute on Aging. (2016, August 18). "Advance Care Planning." National Institute on Aging. Retrieved from https://www.nia.nih.gov/health/publication/advance-care-planning.

Pollack, Keshia M., Morhaim, Dan, and Williams, Michael A. (2010, June 1). "The Public's Perspective on

Advance Directives: Implications for State Legislative and Regulatory Policy." *Health Policy*, vol. 96, no. 1, pp. 57–63.

Weiner, L., and Ballard, E. (2015, September 15). "How I Wish to Be Remembered: The Use of an Advance Care Planning Document in Adolescent and Young Adult Populations." Abstract. Retrieved from http://online.liebertpub.com/doi/abs/10.1089.

19. No Cure for Alzheimer's Disease in My Lifetime*

Norman A. Paradis

Biogen recently announced that it was abandoning its late stage drug for Alzheimer's, aducanumab, causing investors to lose billions of dollars.

They should not have been surprised.

Not only have there been more than 200 failed trials for Alzheimer's, it's been clear for some time that researchers are likely decades away from being able to treat this dreaded disease. Which leads me to a prediction: There will be no effective therapy for Alzheimer's disease in my lifetime.

Clinically, I am an emergency physician. But my research interests include diagnostic biomarkers, which are molecular indicators of disease, and a diagnostic test for Alzheimer's is something of a holy grail.

Alzheimer's sits right at the confluence of a number unfortunate circumstances. Stick with me on this—it's mostly bad news for anyone middle-aged or older, but there's a reward of sorts at the end. If you understand why there won't be much headway on Alzheimer's, you'll also understand a bit more why modern medicine has been having fewer breakthroughs on major diseases.

For decades it was widely believed that the cause of Alzheimer's was the build-up of abnormal proteins called amyloid and Tau. These theories dominated the field and led some to believe we were on the verge of effective treatments—through preventing or removing these abnormal proteins. But had the theories been correct we would likely have had at least one or two positive clinical trials.

In retrospect, the multidecade amyloid fixation looks like a mistake that could have been avoided. Although there is a correlation between amyloid and risk of Alzheimer's, there are elderly people whose brains have significant amounts of the protein and yet are cognitively intact. Versions of this observation date back to at least the 1960s. That's one reason why researchers have questioned the enthusiasm for this one hypothesis.

It was always possible that the classic plaques and tangles first seen by Alois Alzheimer, and now known to be made of abnormal proteins, were epiphenomena of aging

*Originally published as Norman A. Paradis, "No Cure for Alzheimer's Disease in My Lifetime," *The Conversation*, https://theconversation.com/no-cure-for-alzheimers-disease-in-my-lifetime-114114 (April 25, 2019). Reprinted with permission of the publisher.

and not the cause of the disease. Epiphenomena are characteristics that are associated with the disease but are not its cause.

Changes occurring in the brain of people with Alzheimer's disease.

But even more convincing that researchers are closer to the beginning than the end in understanding the cause of Alzheimer's is the long list of alternative theories. This now includes but is not limited to infection, disordered inflammation, abnormal diabetes-like metabolism and numerous environmental toxins.

And the past few years have seen more evidence for viral, bacterial and fungal infections. These viral and bacterial hypotheses were portrayed as eureka moments. But this begs the question: How did powerful tools of epidemiology miss associations with things like cold sores and gum disease?

When Occam's razor—the principle that the simplest solution is often the best—is applied to this laundry list of possible causes, it leads to some profound implications. Either Alzheimer's is not one disease, or many factors can contribute to triggering or promoting it. Some authorities have been trying to make such arguments for some time.

Either of these would be bad news, since we would need to develop multiple effective treatments, possibly in combination.

Unfortunately, our biomedical system is designed for the development and testing of one drug at a time. Combinations of drugs dramatically increase the number of clinical trials needed to test for efficacy and toxicity.

For 50 years after Alzheimer described the first patient, the disease was considered relatively rare. Called pre-senile dementia, it struck relatively early and sometimes ran in families. The much more common dementia of old age—senile dementia—was considered part of aging.

But here's the thing—regardless of type, Alzheimer's has a powerful age-related association. This is true even for patients with early-onset inherited form of Alzheimer's. Give someone the worst possible genome for Alzheimer's—including the dreaded APOE e4 gene that may be associated with a tenfold increase in risk—and that person still needs to age a bit before developing the disease.

Combine the long list of risk factors with the powerful age association and Alzheimer's comes into focus. Neurons may be the high-wire act of cell types, and the senescence of aging inexorably wears on them. Any one of many cellular insults may accelerate neurons toward earlier cell death. The worst of these may be a particularly bad gene you inherited from your parents, but all are additive to a greater or lesser degree.

If correct, this conception of the disease means we're even further away from an effective treatment.

Aging is not disease. It is the normal arc of life and an ineluctable part of being human ("dust unto dust"). As such, the biology of aging didn't get the attention that was bestowed on organ systems and diseases during the golden years of research funding.

In retrospect, I think this may have been a grave mistake. If you list the risk factors for the major diseases of modern life—heart disease, diabetes, dementia—the most powerful is almost always age.

Bottom line: We also lack an understanding of the basic science of Alzheimer's most important risk factor.

While it is widely known that it is not possible to diagnose Alzheimer's accurately during life, a dirty little secret of Alzheimer's research is that a significant fraction of patients cannot be categorized even on autopsy. The classic plaques and tangles that Alois Alzheimer saw through his microscope may not be accurate biomarkers of this disease.

The single absolute requirement for the development of therapies is an accurate diagnostic. You can't begin to develop a drug if you can't accurately identify who has and does not have the disease. Alzheimer's is the quintessential example of this, as it is very difficult to diagnose. In living patients, diseases like vascular dementia and Lewy body dementia can be indistinguishable from Alzheimer's. Some of the newest technologies are actually based on imaging amyloid, which some studies show may not be a reliable diagnostic test.

It takes a long time for the Food and Drug Administration to approve a drug. From the moment a possible drug is first conceived, it is often more than 10 years until it is available.

The brain has few if any repair mechanisms. So when we talk about Alzheimer's treatments, we mean prevention not reversal.

The natural history of Alzheimer's is such that preventive therapy will need to be started early in the course of the disease. This will add years to the drug development cycle. A decade from discovery to bedside would be good news for an Alzheimer's drug.

But history teaches us that the delays could be even worse. Shortly after the discovery of genetic engineering in the early 1980s, it was common to tell patients with diseases like sickle cell that a genetic cure was just a few years away. The sickle cell abnormality and its location in the genome had been known for some time. The organ system involved is easy to access. Thirty years later we have still not successfully cured diseases like sickle cell, and the hubris of those early predictions are painful memories for older physicians like myself.

The situation with Alzheimer's looks much worse than sickle cell disease looked back in the 1980s. We don't know the cause—which is likely multifactorial—and its in a hard to get at organ. And neurological diseases are a particular challenge because the brain is protected behind something called the blood-brain barrier. Even if you have a potentially effective drug, it may not reach its target.

Add all of these considerations together and the long road stretches out ahead.

But no drug for the foreseeable future does not mean there's nothing to do. There is some indication that healthy lifestyle efforts may prevent Alzheimer's. And even if they don't, they're likely effective in preventing vascular dementia, which is almost as common.

20. Guidelines Proposed for Newly Defined Alzheimer's-Like Brain Disorder*

NATIONAL INSTITUTE ON AGING

A recently recognized brain disorder that mimics clinical features of Alzheimer's disease has for the first time been defined with recommended diagnostic criteria and other guidelines for advancing and catalyzing future research. Scientists from several National Institutes of Health-funded institutions, in collaboration with international peers, described the newly named pathway to dementia, Limbic-predominant Age-related TDP-43 Encephalopathy, or LATE, in a report published on April 30, 2019, in the journal *Brain*.

"While we've certainly been making advances in Alzheimer's disease research—such as new biomarker and genetic discoveries—we are still at times asking, 'When is Alzheimer's disease not Alzheimer's disease in older adults?'" said Richard J. Hodes, M.D., director of the National Institute on Aging (NIA), part of the NIH. "The guidance provided in this report, including the definition of LATE, is a crucial step toward increasing awareness and advancing research for both this disease and Alzheimer's as well."

Alzheimer's is the most common form of dementia, which is the loss of cognitive functions—thinking, remembering, and reasoning—and every-day behavioral abilities. In the past, Alzheimer's and dementia were often considered to be the same. Now there is rising appreciation that a variety of diseases and disease processes contribute to dementia. Each of these diseases appear differently when a brain sample is examined at autopsy. However, it has been increasingly clear that in advanced age, a large number of people had symptoms of dementia without the telltale signs in their brain at autopsy. Emerging research seems to indicate that the protein TDP-43—though not a stand-alone explanation—contributes to that phenomenon.

Limbic-predominant Age-related TDP-43 Encephalopathy, or LATE, as seen by microscope and MRI.

---

*Originally published as National Institute on Aging, "Guidelines Proposed for Newly Defined Alzheimer's-Like Brain Disorder," https://www.nia.nih.gov/news/guidelines-proposed-newly-defined-alzheimers-brain-disorder (April 30, 2019).

What Is TDP-43?

TDP-43 (transactive response DNA binding protein of 43 kDa) is a protein that normally helps to regulate gene expression in the brain and other tissues. Prior studies found that unusually misfolded TDP-43 has a causative role in most cases of amyotrophic lateral sclerosis and frontotemporal lobar degeneration. However, these are relatively uncommon diseases. A significant new development seen in recent research is that misfolded TDP-43 protein is very common in older adults. Roughly 25 percent of individuals over 85 years of age have enough misfolded TDP-43 protein to affect their memory and/or thinking abilities.

TDP-43 pathology is also commonly associated with hippocampal sclerosis, the severe shrinkage of the hippocampal region of the brain—the part of the brain that deals with learning and memory. Hippocampal sclerosis and its clinical symptoms of cognitive impairment can be very similar to the effects of Alzheimer's.

"Recent research and clinical trials in Alzheimer's disease have taught us two things: First, not all of the people we thought had Alzheimer's have it; second, it is very important to understand the other contributors to dementia," said Nina Silverberg, Ph.D., director of the Alzheimer's Disease Centers Program at NIA. In the past many people who enrolled in clinical trials likely were not positive for amyloid. "Noting the trend in research implicating TDP-43 as a possible Alzheimer's mimic, a group of experts convened a workshop to provide a starting point for further research that will advance our understanding of another contributor to late life brain changes," Silverberg explained. In addition to U.S. scientists, experts included researchers from Australia, Austria, Sweden, Japan, and the United Kingdom with expertise in clinical diagnosis, neuropathology, genetics, neuropsychology and brain imaging.

Supported by NIA, the workshop was held October 17 and 18, 2018, in Atlanta, and co-chaired by Dr. Silverberg and Peter Nelson, M.D., Ph.D., from the University of Kentucky, Lexington, the lead author on the paper. As published in the report, outcomes included classification guidelines for diagnosis and staging of LATE as well as recommendations for future research directions.

LATE: A New Research Priority

The authors wrote that LATE is an underrecognized condition with a very large impact on public health. They emphasized that the "oldest-old" are at greatest risk and importantly, they believe that the public health impact of LATE is at least as large as Alzheimer's in this group.

The clinical and neurocognitive features of LATE affect multiple areas of cognition, ultimately impairing activities of daily life. Additionally, based on existing research, the authors suggested that LATE progresses more gradually than Alzheimer's. However, LATE combined with Alzheimer's—which is common for these two highly prevalent brain diseases—appears to cause a more rapid decline than either would alone.

"It is important to note that the disease itself is not new. LATE has been there all along, but we hope this report will enable more rapid advancement in research to help us better understand the causes and open new opportunities for treatment," said Dr. Silverberg.

LATE and TDP-43 also were featured as emerging scientific topics at the recent Alzheimer's Disease-Related Dementias Summit 2019, at which presenters foreshadowed research priorities covered in the *Brain* report.

Laying Groundwork for LATE

A key recommendation was for routine autopsy evaluation and classification of LATE. The researchers suggest the autopsy diagnosis be in three stages, according to where in the brain TDP-43 is detected:

- Stage 1: amygdala only
- Stage 2: amygdala and hippocampus
- Stage 3: amygdala, hippocampus and middle frontal gyrus

Additional recommendations include highlighting the great need for the development of biomarkers, further pathological studies, and the generation of new animal models. Suggestions were provided for possible strategies to help guide future therapeutic interventions, including the importance of removing subjects with LATE from other clinical trials, which could significantly improve the chances of successful Alzheimer's breakthroughs. The researchers also discussed the importance of more epidemiological, clinical, neuroimaging and genetic studies to better characterize LATE, and the need for research in diverse populations.

"It can't be emphasized enough that this research wouldn't have gotten this far—and can't go further—without those who are willing to donate brain tissue after death," said Dr. Hodes. "We are grateful for organ donors and their families, as well as all clinical trial participants, who truly are crucial to furthering discoveries that can lead to treatments and cures."

For more information about participating in Alzheimer's disease and related dementias clinical research, go to the NIA website.

REFERENCE

Nelson PT, et al. "Limbic-Predominant Age-Related TDP-43 Encephalopathy (LATE): Consensus Working Group Report." *Brain*. 2019 Apr 30. DOI: 10.1093/brain/awz099.
Funding included grants from NIH: U01AG016976, P01AG003949, R01AG03749, P50AG016574, R01AG054449, P30AG028303, P30AG012300, P30AG049638, P30AG010124, P30AG010161, P50AG047366, P50AG025688, P50AG005131, R37AG011378, R01AG041851, R01AG042210, R01AG017917, R01AG034374, UF1AG053983 and UF1AG057707.

21. As Life Expectancies Rise, So Are Expectations for Healthy Aging[*]

Marcia G. Ory, Basia Belza
and Matthew Lee Smith

The Fountain of Youth may still be a myth, but a longer life expectancy is now a reality.

In fact, life expectancy at birth in the United States has risen by more than 30 years in barely more than a century to a current 78.6 years.

But with the increased life expectancy, a question arises: How do people stay healthy as they age? A new concept of healthy aging has emerged. In fact, some are using a new word for aging baby boomers—"perennials"—to describe people who want to live an active, blossoming life into old age.

What is healthy aging? As members of the Healthy Aging Research Network, we have been researching factors affecting how long Americans will live, ways to stay as healthy as possible, and how best to make extended years quality years. Taking a comprehensive view, we defined healthy aging as "the development and maintenance of optimal physical, mental (cognitive and emotional), spiritual, and social well-being and function in older adults."

But achieving this is something different altogether.

Shifting Demographics, Shifting Views

We now know many of the interacting factors influencing healthy aging—one's genetic makeup, cellular biology, lifestyle behaviors, personal perspectives about aging, social engagement, and environment—and realize the importance of viewing aging as the culmination of all these factors. Despite the accumulation of chronic diseases such as arthritis, dementia, heart disease, diabetes, or cancer, aging is not a "disease" but rather

*Originally published as Marcia G. Ory, Basia Belza, and Matthew Lee Smith, "As Life Expectancies Rise, So Are Expectations for Healthy Aging," *The Conversation*, https://theconversation.com/as-life-expectancies-rise-so-are-expectations-for-healthy-aging-102388 (September 24, 2018). Reprinted with permission of the publisher.

a lifelong process that occurs from birth to death. Social and behavioral determinants are often stronger predictors of premature death than one's biology or healthcare.

Yet, there are fundamental questions about what aging means in the U.S. and abroad. This is important to consider, as stereotypical views of aging can be health hazards themselves, as research has shown that holding negative perceptions of aging can cut 7.5 years from one's life.

In the early 1900s, U.S. life expectancy at birth was under 50 years of age, and only a very small percentage of Americans lived to age 65.

As a result, people did not expect to live to an old age, and the concept of healthy aging was unthinkable. Few people, including older adults, healthcare professionals, or policymakers, could imagine the costs of aging with chronic conditions for individuals and society.

Now, aging is a global phenomenon with 962 million people 60 years and older around the world, including about 78 million North Americans. With average life expectancies hovering around 80 and the possibility of living to 125 on the horizon, there is more attention to the contributors and consequences of living into one's 80s, 90s, 100s, and beyond.

Population aging, older persons comprising an increasingly larger share of the population, is becoming the "new normal" throughout the world. This is resulting in the debunking of some stereotypes about global aging as a phenomenon only occurring in the most developed countries.

Although Japan and European countries have the highest percentages of older people, rates of population aging are actually higher in many developing regions such as Asia, Africa, and Latin America and have huge implications for the welfare of older populations. With rapid globalization and urbanization, families are often more mobile, social support networks are breaking down, healthcare systems are inadequate, and older people are often left in remote villages to fend for themselves or care for young children left behind.

On the positive side, we in the U.S. can learn from how some countries are successfully dealing with their aging populations and age-related conditions by considering "all in" community approaches such as dementia-friendly communities.

Ageism Rampant

Despite the increased proportion of older people in our society, many people still hold stereotypical views of aging and view seniors as less capable. Often, the images they hold depict aging as synonymous with frailty, loneliness, and poverty.

Similarly, depictions of super-aging, such as 90-year-olds running marathons, reflect extreme cases that are not necessarily the reality for most people in their 80s, 90s, or 100s, the age groups increasing most rapidly. Healthy aging does not mean everyone needs to be at peak performance on every dimension; rather, it means everyone should live life to the fullest.

Foremost, it is important to combat ageism in all its forms requiring a shift in our thinking and policies away from negative aging stereotypes.

Recognizing aging as a societal and individual concern, it is important to identify concrete actions at all levels that can make a difference.

For grand-scale change, we believe that multiple sectors—aging services, public health, and healthcare—and policymakers, healthcare professionals, families, and older people themselves can take action. We believe there needs to be more public support enabling the growing number of perennials to engage in the well-documented keys to healthy aging. These include having a positive attitude toward aging, being physically active, having access to healthy foods, being socially connected, and living in safe communities.

Toward this end, several aging advocacy groups have banded together to create a campaign to "reframe" or "disrupt" aging—stressing its positive aspects, but also recognizing the realities of some age-related changes, such as declines in sensory abilities and chronic conditions.

A crucial factor is rethinking the role of older people in society and having meaningful roles throughout one's life, whether paid or unpaid. We need to combat ageist views that make it difficult for older workers to maintain high-paying jobs or find new ones if they find themselves unemployed. As researchers, we have seen the positive impact of evidence-based programs for chronic disease self-management, physical activity, falls prevention, and lifestyle enhancement for promoting health and independence.

The Challenge Isn't Going Away

By 2050, there will be more than two billion older people globally. By 2035, there will be more adults 65 and older than children under the age of 18 in the U.S. This unprecedented transformation can bring about doom-and-gloom projections. While these numbers are game-changing, aging demographics do not need to be destiny.

Such projections can also serve as a catalyst to action to create a society that values older people, fosters social and physical environments that are supportive for healthy aging, encourages intergenerational commonalities over intergenerational conflicts, and emboldens older people to take charge of their own health. However, this requires a commitment to programs and services that help older people maintain their health and functioning.

We want to envision a world where intimate relationships would be seen as natural at any age, most falls are preventable, technology is omnipresent to extend older adults' health and well-being, and caregivers have support to maintain their valuable roles. Most importantly, we believe it is best for society as a whole if perennials do indeed remain in vibrant, productive roles whether at home, in the community, or at work.

22. Research Shows Old Age Is Getting Younger All the Time*

WARREN SANDERSON *and* SERGEI SCHERBOV

In 1985, American Richard Bass accomplished an amazing feat. He had set for himself the task of climbing the world's highest mountains in all seven continents. In that year, at age 55, he completed the climb of the last of his seven mountains, Mt. Everest and in doing so became the first person to climb all seven mountains and the oldest person ever to successfully climb Mt. Everest.

But now Mr. Bass's record has been eclipsed.

The oldest person to climb Mt. Everest is Yuichiro Miura of Japan, who reached the summit in 2013 at age 80. And the oldest person to have climbed all seven mountains in seven continents is Takao Arayama of Tanzania, who climbed the last of those mountains at age 74 in 2010.

Over time, as life expectancy increases and people become healthier, older people can do things which were previously the domain of those younger. Indeed, no one would be surprised if, within the next decade, both the above records were broken.

Well, perhaps not exactly no one.

People who analyze population aging using conventional measures assume that none of the attributes that are important for understanding aging change over time or differ in localities. But a wide variety of attributes can be used to study aging. An important one for 65-year-olds, for example, is their projected remaining life expectancy. Another one is how well those 65-year-olds can remember things.

Our research findings challenge the view that the only thing that matters in the study of aging is chronological age; we also dispute the idea that the attributes of elderly people do not matter.

We believe that it is time for aging measurements to account for the new reality of today's old age, including how well the elderly actually function.

*Originally published as Warren Sanderson and Sergei Scherbov, "Research Shows Old Age Is Getting Younger All the Time," *The Conversation*, https://theconversation.com/research-shows-old-age-is-getting-younger-all-the-time-38556 (April 16, 2015). Reprinted with permission of the publisher.

Limitations of the Conventional View on Aging

In the conventional view used by most demographers and policy-makers it is irrelevant that life expectancy at older ages is increasing. Such views don't account for the observation that older people are healthier and are achieving ever higher scores on cognitive status tests than in the past.

And many find no relevance in the fact that people in their mid–80s and beyond will be able to climb the world's highest mountains in the future.

We seek to challenge this misconception.

An analysis of population aging has two aspects.

First, based on chronological age, most countries of the world are in the process of growing older. The proportions of populations 65+ years old are increasing. The proportions 80+ are increasing even faster and median ages of the populations are also increasing.

The conventional approach to the study of population aging ends here, but in doing so, it ignores the second and equally important aspect of aging.

Today's Elderly Are Not Your Father's Grandparents

The characteristics of people at each age are changing.

For example, in 1950, 65-year-old Swedish men had a life expectancy of 13.5 more years. In 2011, their life expectancy was 18.4 years more, almost five years longer.

In contrast in 2010, 65-year-old Russian men had a life expectancy of 11.9 more years, which is less than that of Swedish men in 1900.

By ignoring changes in the attributes of people and looking only at chronological age, the conventional approach provides a misleading picture of the future.

In a series of articles, we show how to incorporate the changing characteristics of people into measures of population aging. (Go to https://www.iiasa.ac.at/web/home/research/researchPrograms/WorldPopulation/Reaging/Indicators.html.) In particular, we have defined a new measure called "prospective age." Prospective age is a measurement based on the average number of years that people have left to live. We categorize people as being "old" not at age 65, but when people at their age have an average of 15 more years to live.

Using this criterion, a Swedish man in 1900 would be considered old at age 60. In 1960, he would have been considered old at age 63, and in 2010 at age 69. Russian men would have been considered old at age 62 in 1960, about the same age at which Swedish men would have been considered old at that time. In 2010, however, Russian men would have been considered old at age 59, three years younger than in 1960. This reflects the mortality crisis in Russia after the dissolution of the Soviet Union.

In our article in PLOS ONE we describe our discovery of a new and counterintuitive aspect of population aging based on those new measures.

Using measures of aging based on prospective age, we found that these measures of aging increase more slowly when life expectancy increase is faster.

For example, we looked at what would happen to measures of aging based on prospective age, if life expectancy were to continue to increase at its current pace in many developed countries of around 1.5 additional years of life per decade. We also looked at what would happen if increases in life expectancy were to stop. We found that our measures of aging were lower in the scenario in which life expectancy was increasing.

In other words, if people lived longer, healthier and more productive lives, we would have less to worry about, in terms of population aging, than if they lived shorter, less healthy and less productive lives.

Worries About Increases in Life Expectancies

When people think about aging from the conventional perspective, they tend to fear rapid increases in life expectancy for four reasons.

First, rapid increases in life expectancy may affect the sustainability of pension systems. But more and more countries are adopting pension systems that automatically adjust for changes in life expectancy. For this growing list of countries, the challenge of sustaining pension systems has already been successfully addressed. The United States, unfortunately, is not one of those countries, but it could be in the future.

The second fear centers on health-care costs. But health-care costs are highest in the last few years of life and these years occur later as life expectancy increases.

The third fear is that there will be so many seriously disabled people in the future that it will be difficult to care for all of them. The evidence, however, tends not to support this concern because the rates of severe disability at each stage of older age tend to decrease with increasing life expectancy.

The last fear is that when life expectancy increases there will be more people not working. However, simultaneous with the increases in the life expectancy and health of Americans, the labor force participation rates of 65- to 69-year-olds has jumped (according to figures from the U.S. Bureau of Labor Statistics) from 21.8 percent in 1990 to 30.8 percent in 2010.

The life expectancy of a child born in a wealthy country today could well be 100 years. By the end of the century, the populations of many of those countries could have median ages above 65.

We need to think about a future in which more than half of the population would be older than the age at which most people retire today. Pension systems, tax systems, educational systems, and labor markets will all have to adjust.

Population aging does produce challenges. It does us no good, however, to misunderstand those changes based on insufficient measurements. It is time for us to understand aging not just on the basis of how many years people have lived, but on the basis of how well they function. When we understand this, we will be in a better position to plan for the changes that we will have to make.

23. It's Time to Measure 21st Century Aging with 21st Century Tools[*]

WARREN SANDERSON *and* SERGEI SCHERBOV

The populations of most countries of the world are aging, prompting a deluge of news stories about slower economic growth, reduced labor force participation, looming pension crises, exploding healthcare costs and the reduced productivity and cognitive functioning of the elderly.

These stories are dire, in part because the most widely used measure of aging—the old-age dependency ratio, which measures the number of older dependents relative to working-age people—was developed a century ago and implies the consequences of aging will be much worse than they are likely to be. On top of that, this ratio is used in political and economic discussions of topics such as healthcare costs and the pension burden—things it was not designed to address.

Turning 65 in 2016 doesn't mean the same thing as hitting 65 in 1916. So instead of relying on the old-age dependency ratio to figure out the impact of aging, we propose using a series of new measures that take changes in life expectancy, labor participation and health spending into account. When you take these new realities into account, the picture looks a lot brighter.

Our Tools to Measure Aging Have Aged

The most commonly used measure of population aging is the "old-age dependency ratio," which is the ratio of the number of people 65 years or older to those 20 to 64.

But, since the old-age dependency ratio was introduced in the early 1900s, most countries have experienced a century of rising life expectancy, and further increases are anticipated.

For instance, in 1914, life expectancy at birth in Sweden was 58.2 years (average for both sexes). By 2014, it had risen to 82.2 years. In 1935, when the U.S Social Security Act

[*]Originally published as Warren Sanderson and Sergei Scherbov, "It's Time to Measure 21st Century Aging with 21st Century Tools," *The Conversation*, https://theconversation.com/its-time-to-measure-21st-century-aging-with-21st-century-tools-53033 (March 4, 2016). Reprinted with permission of the publisher.

was signed into law, 65-year-olds were expected to live 12.7 more years, on average. In 2013, 65-year-olds may expect to live 19.5 years more.

But these changes aren't reflected in the conventional statistics on aging. Nor is the fact that many people don't just stop working when they turn 65, and that people are staying healthier for longer.

To get a better sense of what population aging really means today, we decided to develop a new set of measures that take these new realities into account to replace the old-age dependency ratio. And instead of one ratio, we created several ratios to evaluate healthcare costs, labor force participation and pensions.

Who Retires at 65 Anymore?

One of these new realities is that the number of people working into their late 60s and beyond is going up. In 1994, 26.8 percent of American men aged 65 to 69 participated in the labor force. That figure climbed to 36.1 percent in 2014 and is forecast to reach 40 percent by 2024. And the trend is similar for even older men, with 17 percent of those aged 75 to 79 expected to still be working in a decade, up from just 10 percent in 1994.

Clearly, these older people did not get the message that they were supposed to become old-age dependents when they turned 65.

This isn't unique to the U.S. Rates like these in many countries have been rising. In the U.K., for instance, the labor force participation rate of 65- to 69-year-old men was 24.2 percent in 2014, and in Israel it was 50.2 percent, up from 14.8 percent and 27.4 percent, respectively, in 2000. In part this is because older people now often have better cognitive functioning than their counterparts who were born a decade earlier.

So, instead of assuming that people work only from ages 20 to 64 and become old-age dependents when they hit 65, we have computed "economic dependency ratios" that take into account observations and forecasts of labor force participation rates. This tells us how many adults not in the labor force there are for every adult in the labor force, giving us a more accurate picture than using 65 as a cutoff point. We used forecasts produced by the International Labour Organization to figure this out.

The old-age dependency ratio in the U.S. is forecast to increase by 61 percent from 2013 to 2030. But using our economic dependency ratio, the ratio of adults in the labor force to adults not in the labor force increases by just 3 percent over that period.

Clearly, doom and gloom stories about U.S. workers having to support so many more nonworkers in the future may need to be reconsidered.

Is the Health Care Burden Going to Be So High?

Another reality is that while healthcare costs will go up with an older population, they won't rise as much as traditional forecasts estimate.

Instead of assuming that healthcare costs rise dramatically on people's 65th birthdays, as the old-age dependency ratio implicitly does, we have produced an indicator that takes into account the fact that most of the healthcare costs of the elderly are incurred in their last few years of life. Increasing life expectancy means those final few years happen at ever later ages.

In Japan, for example, when the burden of the healthcare costs of people aged 65 and up on those 20 to 64 years old is assessed using only the conventional old-age dependency ratio, that burden is forecast to increase 32 percent from 2013 to 2030. When we compute healthcare costs based on whether people are in the last few years of their lives, the burden increases only 14 percent.

Pension Ages Are Going Up

The last reality we considered concerns pensions.

In most OECD countries, the age at which someone can begin collecting a full public pension is rising. In a number of countries, such as Sweden, Norway and Italy, pension payouts are now explicitly linked to life expectancy.

In Germany, the full pension age will rise from 65 to 67 in 2029. In the U.S., it used to be 65, is now 66 and will soon rise to 67.

Instead of assuming that everyone receives a full public pension at age 65, which is what the old-age dependency ratio implicitly does, we have computed a more realistic ratio, called the pension cost dependency ratio, that incorporates a general relationship between increases in life expectancy and the pension age. The pension cost dependency ratio shows how fast the burden of paying public pensions is likely to grow.

For instance, in Germany, the old-age dependency ratio is forecast to rise by 49 percent from 2013 to 2030, but 65-year-old Germans will not be eligible for a full pension in 2030. Our pension cost dependency ratio increases by 26 percent over the same period. Instead of indicating that younger Germans will have to pay 49 percent more to support pensioners in 2030 compared to what they paid in 2013, taking planned increases in the full pension age into account, we see that the increase is 26 percent.

Sixty-five Just Isn't That Old Anymore

In addition to this suite of measures focused on particular aspects of population aging, it is also useful to have a general measure of population aging. We call our general measure of population aging the prospective old-age dependency ratio.

People do not suddenly become old-age dependents on their 65th birthdays. From a population perspective, it makes more sense to classify people as being old when they are getting near the end of their lives. Failing to adjust who is categorized as old based on the changing characteristics of people and their longevity can make aging seem faster than it will be.

In our prospective old-age dependency ratio, we define people as old when they are in age groups where the remaining life expectancy is 15 years or less. As life expectancy increases, this threshold of old age increases.

In the U.K., for instance, the conventional old-age dependency ratio is forecast to increase by 33 percent by 2030. But when we allow the old-age threshold to change with increasing life expectancy, the resulting ratio increases by just 13 percent.

Populations are aging in many countries, but the conventional old-age dependency ratio makes the impact seem worse than it will be. Fortunately, better measures that do not exaggerate the effects of aging are now just a click away.

24. Patients Experiment with Prescription Drugs to Fight Aging[*]

Marisa Taylor

Dr. Alan Green's patients travel from around the country to his tiny practice in Queens, N.Y., lured by the prospect of longer lives.

Over the past two years, more than 200 patients have flocked to see Green after learning that two drugs he prescribes could possibly stave off aging. One 95-year-old was so intent on keeping her appointment that she asked her son to drive her from Maryland after a snowstorm had closed the schools.

Green is among a small but growing number of doctors who prescribe drugs "off-label" for their possible anti-aging effects. Metformin is typically prescribed for diabetes, and rapamycin prevents organ rejection after a transplant, but doctors can prescribe drugs off-label for other purposes—in this case, for "aging."

Rapamycin's anti-aging effects on animals and metformin's on people with diabetes have encouraged Green and his patients to experiment with them as anti-aging remedies, even though there's little evidence healthy people could benefit.

"Many of [my patients] have Ph.D.s," said Green, who is 76 and has taken the drugs for three years. "They have read the research and think it's worth a try."

In fact, it's easier for patients to experiment with the drugs—either legally off-label or illegally from a foreign supplier—than it is for researchers to launch clinical trials that would demonstrate they work in humans.

No rigorous large-scale clinical trials have been conducted aimed at aging. The FDA so far has not agreed that a treatment could be approved for delaying the onset of aging or age-related diseases, citing questions about whether research can demonstrate an overall effect on aging rather than just on a specific disease.

Given such reservations, pharmaceutical companies have little incentive to fund costly, large-scale trials. Also, both metformin and rapamycin are generic and relatively cheap.

*Originally published as Marisa Taylor, "Patients Experiment with Prescription Drugs to Fight Aging," *Kaiser Health News*, https://khn.org/news/patients-experiment-with-prescription-drugs-to-fight-aging/ (March 6, 2019). *Kaiser Health News* is a nonprofit news service covering health issues. It is an editorially independent program of the Kaiser Family Foundation that is not affiliated with Kaiser Permanente.

"There's no profit," said Matt Kaeberlein, a professor of pathology at the University of Washington medical school whose team received a $15 million grant from the National Institutes of Health to study the effects of rapamycin in dogs but has noted the lack of funds for studies in people. "Without profit, there's no incentive."

Supplements with purported anti-aging effects routinely enter the market with little scrutiny and less evidence.

Yet, late last year, the NIH rejected a $77 million grant proposal by a prominent group of researchers to determine whether metformin could target multiple age-related diseases at once. It was the second rejection of the ambitious but unorthodox bid.

"We're going to keep trying," said a lead author of the metformin proposal, Stephen Kritchevsky, a co-director of the Sticht Center for Healthy Aging and Alzheimer's Prevention. "These things take time."

Less is known about rapamycin's anti-aging effects and its possible side effects in the general population, including the possibility it could lead to insulin resistance. Yet a litany of studies show that rapamycin extends animal life spans. It also has been shown in such studies to stave off age-related diseases, from cancer to cardiovascular diseases to cognitive diseases.

"There should have been a clinical trial for rapamycin and Alzheimer's disease years ago," said Kaeberlein, who has publicly urged NIH to use a historic boost in Alzheimer's funding to study the drug's effects. "But the fact is, the clinical trials are really hard and expensive."

Alexander Fleming, a former FDA official and advocate for the metformin proposal, said he believed it was difficult for regulators and funders to grasp that aging can be tackled as a whole—not just one disease at a time.

In fact, NIH reviewers who rejected the metformin proposal cited problems with the project's aim of testing multiple age-related diseases at once. The researchers considered appealing the decision, asserting those reviewers were biased against studying aging as a whole. NIH, which declined to comment, discouraged the attempt.

Dr. Evan Hadley, director of the National Institute on Aging's division of geriatrics and clinical gerontology, told Kaiser Health News that NIH is not ruling out funding projects that target aging, saying such proposals are still "of interest."

The FDA also is open to considering such efforts "based on the scientific evidence presented to us," said FDA spokeswoman Amanda Turney.

Fleming, who oversaw the controversial FDA approval of metformin for Type 2 diabetes, said an argument could be made that it could approve a drug like metformin for preventing age-related diseases instead of just treating them. He points to now widely used statins, which were approved to prevent heart disease.

"There is some kind of belief that the FDA can't approve a therapy to reduce the progress of aging or age-related conditions," said Fleming, an endocrinologist. "It's just not true."

Given the lack of consensus, other researchers have moved ahead with clinical trials focused on specific age-related conditions.

Researchers have shown that a "cousin" of rapamycin boosts the effectiveness of flu shots and lowers the incidence of upper respiratory infections in seniors by up to 30 percent. This group, led by Dr. Joan Mannick, has licensed it from Novartis and is now working on getting approval to target Parkinson's disease.

"We're trying to be pragmatic," Mannick said of her team's approach.

Some doctors and patients have decided not to wait. At a recent scientific forum on aging, one of the researchers on the NIH proposal asked the 300 or so people in attendance to raise their hands if they were already taking metformin for aging.

"Half the audience raised their hands," recalled the researcher, Dr. Nir Barzilai, director of the Institute for Aging Research at the Albert Einstein College of Medicine, who said a pharmaceutical rep recently estimated that metformin sales are up 20 percent.

Barzilai is concerned about the off-label trend, although he sees metformin as promising. He contends that researchers in the longevity field first need to set up a framework for testing in clinical trials. Even if metformin doesn't pan out as the most effective drug, he asserts a model like the metformin proposal is needed for any major clinical trial to proceed. His group is now trying to secure about half the amount of funding it requested from NIH from a mix of nonprofit and private investment.

"Much of the aging field is charlatans," Barzilai said. "They tell you take this or that and you'll live forever. But you have to do a clinical trial that is placebo-controlled and only then can you say what it really is and whether it's safe."

Green nonetheless said he plans to continue prescribing. He estimates about 5 percent of his patients are doctors themselves. Others have backgrounds in science or are in the upper-income bracket. According to his website, he charges $350 for an initial visit and does not accept insurance.

"They fly to see me on their own planes," he said.

But other doctors who are open to prescribing metformin are holding off on rapamycin, given side effects in higher doses in sick patients.

"I need to see more evidence," said Dr. Garth Denyer, a doctor in The Woodlands, a wealthy Houston suburb, who said he prescribed metformin to a small number of patients but is waiting on rapamycin. "I'm hoping to see more data on safety."

Michael Slattery, who has been HIV-positive since 1983, said he is taking both drugs because the virus is likely to shorten his life expectancy.

So far, he has not noticed any side effects or benefits. His partner, however, who is also HIV-positive, stopped taking rapamycin after getting kidney infections.

"I feel I have nothing left to lose," said Slattery, a retired biotech consultant.

Other patients remain hopeful, even though the evidence is unlikely to be definitive anytime soon.

Linda Mac Dougall, 70, of Port Hueneme, Calif., said she participated in a small study that did not have a placebo control. She's uncertain whether it had any effect on her.

"I really haven't noticed anything, but that doesn't mean it didn't work," said Mac Dougall, a massage therapist for seniors. She has slightly more confidence in the wide array of supplements she takes, she said: "If I live until I'm 110, we'll know."

25. A "Fountain of Youth" Pill?*

Sure, if You're a Mouse

Marisa Taylor

Renowned Harvard University geneticist David Sinclair recently made a startling assertion: Scientific data shows he has knocked more than two decades off his biological age.

What's the 49-year-old's secret? He says his daily regimen includes ingesting a molecule his own research found improved the health and lengthened the life span of mice. Sinclair now boasts online that he has the lung capacity, cholesterol and blood pressure of a "young adult" and the "heart rate of an athlete."

Despite his enthusiasm, published scientific research has not yet demonstrated the molecule works in humans as it does in mice. Sinclair, however, has a considerable financial stake in his claims being proven correct, and has lent his scientific prowess to commercializing possible life extension products such as molecules known as "NAD boosters."

His financial interests include being listed as an inventor on a patent licensed to Elysium Health, a supplement company that sells a NAD booster in pills for $60 a bottle. He's also an investor in InsideTracker, the company that he says measured his age.

Discerning hype from reality in the longevity field has become tougher than ever as reputable scientists such as Sinclair and pre-eminent institutions like Harvard align themselves with promising but unproven interventions—and at times promote and profit from them.

Fueling the excitement, investors pour billions of dollars into the field even as many of the products already on the market face fewer regulations and therefore a lower threshold of proof.

"If you say you're a terrific scientist and you have a treatment for aging, it gets a lot of attention," said Jeffrey Flier, a former Harvard Medical School dean who has been critical of the hype. "There is financial incentive and inducement to overpromise before all the research is in."

Elysium, co-founded in 2014 by a prominent MIT scientist to commercialize the molecule nicotinamide riboside, a type of NAD booster, highlights its "exclusive" licensing

*Originally published as Marisa Taylor, "A 'Fountain of Youth' Pill? Sure, if You're a Mouse," *Kaiser Health News*, https://khn.org/news/a-fountain-of-youth-pill-sure-if-youre-a-mouse/ (February 11, 2019). *KHN* senior correspondent Jay Hancock contributed to this report. *Kaiser Health News* is a nonprofit news service covering health issues. It is an editorially independent program of the Kaiser Family Foundation that is not affiliated with Kaiser Permanente.

agreement with Harvard and the Mayo Clinic and Sinclair's role as an inventor. According to the company's press release, the agreement is aimed at supplements that slow "aging and age-related diseases."

Further adding scientific gravitas to its brand, the website lists eight Nobel laureates and 19 other prominent scientists who sit on its scientific advisory board. The company also advertises research partnerships with Harvard and U.K. universities Cambridge and Oxford.

Some scientists and institutions have grown uneasy with such ties. Cambridge's Milner Therapeutics Institute announced in 2017 it would receive funding from Elysium, cementing a research "partnership." But after hearing complaints from faculty that the institute was associating itself with an unproven supplement, it quietly decided not to renew the funding or the company's membership to its "innovation" board.

"The sale of nutritional supplements of unproven clinical benefit is commonplace," said Stephen O'Rahilly, the director of Cambridge's Metabolic Research Laboratories who applauded his university for reassessing the arrangement. "What is unusual in this case is the extent to which institutions and individuals from the highest levels of the academy have been co-opted to provide scientific credibility for a product whose benefits to human health are unproven."

The Promise

A generation ago, scientists often ignored or debunked claims of a "fountain of youth" pill.

"Until about the early 1990s, it was kind of laughable that you could develop a pill that would slow aging," said Richard Miller, a biogerontologist at the University of Michigan who heads one of three labs funded by the National Institutes of Health to test such promising substances on mice. "It was sort of a science fiction trope. Recent research has shown that pessimism is wrong."

Mice given molecules such as rapamycin live as much as 20 percent longer. Other substances such as 17 alpha estradiol and the diabetes drug Acarbose have been shown to be just as effective—in mouse studies. Not only do mice live longer, but, depending on the substance, they avoid cancers, heart ailments and cognitive problems.

But human metabolism is different from that of rodents. And our existence is unlike a mouse's life in a cage. What is theoretically possible in the future remains unproven in humans and not ready for sale, experts say.

History is replete with examples of cures that worked on mice but not in people. Multiple drugs, for instance, have been effective at targeting an Alzheimer's-like disease in mice yet have failed in humans.

"None of this is ready for prime time. The bottom line is I don't try any of these things," said Felipe Sierra, the director of the division of aging biology at the National Institute on Aging at NIH. "Why don't I? Because I'm not a mouse."

The Hype

Concerns about whether animal research could translate into human therapy have not stopped scientists from racing into the market, launching startups or lining up investors. Some true believers, including researchers and investors, are taking the substances themselves while promoting them as the next big thing in aging.

"While the buzz encourages investment in worthwhile research, scientists should avoid hyping specific [substances]," said S. Jay Olshansky, a professor who specializes in aging at the School of Public Health at the University of Illinois at Chicago.

Yet some scientific findings are exaggerated to help commercialize them before clinical trials in humans demonstrate both safety and efficacy, he said.

"It's a great gig if you can convince people to send money and use it to pay exorbitant salaries and do it for 20 years and make claims for 10," Olshansky said. "You've lived the high life and get investors by whipping up excitement and saying the benefits will come sooner than they really are."

Promising findings in animal studies have stirred much of this enthusiasm.

Research by Sinclair and others helped spark interest in resveratrol, an ingredient in red wine, for its potential anti-aging properties. In 2004, Sinclair co-founded a company, Sirtris, to test resveratrol's potential benefits and declared in an interview with the journal *Science* it was "as close to a miraculous molecule as you can find." GlaxoSmithKline bought the company in 2008 for $720 million. By the time Glaxo halted the research in 2010 because of underwhelming results with possible side effects, Sinclair had already received $8 million from the sale, according to Securities and Exchange Commission documents. He also had earned $297,000 a year in consulting fees from the company, according to *The Wall Street Journal*.

At the height of the buzz, Sinclair accepted a paid position with Shaklee, which sold a product made out of resveratrol. But he resigned after *The Wall Street Journal* highlighted positive comments he made about the product that the company had posted online. He said he never gave Shaklee permission to use his statements for marketing.

Sinclair practices what he preaches—or promotes. On his LinkedIn bio and in media interviews, he describes how he now regularly takes resveratrol; the diabetes drug metformin, which holds promise in slowing aging; and nicotinamide mononucleotide, a substance known as NMN that his own research showed rejuvenated mice.

Of that study, he said in a video produced by Harvard that it "sets the stage for new medicines that will be able to restore blood flow in organs that have lost it, either through a heart attack, a stroke or even in patients with dementia."

In an interview with *KHN*, Sinclair said he's not recommending that others take those substances.

"I'm not claiming I'm actually younger. I'm just giving people the facts," he said, adding that he's sharing the test results from InsideTracker's blood tests, which calculate biological age based on biomarkers in the blood. "They said I was 58, and then one or two blood tests later they said I was 31.4."

InsideTracker sells an online age-tracking package to consumers for up to about $600. The company's website highlights Sinclair's support for the company as a member of its scientific advisory board. It also touts a study that describes the benefits of such tracking, which Sinclair co-authored.

Sinclair is involved either as a founder, an investor, an equity holder, a consultant or a board member with 28 companies, according to a list of his financial interests. At least 18 are involved in anti-aging in some way, including studying or commercializing NAD boosters. The interests range from longevity research startups aimed at humans and even pets to developing a product for a French skin care company to advising a longevity investment fund. He's also an inventor named in the patent licensed by Harvard and the Mayo Clinic to Elysium, and one of his companies, MetroBiotech, has filed a patent related to nicotinamide mononucleotide, which he says he takes himself.

Sinclair and Harvard declined to release details on how much money he—or the university—is generating from these disclosed outside financial interests. Sinclair estimated in a 2017 interview with Australia's *Financial Review* that he raises $3 million a year to fund his Harvard lab.

Liberty Biosecurity, a company he co-founded, estimated in Sinclair's online bio that he has been involved in ventures that "have attracted more than a billion dollars in investment." When *KHN* asked him to detail the characterization, he said it was inaccurate, without elaborating, and the comments later disappeared from the website.

Sinclair cited confidentiality agreements for not disclosing his earnings, but he added that "most of this income has been reinvested into companies developing breakthrough medicines, used to help my lab, or donated to nonprofits." He said he did not know how much he stood to make off the Elysium patent, saying Harvard negotiated the agreement.

Harvard declined to release Sinclair's conflict-of-interest statements, which university policy requires faculty at the medical school to file in order to "protect against any faculty bias that could heighten the risk of harm to human research participants or recipients of products resulting from such research."

"We can only be proud of our collaborations if we can represent confidently that such relationships enhance, and do not detract from, the appropriateness and reliability of our work," the policy states.

Elysium advertises both Harvard's and Sinclair's ties to its company. It was co-founded by Massachusetts Institute of Technology professor Leonard Guarente, Sinclair's former research adviser and an investor in Sinclair's Sirtris.

Echoing his earlier statements on resveratrol, Sinclair is quoted on Elysium's website as describing NAD boosters as "one of the most important molecules for life."

Supplement Loophole?

The Food and Drug Administration doesn't categorize aging as a disease, which means potential medicines aimed at longevity generally can't undergo traditional clinical trials aimed at testing their effects on human aging. In addition, the FDA does not require supplements to undergo the same safety or efficacy testing as pharmaceuticals.

The banner headline on Elysium's website said that "clinical trial results prove safety and efficacy" of its supplement, Basis, which contains the molecule nicotinamide riboside and pterostilbene. But the company's research did not demonstrate the supplement was effective at anti-aging in humans, as it may be in mice. It simply showed the pill increased the levels of the substance in blood cells.

"Elysium is selling pills to people online with the assertion that the pills are 'clinically proven'" said O'Rahilly. "Thus far, however the benefits and risks of this change in chemistry in humans is unknown."

"Many interventions that seem sensible on the basis of research in animals turn out to have unexpected effects in man," he added, citing a large clinical trial of beta carotene that showed it increased rather than decreased the risk of lung cancer in smokers.

Elysium's own research documented a "small but significant increase in cholesterol," but added more studies were needed to determine whether the changes were "real or due to chance." One independent study has suggested that a component of NAD may influence the growth of some cancers, but researchers involved in the study warned it was too early to know.

Guarente, Elysium's co-founder and chief scientist, told *KHN* he isn't worried about any side effects from Basis, and he emphasized that his company is dedicated to conducting solid research. He said his company monitors customers' safety reports and advises customers with health issues to consult with their doctors before using it.

If a substance meets the FDA's definition of a supplement and is advertised that way, then the agency can't take action unless it proves a danger, said Alta Charo, a former bioethics policy adviser to the Obama administration. Pharmaceuticals must demonstrate safety and efficacy before being marketed.

"A lot of what goes on here is really, really careful phrasing for what you say the thing is for," said Charo, a law professor at the University of Wisconsin. "If they're marketing it as a cure for a disease, then they get in trouble with the FDA. If they're marketing it as a rejuvenator, then the FDA is hamstrung until a danger to the public is proven.

"This is a recipe for some really unfortunate problems down the road. We may be lucky and it may turn out that a lot of this stuff turns out to be benignly useless. But for all we know, it'll be dangerous."

The debate about the risks and benefits of substances that have yet to be proven to work in humans has triggered a debate over whether research institutions are scrutinizing the financial interests and involvement of their faculty—or the institution itself—closely enough. It remains to be seen whether Cambridge's decision not to renew its partnership will prompt others to rethink such ties.

Flier, the former dean of Harvard Medical School, had earlier heard complaints and looked into the relationships between scientists and Elysium after he stepped down as dean. He said he discovered that many of the board members who allowed their names and pictures to be posted on the company website knew little about the scientific basis for use of the company's supplement.

Flier recalls that one scientist had no real role in advising the company and never attended a company meeting. Even so, Elysium was paying him for his role on the board, Flier said.

Caroline Perry, director of communications for Harvard's Office of Technology Development, said agreements such as Harvard's acceptance of research funds from Elysium comply with university policies and "protect the traditional academic independence of the researchers."

Harvard "enters into research agreements with corporate partners who express a commitment to advancing science by supporting research led by Harvard faculty," Perry added.

Like Harvard, the Mayo Clinic refused to release details on how much money it would make off the Elysium licensing agreement. Mayo and Harvard engaged in "substantial diligence and extended negotiations" before entering into the agreement, said a Mayo spokeswoman.

"The company provided convincing proof that they are committed to developing products supported by scientific evidence," said the spokeswoman, Duska Anastasijevic.

Guarente of Elysium refused to say how much he or Elysium was earning off the sale of the supplement Basis. MIT would not release his conflict-of-interest statements.

Private investment funds, meanwhile, continue to pour into longevity research despite questions about whether the substances work in people.

One key Elysium investor is the Morningside Group, a private equity firm run by Harvard's top donor, Gerald Chan, who also gave $350 million to the Harvard School of Public Health.

Billionaire and WeWork co-founder Adam Neumann has invested in Sinclair's Life Biosciences.

An investment firm led by engineer and physician Peter Diamandis gave a group of Harvard researchers $5.5 million for their startup company after their research was publicly challenged by several other scientists.

In its announcement of the seed money, the company, Elevian, said its goal was to develop "new medicines" that increase the activity levels of the hormone GDF11 "to potentially prevent and treat age-related diseases."

It described research by its founders, which include Harvard's Amy Wagers and Richard Lee, as demonstrating that "replenishing a single circulating factor, GDF11, in old animals mirrors the effects of young blood, repairing the heart, brain, muscle and other tissues."

Other respected labs in the field have either failed to replicate or contradict key elements of their observations.

Elevian's CEO, Mark Allen, said the early scientific data on GDF11 is encouraging, but "drug discovery and development is a time-intensive, risky, regulated process requiring many years of research, preclinical [animal] studies, and human clinical trials to successfully bring new drugs to market."

Flier worries research in the longevity field could be compromised, although he recognizes the importance and promise of the science. He said he's concerned that alliances between billionaires and scientists could lead to less skepticism.

"A susceptible billionaire meets a very good salesman scientist who looks him deeply in the eyes and says, 'There's no reason why we can't have a therapy that will let you live 400 or 600 years,'" Flier said. "The billionaire will look back and see someone who is at MIT or Harvard and say, 'Show me what you can do.'"

Despite concerns about the hype, scientists are hopeful of finding a way forward by relying on hard evidence. The consensus: A pill is on the horizon. It's just a matter of time—and solid research.

"If you want to make money, hiring a sales rep to push something that hasn't been tested is a really great strategy," said Miller, who is testing substances on mice. "If instead you want to find drugs that work in people, you take a very different approach. It doesn't involve sales pitches. It involves the long, laborious, slogging process of actually doing research."

26. Strengthening the National Family Caregiver Support Program[*]

The Time Has Come

Lynn Friss Feinberg

The creation of the National Family Caregiver Support Program (NFCSP) nearly two decades ago marked the first federal recognition of the central role families play in the provision of long-term services and supports (LTSS). In the field of aging and caregiving, the NFCSP, created in 2000 under the Older Americans Act (originally enacted in 1965), was a game changer. Why? Because the federal program made it possible for every state to address family related matters that historically were thought to be too private for a public response.

Today, the NFCSP remains a key federal program that directly addresses the service and support needs of families in their caregiving role. The program provides information to caregivers about available services, assistance to caregivers in accessing supportive services, individual counseling, support groups and caregiver trainings, respite care, and supplemental services. The NFCSP has proven both cost-effective and successful at supporting family caregivers and the important work they do.

Inadequate Reach

Family caregivers are crucial to both the healthcare and LTSS systems. An estimated 40 million family caregivers provide about $470 billion annually in unpaid care to their adult relatives and friends with limitations in daily activities. Yet in 2016, the NFCSP provided support services to only about 740,000 family caregivers nationwide. This was due, in large part, to inadequate funding, as the NFCSP that year had a budget of slightly over $150 million. While not all family caregivers need help, the NFCSP is not reaching many of those who need the program's support.

In recent years, experts have called for increased funding for the NFCSP. A new

*Originally published as Lynn Friss Feinberg, "Strengthening the National Family Caregiver Support Program: The Time Has Come," AARP Policy Institute, https://blog.aarp.org/2019/03/11/strengthening-the-national-family-caregiver-support-program-the-time-has-come/?_ga=2.115967173.272735043.15579 74402-2040342837.1557974402 (March 11, 2019). Reprinted with permission of the publisher.

report from the AARP Public Policy Institute confirms that need, showing how Older Americans Act funding, including funding for the NFCSP, has not kept pace with inflation and the demographic reality of an aging population.

Effective Support

Data confirm that NFCSP services help families continue in their caregiving roles. A recent NFCSP outcome evaluation, for example, shines a light on the importance of assessing and addressing the needs of family caregivers. Key among the evaluation's findings are that NFCSP respite services are effective in reducing caregiver burden, and that other caregiver support services—including education and skills training, support groups and counseling—increase caregiver confidence. The findings also suggest that NFCSP services reduce burnout and help family members and close friends who take on a caregiving role to continue providing care for their loved one at home and in the community—an outcome that delays or prevents nursing home use and unnecessary hospitalizations.

The Family Caregiver Assessment Need

A key area in which the NFCSP can be more effective is by making family caregiver assessments standard practice. The outcome evaluation found that Area Agencies on Aging (AAAs) that examined the impact of caregiving in their assessment process were effective at targeting the family caregivers with the greatest caregiver burden. Yet while most (69 percent) AAAs already use a standardized assessment tool, only one-third (35 percent) use the information gained from it in this way—that is, to prioritize who receives caregiver support services.

Moving forward, the use of comprehensive, standardized assessment tools helps ensure direct contact with the family caregiver—listening to their goals, needs, resources, and strengths. Such tools will also help service providers to better understand family needs and preferences, and to consistently address those needs to ensure that family caregivers most at-risk are being well served.

The NFCSP evaluation provides guidance in implementing a standardized assessment process, in addition to identifying priorities for increased funding and expanding support services. With additional funding, NFCSP services could serve as a key mechanism for disseminating evidence-based services and make them available, accessible, and affordable to the families who need them.

Moving Toward a Coordinated Policy Framework

Meanwhile, other positive family caregiving developments are occurring at the federal level that impact the NFCSP and its evolution. In the near future, the Administration for Community Living in the U.S. Department of Health and Human Services will be forming a federal Family Caregiving Advisory Council under the Recognize, Assist, Include, Support, and Engage (RAISE) Family Caregivers Act of 2017 (Public Law 115–119).

Among other responsibilities, the Advisory Council will advise and provide recommendations to the Secretary of Health and Human Services on ways to improve coordination of services and activities across federal government programs to better recognize and support family caregivers. The development of a national caregiving strategy may be an opportunity to strengthen the NFCSP based on findings from the national evaluation.

In the meantime, we urge Congress to reauthorize the Older Americans Act, make assessment of family caregivers' needs standard practice, and increase the authorized funding level for the NFCSP to provide meaningful and practical supports to the families who need information and support services. Families can ill afford to wait for help. Surely, we can do better.

27. Frail Seniors Find Ways to Live Independently*

Judith Graham

Pauline Jeffery had let things slide since her husband died. Her bedroom was a mess. Her bathroom was disorganized. She often tripped over rugs in her living and dining room.

"I was depressed and doing nothing but feeling sorry for myself," said the 85-year-old Denver resident.

But Jeffery's inertia faded when she joined a program for frail low-income seniors: Community Aging in Place—Advancing Better Living for Elders (CAPABLE). Over the course of several months last year, an occupational therapist visited Jeffery and discussed issues she wanted to address. A handyman installed a new carpet. A visiting nurse gave her the feeling of being looked after.

In short order, Jeffery organized her bedroom, cleaned up her bathroom and began to feel more upbeat. "There's a lot of people like myself that just need a push and somebody to make them feel like they're worth something," she said. "What they did for me, it got me motivated."

New research shows that CAPABLE provides considerable help to vulnerable seniors who have trouble with "activities of daily living"—taking a shower or a bath, getting dressed, transferring in and out of bed, using the toilet or moving around easily at home. Over the course of five months, participants in the program experienced 30 percent fewer difficulties with such activities, according to a randomized clinical trial—the gold standard of research—published in *JAMA Internal Medicine*.

"If someone found a drug that reduced disability in older adults by 30 percent, we'd be hearing about it on TV constantly," said John Haaga, director of the Division of Behavioral and Social Research at the National Institute on Aging, which provided funding for the research.

Positive findings are especially notable given the population that was studied: 300 poor or near-poor older adults, nearly 90 percent women, over 80 percent black, with

*Originally published as Judith Graham, "Frail Seniors Find Ways to Live Independently," *Kaiser Health News*, https://khn.org/news/frail-seniors-find-ways-to-live-independently/ (January 31, 2019). *Kaiser Health News* is a nonprofit news service covering health issues. It is an editorially independent program of the Kaiser Family Foundation that is not affiliated with Kaiser Permanente.

an average age of 75 and multiple chronic medical conditions such as heart disease, arthritis and chronic obstructive pulmonary disease. While about one in three older adults in the U.S. need help with one or more daily activities, rates of disability and related healthcare costs are higher in this challenged population.

Half of the older adults in the trial received the CAPABLE intervention, which includes six visits by an occupational therapist, four visits by a registered nurse, and home repair and modification services worth up to $1,300. The control group received 10 visits of equal length from a research assistant and were encouraged to use the internet, listen to music, play board games or reminisce about the past, among other activities.

Both groups experienced improvements at five months, but older adults who participated in CAPABLE realized substantially greater benefits. Eighty-two percent strongly agreed that the program made their life easier and their home safer. Nearly 80 percent said it enabled them to live at home and increased their confidence in managing daily challenges.

Sarah Szanton, who developed CAPABLE and directs the Center for Innovative Care in Aging at the Johns Hopkins School of Nursing, attributes positive results to several program elements. Instead of telling an older adult what's wrong with them, a mainstay of medical practice, CAPABLE staff ask older adults what they'd like to be able to do but can't do now.

Seniors often say they want to cook meals for themselves, make their beds, use the stairs, get out of the house more easily, walk around without pain or go to church.

The focus then turns to finding practical solutions. For someone who wants to cook but whose legs are weak, that could mean cutting vegetables while sitting down before standing up at the stove. A bed may need to be lifted on risers and a grab bar positioned between the mattress and box spring so a person can push herself up to a standing position more easily. Or, a nurse may need to go over medications and recommend potential changes to a person's primary care doctor.

"Why does it work? Because we're guided by what people want, and in order to get better, you have to want to get better: It has to be important to you," said Amanda Goodenow, program manager for CAPABLE at the Colorado Visiting Nurse Association, the agency that assisted Jeffery. In Colorado, CAPABLE has been funded by a local foundation and Habitat for Humanity, which supports the program in six markets.

Hattie Ashby, 90, who has lived in the same two-story house in Aurora, a city adjacent to Denver, for 43 years, told Goodenow last summer that she wanted to get up and down the stairs more easily and walk around outside the house. Ashby has high blood pressure and COPD.

"They gave me a walker and made arrangements for me to put my oxygen tank on it so I could go to the mall," she said, recalling some of what the CAPABLE staff did. "They fixed the wall in my bathroom and put something I could hold onto to get in and out of my bathtub. And going up and down my stairs, they put another rail on the wall where I would be able to hold onto."

"It is a remarkable service for a senior citizen to be encouraged, to be helped, to be supported that way," Ashby said.

It also turns out to be a cost-effective investment. For every dollar spent on CAPABLE, nearly $10 in combined savings accrues to Medicare and Medicaid, largely because of hospitalizations and nursing home placements that are prevented, research by Szanton and others has shown. (Many CAPABLE participants are eligible for both government health insurance programs because of their low incomes.) The average program cost per person is $2,825, far below the average $7,441 monthly cost of a semiprivate room in a nursing home in 2018.

With a new grant of nearly $3 million from the Rita & Alex Hillman Foundation, Szanton is turning her attention to expanding CAPABLE across the country. Currently, the program is available at 26 locations in 12 states, and Medicaid programs in Massachusetts and Michigan have adopted a version of it for some members. A major challenge is securing funding, since public and private insurers don't typically pay for these kinds of services. So far, foundation and grant funding has been a major source of support.

Szanton hopes to persuade Medicare Advantage plans, which cover about 19 million Medicare recipients and can now offer an array of nonmedical benefits to members, to adopt CAPABLE. Also, Johns Hopkins and Stanford Medicine have submitted a proposal to have traditional Medicare offer the program as a bundled package of services. Accountable care organizations, groups of hospitals and physicians that assume financial risk for the health of their patients, are also interested, given the potential benefits and cost savings.

Another priority will be looking at how to extend CAPABLE's impact over time. Since benefits diminished over a 12-month period in the just-published clinical trial, additional program elements—phone calls, extra visits and follow-up assessments—will probably be needed, said Dr. Kenneth Covinsky, a professor of geriatrics at the University of California–San Francisco and co-author of an editorial on CAPABLE that accompanied the study.

He's bullish on CAPABLE's prospects. "As clinicians, when we see older patients with conditions we can't reverse, we need to understand we haven't run out of things we can do," Covinsky said. "Referring patients to a program like CAPABLE is something that could make a big difference."

28. Seniors Helping Seniors[*]

Maximizing Potentials

SUNDAY AKIN OLUKOJU

Two seniors, Donald Trump and Hillary Clinton, ran very vigorous campaigns in the 2016 U.S. general election. Both displayed a vigor and energy never imagined and proved that many older people are still active, resourceful and productive.

According to a report compiled by the U.S. Administration on Aging, there is an "increase in the percent of the population 60 and older from 6 percent in 1900 to 16 percent in 2000," while "the percent of the population 65 and older" increased "from 4 percent in 1900 to 12 percent in 2000." The report also shows a percentage increase "from 0.2 percent in 1900 to 1.5 percent in 2000 of the population 85 and older."

Trend in Population Growth

The projected increase for 60+ Americans is "25 percent in 2030 and 26 percent in 2050," while Americans who are 65 years and older are "projected to be 19 percent in 2030 and 20 percent in 2050." The group that will likely be most dependent, the 85 years and older population, is projected to increase by "2.3 percent in 2030 and 4.3 percent in 2050."

The younger cohort of seniors (60+) will constitute a higher population than more dependent ones (85+). If properly harnessed, a huge pool of younger seniors could become a reliable resource for needy seniors, especially as "8.8 million (18.9 percent) Americans age 65 and over were in the labor force in 2015." Despite this, "over 4.5 million people age 65 and over (10 percent) were below the poverty level in 2014."

In Canada, according to the Canadian Medical Association (CMA), seniors are Canada's fastest growing demographic as "the first of the baby boomer generation turned 65 and Canada's senior population reached 5 million" in 2011. With reports by the Canadian Institute for Health Information that "seniors accounting for less than 15 percent of the population today" will "consume approximately 45 percent of public health spending," something urgent has to be done in addressing the rising costs.

---

*Originally published as Sunday Akin Olukoju, "Seniors Helping Seniors: Maximizing Potentials," *PA Times*, https://patimes.org/seniors-helping-seniors-maximizing-potentials/ (December 6, 2016). Reprinted with permission of the publisher.

Seniors and Volunteering

Chappell and Prince, writing on the "Reasons Why Canadian Seniors Volunteer" in the 1997 *Canadian Journal on Aging*, concluded that "volunteering has become increasingly recognized as governments try to shrink the public purse." They found that seniors "volunteer for reasons of obligation and social value," and "are more likely to be involved in service provision." Hence, younger seniors should be sensitized, mobilized and deployed to help older seniors in various ways.

First, issues identified by Vanessa Sink of the National Council on Aging (NCOA) such as the renewal of the Older Americans Act (OAA) and Elder Justice Act (EJA), restoration of investments in aging services, advancement of legislation to improve access to Medicaid home and community-based services and finance long-term care (LTC), improvement of chronic care under Medicare, and the introduction of legislation to address the Medicare low-income protection cliff should be pursued using younger seniors as advocacy hawks to pursue lawmakers in their local jurisdictions.

Second, younger seniors between 60 and 65 could offer transportation services at a reduced rate to older seniors to cut rising cost. Fei and Chen, writing in the 2015 *Case Studies on Transport Policy* referenced the impact of the Americans with Disabilities Act of 1990 (ADA) and how the Greater Richmond Transit Company (GRTC) in Virginia had "a significant operating deficit in providing its paratransit service" because "it is also the most expensive" despite being "one of the most efficient ways to help move people with disabilities and the elderly." A "senior-helping-senior arrangement" could eliminate the shortfall.

Third, and consistent with Roberto's suggestion of multiple solutions with multiple players in multiple settings to eradicate elder abuse, younger seniors (60+) in various fields should be part of such a collective approach. As noted by Roberto in the 2016 *American Psychologist*, elder abuse affects at "least 1 in 10 older Americans."

Fourth, younger seniors (60+) can assist older seniors (70+) overcome what Xie and Jaeger described in the March 2008 *Journal of Cross-Cultural Gerontology* as "ambivalence and negative attitudes toward political activities online." Gleaning from Wicks' research on "Older Adults and Their Information Seeking" published in the 2004 *Behavioral & Social Sciences Librarian*, younger seniors should help older seniors navigate the internet while seeking information, including voting online, given their "effort expectancy" identified by Powell et al. in "e-Voting Intent: A Comparison of Young and Elderly Voters" published in the *2012 Government Information Quarterly*.

Conclusion

According to Administration on Aging, "persons 65 years or older" numbering 46.2 million in 2014. With "over 4 million low-income adults over age 60 relying on the Supplemental Nutrition Assistance Program to stay healthy and make ends meet," according to the National Council on Aging, using younger seniors to encourage older seniors to apply for SNAP is no longer an option, especially as "3 out of 5 seniors who qualify for SNAP do not apply." This means 5.2 million seniors are without benefits. Barriers that cause low participation are "mobility, technology and stigma." Involvement of younger seniors as partners in progress can alleviate these factors.

29. A Critical Examination of Long-Term Care in the San Francisco Bay Area[*]

IRINA REYKHEL *and* WILLIE LEE BRITT

As millions of Americans age, the consequence of such an ordinary progression of life proves to be devastating and life-altering for those who are unprepared for its repercussions. Despite the frenzy of attention that hot topics such as healthcare receive, the issue of long-term care is far less scrutinized. For this reason, many Americans do not take initiative in preparing for the long term. However, it is important to note that with many improvements in medicine and technology, Americans tend to live longer than former generations, creating a higher probability of needing long-term care services.

Research Purpose and Approach

The purpose of the research was to determine whether specific barriers prevented San Francisco Bay Area residents from having adequate knowledge of the long-term care system. The specific barriers included: (1) misperception of public and private programs; (2) lack of knowledge and denial; (3) the complexity of products; and, (4) affordability surrounding long-term care.

The goal of the research was to help contribute to the body of knowledge on long-term care and long-term care insurance. The primary focus of attention of the research was to provide residents who have little or no knowledge of the available options in the long-term care system. Interview data with key experts provided insights into the problems with the long-term care system. Survey data from the research from San Francisco Bay Area residents described the levels of knowledge of the long-term care system. Demographic factors were taken into consideration to reveal whether socioeconomic aspects affect people's understanding and knowledge of long-term care.

*Published with permission of the authors.

Definition

Long-term care "refers to a broad range of health and social services needed by people with a limited capacity for self-care due to a physical, cognitive, or mental disability or condition that results in functional impairment and dependence on others for an extended period of time." The need for long-term care services is measured by the individual's limitations in performing activities such as eating, bathing, using the toilet, dressing, walking across a room, and transferring (getting in and out of a chair).

In addition, instrumental activities of daily living (IADLs) are also used to measure an individual's capacity in living alone. IADLs include "preparing meals, managing money, shopping for groceries or personal items, performing housework, using a telephone, doing laundry, getting around outside the home, and taking medications. There are a variety of ways in which individuals receive the long-term care services they need."

A significant percentage of long-term care is provided by friends and families of disabled people. These care providers generally do not receive compensation for their service. However, livelihoods are very likely to be disrupted as a result. For instance, members in a family may have to quit their jobs in order to adequately take care of the disabled family member, which may result in financial strain.

Summary of Findings

Overall, despite the diversity of each key informant, several similarities existed in the responses. Whether the key informant responded tersely or verbosely, many of them reaffirmed the findings from the literature review as well as the assumptions of the research. Barriers existed in the long-term care insurance market and government had done a poor job of addressing this dynamic market. Furthermore, there was definitely misperception of public programs. In addition, the institutional bias of programs such as Medicare and Medicaid was apparent. Due to the diverse eligibility criteria of government sponsored programs, portions of the population may not be eligible for the care and services they need. Denial and affordability were mentioned by several key informants as barriers in the long-term care insurance market. The general attitude of the key informants was a mutual agreement that the long-term care system needs improvement.

The findings of the survey revealed that a large portion of the population lacked knowledge of long-term care insurance. In addition, numerous respondents were simply not thinking about long-term care needs. Interestingly, most key informants did not list lack of knowledge as a barrier to the long-term care market. The diverse views of the key informants did relate to the opinions of the survey respondents in some ways. It appeared that only a small portion of the respondents felt that government would pay for their long-term care services. This corresponded to the key informants agreeing that government was not prepared adequately. For this reason, it was clear to not only experts in the field of long-term care but also to the general population that government needed to improve its role and approach in promoting a stable and well-functioning long-term care system. Lastly, the survey respondents felt that long-term care insurance policies are too expensive. These attitudes corresponded to the key informants who also listed price and affordability as a major barrier in the long-term care market.

Conclusions and Recommendations

Based on the literature review and the results and findings portion of the research, it is apparent that not only the public sector but the private sector as well needs to have a more meaningful role in the long-term care market. Many barriers exist that deter individuals from purchasing long-term insurance. The results can be devastating when an individual is unprepared for the long term. For instance, some individuals need to exhaust all of their financial savings and assets before they can be eligible for Medicaid. In other instances, family members and friends are forced to care for the disabled individual. This may result in a strain on the family members and friends' livelihoods since they may have to take time off work or even leave their jobs in order to provide the care. This leads to the conclusion that, generally, the effects of being unprepared for the long-term can be devastating. This is especially unnerving since there are a number of advances in medicine and technology which create longevity. With longevity, more people will need long-term care services. These are all factors which must be taken into consideration in order to ensure that the nation can provide services that are needed.

Many key informants provided similar views on the shortcomings of the long-term care system. The consensus among the key informants was that the government was unprepared and inadequately addressing an impending crisis in terms of long-term care. It appeared that some of the key informants believed that the long-term care insurance market can only play a small role in alleviating the long-term care crisis. This was due to affordability issues, inflation rates and the high premium costs associated with the insurance. Most importantly, each key informant believed that the current system of long-term care was failing to a large degree. Despite the issues with the long-term insurance market, it must be acknowledged. Long-term care insurance provides independence to an individual since he or she will not need to rely on family and friends to provide needed care. In addition, by purchasing long-term care insurance, an individual is able to protect his or her assets and will not need to be on the brink of poverty in order to be eligible for Medicaid. Also, when long-term care insurance is purchased in advance, it is more affordable and ensures that an individual is able to receive the needed care he or she needs when it is needed. Another important factor of long-term care insurance is that it protects living standards; more specifically, the cost of a person's care will not affect friends and family.

Recommendations

A great amount of work needs to be done in order to repair the current broken long-term care system. Three recommendations were offered:

Government action: The federal government should take actions in addressing the long-term care crisis. Federal government policymakers must recognize the dire need in reforming the current system to ensure that the nation's citizens will receive adequate care and attention when it is needed. With the longevity in life, the government will not be able to financially sustain a well-functioning long-term care system, especially through the Medicare and Medicaid programs.

As part of the Patient Protection and Affordable Healthcare Act of 2010, Congress made an attempt to address the long-term care expenses through the Community Living

Assistance Services and Supports program (the CLASS Act). However, the CLASS Act was suspended in its implementation and declared to have "no viable path forward" by Speaker of the House of Representatives John A. Boehner in 2011.

A better alternative in addressing the long-term care crisis would be through government mandated education programs. Instead of figuring out a way to finance citizens' long-term care needs, the federal government should first create mandated educations programs which would be administered by the states that would then create specific requirements on local governments. Although creating a sustainable and well-function education program may take time, the government must set a stringent deadline in accomplishing this.

Long-term care insurance incentive: The long-term insurance market was appealing to individuals who had substantial assets. Many deterrents existed for the remainder of the population due to the high cost of a policy, the rising premiums, and the complexity of the product and the uncertainty of when the product would actually be needed. In order to create more balance and get a higher rate of the public to purchase long-term care insurance, several features must be modified. First, the cost of long-term care insurance must be cheaper to some extent so that more people can afford it. Next, there must be more stability in premiums. The outrageous increases in premiums make long-term care insurance unaffordable for many. If there is stability in prices, more people will have confidence and less worry in regard to the long-term care insurance market. Uncertainty and change are major deterrents. Therefore, stability in price and premiums must be achieved in order to incentivize people to purchase policies.

Education on long-term insurance: Most importantly, there must be more education on long-term care insurance. Lack of knowledge was the major barrier which has prevented people from obtaining long-term care insurance according to the survey administered. As stated in the first recommendation, government must educate the public about long-term care needs. With the increasing aging population and the longevity of life, the effects of a lack of education will be devastating. Government at all levels must cooperate with private insurance companies as well as any other necessary agencies to devise a plan of how to best educate the nation on long-term care insurance. Several factors should be taken into consideration on the best approach of educating populations with diverse incomes and capacities. Also, long-term care may be a sensitive subject to some. For that reason, the approach in educating people must be thorough yet ethically sound.

REFERENCE

Portnoy, Irina. "A Critical Examination of Long-Term Care in the San Francisco Bay Area." San Francisco: Golden Gate University, 2001.

30. Without Safety Net
of Kids or Spouse, "Elder Orphans"
Need Fearless Fallback Plan[*]

JUDITH GRAHAM

It was a memorable place to have an aha moment about aging.

Peter Sperry had taken his 82-year-old father, who'd had a stroke and used a wheelchair, to Disney World. Just after they'd made their way through the Pirates of the Caribbean ride, nature called. Sperry took his father to the bathroom where, with difficulty, he changed the older man's diaper.

"It came to me then: There isn't going to be anyone to do this for me when I'm his age, and I needed to plan ahead," said Sperry, now 61, recalling the experience several years ago.

Sperry never married, has no children and lives alone.

Like other "elder orphans" (older people without a spouse or children on whom they can depend) and "solo agers" (older adults without children, living alone), he's expecting to move through later life without the safety net of a spouse, a son or a daughter who will step up to provide practical, physical and emotional support over time.

About 22 percent of older adults in the U.S. fall into this category or are at risk of doing so in the future, according to a 2016 study.

"This is an often overlooked, poorly understood group that needs more attention from the medical community," said Dr. Maria Carney, the study's lead author and chief of the division of geriatrics and palliative medicine at Northwell Health in New York. It's also an especially vulnerable group, according to a recently released survey of 500 people who belong to the Elder Orphan Facebook Group, with 8,500 members.

Notably, 70 percent of survey respondents said they hadn't identified a caregiver who would help if they became ill or disabled, while 35 percent said they didn't have "friends or family to help them cope with life's challenges."

*Originally published as Judith Graham, "Without Safety Net of Kids or Spouse, 'Elder Orphans' Need Fearless Fallback Plan," *Kaiser Health News*, https://khn.org/news/without-safety-net-of-kids-or-spouse-elder-orphans-need-fearless-fallback-plan/ (October 4, 2018). *Kaiser Health News* is a nonprofit news service covering health issues. It is an editorially independent program of the Kaiser Family Foundation that is not affiliated with Kaiser Permanente. KHN's coverage related to aging and improving care of older adults is supported in part by the John A. Hartford Foundation.

"What strikes me is how many of these elder orphans are woefully unprepared for aging," said Carney, who reviewed the survey at my request.

Financial insecurity and health concerns are common among the survey respondents: a non-random sample consisting mostly of women in their 60s and 70s, most of them divorced or widowed and college-educated.

One-quarter of the group said they feared losing their housing; 23 percent reported not having enough money to meet basic needs at least once over the past year; 31 percent said they weren't secure about their financial future.

In the survey, 40 percent of people admitted to depression; 37 percent, to anxiety. More than half (52 percent) confessed to being lonely.

Carol Marak, 67, who runs the Facebook group, understands members' insecurities better than ever since suffering an accident several weeks ago. She cut her finger badly on a meat grinder while making chicken salad for dinner guests. Divorced and childless, Marak lives alone in an apartment tower in Dallas. She walked down the hall and asked neighbors—a married couple—to take her to the emergency room.

"I freaked out—and this wasn't even that big of a deal," Marak said. "Imagine people like me who break a hip and have a long period of disability and recovery," she said. "What are they supposed to do?"

Sperry has thought a lot about who could be his caregiver down that road in a circumstance like that. No one fits the bill.

"It's not like I don't have family or friends: It's just that the people who you can count on have to be specific types of family and friends," he said. "Your sister or brother, they may be willing to help but not able to if they're old themselves. Your nieces and nephews, they may be able, but they probably are not going to be willing."

The solution Sperry thinks might work: moving to a continuing care retirement community with different levels of care when he begins to become less independent. That's an expensive proposition—entry fees range from about $100,000 to $400,000 and monthly fees from about $2,000 to $4,000.

Sperry, a longtime government employee, can afford it, but many people aging alone can't.

Sperry also has a short-term plan: He wants to retire next year and relocate from Woodbridge, Va., to Greenville, S.C.—a popular retirement haven—in a home with design features to help him age in place. Those plans could be upended, however, if his widowed mother in Pennsylvania requires extra care.

In the meantime, Sperry is resolved to be pragmatic. "Do I look at my situation and say 'Gee, there's not going to be anyone there for me' and start feeling sorry for myself? Or do I say 'Gee, I'd better figure out how I'm going to take care of myself?' I'm not going with pity—I don't think that would be very pleasant," he said.

Planning for challenges that can arise with advancing age is essential for people who go it alone, advised Sara Zeff Geber, a retirement coach and author of "Essential Retirement Planning for Solo Agers: A Retirement and Aging Roadmap for Single and Childless Adults." A good way to start is to think about things that adult children do for older parents and consider how you're going to do all of that yourself or with outside assistance, she said.

In her book, Geber lists the responsibilities that adult children frequently take on: They serve as caregivers, help older parents figure out where to live, provide emotional and practical support, assist with financial issues such as managing money, and agree to serve as healthcare or legal decision-makers when a parent becomes incapacitated. Also, older parents often rely on adult children for regular social contact and a sense of connectedness.

In New York, Wendl Kornfeld, 69, began running year-long workshops for small groups of solo agers four years ago. Though married, she and her 80-year-old husband consider themselves future solo agers living together. "We figured out a long time ago one of us was going to survive the other," she said.

At those gatherings, Kornfeld asked people to jettison denial about aging and imagine the absolute worst things that might happen to them, physically and socially. Then, people talked about how they might prepare for those eventualities.

"The whole purpose of these get-togethers was to be fearless, face issues head-on and not keep our heads in the sand," Kornfeld said. "Then, we can plan for what might happen, stop worrying and start enjoying the best years of our lives."

Kornfeld took her program to New York City's Temple Emanu-El three years ago and is working with several synagogues and churches interested in launching similar initiatives. Meanwhile, elder orphans have begun meeting in-person in other cities, including Chicago; Dallas; Portland, Ore.; San Diego; and Seattle, after getting to know each other virtually on the Elder Orphan Facebook Group.

Kornfeld applauds that development. "So many solo agers identify as being introverted or shy or impatient with other people. They have a million reasons why they don't go out," she said. "I tell people, this may be hard for you, but you've got to leave the house because that's where the world is."

31. Understanding Loneliness in Older Adults— And Tailoring a Solution[*]

JUDITH GRAHAM

For years, Dr. Linda Fried offered older patients who complained of being lonely what seemed to be sensible guidance. "Go out and find something that matters to you," she would say.

But her well-meant advice didn't work most of the time. What patients really wanted were close relationships with people they care about, satisfying social roles and a sense that their lives have value. And this wasn't easy to find.

We need "new societal institutions that bring meaning and purpose" to older adults' lives, Fried recently told a committee of the National Academies of Sciences investigating loneliness and social isolation among older adults. (Fried is a geriatrician and dean of the Mailman School of Public Health at Columbia University.)

The committee's deliberations come amid growing interest in the topic. Four surveys (by Cigna, AARP, the Kaiser Family Foundation and the University of Michigan) have examined the extent of loneliness and social isolation in older adults in the past year. And health insurers, healthcare systems, senior housing operators and social service agencies are launching or expanding initiatives.

Notably, Anthem Inc. is planning a national rollout to Medicare Advantage plans of a program addressing loneliness developed by its subsidiary CareMore Health, according to Robin Caruso, CareMore's chief togetherness officer. UnitedHealthcare is making health navigators available to Medicare Advantage members at risk for social isolation. And Kaiser Permanente is starting a pilot program that will refer lonely or isolated older adults in its Northwest region to community services, with plans to eventually bring it to other regions, according to Lucy Savitz, vice president of health research at Kaiser Permanente Northwest.

The effectiveness of these programs and others remains to be seen. Few have been

*Originally published as Judith Graham, "Understanding Loneliness in Older Adults—And Tailoring a Solution," *Kaiser Health News*, https://khn.org/news/understanding-loneliness-in-older-adults-and-tailoring-a-solution/ (March 14, 2019). *Kaiser Health News* is a nonprofit news service covering health issues. It is an editorially independent program of the Kaiser Family Foundation that is not affiliated with Kaiser Permanente.

rigorously evaluated, and many assume increased social interaction will go a long way toward alleviating older adults' distress at not having meaningful relationships. But that isn't necessarily the case.

"Assuaging loneliness is not just about having random human contact; it's about the quality of that contact and who you're having contact with," said Dr. Vyjeyanthi Periyakoil, an associate professor of medicine at Stanford University School of Medicine.

A one-size-fits-all approach won't work for older adults, she and other experts agreed. Instead, varied approaches that recognize the different degrees, types and root causes of loneliness are needed.

Degrees of Loneliness

The headlines are alarming: Between 33 and 43 percent of older Americans are lonely, they proclaim. But those figures combine two groups: people who are sometimes lonely and those who are always lonely.

The distinction matters because people who are sometimes lonely don't necessarily stay that way; they can move in and out of this state. And the potential health impact of loneliness—a higher risk of heart disease, dementia, immune dysfunction, functional impairment and early death—depends on its severity.

People who are severely lonely are at "high risk," while those who are moderately lonely are at lower risk, said Julianne Holt-Lunstad, a professor of psychology and neuroscience at Brigham Young University.

The number of people in the highest risk category is relatively small, as it turns out. When AARP asked adults who participated in its survey last year "How often do you feel lonely or isolated from those around you?" 4 percent said "always," while 27 percent said "sometimes." In the University of Michigan's just-published survey on loneliness and social isolation, 8 percent of older adults (ages 50–80) said they often lacked companionship (a proxy for loneliness), while 26 percent said this was sometimes the case.

"If you compare loneliness to a toxin and ask 'How much exposure is dangerous, at what dose and over what period of time?' the truth is we don't really know yet," Periyakoil said.

Why it matters: Loneliness isn't always negative, and seniors shouldn't panic if they sometimes feel this way. Often, loneliness motivates people to find a way to connect with others, strengthening social bonds. More often than not, it's inspired by circumstances that people adjust to over time, such as the death of a spouse, close family member or friend; a serious illness or injury; or a change in living situation.

Types of Loneliness

Loneliness comes in different forms that call for different responses. According to a well-established framework, "emotional loneliness" occurs when someone feels the lack of intimate relationships. "Social loneliness" is the lack of satisfying contact with family members, friends, neighbors or other community members. "Collective loneliness" is the feeling of not being valued by the broader community.

Some experts add another category: "existential loneliness," or the sense that life lacks meaning or purpose.

Dr. Carla Perissinotto, associate chief for geriatrics clinical programs at the University of California–San Francisco, has been thinking about the different types of loneliness recently because of her 75-year-old mother, Gloria. Widowed in September, then forced to stay home for three months after hip surgery, Gloria became profoundly lonely.

"If I were a clinician and said to my mother, 'Go to a senior center,' that wouldn't get at the core underlying issues: my mother's grief and her feeling, since she's not a native to this country, that she's not welcome here, given the political situation," Perissinotto said.

What's helped Gloria is "talking about and giving voice to what she's experiencing," Perissinotto continued. Also, friends, former co-workers, family members and some of Perissinotto's high school buddies have rallied around Gloria. "She feels that she's a valuable part of her community, and that's what's missing for so many people," Perissinotto said.

"Look at the older people around you who've had a major life transition: a death, the diagnosis of a serious illness, a financial setback, a surgery putting them at risk," she recommended. "Think about what you can offer as a friend or a colleague to help them feel valued."

Why it matters: Listening to older adults and learning about the type of loneliness they're experiencing is important before trying to intervene. "We need to understand what's driving someone's loneliness situation before suggesting options," Perissinotto said.

Root Causes of Loneliness

One of the root causes of loneliness can be the perception that other people have rejected you or don't care about you. Frequently, people who are lonely convey negativity or push others away because of perceived rejection, which only reinforces their isolation.

In a review of interventions to reduce loneliness, researchers from the University of Chicago note that interventions that address what they call "maladaptive social cognition"—distrust of other people, negativity and the expectation of rejection—are generally more effective than those that teach social skills or promote social interactions. Cognitive behavior therapy, which teaches people to recognize and question their assumptions, is often recommended.

Relationships that have become disappointing are another common cause of loneliness. This could be a spouse who's become inattentive over time or adult children or friends who live at a distance and are rarely in touch.

"Figuring out how to promote quality relationships for older adults who are lonely is tricky," Holt-Lunstad said. "While we have decades of research in relationship science that helps characterize quality relationships, there's not a lot of evidence around effective ways to create those relationships or intervene" when problems surface.

Other contributors to loneliness are easier to address. A few examples: Someone who's lost a sense of being meaningfully connected to other people because of hearing loss—the most common type of disability among older adults—can be encouraged to use a hearing aid. Someone who can't drive anymore and has stopped getting out of the house can get assistance with transportation. Or someone who has lost a sibling or a spouse can be directed to a bereavement program.

"We have to be very strategic about efforts to help people, what it is they need and what we're trying to accomplish," Holt-Lunstad said. "We can't just throw programs at people and hope that something is better than nothing."

She recommends that older adults take mental stock of the extent to which they feel lonely or socially isolated. Am I feeling left out? To what extent are my relationships supportive? Then, they should consider what underlies any problems. Why don't I get together with friends? Why have I lost touch with people I once spoke with?

"When you identify these factors, then you can think about the most appropriate strategies to relieve your discomfort and handle any obstacles that are getting in the way," Holt-Lunstad said.

32. Social Isolation, Loneliness in Older People Pose Health Risks*

NATIONAL INSTITUTE ON AGING

Human beings are social creatures. Our connection to others enables us to survive and thrive. Yet, as we age, many of us are alone more often than when we were younger, leaving us vulnerable to social isolation and loneliness—and related health problems such as cognitive decline, depression, and heart disease. Fortunately, there are ways to counteract these negative effects.

National Institute on Aging-supported researchers are studying the differences between social isolation and loneliness, their mechanisms and risk factors, and how to help people affected by these conditions. "NIA is interested in exploring potential interventions to address social isolation and loneliness, which are both risk factors for poor aging outcomes," said Lisbeth Nielsen, Ph.D., of NIA's Division of Behavioral and Social Research.

Social isolation and loneliness do not always go together. About 28 percent of older adults in the United States, or 13.8 million people, live alone, according to a report by the Administration for Community Living's Administration on Aging of the U.S. Department of Health and Human Services, but many of them are not lonely or socially isolated. At the same time, some people feel lonely despite being surrounded by family and friends.

"A key scientific question is whether social isolation and loneliness are two independent processes affecting health differently, or whether loneliness provides a pathway for social isolation to affect health," Dr. Nielsen noted.

Research has linked social isolation and loneliness to higher risks for a variety of physical and mental conditions: high blood pressure, heart disease, obesity, a weakened immune system, anxiety, depression, cognitive decline, Alzheimer's disease, and even death.

People who find themselves unexpectedly alone due to the death of a spouse or partner, separation from friends or family, retirement, loss of mobility, and lack of transportation are at particular risk.

Conversely, people who engage in meaningful, productive activities with others tend

---

*Originally published as National Institute on Aging, "Social Isolation, Loneliness in Older People Pose Health Risks," https://www.nia.nih.gov/news/social-isolation-loneliness-older-people-pose-health-risks (April 23, 2019).

to live longer, boost their mood, and have a sense of purpose. These activities seem to help maintain their well-being and may improve their cognitive function, studies show.

Breaking Ground in Loneliness Research

Much of what we know about the causes and effects of social isolation and loneliness comes from the groundbreaking research of the late John T. Cacioppo, Ph.D., former director of the Center for Cognitive and Social Neuroscience at the University of Chicago and an NIA grantee.

Dr. Cacioppo's research found that being alone and loneliness are different but related. Social isolation is the objective physical separation from other people (living alone), while loneliness is the subjective distressed feeling of being alone or separated. It's possible to feel lonely while among other people, and you can be alone yet not feel lonely.

A pioneer in the field of social neuroscience, Dr. Cacioppo passed away in March 2018. His wife and collaborator, Stephanie Cacioppo, Ph.D., continues this work as assistant professor of psychiatry and behavioral neuroscience at the University of Chicago and director of the university's NIA-supported Brain Dynamics Laboratory.

"The misery and suffering caused by chronic loneliness are very real and warrant attention," she said. "As a social species, we are accountable to help our lonely children, parents, neighbors, and even strangers in the same way we would treat ourselves. Treating loneliness is our collective responsibility."

Although there is more to learn, the understanding of the mechanisms of action of loneliness and its treatment has increased dramatically since scientific investigation began more than two decades ago, according to Dr. Stephanie Cacioppo. Among the novel predictions from the Cacioppo Evolutionary Theory of Loneliness is that loneliness automatically triggers a set of related behavioral and biological processes that contribute to the association between loneliness and premature death in people of all ages. Research is headed toward the systematic study of these processes across generations, Dr. Cacioppo explained.

Understanding the Biology of Loneliness

Losing a sense of connection and community changes a person's perception of the world. Someone experiencing chronic loneliness feels threatened and mistrustful of others, which activates a biological defense mechanism, according to Steve Cole, Ph.D., director of the Social Genomics Core Laboratory at the University of California, Los Angeles. His NIA-funded research focuses on understanding the physiological pathways of loneliness (the different ways that loneliness affects how your mind and body function) and developing social and psychological interventions to combat it.

For example, loneliness may alter the tendency of cells in the immune system to promote inflammation, which is necessary to help our bodies heal from injury, Dr. Cole said. But inflammation that lasts too long increases the risk of chronic diseases.

Loneliness acts as a fertilizer for other diseases," Dr. Cole said. "The biology of loneliness can accelerate the buildup of plaque in arteries, help cancer cells grow and spread, and promote inflammation in the brain leading to Alzheimer's disease. Loneliness promotes several different types of wear and tear on the body."

"People who feel lonely may also have weakened immune cells that have trouble fighting off viruses, which makes them more vulnerable to some infectious diseases," he added.

NIA-supported research by Dr. Cole and others shows that having a sense of mission and purpose in life is linked to healthier immune cells. Helping others through caregiving or volunteering also helps people feel less lonely.

"Working for a social cause or purpose with others who share your values and are trusted partners puts you in contact with others and helps develop a greater sense of community," he noted.

Researching Genetic and Social Determinants of Loneliness

In another NIA-funded study, researchers are trying to understand the differences between social isolation and loneliness and how they may influence health. They are also trying to identify potential interactions between genes and the environment of older adults affected by social isolation and loneliness.

Previous studies have estimated the heritability of loneliness between 37 percent and 55 percent using twins and family-based approaches. "Individuals who are not prone genetically to feeling lonely may, for example, suffer much less from social isolation, while others feel lonely even though they are surrounded and part of a rich social life," according to Nancy Pedersen, Ph.D., a professor of genetic epidemiology at the Karolinska Institutet in Stockholm, Sweden. "We are also interested in understanding what role socioeconomic status plays in such associations."

Using data from twin studies, Dr. Pedersen and researchers found that both social isolation and loneliness are independent risk factors, and that genetic risk for loneliness significantly predicted the presentation of cardiovascular, psychiatric (major depressive disorder), and metabolic traits. Family history does not strongly influence this effect.

"We need to identify people who are most prone to suffer from social isolation and loneliness and those who would benefit most from interventions," said Dr. Pedersen. "Interventions for social isolation may look very different from interventions for those who feel lonely."

Beyond genetics, understanding social determinants of health, and the role of social and interpersonal processes in healthy aging and longevity, is another research direction at NIH. Scientists are beginning to apply this framework to research on social isolation and loneliness.

"Future research will need to clarify the extent to which loneliness and social isolation are malleable, and if so, what are the most effective approaches? Demonstrating that we can move the needle on these risk factors is a critical first step toward developing effective interventions," said Dr. Nielsen. Research is also needed to clarify how great a change in loneliness or social isolation is required to achieve a meaningful change in health, she added.

Living Alone with Cognitive Impairment

Older adults living alone with cognitive impairment—a growing and vulnerable population—face unique challenges. Elena Portacolone, Ph.D., assistant professor of sociology at the University of California, San Francisco, leads an NIA-funded study to understand their daily experiences, social networks, and decision-making ability, with the aim of designing culturally sensitive interventions to improve their health, well-being, and social integration.

"Whereas most researchers of isolation study the personal traits and behaviors of isolated individuals, my research focuses on the role that *structural* factors (i.e., institutions, social policies, ideologies) play in exacerbating the social isolation of vulnerable individuals," said Dr. Portacolone. "For example, in my prior investigation of older residents of high-crime neighborhoods, who were mostly African American older adults, a tension emerged between participants' longing to participate in society and obstacles that made this participation difficult to attain."

These structural obstacles included fear of being robbed, distrust of neighbors, limited availability of appropriate services, dilapidated surroundings, and limited meaningful and positive relationships. Having few friends or family members attuned to their concerns was another factor exacerbating social isolation. Study participants expressed a desire to be socially integrated, an idea that runs against the prevailing assumption that isolated older adults are alone by choice.

Similar patterns emerge in Dr. Portacolone's ongoing investigation of older adults with cognitive impairment living alone. "One African American study participant told me of her tendency to lock herself in the bathroom during family gatherings to cry and 'let the tension out' because her family members realize how concerned she is about her memory loss," recalled Dr. Portacolone. "Other participants with Alzheimer's disease noted that their friends were less eager to see them after they shared their diagnosis."

Another structural obstacle is limited affordable services that address the specific needs of cognitively impaired people living alone. Home care aides are seldom trained to support older adults with cognitive impairment, and their fees are often too high for most older adults on a long-term basis, explained Dr. Portacolone. In addition, some older adults with cognitive impairment have had their driver's license revoked, but they do not get help with replacement transportation, which dramatically increases their isolation.

As a result, older adults with cognitive impairment living alone spend much of their time managing their household and their health, Dr. Portacolone said. They are often reluctant to show they need help because they fear being forced to move from their homes.

"The primary takeaway from this research is that interventions to increase older adults' social integration should address not only their behaviors, but their overall surroundings. We need to concentrate our attention on the influence of social policies, institutions, and ideologies in the everyday experience of isolated older adults," Dr. Portacolone said.

REFERENCES

Administration on Aging. "A Profile of Older Americans: 2017" (PDF, 712K). April 2018.
Cacioppo, J.T., and Cacioppo, S. "The Growing Problem of Loneliness." *Lancet* 2018; 391(10119):426.

Cacioppo, J.T., and Cacioppo, S. "Loneliness in the Modern Age: An Evolutionary Theory of Loneliness (ETL)." *Advances in Experimental Social Psychology* 2018; 58:127–197.

Cacioppo, J.T., and Cacioppo, S. "Older Adults Reporting Social Isolation or Loneliness Show Poorer Cognitive Function 4 Years Later." *Evidence-Based Nursing* 2014; 17(2):59–60.

Cacioppo, J.T., and Hawkley, L.C. "Perceived Social Isolation and Cognition." *Trends in Cognitive Sciences* 2009; 13(10):447–454.

Cacioppo, S., Capitanio, J.P., Cacioppo, J.T. "Toward a Neurology of Loneliness." *Psychological Bulletin* 2014; 140(6):1464–1504.

Cacioppo, S., Grippo, A.J., London, S., et al. "Loneliness: Clinical Import and Interventions." *Perspectives on Psychological Science* 2015; 10(2):238–249.

Cole, S.W., Capitanio, J.P., Chun, K., et al. "Myeloid Differentiation Architecture of Leukocyte Transcriptome Dynamics in Perceived Social Isolation." *Proceedings of the National Academy of Sciences USA* 2015; 112(49):15142–15147.

Cole, S.W., Hawkley, L.C., Arevalo, J.M., et al. "Transcript Origin Analysis Identifies Antigen-Presenting Cells as Primary Targets of Socially Regulated Gene Expression in Leukocytes." *Proceedings of the National Academy of Sciences USA* 2011; 108(7):3080–3085.

Portacolone, E. "On Living Alone with Alzheimer's Disease." *Care Weekly* 2018; 1–4.

Portacolone, E. "Structural Factors of Elders' Isolation in a High-Crime Neighborhood: An In-Depth Perspective." *Public Policy and Aging Report* 2018; 27(4):152–155.

Portacolone, E., Covinsky, K.E., Rubinstein, R.L., et al. "The Precarity of Older Adults Living Alone with Cognitive Impairment." *The Gerontologist* 2019; 59(2):271–280.

Portacolone, E., Johnson, J.K., Covinsky, K.E., et al. "The Effects and Meanings of Receiving a Diagnosis of Mild Cognitive Impairment or Alzheimer's Disease When One Lives Alone." *Journal of Alzheimer's Disease* 2018; 61(4):1517–1529.

Portacolone, E., Perissinotto, C.M., Yeh, J., et al. "'I feel trapped': The Tension Between Personal and Structural Factors of Social Isolation and the Desire for Social Integration Among Older Residents of a High-Crime Neighborhood." *The Gerontologist* 2018; 58(1):79–88.

Portacolone, E., Segal, S.P., Mezzina, R., et al. "A Tale of Two Cities: The Exploration of the Trieste Public Psychiatry Model in San Francisco." *Culture, Medicine, and Psychiatry* 2015; 39(4):680–697.

• *D. Housing and Accommodations* •

33. Housing Policy Solutions to Support Aging with Options[*]

SHANNON GUZMAN, JANET VIVEIROS
and EMILY SALOMON

The phrase "home is where the heart is" captures the sentiments of many older adults when it comes to making choices about where they live as they age. Seventy-eight percent of adults ages 45 and older surveyed in 2014 stated that they would prefer to remain in their homes indefinitely as they age. Should they find themselves unable to do so, 80 percent of the people surveyed agreed with the statement, "What I'd really like to do is remain in my local community for as long as possible."[1] Social connections with friends and neighbors, familiarity with local amenities, and proximity to services and even doctors are among the many things that may be lost when an older adult has to move from his or her community.

Population projections indicate that by 2030, one in five people will be age 65 or older.[2] Communities must prepare for the housing and service needs of older adults. Local decision makers and other community stakeholders can act now to put policies in place that will address challenges that community members may face as they age.

Implementing policies that tackle issues of housing affordability, accessibility, and supportive services is a key action local officials can take to improve community livability and support people at all life stages.

What Is Aging in Place?

"Aging in place" describes older adults living independently in their current residence or community for as long as possible. Policies to promote aging in place often provide services and supports in the home, but the ability to age in place is also determined by the physical design and accessibility of the home, as well as community features such as the availability of nearby services and amenities, affordable housing, and transportation

---

[*]Originally published as Shannon Guzman, Janet Viveiros, and Emily Salomon, "Housing Policy Solutions to Support Aging with Options," AARP Policy Institute, https://www.aarp.org/content/dam/aarp/ppi/2017/06/housing-policy-solutions-to-support-aging-with-options.pdf (July 2017). Reprinted with permission of the publisher.

options. The AARP report "Aging in Place: A State Survey of Livability Policies and Practices" highlights examples of what states are doing for locals who want to age in their homes and communities.[3]

Studies have found that aging in place can lead to better health outcomes, life satisfaction, and self-esteem, compared with aging in a nursing home.[4] In addition, aging in place is typically more affordable than moving to an assisted living facility or nursing home. For example, the median annual cost for a private room in an assisted living facility exceeded $43,000 in 2016, and a semi-private room in a nursing facility was nearly twice as costly.[5] By comparison, the average annual costs for a home health aide working 30 hours a week is much lower, at $31,000.[6]

Housing Challenges and Policy Solutions

Following are some of the principal obstacles to aging in homes and communities, along with potential solutions for meeting those challenges.

Challenge: The population of older adults is rapidly rising and expected to reach 20 percent of the U.S. population by 2030. Many communities are lagging behind in supporting policies and programs that will address the needs, including housing, of older adults.

A MetLife survey, from 2011, found that many municipalities and counties across the country are struggling to set policies and provide services for older adults who wish to remain in their communities as they age.[7] Survey respondents indicated that their greatest challenges were providing housing- and transportation-related programs and services to older adults due to financial constraints as a result of the Great Recession.[8]

Additionally, the findings reveal that the majority of jurisdictions are not considering the needs of older adults when developing strategic and long-term community plans. Localities are failing to include the voices of older adults in their community planning activities and reflecting their needs in strategic plans.[9] Neglecting older adults may put localities at a disadvantage both in preparing for the health and well-being of their communities as residents age and in losing older adults' knowledge and experience that they may bring to discussions about shaping the future of their neighborhoods.

Solution: Local jurisdictions can use programs such as the AARP Network of Age-Friendly Communities or similar initiatives to address the housing and other needs of all residents regardless of age.

AARP is the U.S. affiliate for the World Health Organization's Age-Friendly Cities and Communities program.[10] When communities join the AARP Network of Age-Friendly Communities (AFC), they commit to take programmatic and policy actions to improve the lives of their residents at every life stage. Since 2012, over 170 communities (cities, counties, and towns) have joined the AFC, covering a population of more than 65 million people.[11]

The initiative's framework highlights the importance of key community characteristics that support the ability of community members to remain independent and active participants in community life as they age. These characteristics cover the built environment, amenities, and services across several areas called domains. These include housing, transportation, health, civic participation, and education, among others, that have an impact on the health and well-being of residents.[12] For example, an age-friendly community has affordable options for households with varying income levels and has homes with design features to accommodate people with limited mobility.

Member jurisdictions engage community members, local organizations, and businesses to develop an action plan that prioritizes strategies to address their locality's critical and unique challenges and to align their actions with these valued community features.[13]

The collaboration between local leaders and residents is important not only to obtain the diverse perspectives of each party, but also to begin forming coalitions that can work together toward solving their most pressing issues.

Each community is different and has its own unique set of assets and challenges, especially when considering the needs of people as they age. Local leaders can make crucial decisions today that can have a positive impact on older adults' lives now and in the future by taking steps toward being more age friendly. The AFC is one program, among several others, such as Grantmakers in Aging's Agenda grants, helping communities do so successfully.[14]

Challenge: As people age, some will need assistance with daily tasks.

Many older adults develop chronic conditions and mobility challenges that make it difficult to care for themselves and their home. The older the members of a household, the more likely they are to have a disability. Older and low-income individuals are at greatest risk of developing a disability.[15] Having a disability or chronic condition can make it difficult for older adults to complete activities of daily living such as bathing, dressing, or eating, as well as instrumental activities of daily living such as cooking, shopping, and managing medications on their own.

If older adults' health and mobility change and they need assistance with these activities, they are faced with a decision on how to get the help they need in order to live safely. They may rely on family members to serve as caregivers, hire personal care assistants to help them in their homes, or move to an assisted living or nursing facility. However, most older adults would prefer to age in their home or community instead of an assisted living or nursing facility; moreover, the costs of these facilities can pose financial hardships.

Solution: Offering supportive services at home or close by in the community can help older adults continue to live safely in their homes.

Supportive services can include a variety of forms of help, ranging from personal care assistance to medication management, that are focused on aiding individuals in completing daily tasks and managing their health and well-being. In urban communities, supportive service programs offered in home and community settings can take the form of collaborations between housing providers and health providers who understand the important role of stable housing in supporting health and well-being. In New York State, the Office for the Aging funds Naturally Occurring Retirement Community Supportive Service Programs (NORC-SSP) in multifamily buildings having a concentration of older adults. The program provides supports and services to facilitate aging at home and in communities.

The success of many of these programs at supporting aging is in part the result of the cooperation of housing providers who promote participation. Housing providers also share information on the well-being of residents with healthcare provider partners so they can better tailor services to individuals' needs.

Since its inception, NORC-SSP in New York State has served over 19,000 adults ages 60 or older.[16] Around the country, similar home- and community-based programs are offered in senior and community centers in suburban and rural communities by social service agencies and health provider networks.

In fact, contrary to common assumptions, quality support isn't just an option for cities. Whether older adults rent or own, or live in a high-rise building in the city or a single-family home in a rural community, a variety of models are available for offering services that support healthy aging.[17] Some programs offer services onsite in multifamily buildings or through home visits, while other programs are based in central and accessible community centers.

Local governments can facilitate the development and expansion of new and existing home- and community-based supportive service programs by offering grants to fund programs to ensure that services are affordable to low-income older adults. They can also support programs by making space available at low or no cost in community centers so that programs can operate in central and accessible locations. State governments also play an important role by funding supportive service programs for aging through grants from various sources.

Challenge: An older adult's home is not physically accessible or requires burdensome or expensive upkeep.

Structural barriers, such as narrow doorways and the absence of a first-floor bathroom, can make it difficult for older adults with mobility limitations to meet their daily needs and engage in routine activities.

A home's age and size have implications for the amount of time and effort required to keep it well maintained, up to local building codes, and accessible to an aging individual. Older homes (which are often where older individuals may reside if they have lived there a long time) typically require more maintenance than newer homes and can pose a barrier to aging in place. Residents may be unable to manage upkeep or improve accessibility because of physical or financial restrictions.

Solution: Existing homes can be modified to improve accessibility and safety for older residents, while communities can implement innovative programs to enable such improvements.

A simple modification might be installing handrails to make it easier to use stairs; a more complex modification might involve adding a bedroom on a home's first floor or widening doorways to accommodate a wheelchair. Modifications such as grab bars and railings make homes more accessible and can reduce the risk of falls needing medical treatment, a prevalent cause of injury among older adults, by about 20 percentage points.[18]

Local governments can take numerous steps to support home modifications for older adults, including adopting expedited permitting and review policies, certifying home improvement contractors that specialize in aging-in-place modifications, and allocating resources from housing trust funds or other revenue streams to subsidize the cost of home modifications for income-eligible residents.[19]

Home modifications can be a viable option to enable homeowners to remain in their homes as they age; however, renters are generally at a disadvantage because they have less control over the features of their homes. Accessibility requirements of the Fair Housing Act do not apply to buildings with fewer than four units, so older renters in single-family homes, duplexes, and other small structures can often face hardships as a result. Although the Fair Housing Act permits renters with disabilities in single-family homes to make "reasonable modifications" to improve accessibility in their homes, they must do so at their own expense,[20] which can present a challenge for those with limited financial resources.

Communities can provide assistance to landlords to make modifications that accommodate the needs of their tenants. In Boston, for example, landlords who rent to older adults or people with disabilities are eligible to apply for the Metropolitan Boston Housing Partnership's zero- and low-interest home modification loans. The program issued nearly 2,000 home modification loans between 2000 and 2013.[21]

In the case of new construction, jurisdictions should consider building codes that require accessibility features to accommodate residents as they age, thus reducing the prevalence of barriers and minimizing the need for future home modifications.

Challenge: In many communities, the existing housing stock does not offer a range of choices for older adults wishing to remain in their community by moving to homes that are smaller or closer to transit, shops, places of worship, and other destinations.

Almost 60 percent of adults over age 50 live in single-family detached homes.[22] Those homes may be too large, too expensive, and too automobile dependent for many residents. Restrictive zoning laws and other land-use policies or strong "NIMBY" (not in my backyard) sentiment can make it difficult for developers to build multifamily housing, accessory dwelling units (ADUs), or other, often smaller, more affordable and accessible alternatives to single-family homes.

Meanwhile, land-use policies that separate homes from services and amenities can make aging more difficult for people who want to remain in their homes and communities. For example, healthcare and social service facilities that are permitted only in areas far from where many older adults live can make it difficult for them to receive the care they need, especially if public transportation services are inadequate and driving is not an option.

Solution: Local governments can revisit their zoning policies and encourage a mix of housing types and affordability levels to accommodate older adults and others interested in multifamily housing.

For example, communities can rezone areas to accommodate more compact residential development near transit stops and in mixed-use, walkable communities—increasing accessibility for older adults who are unable or choose not to drive. By coordinating this development with their affordable housing policies, communities can ensure that a portion of these units are affordable to low- or moderate-income households.

Another possibility is to promote the use of ADUs, which are self-contained residential units located either within a single-family home or on the same property. Many local communities have adopted ADU policies. The city of Santa Cruz, California, for example, developed "ADU Plan Sets Books," which include ADU plans designed by architects and a homeowner manual for how to plan, design, and obtain permits for an ADU.[23] Since ADUs are built on existing properties rather than on the fringe of the community, they are more commonly located near city amenities and bus routes. They also tend to be smaller and more affordable than stand-alone units.

Challenge: As older adults age, incomes often do not keep pace with housing costs.

Housing costs in excess of what older adults can afford may also present a barrier to aging in place, particularly for those with limited financial resources. Nearly one-third of adults between the ages of 50 and 80 spend more than 30 percent of their income on housing costs, while almost 40 percent of adults 80 years or older spend more than 30 percent of their incomes on housing.[24] Spending more than 30 percent of income on housing may reduce the available funds that families have for other vital household expenses. Although both owners and renters are susceptible to housing cost burdens, the two groups face very different affordability challenges.

More than 80 percent of households headed by adults 65 or older own their homes.[25]

Historically, housing affordability problems for older homeowners could be traced to rising property taxes, utility costs, or costly property insurance. Recently, however, challenges have evolved, particularly with so many Americans relying on their homes as a key financial asset. The Great Recession during the past decade and the subsequent collapse in the housing market impacted many older homeowners when property values tumbled. The depressed housing prices in many markets contributed to the decline in the net wealth (primarily home equity) of low-income older homeowners. Between 2007 and 2010, the median net wealth of low-income homeowners ages 50 and older fell by about 30 percent.[26] This loss of wealth poses a major challenge to homeowners who were planning on using the proceeds of the sale of their home to pay for healthcare or supportive services that they may need as they age.

For renters, hundreds of thousands of government-subsidized units affordable to low- and moderate-income households are at risk of being lost as their landlords reach the end of their required affordability periods.[27] Historically affordable rental homes, particularly those that lack government subsidies, are also at risk of becoming less so as they are upgraded, or as homeowners displaced by foreclosure increase demand (and rents) for low-cost rental housing. Thus, growing competition and rising rents may make it difficult for older adults to remain in their communities.

Solution: Whether renting or owning, older adults can benefit from programs that increase or preserve the stock of affordable housing units and reduce costs for existing units.

Localities have a wide variety of policy tools at their disposal to produce and preserve affordable housing for older adults. Jurisdictions should consider developing a comprehensive housing strategy to assess both the supply of and demand for affordable units targeted to older adults and to coordinate housing policies to meet the needs of the community. In some jurisdictions, for example, it may be appropriate to create a housing trust fund and use the revenue to increase the affordable stock. In others, states and localities may wish to prioritize efforts to preserve the affordability of subsidized rental housing by maintaining or adding subsidies, refinancing existing debts, or taking other rental preservation steps. In communities with an ample supply of moderately priced units, tenant-based rental subsidies may be the right solution to alleviate cost burdens for older adults. Because housing affordability problems are often multidimensional, a coordinated series of complementary policy solutions that cut across industries is likely the needed strategy in many communities.

Many states seek to reduce housing costs for older adults by providing tax relief to current residents. One example is a homestead exemption, authorized by states and administered by localities, which reduces the portion of a property's assessed value that is subject to taxation. Another example is a property tax deferral program that allows older homeowners to postpone payment of all or part of their property taxes until death or the sale of their property.[28]

To date, 33 states and Washington, D.C., use such "circuit breakers" to reduce the property tax burden of homeowners, and many also extend the program to renters.[29] Although renters do not pay property taxes directly, renter circuit breakers offer a tax credit to income- or age-eligible households based on the assumption that property tax is implicitly part of their monthly rent payment. Credits range from 6 to 25 percent of the total rent paid.[30] In Maryland, the state's circuit breaker property tax relief program targets low-income homeowners and renters, including people with disabilities. In 2014, 80 percent of the more than 49,000 tax credits issued to older adult homeowners ages 60 and over in the state had an average value of $1,219.[31] Maryland's tax credit program for renters is open to older adults ages 60 and older, people with disabilities, and households with children. In that same year, the average tax credit for renters in Maryland was $307.[32]

By supporting both policies that expand the availability of affordable housing and those that reduce the housing cost burden for residents, states and localities can provide comprehensive solutions to address the affordable housing needs of older adults.

Federal Policy to Expand Home- and Community-Based Services

Some provisions of the Affordable Care Act (ACA) have the potential to expand aging-in-place options by better connecting low-income older adults with supportive services. The ACA creates options and incentives for states to offer more home- and community-based supportive service programs to Medicaid enrollees in order to reduce overall Medicaid long-term care spending. In 2013, older adults made up approximately 9 percent of the Medicaid enrollees but accrued 21 percent of total Medicaid expenditures.[33]

This policy direction helps states serve more Medicaid enrollees through home- and community-based services, which are both more cost effective and better aligned with the personal preferences of people who want to age at home instead of in institutional settings. These changes make it possible for states to significantly expand the number of people they serve in home- and community-based settings, making it easier for more low-income older adults to age in place. Potential action to repeal or remove aspects of the ACA could hinder the ability for states to provide the services to those who desire to stay in their homes and communities as they age.

Notes

1. Linda Barrett, "Home and Community Preferences of the 45+ Population 2014" (Washington, DC: AARP Research Center, September 2014).

2. Rodney Harrell, Jana Lynott, and Shannon Guzman, "Is This a Good Place to Live? Measuring Community Quality of Life for All Ages" (Washington, DC: AARP, April 2014).

3. Nicholas Farber, Douglas Shinkle, Jana Lynott, Wendy Fox-Grage, and Rodney Harrell, "Aging in Place: A State Survey of Livability Policies and Practices" (Washington, DC: National Conference of State Legislatures and AARP, December 2011).

4. Jordana Maisel, Eleanor Smith, and Edward Steinfeld, "Increasing Home Access: Designing for Visitability" (Washington, DC: AARP, August 2008); Janet Viveiros and Maya Brennan, Aging in Every Place: Supportive Service Programs for High and Low Density Communities (Washington, DC: National Housing Conference, 2014).

5. Genworth 2016 Cost of Care Survey, conducted by CareScout, April 2016, accessed November 3, 2016, https://www.genworth.com/about-us/industry-expertise/cost-of-care.html.

6. AARP estimates that the average work week for a home health aide is 30 hours per week. This figure is based on Genworth's 2016 Cost of Care Survey showing a national median hourly rate of $20.

7. N4a and MetLife Foundation, "The Maturing of America: Communities Moving Forward for an Aging Population" (Washington, DC: N4a and MetLife Foundation, June 2011).

8. N4a and MetLife Foundation, "The Maturing of America."

9. N4a and MetLife Foundation, "The Maturing of America."

10. The AARP Network of Age-Friendly Communities website, accessed December 6, 2016, http://www.aarp.org/livable-communities/network-age-friendly-communities/.

11. "The Member List," The AARP Network of Age-Friendly Communities, accessed December 6, 2016, http://www.aarp.org/livable-communities/network-age-friendly-communities/info-2014/member-list.html.

12. "Getting Started," The AARP Network of Age-Friendly Communities, accessed December 6, 2016, http://www.aarp.org/livable-communities/network-age-friendly-communities/info-2014/getting-started.html.

13. The AARP Network of Age-Friendly Communities website.

14. "Community AGEnda: Q and A," Grantmakers in Aging, last modified October 2014, accessed January 9, 2017, http://www.giaging.org/documents/141015_CommunityAGEnda_QA_FINAL.pdf.

15. Barbara Lipman, Jeffrey Lubell, and Emily Salomon, "Housing an Aging Population: Are We Prepared?" (Washington, DC: Center for Housing Policy, 2012), http://www.nhc.org/2012-housing-an-aging-population.

16. These are the latest data available from the New York State Office for the Aging. "Naturally Occurring Retirement Community Supportive Service Program (NORC-SSP) and Neighborhood NORC (NNORC)," New York State Office for the Aging, accessed July 14, 2016, http://www.aging.ny.gov/NYSOFA/Programs/CommunityBased/NORC-NNORC.cfm.

17. Viveiros and Brennan, "Aging in Every Place."

18. Michael D. Ericksen, Nadia Greenhalgh-Stanley, and Gary V. Engelhardt, "Home Safety, Accessibility, and Elderly Health: Evidence from Falls," *Journal of Urban Economics,* vol. 87, pp. 14–24, May 2015, http://papers.ssrn.com/sol3/papers.cfm?abstract_id=2344916.

19. Aging in Place Initiative, "A Blueprint for Action: Developing a Livable Community for All Ages" (Washington, DC: National Association of Area Agencies on Aging and Partners for Livable Communities, May 2007).

20. "Fair Housing—It's Your Right," U.S. Department of Housing and Urban Development, accessed October 14, 2016, http://portal.hud.gov/hudportal/HUD?src=/program_offices/fair_housing_equal_opp/FHLaws/yourrights.

21. "Home Modification Loan Program (HMLP)," Massachusetts Rehabilitation Commission, accessed July 14, 2016, http://www.mass.gov/eohhs/docs/mrc/hmlp-fact-sheet-2014.pdf.

22. Joint Center for Housing Studies, "Housing America's Older Adults: Meeting the Needs of an Aging Population" (Cambridge, MA: Harvard University, 2014), Appendix Table A-6, Characteristics of Stock Occupied by Older Adults: 2011.

23. Natalie Burg, "Affordable Housing: What Ann Arbor Can Learn from Santa Cruz, CA," *Concentrate,* http://www.secondwavemedia.com/concentrate/features/santacruzADUs0230.aspx.

24. Joint Center for Housing Studies, "Housing America's Older Adults," Appendix Table A-10, Housing Cost Burdened.

25. Joint Center for Housing Studies, "Housing America's Older Adults," Appendix Table A-6.

26. Joint Center for Housing Studies, "Housing America's Older Adults."

27. National Low Income Housing Coalition, "Project-Based Rental Assistance," in "2014 Advocates' Guide to Housing and Community Development Policy" (Washington, DC: National Low Income Housing Coalition, 2014).

28. David Baer, "State Programs and Practices for Reducing Residential Property Taxes" (Washington, DC: AARP Public Policy Institute, May 2003).

29. These are the latest data available from the Lincoln Institute of Land Policy. "Significant Features of the Property Tax," Lincoln Institute of Land Policy and George Washington Institute of Public Policy. ("Residential Property Tax Relief Programs," accessed October 14, 2016, http://datatoolkits.lincolninst.edu/subcenters/significant-features-property-tax/Report_Residential_Property_Tax_Relief_Programs.aspx).

30. Karen Lyons, Sarah Farkas, and Nicholas Johnson, "The Property Tax Circuit Breaker: An Introduction and Survey of Current Programs" (Washington, DC: Center on Budget and Policy Priorities, March 2007).

31. Department of Assessments and Taxation, "The Seventieth Annual Report of the State Department of Assessments and Taxation for Fiscal Year 2014," http://dat.maryland.gov/Pages/Statistics-Reports.aspx.

32. *Ibid.*

33. Center for Budget and Policy Priorities, "Policy Basics: Introduction to Medicaid, What Is Medicaid?" (Washington, DC: June 2015), http://www.cbpp.org/sites/default/files/atoms/files/policybasics-medicaid_0.pdf.

34. The Need for Safe and Healthy Homes in Order to Age in Place[*]

RACHEL L. FONTENOT *and* WILLIE LEE BRITT

This chapter focuses on the impact that home repair and safety modifications completed by Rebuilding Together San Francisco, a non-profit organization, has on making it possible for the elderly homeowners they serve to age safely in their homes. Various perspectives were sought to measure this impact. Also, homeowners who requested service but did not receive home repair assistance were surveyed to determine if not receiving services adversely affected their ability to remain safe and healthy in their homes. Next, homeowners who did receive home repair and safety modifications were surveyed to explore the impact the services they received had on their ability to remain safe in their homes since repairs were made. Finally, key stakeholders were interviewed to obtain insights on what factors do and do not make the services provided by Rebuilding Together San Francisco vital to allowing seniors to age in place.

The number of seniors within the City of San Francisco is growing and challenging the existing public service system to meet their housing and healthcare needs at a time when financial resources are limited. As people age, there are frequent changes and modifications required and made in their living environment to help eliminate risks of falls and potential health hazards. Rebuilding Together San Francisco is a community-based organization that leverages volunteer labor with corporate donations to provide repairs and install safety modifications, free of charge, to low income seniors.

This study was designed to determine if the housing repair and modification services offered by Rebuilding Together San Francisco are making the homes of low income elderly safer and healthier. As of the date of the research in 2014, there had been no research targeting the scope of services provided by this type of service organization and the impact they have on older individuals in a metropolitan city such as San Francisco. The research question studied was: Is Rebuilding Together San Francisco making the homes they serve safer and healthier? The researcher's hypothesis was: Rebuilding Together San Francisco is making the homes they serve safer and healthier. The independent variable in this research was Rebuilding Together San Francisco's services and the dependent variable was the impact result of making the homes of seniors safer and healthier. Although there is only one organization called Rebuilding Together San Fran-

---

*Published with permission of the authors.

cisco, the scope of their service can vary according to funding and volunteer labor. This organization also categorizes potential clients based on the nature of their need. If callers report the need for safety equipment, they are put on a list for volunteers to install home safety equipment. If they report needing larger scopes of work, such as painting, step repairs and roofing, they are added to a list that is matched with larger volunteer groups and sponsors. For the purposes of this research, all individuals who had requested services were merged into one list and sorted randomly.

The dependent variable, making homes safer and healthier, was expected to be a subjective evaluation made by the individuals being served and key informants.

Specific standards have been developed by the National Center for Healthy Housing that have been determined to represent a safe and healthy home. However, clients who have received services from Rebuilding Together San Francisco have not received training on this material.

For the purposes of this research, the following operational definitions were used:

1. Rebuilding Together San Francisco is a non-profit organization located in San Francisco California that leverages volunteers to provide home repairs.

2. A home is a dwelling, either single or multi-family, whose legal owner is the individual being served.

3. Seniors will refer to individuals over the age of 60 who received services from Rebuilding Together San Francisco during the 2014 calendar year.

4. The terms safer and healthier will refer to the standards identified by the National Center for Healthy Housing targeting 22 risk factors associated unsafe and unhealthy homes as described in the research.

Data Collection Process Overview

Primary data was collected by conducting telephone interviews with two groups of seniors as well as key informants. Group One was comprised of seniors who had received services from Rebuilding Together San Francisco. Group Two had requested services but had not received services as of the time of the interview. Key Informants consisted of professionals in the fields of aging and Rebuilding Together San Francisco administration. The purpose of the interview was to determine what, if any, impact Rebuilding Together San Francisco had by providing or not providing services. A list of 168 names and phone numbers was provided to the researcher by Rebuilding Together San Francisco and identified as individuals who had received services from the organization during the 2014 calendar year. A similarly compiled list of 50 individuals who had requested services but had not received services to date was also provided. These lists did not include any service or need-related information. The people in Group 1, those who had received services from Rebuilding Together San Francisco, were asked to respond to four questions which were designed to obtain information about the impact, if any, the services provided to them had made on the health and safety of their home. The people in Group 2, who had requested but not received services, were asked three questions to determine if they were able to coordinate home repair needs without the assistance of Rebuilding Together San Francisco.

Four key informants were surveyed to obtain their perspective on the needs of aging individuals in San Francisco and the impact Rebuilding Together San Francisco has made toward helping this population age in place. The executive director of the San Francisco Department of Aging and Adult Services represents the City agency responsible for advocating, coordinating and funding services for older adults and individuals with disabilities. The director of aging services for Catholic Charities in San Francisco leads a large community-based effort to provide support to aging individuals in order to allow them to age in their homes. The executive director of Rebuilding Together San Francisco had extensive experience in coordinating home modification and repair services to low income seniors in San Francisco. The president of Rebuilding Together San Francisco's board of directors had experience as a rebuilding project leader for teams that conduct repair services as well as the administrative vision for Rebuilding Together San Francisco.

Potential factors affecting the internal validity of this study included unexpected health conditions of the individuals being interviewed. Many conditions cannot be eliminated or prevented through the implementation of health and safety modifications and may prevent an individual from remaining in their home despite the availability of a safe environment. Additionally, personal finances may prohibit an individual from being able to pay required mortgages, taxes or utilities in order to remain in their home. In order to reduce the impact of these internal variables, the individuals included in the two interview groups had been screened for financial eligibility and determined to be in no immediate risk of eviction by Rebuilding Together San Francisco prior to providing the list to this researcher.

This research was externally valid to other national Rebuilding Together Affiliates of similar size to Rebuilding Together San Francisco. There were no other nonprofit community-based organizations that offer free home repair and safety modification services to low-income homeowners in the San Francisco area. However, this research would be pertinent to medical service organizations that offer healthcare to low income seniors, families as well as the general public. The issue of safe and healthy housing has the potential to impact everyone because the home environment can impact all aspects of personal health.

Key Findings from Survey Data

As the survey data indicated, service recipients did not associate the services they received from Rebuilding Together San Francisco with making their homes safer and healthier. The majority of respondents associated the terms safe and healthy with their personal safety in their neighborhoods and their personal health conditions. These respondents recognized the changes that had been made to their homes but did not recognize the homes as being safe and healthy.

Survey data clearly showed that individuals who had not received services from Rebuilding Together San Francisco but had requested assistance, had not been successful in finding alternative methods to having the needed repairs made. Furthermore, data reflected falling, tripping and safety as a primary concern for all individuals who had and those who were still waiting for services. The research data reflected unmet needs among some service recipients. The researcher concluded that the repairs remaining as needed were costly and require a greater level of skills than smaller repairs. Roofing problems, windows, furnace replacement and other structural problems are very expensive to perform. Key stakeholders were selected based on their familiarity and experience in the field of aging services in San Francisco and their knowledge of services provided by Rebuilding Together San Francisco. Two questions were asked to obtain qualitative and quantitative information:

1. What do you see as the biggest barrier to seniors being able to age safely in their homes in San Francisco?
2. What impact do the services provided by Rebuilding Together San Francisco have on making homes of seniors safer and healthier?

Key Findings

Key Informants unanimously identified lack of funds as the primary barrier to seniors being able to age safely in their homes. Because the homes in San Francisco are predominantly multi-floor, modifications will more than likely be required to assist aging homeowners with going up and down stairs, using the bathroom and safely maneuvering narrow hallways. Lack of knowledge of available resources was also reported as a barrier. Key Informants clearly supported the research hypothesis that Rebuilding Together San Francisco is making the homes they serve safer and healthier.

Research data clearly highlighted the areas in which Rebuilding Together San Francisco is successfully helping the low-income seniors they serve. Safety modifications and minor repairs were reported as having a significant impact on the service recipients. However, data also pointed out that this organization does not currently have the capacity to address the more expensive and structural repairs that are needed by a large number of seniors. Additionally, key informants clearly expressed their belief that Rebuilding Together San Francisco was making the homes of the seniors they serve safer and healthier. However, the majority of service recipients' did not agree. It is worth pointing out that the difference in responses is reflective of the service recipients' lack of clinical understanding of a safe and healthy home.

Conclusions and Recommendations

Conclusion 1: Based on the majority of responses obtained from Group 1, aging individuals would benefit by receiving education on health and safety risk factors in their homes. Data revealed that most respondents considered a state of health and safety to be applicable to their person and not their homes. Materials and training could help educate older residents of potential dangers and risks in their homes. However, it is also interesting to note that several respondents claimed that they did not know why they were referred or what the nature of their needs was. A possible explanation for this response could be that these individuals had a representative who requested assistance on their behalf, leaving the respondent unaware of the nature of the risks in the home.

Conclusion 2: Due to lack of funding, Rebuilding Together San Francisco was unable to perform repairs that are expensive and structurally complicated. The needs remaining for service recipients represented in Group 1 consists of stairs, windows, furnaces and foundations. Additional public funding for home repairs and modifications would allow a large portion of low-income seniors to be served and allow Rebuilding Together San Francisco to make a greater impact.

Conclusion 3: The scope of repairs Rebuilding Together San Francisco was able to complete is limited by their funding and skills capacity. As survey data indicated, some needed repairs were not addressed due to funding limitations and the skills needed to install the modifications. Additional funding would allow Rebuilding Together San Francisco to purchase the supplies and skill required to make such repairs.

Conclusion 4: Rebuilding Together San Francisco did not have the name recognition necessary to obtain additional funding from private corporations and donors. Additionally, low income seniors may not have been aware of the assistance available from Rebuilding Together.

Recommendation 1: By December 2015, Rebuilding Together San Francisco should develop educational materials addressing safe and healthy housing. Such materials should provide to seniors and families when being assessed and oriented for service. This material may also be shared with other direct service providers who serve the aging population in an effort to reach as many seniors as possible.

Recommendation 2: By August 1, 2015, Rebuilding Together San Francisco should contact the City of San Francisco Mayor's Office on Housing and Community Development to request additional funds. An initial funding request of $300,000, leveraged with volunteer labor and discounted materials would make it possible for Rebuilding Together San Francisco to address approximately 50 percent of the unmet need identified in this research.

Recommendation 3: By April 1, 2015, Rebuilding Together San Francisco should expand their reach into multiple funding options and investigate additional funding from healthcare institutions, medical insurance providers and long-term care providers.

Recommendation 4: By September 1, 2015, Rebuilding Together San Francisco should develop a marketing plan to guide the organization to new level of exposure and access to funding options.

These recommendations were developed to improve Rebuilding Together San Francisco's capacity to provide the help most needed by low income seniors in order for them to safely age in place.

Update 2019

Since completing the research in 2014, Rebuilding Together San Francisco has expanded their educational outreach to low-income homeowners in San Francisco to educate them about potential health hazards in the home. They have also released a very successful initiative called SHE BUILDS over the past four years that has significantly increased the volunteer skill capacity and funding to make much needed repairs. Women in the construction industry have demonstrated a commitment to working together to expand the number of seniors helped. In conjunction with National Rebuilding Day, the last Saturday in April, teams of female carpenters, plumbers, engineers, attorney's, and general labor have joined together to provide a much-needed boost to Rebuilding Together San Francisco's impact.

Thought for the future: "Improving the material integrity of one's home instills personal dignity, allowing safe and independent living as well as renewed pride in the home and one's history."

REFERENCE

Fontenot, Rachel L. "The Need for Safe and Healthy Homes in Order to Aging in Place: Evaluating Rebuilding Together San Francisco's Impact." San Francisco: Golden Gate University, 2014.

35. Engaging Nonprofit Sector Institutions for Housing Seniors*

Joshua Odetunde

Effective engagement of nonprofit sector institutions is indispensable to ensure social justice in community development and urban planning for seniors. Commonly, it is assumed economic development land use planning issues are parallel to institutionalized social issues in the processes of public policy formulation and implementation. Community participation does not always correct this misconception because "efforts to achieve public participation are often less sophisticated," as pointed out in a November 2016 *PA Times* issue. Sometimes, recognizing related issues requires professional knowledge. A case in point is real estate management issues intertwined with public policy issues in community development and urban planning. Often, they are kept separate to protect individual rights and privacy. Sometimes, this results in absurdity. For example, although it is public policy to ensure that every American family has a decent home, homelessness remains a concurrent problem with vacant and abandoned residential properties in many cities in the United States. Nonprofit sector institutions with professional capacities are needed to link economic efforts of institutions in both private and public sectors.

At present, nonprofit sector institutions commonly engage as charitable social service agencies providing housing assistance subsidies where relevant to their mission goals. This approach has not effectively impacted the local housing markets because currently the public perceives housing needs as private social issues such as basic need for shelter. Community development and urban planning for seniors should link their housing needs with their private social needs. Housing needs are not necessarily the same as social needs because housing units are not just shelters for living. Housing units are investments in landed properties. They are capital assets which can generate incomes for seniors who are homeowners. However, their housing needs as seniors have to be linked with real estate management of their capital assets. This will involve reconciling some conflicting public policy issues because of the general tendency to separate social and economic needs.

*Originally published as Joshua Odetunde, "Engaging Nonprofit Sector Institutions for Housing Seniors," *PA Times*, https://patimes.org/engaging-nonprofit-sector-institutions-housing-seniors/ (February 3, 2017). Reprinted with permission of the publisher.

Social change is needed in the current public perception of housing as consumption goods. Residential landed properties are investment goods. Public policy in housing finance could also promote the social change. At present, financial institutions such as mortgage companies and credit card companies use various strategies to indirectly force homeowners to refinance instead of preserving their equities. Many homeowners, including seniors, may not have enough equities to make necessary changes in their housing needs. Worse still, most foreclosure processes do not include adequate protection of equitable landed property interests of homeowners. Hence, real estate dealers prey on many low income homeowners including seniors in their local housing markets. Therefore, public policy news to complement nonprofit sector institutions in various local housing markets to ensure social change.

Furthermore, while focusing on their charitable missions, nonprofit sector institutions tend to underestimate the economic force of the sector in community development programs. As a result, either some critical economic goods and services are undervalued, or those critical goods and services cannot be attracted for implementing development programs. Where those critical elements are appropriately valued and involved, nonprofit sector institutions may have to compete with for-profit private establishments to achieve their mission goals. Rather than take on competition in terms of financial outcomes however, the mission goals of the nonprofit sector institutions should clearly identify the unique social justice outcome of programs. One of such social justice outcomes is to ensure seniors are not perceived as economic liabilities because their social and economic needs are severed. Well-blended nonprofit charitable social services could constitute significant economic force in community development.

For promoting social change, public policy administrators particularly need to engage with nonprofit sector institutions in community real estate management for mutual benefits in local housing markets across the United States. The public policy issue of housing affordability is being confused with housing needs as landed properties in local housing markets. Rather than encouraging effective real estate management of existing housing stock as investments, public policy administrators are seeking for solutions in developments and designs to meet housing needs. The current public policy approach has resulted in ambivalent dichotomy in local housing markets comprising of market rate and subsidized housing units. Therefore, many low-income households including seniors are either homeless or occupying inadequate housing while some residential properties are vacant or abandoned. Also, foreclosures and tenant evictions remain common features of local housing markets. According to the 2014 study on housing America's older adult by the Joint Center for Housing Studies of Harvard University, it is projected one out of five people will be 65 years or older by 2030. A decent home is the linchpin of well-being. The need for social change is urgent. Engagement of nonprofit sector institutions in community real estate management is needed to complement public policy in local housing markets for social change.

An example is the Community Housing Market Support Network, Inc. (CHMSN), a 501(c)3 Christian-faith-based nonprofit organization under the Internal Revenue Service code. The organization is based on the concept that low-income families and the poor will always be an integral part of any country's economy while they depend on charitable assistance and generosity to one another in their communities (Deuteronomy 15: 4 & 11). Therefore, CHMSN provides nonprofit real estate services and management for low-income households and the poor as leverage in line with the Christian principles of associating with those in low positions (Romans 12: 16). Since houses are capital resource assets, every family directly or indirectly receives some public assistance or leverage through financial engineering of the housing industry. The financial engineering makes helping families to meet their housing needs go beyond the traditionally charitable assistance. The housing market has evolved into the communal strategy of leveraging one another through home mortgage loans. Therefore, community-based nonprofit organizations are needed to complement public policy in the housing market and ensure social justice.

Such nonprofit organizations are needed because public policymakers have translated the invaluable mutual benefits of the communal strategy into monetary values for property tax, sales tax, user fees, and utility surcharges making complementary public policy imperative in local housing marketplaces. Otherwise, the housing finance system cannot evolve into equitable access for every family to have a decent home as reasonably envisaged in the goal of the United States Housing Act of 1949. The mainstream thinking about the free market economy remains dominated by individualism, personal achievements, and competition with unsettled gaps in knowledge and practice in local housing marketplaces. While policymakers now tend to rely less on the traditional progressive income tax principles for economic efficiency to promote capitalism, renting homes to meet their housing needs has become the necessity for low-income households.

Therefore, our networking and innovative real estate management strategies in Louisville metro will involve:

- helping individuals and families to find affordable housing and to become homeowners.
- helping families to become a network of investors collaborating to protect their home equities.
- helping low-income households to prevent foreclosures.
- providing homeownership counseling to help low-income households build equity in their homes.
- helping to rehabilitate the homeless and providing a range of temporary shelter for households.
- providing real estate management and services for single-family homes, small-scale investors, and landlords.

36. Advancing Independence, Integration and Inclusion Throughout Life*

ADMINISTRATION FOR COMMUNITY LIVING

The Administration for Community Living (ACL) was created around the fundamental principle that older adults and people of all ages with disabilities should be able to live where they choose, with the people they choose, and with the ability to participate fully in their communities.

By funding services and supports provided by networks of community-based organizations, and with investments in research, education, and innovation, ACL helps make this principle a reality for millions of Americans.

Mission and Strategic Plan

All Americans—including people with disabilities and older adults—should be able to live at home with the supports they need, participating in communities that value their contributions. To help meet these needs, the U.S. Department of Health and Human Services (HHS) created the Administration for Community Living in 2012.

ACL brings together the efforts and achievements of the Administration on Aging (AoA), the Administration on Intellectual and Developmental Disabilities (AIDD), and the HHS Office on Disability to serve as the Federal agency responsible for increasing access to community supports, while focusing attention and resources on the unique needs of older Americans and people with disabilities across the lifespan.

Mission: Maximize the independence, well-being, and health of older adults, people with disabilities across the lifespan, and their families and caregivers.

Vision:

- For all people, regardless of age and disability, to live with dignity, make their own choices, and participate fully in society. Therefore, we will:
- For the people we serve: Promote strategies that enable people to live in their communities.

---

*Originally published as Administration for Community Living, "Advancing Independence, Integration, and Inclusion Throughout Life," https://acl.gov/about-community-living.

- For our networks: Provide leadership and support.
- For our partners: Be a source of collaboration, innovation, and solutions.
- For our employees: Support their contributions, professional growth, and work-life balance.
- For the public: Be effective stewards of public resources and a source for information.

All people, regardless of age or disability, should be able to live independently and participate fully in their communities. Every person should have the right to make choices and to control the decisions in and about their lives. This right to self-determination includes decisions about their homes and work, as well as all the other daily choices most adults make without a second thought.

Why Community Living?

In survey after survey, when older adults and people with disabilities are asked where they would prefer to live, they say they want to live in their communities, not in institutions.

Many people have deep ties to their communities that go back decades, if not generations. Remaining in the community allows people to preserve a critical connection to meaningful memories, people, places, and things. These connections with the familiar can be particularly important for older adults.

Living in the community can also offer a level of social connection that is hard to find in a nursing home or other institutional setting. It offers the opportunity to interact with family members, friends, and neighbors. Being integrated in the community means having the opportunity to live with, and work alongside, people of all different abilities.

Community living offers many benefits for individuals and their families, but it also offers many benefits to the communities themselves. Communities miss out on valuable voices and perspectives when people with disabilities and older adults are left out. They are deprived of co-workers, volunteers, mentors, and friends who offer new ways of thinking about, and navigating, the world as well as wisdom collected over many decades. Older adults also often serve the critical roles of family historians and keepers of a community's memories.

Not only is community living rewarding for individuals and communities, but also happens to be less expensive than other options for most people. Skilled nursing facilities can cost an average of $75,000 a year and public residential facilities for people with disabilities average $225,000 a year. In most cases, these costs are not covered by Medicare or private health insurance.

Finally, a series of laws, court decisions, and administrative rules have established community living as a legal right. Most notably, in 1999, the U.S. Supreme Court ruled in Olmstead v. L.C. that people with disabilities must receive services in the most integrated settings possible. This landmark decision has been a critical tool in protecting the rights of people with disabilities and older adults alike.

Supporting People in the Community

Many older adults and people with disabilities need help with the daily tasks of life. For some people this is physical help such as help with dressing and eating. For others, it is help with making decisions and planning. Still others require a blend of supports. Each person is unique, and the help they may need is unique as well.

At ACL, we believe that the preferences and needs of older adults and people with disabilities who need assistance belong at the center of the system of services and supports that enable them to live the lives they want to live. We further believe that those needs and preferences should be defined by the individual receiving services and supports.

At the same time, ACL recognizes that some people with disabilities and some older adults experience challenges in understanding and communicating their preferences and needs, and family members and caregivers often play a critical role in ensuring that those preferences are honored and needs are met.

We also recognize that the preferences of the individual are not the only factor in determining how to best support that person. The availability of services and supports in a variety of settings, the resources and availability of family caregivers, and other factors also must be considered.

Making Community Living Work for You and Your Family

The realization that you or someone you love will need additional services or supports to stay in the community can feel overwhelming, especially after an unexpected event such as a fall or an accident. Many people do not know what services are available, to whom to turn for help, or where to start.

In many states, Aging and Disability Resource Centers can act as a gateway to a broad range of services and supports for older adults and people with disabilities.

For people with disabilities of all ages, Centers for Independent Living are a great first stop. These community-based centers are run by and for people with disabilities and offer a broad range of services to empower and enable people to stay in the community.

People with disabilities of all ages may also benefit from assistive technology (AT) devices and services. AT includes everything from "low tech" helping tools like utensils with big handles to high tech solutions like talking computers. Every state and territory has an Assistive Technology Act program that can help people find, try, and obtain AT.

For older adults, ACL's Eldercare Locator is a great place to start. Visit www.eldercare. gov or call 800-677-1116 to be connected with your local area agency on aging or aging and disability resource center. Those organizations can help you understand what services are available in your community and help you sign up.

37. Accessibility Solutions for Colton Hall[*]

Claire M. Rygg *and* Willie Lee Britt

The adequacy of handicap access to public historical sites is often overlooked and not considered significant unless you have a family member or friend who is adversely impacted. This may limit the opportunity to simply visit, never mind enjoying, what is often taken for granted by those who are not physically impaired (mobility, vision or hearing).

The City of Monterey, California, is not only a tourist destination for those who want to explore the beauty of Monterey Bay and surrounding areas, but it also offers a rich history and cultural heritage, spanning from early colonial California to the sardine capital of the world. Approximately 4 million tourists come each year and many visit the Monterey Old Town Historic District, "an area that generally includes within its boundaries a significant concentration of properties linked by architectural style or a past event." This is prevalent throughout many cities and towns in the United States. In Monterey, several 19th century historic adobes and buildings are under the stewardship of the Monterey State Historic Park Association and the City of Monterey, including Colton Hall. Colton Hall is the original site of California's 1849 Constitutional Convention ("the birthplace of California"). Colton Hall is owned and stewarded by the city.

According to Melvyn Green, principal engineer of Melvyn Green & Associates, Inc., who wrote the "Historic Structure Report for Colton Hall" (Green, 1991), Colton Hall is "an interesting and unusual mixture of the prevalent California style and the Greek Revival buildings...[and] eminently worthy of preservation at any cost." The upper floor of the two-story building is a history museum that was established in 1948. City offices occupy the first floor. "One of the more remarkable facts about Colton Hall is that it has been in continuous use as a public building since its construction" (Conway, 2003).

Three part-time museum guides welcome over 14,000 annual visitors and interpret the history of the hall and of its multi-use significance as the site of the first California constitutional convention, a town hall and an elementary school, courthouse, and other various municipal, county, state and federal agencies. In 2012 on some occasions, the guides would meet with individuals in front of Colton Hall who could not access the second-story museum to interpret the history and the site. The hall is also a gathering

---

*Published with permission of the authors.

place for special events such as proclamations by the mayor, an annual reenactment of the 1849 Constitutional Convention, the venue for annual winter evening music concerts, art exhibits, hosting visiting dignitaries, for recognizing members of the community or professional organizations, and visiting educational and cultural groups.

In 1993, city engineers estimated the cost of a mechanical lift for the rear second-story entrance of Colton Hall would be $75,000 excluding a building electrical upgrade and would have to be approved by the City Council as a capital improvement project budget or funded from an alternative source. In 2005, museum staff presented the subject of accessibility to Colton Hall and recommended the legislative body for policy on Colton Hall, the Colton Hall Museum and Cultural Arts Commission to consider "alternative approaches to making Colton Hall exhibits and services accessible to people with disabilities, rather than recommending construction of a lift to the second floor" (Conway, 2005). The commission directed museum staff to gather information on web-based technology or closed-circuit television as alternatives to improve visitor access to Colton Hall. From that direction, the city explored the use of audio tours by cellphone and added flash tours (graphical representation or virtual tour of a site via internet browser) of some of the city's historic sites to its website, www.monterey.org. In October 2011, the city began its development of a cellphone tour with two-minute descriptive audio-narrative for approximately twenty historic sites, and in January 2012, the cell tours became available to the public.

What happened between January 2012 and December 2017? The city decided that it needed to bid work for compliance with ADA accessibility requirements and an access compliance survey was performed in 2013 for the entire city, including Colton Hall. A proposal for an ADA accessibility study with recommendations was granted, the study completed, and the ADA accessibility improvements for Colton Hall was advertised on December 6, 2017. The project description was: "In general, the work consists of, but is not limited to, improvements to Colton Hall and City Hall buildings to comply with ADA accessibility requirements, including the reconstruction of parking stalls, installation of an elevator at Colton Hall and a lift at City Hall, construction of an access ramp to access the Planning Office (Colton Hall), construction of an ADA-compliant bathroom (Colton Hall), and construction of an ADA-compliant path around both buildings."

By October 2018, for the first time in its 169-year history, Colton Hall was accessible to visitors with special needs. The city has completed a $353,000 improvement project, which includes a reconstruction of the back stairs and deck, a new Limited Use/Limited Access (LULA) lift to provide Americans with Disabilities Act access to the second floor. Additionally, a new ADA compliant restroom that can accommodate a wheelchair, an access ramp in the rear courtyard, and an adjacent ADA parking area were added.

With the passage of the Americans with Disabilities Act in 1990, many persons with disabilities have gained their civil rights and enjoy a life of independence. The ADA is a civil rights law that prohibits discrimination against individuals with disabilities in all areas of public life, including jobs, schools, transportation, and all public and private places that are open to the general public.

However, there were/are obstacles that made/make accessibility to historic buildings, such as Colton Hall, difficult for this minority group, because of the goal to preserve the building's historic integrity. A review of literary sources revealed how public venues accommodate people with disabilities, how individuals perceive of the effectiveness of the ADA, and how handheld technology may be used to provide accessibility to historic building.

In reviewing the intent and provisions of the ADA, some key observations have been made that appear relevant for the issues of accessibility for historic buildings while preserving their structural integrity:

Griff Hogan in *Inclusive Corporation: A Disability Handbook for Business Professions* (2003) referenced that O'Quinn cautioned that: "legislation enacted with the least partisan dispute often turns out to be the worst law because its provisions were never really tested in any serious public debate.... Congress drafted the ADA broadly, using imprecise and undefined terms, and consequently left the task fleshing out the meaning of its provision to the federal judiciary.... Contrary to the claims of its proponents, the ADA imposes significant costs on American business firms and government entities (pp. 27–28).

For a greater understanding of the complexities involved with public accommodation, the authors listed below provide relevant insights:

Kozue Handa, Hitoshi Dairoku and Yoshiko Toriyanna sought adult members of the visually impaired community and conducted a study titled "The Investigation of Priority Needs in Terms of Museum Service Accessibility for Visually Impaired" (2010), analyzing facilities for wayfinding, exhibitions, information in Braille, audio or large print, and how museum staff would assist those who required those services.

Thomas Jester and Sharon Park listed recommendations in their preservation brief "Making Historic Properties Accessible" (www.nps.gov, 1995) without destroying the historic integrity of the building.

Ellen Giusti in her article "Improving Visitor Access" (2008) briefly described the creation and advancement of audio tour technology, and that today's consumer's cell or smartphone technology has rapidly advanced to become the wayfinding agents with "audience-specific narration" which provides independence for the museum visitor. C. Reich and A. Lindgren-Streicher state (as cited in Giusti, 2008) that access is more than just physical:

> While the publication of [disability regulation] ...have led to significant changes in the industry, they predominantly focused on providing physical access to museums and did not address providing intellectual access to learning. Understanding physical difference among individuals and the resulting space and architectural requirements are important first steps. However, this information is not sufficient for providing true access to learning for all. Universal design for learning goes beyond physical accessibility. It involves creating multisensory, multimodal learning experiences from which all visitors can learn by touching, seeing, listening, smelling and sometimes even tasting.

In 2011, research was done relative to Colton Hall's accessibility. Members from the sensory and physically impaired communities participated in a brief survey, and disability service coordinators, representatives from municipal government, and ADA professionals were interviewed for their insights on priority needs for accessing a historic museum building in order to receive its history interpretive services and cultural arts programs. The results of this research are summarized to provide further information to other public and private entities that are responsible for the stewardship of historic buildings. This may be of some significance to enhance the overall view for accessibility and may inspire more innovative solutions for access for persons with disabilities.

Policy Recommendations and Future Research

In 2012, Claire M. Rygg provided policy recommendations, some she indicated may be implemented within a few months to two years (Phase I), and some may span over a few years (Phase II):

Phase I

- Install larger font exhibit labels in Colton Hall for the visually impaired. The museum staff may recommend to the Colton Hall Museum and Cultural Art Commission that the installation of larger font exhibit labels may be beneficial to the visually impaired.
- Build collaborative partnerships between the City of Monterey and local sensory impaired service centers in an effort to develop an outreach program to present informal lectures on early California history, for example, an annual event consisting of one, half-hour presentation during a luncheon at the Blind and Visually Impaired Center.
- Develop a training program for museum docents to guide blind and visually impaired individuals upon their request and provide history interpretive services on Colton Hall and early California history.
- Install Quick Response (QR) Codes on the City's "Explore Monterey" cell phone tours so the deaf may access a video of an American Sign Language interpreter signing historical information about Colton Hall and each of the other twenty-one historic sites listed on the tour.
- Develop a policy on access to the Colton Hall Museum. This policy may explain to interested individuals some of the standards of the American with Disabilities Act and the National Preservation Act for providing access to public services in a historically significant building.
- Review feasibility of a vertical lift system for Colton Hall. Once the final Access Compliance Survey has been completed, further action may be taken by the municipal leadership upon the counsel of the ADA consultant, the architect preservation professional staff who assess the historic integrity of Colton Hall and submits its findings in a historic structures report to the City's Museum and Cultural Arts Division and Planning and Historic Preservation staff.

Phase II

- Develop plan for future phase funding via grants for access solutions for Colton Hall. This may be dependent upon the results of the feasibility study as suggested in Phase I.
- Revisit Phase I policy recommendations after one year.

Future Research

- Conduct a follow-up survey with a larger population of people with disabilities and inquire about their level of satisfaction of the types of effectiveness of accessible solutions at historic buildings and museums in Monterey County.
- Conduct a survey of the stewards of historic buildings and museums to find out if accessibility for persons with disabilities exist and if they are implemented.
- Collaborate with other public and private entities to develop and implement a display of cultural heritage outreach program and accessibility service listings via the Internet and/ or a cell phone application.

2019 Update

Based on the 2012 proposed recommendations and areas for future research, a follow-up was completed at the beginning of 2019. Those results are below:

Construction for a rear stairway including a Limited Use/Limited Access (LULA) lift, an ADA accessible restroom and parking spaces was completed at historic Colton Hall in the fall of 2018. The funding for the project was obtained by the City's capital improvement and Neighborhood Improvement Programs, and foundation grants.

The Museums and Cultural Arts Commission reviewed their strategic plan for 2017/2019, and a subcommittee for the Colton Hall Museum and Old Monterey Jail was formed in 2017 with three Commission members who will assist museum staff to identify interpretive plan elements including technology (MCAC Minutes; Strategic Plan Goals for FY 17/19, August 28, 2017). The subcommittee met on December 18, 2018, to review the staff's work plan for short-term interpretive plan recommendations, electronic media display, and discussed exterior signage identifying Colton Hall.

Some of the recommendations listed in Phases I and II of this chapter may be reviewed by staff and brought forth for consideration in the future to the Colton Hall Museum and Old Monterey Jail subcommittee and it will make recommendations to the Museums and Cultural Arts Commission for action that can be taken to the City Council. Staff may want to prioritize the recommendations in Phase I and develop a policy for access to Colton Hall with additional explanations about the ADA and the National Preservation Act. In addition, a phase funding plan needs to be developed for interpretation for those with sensory challenges or who are differently abled.

The commission also has purview over other historic sites: the Presidio of Monterey Museum located at the Lower Presidio Historic Park, the three historic Worker Shacks and the Pacific Biological Laboratories (also known as Ed Ricketts's Lab), both located at Cannery Row. The city was awarded a foundation grant to develop an ADA accessibility study for the Pacific Biological Laboratories.

All of these historic sites require responsible stewardship, and stewardship requires not only funding but the vision and support of local citizens and city officials who are determined to keep these historic sites available for future generations to enjoy.

REFERENCE

Rygg, Claire. "Accessibility Solutions for Colon Hall." Golden Gate University, February 27, 2012.

38. Township Taps Former Mayor for Age-Friendly Initiative[*]

INTERNATIONAL CITY/COUNTY
MANAGEMENT ASSOCIATION

As the U.S. population ages, most communities will wrestle with a variety of issues related to elderly residents. Top of mind would be emergency services, transportation, engagement and activities, and appropriate housing.

Teaneck, New Jersey (pop. 40,000), is getting ahead of the curve with a program called Age-Friendly Teaneck. The planning phase of the program began in January 2016 and the three-year implementation began in October 2016.

"My many years in Teaneck have made me realize what a priority it should be to keep our residents here, safe and engaged," said Township Manager William Broughton.

Age-Friendly Teaneck

The group launched a website, www.agefriendlyteaneck.org, and Twitter channel, @AFTeaneck, which is full of resources for the town's elderly population. The group has formed task forces and developed materials and ancillary programs in support of its initiative to make Teaneck an age-friendly and livable community. Already, the initiative has 16 steering committee members, 60 residents serving on five task forces, and partnerships are emerging quickly.

None of this would have been accomplished without the involvement of the former mayor, Jacqueline Kates. "Mrs. Kates and her drive have really helped the Age Friendly Initiative come to fruition," said Broughton.

"Most people would like to age in place, near the people and activities that have been part of their lives. But most cities, towns, and villages are not organized to help residents stay connected and engaged, may not have safe and affordable housing options, do not provide adequate access to transportation and mobility, enable economic opportunity, or allow seniors to be financially secure as they age," said Kates, who is project

*Reprinted with permission from "Township Taps Former Mayor for Age-Friendly Initiative" by ICMA, 2017, April, https://icma.org/articles/article/success-story-township-taps-former-mayor-age-friendly-initiative.

coordinator for Age-Friendly Teaneck. "Communities are often unprepared for the increasing number of older people, but we want to make sure that Teaneck is a community where we can remain and enjoy living, whatever age we are."

Starts with a Survey

The initiative began with a survey in which older adults identified these top concerns:

- Staying in their homes despite reduced incomes, higher taxes, and accessibility issues.
- Maintaining their homes when funds, information, and resources are scarce.
- Transportation when driving is no longer an option.
- Access to the adequate community, medical, and healthcare resources.
- Continued access to the Richard Rodda Community Center for activities and social interaction even if they are living alone.
- Managing finances and access to related resources and economic assets

"Our task forces are addressing the issues of concern that were identified during the planning phase, through the survey, as well as interviews and focus groups," Kates said. Task forces include:

- Transportation and Pedestrian Safety Task Force
- Health and Social Engagement Task Force
- Community Resources and Communications Task Force
- Housing Options Task Force
- Business and Banking Task Force.
- Street Safety

The first successful advocacy effort was led by Broughton, who responded to the concerns of the Age-Friendly group by interceding with Bergen County to increase crossing time at an intersection.

"That doesn't sound like a lot, but it really does make a difference for anyone crossing that intersection who can now walk at a slower and safer pace, without feeling the need to run and possibly fall in the street," Kates said. "People are very happy about that. And this safety issue demonstrates that age-friendly improvements can benefit everyone in the community."

Continuing this effort, and in response to an unfortunate rash of pedestrian fatalities, Broughton's office has started working with an expert in Complete Streets at Rutgers University to incorporate ideas into the town's master plan for roads and intersections.

The Transportation and Pedestrian Safety Task Force also is trying to find more ways to expand the township's Senior Transportation Services to help those who don't drive and need to get to doctors' appointments, the supermarket, or the beauty salon. Options include the Independent Transportation Network of volunteer drivers and the Go Go Grandparent program that use Uber and Lyft.

The Community Resources and Communications Task Force is in the process of developing a directory of essential Teaneck resource phone numbers for first responders to leave behind when they respond to emergency calls. "We have learned from the first responders that people call 911 even when there isn't a true emergency because they know they'll get a response, and they don't know where else to turn for help," Kates said.

First responders will distribute the directory that people can put on their refrigerators or near their telephones so they can call the proper number for a problem that is important but does not require police, fire truck or ambulance. The cooperative project is being underwritten by Five Star Senior Premier Living, one of the program's community partners.

On the flip side, Age Friendly Teaneck is promoting the Fire Department's Good Morning Check-In program for those who live alone. Residents who register with the Fire Department will receive a daily call to make sure they are okay, and if there's no response, a hose and ladder fire truck will be there to help.

The Health and Social Engagement Task Force and the Township and the Holy Name Medical Center are cosponsoring a series of four events, Conversation of Your Life, to raise awareness of the importance of anyone over 18 having an Advance Medical Directive.

Housing Concerns Abound

"Housing is one of the biggest concerns of older adults who want to stay in Teaneck," said Kates. "I hear about that issue more often than any other. If there had been housing options in Teaneck for us to downsize, my husband and I would never have considered moving," added Kates, who had lived in Teaneck since she was in elementary school.

For those on limited incomes, the options are few. The Brookdale subsidized independent housing building for older adults opened in April 2016 and has a 10-year waiting list. And while the township council is supportive of residential housing projects, with several new developments approved, Kates does not think any are specifically targeted for older people, with the required amenities that would make it more comfortable to live there.

Thus, the Housing Task Force is exploring options for seniors on a college campus, with residents benefiting from the educational and cultural stimulation of college life, since they would be required to take a number of credits as a condition of becoming a resident. The task force also is looking into publicizing information on home-sharing options that can formalize these situations and protect the elderly with follow-up visits and other parameters set forth in agreements.

For those having difficulty maintaining their homes, the task force is publicizing agencies that can give free volunteer repair and maintenance help to older adults, such as the Chore Service of Bergen Volunteer Center and Rebuilding Together North Jersey. These groups perform minor repairs, install grab bars, and other equipment needed by the elderly.

The task forces also are working with business and banks to ensure that the economic assets of older adult consumers are being maximized and special needs are being met, by improving lighting, using larger fonts on materials and advertising and providing access to public restrooms. Training bank and business staff to recognize signs of financial and physical elder abuse also are on the agenda.

The Teaneck program is funded by the Henry and Marilyn Taub Foundation. The planning phase grant was $35,000 and the implementation grant is for up to $75,000 per year for three years. Resources for local governments in the Aging topic area on the ICMA website.

39. Seniors and the California Courts*

Ruth Astle Samas

Seniors and Jury Service

Seniors may continue to receive jury summonses as long as their names appear on either the DMV or voter registration records. Senior citizens comprise a significant percentage of the prospective jurors who are summoned, and as a group, they tend to be very dedicated and do an exemplary job when called to serve. Often seniors have the time to serve on a jury. Payment is $15 a day after the first day of service. However, it can be difficult to sit for long periods of time and senior jurors may need breaks more often than the customary court breaks. The court may be willing to accommodate these needs. Let the court know at the time you are questioned during *voir dire* (a preliminary examination of a juror by a judge or counsel).

Age and Health

You may be excused if you are over 70 and have a serious health problem. If you are sick or disabled, you may postpone your service or request an excuse. Follow the directions on the summons for postponement or excuse. A doctor's note may be required if you are under 70 years old. If you need special accommodations, contact the court right away.

Persons with disabilities, including seniors, can request reasonable accommodations. (See Rule 1.100 2019 California Rules of Court.) Reasonable accommodations will be made to allow you to serve, including, but not limited to wheelchair access, readers, assistive listening devices, sign language interpreters, or real-time captioning. Contact the phone number on your summons as soon as possible to allow the court time to provide the accommodation.

And what should seniors do if they feel they have a legitimate excuse from jury duty? You should complete and return the jury questionnaire, requesting an excuse if applicable. If you are older than 70 and claim a disability on the juror questionnaire, you

---

*Published with permission of the author.

are automatically excused for that session and do not have to provide a physician's statement to support your disability claim.

2019 California Rules of Court

Rule 1.100. Requests for accommodations by persons with disabilities

(a) Definitions
As used in this rule:

(1) "Persons with disabilities" means individuals covered by California Civil Code section 51 et seq.; the Americans with Disabilities Act of 1990 (42 U.S.C. §12101 et seq.); or other applicable state and federal laws. This definition includes persons who have a physical or mental medical condition that limits one or more of the major life activities, have a record of such a condition, or are regarded as having such a condition.

(2) "Applicant" means any lawyer, party, witness, juror, or other person with an interest in attending any proceeding before any court of this state.

(3) "Accommodations" means actions that result in court services, programs, or activities being readily accessible to and usable by persons with disabilities. Accommodations may include making reasonable modifications in policies, practices, and procedures; furnishing, at no charge, to persons with disabilities, auxiliary aids and services, equipment, devices, materials in alternative formats, readers, or certified interpreters for persons who are deaf or hard-of-hearing; relocating services or programs to accessible facilities; or providing services at alternative sites. Although not required where other actions are effective in providing access to court services, programs, or activities, alteration of existing facilities by the responsible entity may be an accommodation.

(Subd [a] amended effective July 1, 2017; adopted as subd [b] effective January 1, 1996; previously amended effective January 1, 2006, amended and relettered effective January 1, 2007.)

(b) Policy
It is the policy of the courts of this state to ensure that persons with disabilities have equal and full access to the judicial system. To ensure access to the courts for persons with disabilities, each superior and appellate court must delegate at least one person to be the ADA coordinator, also known as the access coordinator, or designee to address requests for accommodations. This rule is not intended to impose limitations or to invalidate the remedies, rights, and procedures accorded to persons with disabilities under state or federal law.

(Subd [b] adopted effective January 1, 2007.)

(c) Process for requesting accommodations
The process for requesting accommodations is as follows:

(1) Requests for accommodations under this rule may be presented *ex parte* on a form approved by the Judicial Council, in another written format, or orally.

Requests must be forwarded to the ADA coordinator, also known as the access coordinator, or designee, within the time frame provided in (c)(3).

(2) Requests for accommodations must include a description of the accommodation sought, along with a statement of the medical condition that necessitates the accommodation. The court, in its discretion, may require the applicant to provide additional information about the medical condition.

(3) Requests for accommodations must be made as far in advance as possible, and in any event must be made no fewer than five court days before the requested implementation date. The court may, in its discretion, waive this requirement.

(4) The court must keep confidential all information of the applicant concerning the request for accommodation, unless confidentiality is waived in writing by the applicant or disclosure is required by law. The applicant's identity and confidential information may not be disclosed to the public or to persons other than those involved in the accommodation process. Confidential information includes all medical information pertaining to the applicant, and all oral or written communication from the applicant concerning the request for accommodation.

(Subd [c] amended effective July 1, 2017; previously amended effective January 1, 2006, and January 1, 2007.)</NUMLIST>

(d) Permitted communication

Communications under this rule must address only the accommodation requested by the applicant and must not address, in any manner, the subject matter or merits of the proceedings before the court.

(Subd [d] amended effective January 1, 2006.)

(e) Response to accommodation request

The court must respond to a request for accommodation as follows:

(1) In determining whether to grant an accommodation request or provide an appropriate alternative accommodation, the court must consider, but is not limited by, California Civil Code section 51 *et seq.*, the provisions of the Americans with Disabilities Act of 1990 (42 U.S.C. § 12101, et seq.), and other applicable state and federal laws.

(2) The court must promptly inform the applicant of the determination to grant or deny an accommodation request. If the accommodation request is denied in whole or in part, the response must be in writing. On request of the applicant, the court may also provide an additional response in an alternative format. The response to the applicant must indicate:

(A) Whether the request for accommodation is granted or denied, in whole or in part, or an alternative accommodation is granted;

(B) If the request for accommodation is denied, in whole or in part, the reason therefor;

(C) The nature of any accommodation to be provided;

(D) The duration of any accommodation to be provided; and

(E) If the response is in writing, the date the response was delivered in person or sent to the applicant.

(Subd [e] amended effective January 1, 2010; previously amended effective January 1, 2006, and January 1, 2007.)

(f) Denial of accommodation request

A request for accommodation may be denied only when the court determines that:

(1) The applicant has failed to satisfy the requirements of this rule;

(2) The requested accommodation would create an undue financial or administrative burden on the court; or

(3) The requested accommodation would fundamentally alter the nature of the service, program, or activity.

(Subd [f] amended effective January 1, 2007; previously amended effective January 1, 2006.)

(g) Review procedure

(1) If the determination to grant or deny a request for accommodation is made by nonjudicial court personnel, an applicant or any participant in the proceeding may submit a written request for review of that determination to the presiding judge or designated judicial officer. The request for review must be submitted within 10 days of the date the response under (e)(2) was delivered in person or sent.

(2) If the determination to grant or deny a request for accommodation is made by a presiding judge or another judicial officer, an applicant or any participant in the proceeding may file a petition for a writ of mandate under rules 8.485–8.493 or 8.930–8.936 in the appropriate reviewing court. The petition must be filed within 10 days of the date the response under (e)(2) was delivered in person or sent to the petitioner. For purposes of this rule, only those participants in the proceeding who were notified by the court of the determination to grant or deny the request for accommodation are considered real parties in interest in a writ proceeding. The petition for the writ must be served on the respondent court and any real party in interest as defined in this rule.

(3) The confidentiality of all information of the applicant concerning the request for accommodation and review under (g)(1) or (2) must be maintained as required under (c)(4).

(Subd [g] amended effective January 1, 2010; previously amended effective January 1, 2006.)

(h) Duration of accommodations

The accommodation by the court must be provided for the duration indicated in the response to the request for accommodation and must remain in effect for the period specified. The court may provide an accommodation for an indefinite period of time, for a limited period of time, or for a particular matter or appearance.

Elder Court in California

Two counties in California have initiated special courts for elders/seniors: Contra Costa County and Ventura County

Superior Court of California, County of Contra Costa Elder Court

The Elder Court program is a partnership of the court and community to ensure justice for elders. Under the leadership of a committed judge, the Superior Court created a multidisciplinary task force to examine how to coordinate the numerous services for elders in the community. The task force's efforts led to the creation of the Elder Court in 2008. The Contra Costa Elder Court exemplifies best practices for managing elder abuse cases and integrating the missions and resources of stakeholders to provide more comprehensive and appropriate remedies for older victims. For an overview and video of the Contra Costa Elder Court, visit http://www.courts.ca.gov/14124.htm

- A single judge hears all case types involving senior citizens: elder abuse, restraining orders, felonies and misdemeanors, landlord tenant disputes, probate matters, small claims and others.
- The District Attorney's Office uses vertical prosecution with a designated prosecutor who brings all criminal elder abuse cases (Code 368) to the attention of the court.
- The Elder Court accommodates physical needs of elders in several ways, including holding hearings in the late morning and providing a wheelchair, assistive listening devices and a document magnifier in the Elder Court courtroom.
- Volunteer Senior Peer Counselors assist elders seeking a restraining order and offer emotional support to before and after hearings to help elders understand the process and the outcomes.
- The court coordinates other services, including free legal advice for indigent seniors from experienced attorneys, in-home counseling, transportation assistance and referrals to community-based resources.

Superior Court of California, County of Ventura Elder Abuse Court

In 2009, the California Superior Court, County of Ventura, established an elder abuse court to hear Penal Code section 368 cases. (See Penal Code section 369, below.) Cases eligible for the court are identified by the District Attorney's Office and heard by a designated judge in a courtroom that has a separate observation room for vulnerable witnesses and victims. The ability of the court to identify and focus on "368" cases stems from a collaboration between courts, prosecutors, public defenders, legal aid, and local service providers. For more information (see Elder Abuse Cases: Proposed Performance Measures for Courts).

Penal Code section 368

(a) The Legislature finds and declares that crimes against elders and dependent adults are deserving of special consideration and protection, not unlike the special protections provided for minor children, because elders and dependent adults may be confused, on various medications, mentally or physically impaired, or incompetent, and therefore less able to protect themselves, to understand or report criminal conduct, or to testify in court proceedings on their own behalf.

(b)(1) Any person who knows or reasonably should know that a person is an elder or dependent adult and who, under circumstances or conditions likely to produce great bodily harm or death, willfully causes or permits any elder or dependent adult to suffer, or inflicts thereon unjustifiable physical pain or mental suffering, or having the care or custody of any elder or dependent adult, willfully causes or permits the person or health of the elder or dependent adult to be injured, or willfully causes or permits the elder or dependent adult to be placed in a situation in which his or her person or health is endangered, is punishable by imprisonment in a county jail not exceeding one year, or by a fine not to exceed six thousand dollars ($6,000), or by both that fine and imprisonment, or by imprisonment in the state prison for two, three, or four years.

(2) If, in the commission of an offense described in paragraph (1), the victim suffers great bodily injury, as defined in *Section 12022.7*, the defendant shall receive an additional term in the state prison as follows:

(A) Three years if the victim is under 70 years of age.

(B) Five years if the victim is 70 years of age or older.

(3) If, in the commission of an offense described in paragraph (1), the defendant proximately causes the death of the victim, the defendant shall receive an additional term in the state prison as follows:

(A) Five years if the victim is under 70 years of age.

(B) Seven years if the victim is 70 years of age or older.

(C) Any person who knows or reasonably should know that a person is an elder or dependent adult and who, under circumstances or conditions other than those likely to produce great bodily harm or death, willfully causes or permits any elder or dependent adult to suffer, or inflicts thereon unjustifiable physical pain or mental suffering, or having the care or custody of any elder or dependent adult, willfully causes or permits the person or health of the elder or dependent adult to be injured or willfully causes or permits the elder or dependent adult to be placed in a situation in which his or her person or health may be endangered, is guilty of a misdemeanor.   A second or subsequent violation of this subdivision is punishable by a fine not to exceed two thousand dollars ($2,000), or by imprisonment in a county jail not to exceed one year, or by both that fine and imprisonment.

(D) Any person who is not a caretaker who violates any provision of law proscribing theft, embezzlement, forgery, or fraud, or who violates *Section 530.5* proscribing identity theft, with respect to the property or personal identifying information of an elder or a dependent adult, and who knows or reasonably should know that the victim is an elder or a dependent adult, is punishable as follows:

(1) By a fine not exceeding two thousand five hundred dollars ($2,500), or by imprisonment in a county jail not exceeding one year, or by both that fine and imprisonment, or by a fine not exceeding ten thousand dollars ($10,000), or by imprisonment pursuant to subdivision (h) of Section 1170 for two, three, or four years, or by both that fine and imprisonment, when the moneys, labor, goods, services, or real or personal property taken or obtained is of a value exceeding nine hundred fifty dollars ($950).

(2) By a fine not exceeding one thousand dollars ($1,000), by imprisonment in a county jail not exceeding one year, or by both that fine and imprisonment, when the moneys, labor, goods, services, or real or personal property taken or obtained is of a value not exceeding nine hundred fifty dollars ($950).

(E) Any caretaker of an elder or a dependent adult who violates any provision of law proscribing theft, embezzlement, forgery, or fraud, or who violates *Section 530.5* proscribing identity theft, with respect to the property or personal identifying information of that elder or dependent adult, is punishable as follows:

(1) By a fine not exceeding two thousand five hundred dollars ($2,500), or by imprisonment in a county jail not exceeding one year, or by both that fine and imprisonment, or by a fine not exceeding ten thousand dollars ($10,000), or by imprisonment pursuant to subdivision (h) of Section 1170 for two, three, or four years, or by both that fine and imprisonment, when the moneys, labor, goods, services, or real or personal property taken or obtained is of a value exceeding nine hundred fifty dollars ($950).

(2) By a fine not exceeding one thousand dollars ($1,000), by imprisonment in a county jail not exceeding one year, or by both that fine and imprisonment, when the moneys, labor,

goods, services, or real or personal property taken or obtained is of a value not exceeding nine hundred fifty dollars ($950).

(F) Any person who commits the false imprisonment of an elder or a dependent adult by the use of violence, menace, fraud, or deceit is punishable by imprisonment pursuant to *subdivision (h) of Section 1170* for two, three, or four years.

(G) As used in this section, "elder" means any person who is 65 years of age or older.

(H) As used in this section, "dependent adult" means any person who is between the ages of 18 and 64, who has physical or mental limitations which restrict his or her ability to carry out normal activities or to protect his or her rights, including, but not limited to, persons who have physical or developmental disabilities or whose physical or mental abilities have diminished because of age. "Dependent adult" includes any person between the ages of 18 and 64 who is admitted as an inpatient to a 24-hour health facility, as defined in *Sections 1250, 1250.2,* and *1250.3 of the Health and Safety Code.*

(I) As used in this section, "caretaker" means any person who has the care, custody, or control of, or who stands in a position of trust with, an elder or a dependent adult.

(J) Nothing in this section shall preclude prosecution under both this section and *Section 187* or *12022.7* or any other provision of law. However, a person shall not receive an additional term of imprisonment under both paragraphs (2) and (3) of subdivision (b) for any single offense, nor shall a person receive an additional term of imprisonment under both *Section 12022.7* and paragraph (2) or (3) of subdivision (b) for any single offense.

(K) In any case in which a person is convicted of violating these provisions, the court may require him or her to receive appropriate counseling as a condition of probation. Any defendant ordered to be placed in a counseling program shall be responsible for paying the expense of his or her participation in the counseling program as determined by the court. The court shall take into consideration the ability of the defendant to pay, and no defendant shall be denied probation because of his or her inability to pay.

(L) Upon conviction for a violation of subdivision (b), (c), (d), (e), or (f), the sentencing court shall also consider issuing an order restraining the defendant from any contact with the victim, which may be valid for up to 10 years, as determined by the court. It is the intent of the Legislature that the length of any restraining order be based upon the seriousness of the facts before the court, the probability of future violations, and the safety of the victim and his or her immediate family. This protective order may be issued by the court whether the defendant is sentenced to state prison or county jail, or if imposition of sentence is suspended and the defendant is placed on probation.

Elder Abuse and Dependent Adult Civil Protection Act

Under Welfare and Institutions Code sections 15600 to 15675 California law recognizes that elders and dependent adults may be subjected to abuse, neglect, or abandonment and that this state has a responsibility to protect these persons. The court has jurisdiction to grant restraining orders and conservatorships. The court can appoint a responsible person of organization to care for another adult who cannot care for himself or herself or mange their own finances. Some definitions under Welfare and Institutions Code section 15610.07 include:

(a) "Abuse of an elder or a dependent adult" means any of the following:

(1) Physical abuse, neglect, abandonment, isolation, abduction, or other treatment with resulting physical harm or pain or mental suffering.

(2) The deprivation by a care custodian of goods or services that are necessary to avoid physical harm or mental suffering.

(3) Financial abuse, as defined in Section 15610.30.

Conclusion

California has significant protections for elders through the criminal and civil courts. The type of court exemplified by the Contra Costa County Elder Court program should be expanded to other counties to give special protection to those who are most vulnerable in our society.

40. Social Security[*]

Who's Counting on It?

ALISON SHELTON

- In 2013, almost 58 million people received a Social Security benefit.
- In 2012, Social Security kept 35 percent of older Americans out of poverty.
- In 2012, almost 24 percent of people age 65 and older lived in families that depended on Social Security for 90 percent or more of their family income.

Social Security insures families against the loss of income caused by retirement, disability, or death.[1] Social Security is particularly important to older Americans because it provides a stable source of income to about 88 percent of Americans age 65 and over.[2] It has kept many older Americans out of poverty.[3] The program, however, faces a long-term financial challenge.

Over the next 75 years, Social Security's shortfall—the amount by which scheduled payments will exceed revenue ("actuarial deficit")—is projected to be 2.72 percent of taxable payroll.[4] This deficit should be addressed soon. Here are some important facts to remember as the future of Social Security is discussed.

All Age Groups Protected: In 2013, almost 58 million people, including 17 million under age 65, received some sort of Social Security benefit.[5] Social Security not only provides retirement income for older Americans but also protects workers of all ages and their families against the risks of death and disability.

- Among people ages 20 to 49 who pay Social Security taxes, 96 percent have earned survivorship protections for their families.[6]
- Among people ages 21 to 64 who pay Social Security taxes, 90 percent can depend on a monthly cash benefit in the case of a severe and prolonged disability.[7]

Benefits Are Fully Funded for Another 19 Years: The Social Security trust funds had accumulated about $2.8 trillion in reserves at the end of 2013.[8] Their value is estimated to peak at $2.9 trillion by the end of 2020.[9] After that year, the trust funds' reserves will begin to be drawn down in order to pay full benefits.

---

*Originally published as Alison Shelton, "Social Security: Who's Counting on It?," AARP Policy Institute, https://www.aarp.org/ppi/info-2015/social-security-who-is-counting-on-it.html (April 2014). Reprinted with permission of the publisher.

According to the Social Security trustees, the Social Security trust funds' reserves will be depleted in 2033. Without any changes, Social Security revenue (primarily payroll taxes) still will be enough to pay 77 percent of scheduled benefits in 2033 and 72 percent of scheduled benefits in 2087.[10]

It is important that reforms necessary to make the program solvent be made sooner rather than later. The sooner action is taken, the less severe the changes to the program must be. For example, either an immediate increase in the payroll tax of 2.66 percentage points or a 16.5 percent decrease in all current and future benefits would close the shortfall in the Social Security trust funds, whereas waiting until the point of reserve depletion in 2033 would require either a 4.1 percentage point increase in the payroll tax or a 23 percent reduction in benefits.[11]

Just as important, the sooner changes are made, the more time there will be for phasing in the changes, and the more time there will be for future retirees to adjust their retirement plans in the event that benefits are reduced.

Social Security Is the Principal Source of Family Income for Nearly Half of Older Americans: Among individuals ages 65 and older, 88 percent include Social Security benefits as a source of family income, which is double the percentage of people who have family income from pensions and retirement savings.

For most older Americans, Social Security is the only retirement income source that is guaranteed for life and adjusted to keep pace with inflation. In contrast, pensions are rarely indexed to inflation, causing a decline in purchasing power over time, and retirees may outlive their retirement assets.

Almost 24 percent of people age 65 and older live in families that depend on Social Security benefits for 90 percent or more of their income. Another 26 percent receive at least half but less than 90 percent of their family income from Social Security.[12]

Additionally, reliance on Social Security as a source of guaranteed income increases with age: about 35 percent of people ages 65 to 69 depend on Social Security for 50 percent or more of their family income, compared to 61 percent of people age 80 and over.

Social Security benefits are particularly important for women because, on average, women live longer and earn less than do men, so they are more dependent than are men on Social Security's progressive benefit and inflation-adjusted, lifetime income. Among women age 65 and older, 27 percent depend on Social Security benefits for 90 percent or more of their family income, compared to 20 percent of men.[13]

Social Security Provides Critical Income Support to Minorities: African Americans and Hispanics are more likely to earn low or moderate wages. The progressive Social Security benefit formula ensures that those lower-wage workers and their families receive a higher benefit relative to their preretirement earnings than do higher-wage workers.

Older minorities are less likely than are whites to have family income from pensions and other retirement savings or assets. However, 82 percent of African Americans and 78 percent of Hispanics age 65 and older have family income from Social Security. Older African Americans and Hispanics are more likely than are older whites to depend on Social Security for 90 percent or more of their family income.

Social Security Keeps Older Americans Out of Poverty: As the only guaranteed source of income in retirement, Social Security has kept millions of older Americans out of poverty. In 2012, Social Security income kept roughly 35 percent of older Americans, about 15 million people, out of poverty.

The poor (income below poverty line) and near poor (income between 100 and 150 percent of the poverty line) rely on Social Security for a significant share of their family income. In 2012, about 58 percent of the poor and 64 percent of the near poor relied on Social Security for 90 percent or more of their family income.

Social Security Is the Foundation of Workers' Retirement Security, but It Was Never Intended to Be the Only Source: Social Security was intended to provide vital basic protections for workers and their families. Savings and pensions are also important components of overall retirement income security. For a comfortable retirement, many financial planners suggest that an individual's total income from pensions, personal savings, and Social Security should replace at least 70 percent of preretirement income.[14] However, Social Security replaces only 41 percent of the preretirement wages of a worker with average earnings over his or her career.[15]

Benefit Reductions May Begin in 2033: Without a legislative change, the Social Security program faces a financial shortfall that—if left unaddressed—will require an across-the-board benefit reduction starting in 2033. The sooner policy makers agree on how to achieve long-term solvency, the less drastic any changes would need to be. Any changes to the program should be made gradually—so that people can plan for their futures—and should protect those in or near retirement.

Solvency should not, however, be the only goal of Social Security reform. Reforms to the program must ensure that Social Security benefits continue as the foundation of a lifetime, guaranteed, inflation-protected retirement income. In addition, reform should strengthen, not erode, the protections for vulnerable workers and their families.

For many Americans age 65 and older, Social Security is the principal or only source of guaranteed retirement income. It is the most effective antipoverty program in the United States, keeping about 35 percent of Americans age 65 and older out of poverty. Policy makers must keep these facts in mind as debate about Social Security reform progresses.

NOTES

1. This is an update of "Social Security: Who's Counting on It?," Fact Sheet 178, using 2013 administrative data and 2012 survey data.

2. Social Security Administration, "Social Security Program Fact Sheet, December 31, 2013," http://www.ssa.gov/OACT/FACTS/.

3. This fact sheet relies on the U.S. Census Bureau's poverty thresholds, http://www.census.gov/hhes/www/poverty/data/threshld/index.html. In 2012, the poverty threshold was $11,011 for a single person age 65 and older and was $13,878 for a couple with a householder age 65 and older.

4. Board of Trustees, Federal Old-Age and Survivors Insurance and Federal Disability Insurance Trust Funds, the 2013 Annual Report of the Board of Trustees of the Federal Old-Age and Survivors Insurance and Federal Disability Insurance Trust Funds (Washington, DC: Social Security Administration, May 31, 2013), http://ssa.gov/OACT/TR/2013/tr2013.pdf. The actuarial deficit of 2.72 percent, expressed as a percentage of taxable payroll, is the difference between income (payroll tax contributions and income from the taxation of scheduled benefits) and scheduled benefits and administrative costs.

5. Social Security Administration, "Social Security Program Fact Sheet, December 31, 2013," http://www.ssa.gov/OACT/FACTS/.

6. *Ibid.*

7. *Ibid.*

8. Social Security Administration, "Trust Fund Data" and "Time Series Report," http://www.ssa.gov/OACT/ProgData/investheld.html.

9. Board of Trustees, Federal Old-Age and Survivors Insurance and Federal Disability Insurance Trust Funds, the 2013 Annual Report of the Board of Trustees of the Federal Old-Age and Survivors Insurance and Federal Disability Insurance Trust Funds, table VI.C6 (Washington, DC: Social Security Administration, May 31, 2013), http://ssa.gov/OACT/TR/2013/tr2013.pdf.

10. Board of Trustees, figure II.D2.

11. Board of Trustees, pages 22–23. The estimated tax rate of 2.66 percent that would lead to solvency for 75 years differs from the actuarial deficit of 2.72 percent because the 2.66 percent figure does not include an ending reserve equal to one year of benefit payments, while the 2.72 percent figure includes this ending reserve. Also, the 2.66 percent figure includes assumed behavioral responses to an increase in payroll taxes, but the 2.72 percent figure does not.

12. These tabulations take account of the income of the entire family in estimating the extent to which older individuals depend on Social Security.

13. A. Shelton, "Social Security: A Key Retirement Resource for Women," AARP Public Policy Institute Fact Sheet 305, April 2014.

14. Investopedia.com, "Mutual Funds: Introduction" (2013), http://www.investopedia.com/university/mutualfunds/.

15. Social Security Administration, "2014 Social Security/SSI/Medicare Information" (2013), http://www.ssa.gov/legislation/2014factsheet.pdf. The figure of 41 percent is for the Social Security Administration's "scaled medium earner" with career average earnings approximately equal to the Administration's Average Wage Index, which is an index of mean earnings nationwide.

41. Five Things to Consider Before You Collect Your Social Security Benefits[*]

STACY CANAN *and* HECTOR ORTIZ

If you're approaching retirement, you're probably thinking about when to start collecting your Social Security retirement benefits.

To help you make a more informed decision about when to claim, the federal Consumer Financial Protection Bureau created a new tool, "Planning for Retirement." You'll see how your claiming age affects your benefits and get tips relevant to your situation, which can help you start the conversation about your retirement needs and goals. We encourage you to try it out!

In addition to using the tool, consider these five tips to help you plan ahead and make the best decision for yourself and your family:

1. Know your "full retirement age."

The age at which you get your full retirement benefits from Social Security ranges from 66 to 67 depending on the year you were born. Claiming before your full retirement age leads to a permanent decrease in monthly benefits, while claiming after leads to a permanent increase. The full retirement age is the age at which you can start working and collecting simultaneously without facing a reduction in benefits.

Did you know? One recent survey found that seven in ten consumers believe that 65 is their *full retirement age*. In fact, the *full retirement age* actually varies depending on the year in which they were born.

2. Don't claim early if you don't have to.

Allowing your benefits to grow for one year makes a difference in your benefits. You'll get an additional five to eight percent in monthly benefits for every year you wait to claim after age 62, maxing out at age 70. A higher monthly benefit could be important when you are older, which is when Social Security may play a more central role in your retirement income. At that point, your other sources of income and savings may be depleted and your health-related costs may be higher.

---

[*]Originally published as Stacy Canan and Hector Ortiz, "Five Things to Consider Before You Collect Your Social Security Benefits," https://www.consumerfinance.gov/about-us/blog/5-things-to-consider-before-you-collect-your-social-security-benefits/ (November 17, 2015).

Did you know? You could see as much as a 30 percent reduction in monthly benefits by claiming before your full retirement age; whereas you can get as much as a 32 percent permanent increase (8 percent per year) by claiming after your full retirement age—up to age 70.

3. Know your retirement budget.

Start with a simple budget that accounts for your income and expenses. Consider both your actual income and expenses before retirement and your expected income and expenses after you retire. This can help you understand how a reduced or increased benefit will affect your ability to meet your needs in retirement. In addition, this kind of budgeting can help you decide if you should reduce your expenses and pay off any debts before retiring.

Did you know? Retirement years may be more expensive than retirees expect, as many will incur increased health and housing expenses in their later years, and many carry mortgages and other debts into retirement.

4. Keep working if you can.

Staying in the workforce—full or part time—for even one or two additional years can earn you an even bigger increase in your Social Security benefit by replacing years with low or no earnings from your earnings record. Working longer also gives you more time to save for retirement.

Did you know? Many people (45 percent) believe that their benefits are based on how long they work as well as their pay during only the last five years of employment, when in fact they are based on their highest 35 years of earnings.

5. Consider your spouse's long-term needs.

Your decision of when to claim your Social Security benefits could affect the benefits your spouse will receive after you die. Because surviving spouses receive the higher of the two spouses' benefits, it often makes sense for higher earning spouses to claim at or after their full retirement age to get their full or highest possible benefit. This can minimize the reduction in income a surviving spouse may experience. Talk to your spouse about your claiming options so you can make this important decision together.

Did you know? On average, a married couple reaching age 65 can expect that one spouse will outlive the other for about 10 years or more.

42. Top 11 Elder Scams*

U.S. Consumer Financial Protection Bureau

Financial institutions are seeing vast numbers of their older customers fall prey to financial exploitation by perpetrators ranging from offshore scammers to close family members—and they're filing hundreds of thousands of reports with the federal government about these suspicions. In February 2019, the Consumer Financial Protection Bureau's Office of Financial Protection for Older Americans released a report about key facts, trends, and patterns revealed in these Suspicious Activity Reports—or SARs—filed by banks, credit unions, casinos, and other financial services providers. The Bureau analyzed 180,000 elder financial exploitation SARs filed with the Financial Crimes Enforcement Network (FinCEN) from 2013 to 2017, involving more than $6 billion. This first-ever public analysis provides a chance to better understand elder fraud and to find ways to improve prevention and response.

What We Learned

- SAR filings on elder financial exploitation quadrupled from 2013 to 2017. In 2017, financial institutions filed 63,500 SARs reporting elder financial abuse. Yet these SARs likely represent only a tiny fraction of the actual 3.5 million incidents of elder financial exploitation estimated to have happened that year.
- Elder financial exploitation isn't just happening at banks or credit unions. Money services businesses, used by many people to wire money, have filed an increasing share of these SARs (58 percent in 2017).
- Older adults ages 70 to 79 lost on average $43,300. And when the older adult knew the suspect, the average loss was even larger–about $50,000.
- While financial institutions are increasingly filing elder financial exploitation SARs, they often do not indicate that they reported the suspicious activity directly to first responders. Fewer than one-third of elder financial exploitation SARs specify that the financial institution reported the activity to adult protective services, law enforcement, or other authorities. If the financial

*Originally published as U.S. Consumer Financial Protection Bureau, "Top 11 Elder Scams," https://www.consumerfinance.gov/documents/7304/cfpb_suspicious-activity-reports-elder-financial-exploitation_report.pdf.

institution is not reporting to these authorities, this is a missed opportunity to strengthen prevention and response.

Top 11 Scams

1. Medicare/Health Insurance Scam

Every U.S. citizen over the age of 65 automatically qualifies for Medicare, so scammers do not have to research which health insurance provider they are using. The scam artists pose as Medicare representatives and try to get seniors' personal information. They may offer services that the senior doesn't need via the telephone or a "mobile unit" then try to bill Medicare for these fake or unnecessary tests/medications/etc. Seniors may get in trouble with Medicare or even be out money for "co-pays."

2. Counterfeit Prescription Drugs

Mostly online scams, the FDA investigates upwards of 20 counterfeit prescription drug scams per year, up from five annually in the 1990s. Not only are seniors losing money on fraudulent prescriptions, they may also harm themselves by taking unsafe substances rather than their real medication. Cheaper is not always better.

3. Funeral and Cemetery Scams

Scammers scour the obituaries or funeral home websites and reach out to survivors right before, during or right after the funeral to inform the bereaved family that the deceased owes a debt that was overdue at his/her death and needs to be repaid post haste to prevent besmirching the deceased's reputation. The scammer plays on the grief of the bereaved family while seemingly being sympathetic.

Another situation that can happen is that disreputable funeral homes will take advantage of grieving families who are unfamiliar with the details around funeral costs, adding on unnecessary or fraudulent extras to the bill. They play on the grief of the bereaved family by reassuring them that they want the absolute best for their loved one, including a very expensive casket for a cremation when only a cardboard box is required.

4. Fraudulent Anti-aging Products

In a society that stigmatizes aging, it is easy to understand why people may fall for scams that offer them the fountain of youth.

Many older Americans seek out new treatments and medications to maintain a youthful appearance, putting them on scammers' radars. Whether it's the ever-popular fake Botox or fraudulent "homeopathic" remedies that do absolutely nothing, there is big money in the anti-aging business.

Botox scams are particularly unsettling, because renegade labs creating versions of the real thing may still be working with the root ingredient, botulism neurotoxin, which is one of the most toxic substances known to science. A bad batch can have serious health consequences. As a result, the consumer may also have to incur unexpected medical expenses to address any adverse effects in addition to paying for the fake Botox.

5. Telemarketing/Phone Scams

Since many seniors are happy to talk to anyone willing to talk to them, phone scams are highly prevalent. Seniors also are more likely to purchase items over the telephone versus the internet, so there is no paper trail, making these transactions almost impossible to trace. Also, once a scammer is successful with a telemarketing scam, s/he may "share the wealth" by spreading the susceptible senior's information. There are several types of telemarketing scams including:

a. The pigeon drop: scammer tells the senior they found a large sum of money that they are willing to split if the senior will provide a "good faith" payment by withdrawing money from their bank account. Often, there is a second con artist involved who portrays a "trustworthy" participant, such as a lawyer or officer.

b. Fake accident: the scammer convinces the senior that a relative or close friend has been in an accident and needs the money for treatment.

c. Fake charities: scammers will call seniors soliciting donations for fake charities. Names will be similar to well-known charities to create the belief that they are legitimate. These scams are particularly popular after natural disasters.

6. Internet Scams

Seniors fall victim to clicking on pop-up windows offering updated virus protection that look legitimate. In reality, they are scams that will either require a large sum to "purchase" or upload an actual virus to the computer that grants the scammer access to personal information. The scammer may even install ransomware and request a payment to regain control of their information.

Email phishing scams are also popular. Someone pretends to be from their bank, the IRS or some other official entity that needs to verify the personal information of the senior.

Seniors may also fall victim to a "Work from Home" money claim from an Internet ad or email. The offer may involve the senior needing to pay for "training" or special "equipment" in order to begin making the money.

7. Investment Schemes

When they retire, seniors are often looking for ways to maximize their savings while minimizing risks. Pyramid schemes, such as investment opportunities offered by a fabled Nigerian prince, are simply too good to be true. They are designed to take advantage of people and steal their financial resources. No legitimate investment will require up front money to reap astronomical returns within unrealistic timeframes.

8. Homeowners/Reverse Mortgage Scams

This encompasses two distinct scams. The first involves a con artist who poses as a tax official offering to reassess the senior's property for tax purposes. The scam is predicated on the notion that the senior's tax debt would be lowered. The con artist charges a fee for this "reassessment," which is fraudulent.

The second revolves around pressuring seniors to obtain a reverse mortgage to access the equity in their home. Typically, scammers are lurking to perform "necessary home repairs" to take advantage of the windfall of cash the senior receives from the reverse mortgage. Since real estate generally encompasses a large portion of a senior's wealth, obtaining a reverse mortgage may effectively deplete their largest asset.

9. Sweepstakes and Lottery Scams

While not limited to seniors, these scams use the lure of free money to convince consumers to divulge sensitive information or send funds to a con artist. Seniors receive a communication via email, mail, phone call or sometimes even in person. They have won a prize from some contest they don't even remember entering. Before they can get the entire amount, they have to deposit a partial amount to "verify" their bank account information. They are then asked to repay that amount to the scammer before the fraudulent check has been returned. By the time the check is returned as a fraud, the scammer is long gone with money they got from the senior.

10. Imposter Scam

This one seems particularly egregious because it can pull on the heartstrings of the senior involved depending on the persona adopted by the scammer. The scammer may call and pretend to be an IRS agent or from another official entity, such as the local utility company or even their bank. The scammer will then claim that the senior owes money that must be repaid immediately or charges will be filed.

Alternatively, the scammer may try a more personal approach by self-identifying as the senior's favorite grandchild/niece/nephew/etc., in need of money. It may just be a "loan," to address an urgent situation like a car repair, late rent, school tuition, or something along those lines. The scammer implores the senior not to tell mom or dad and states that s/he will pay the senior back. The scammer will then provide a Western Union or MoneyGram location to pick up the money.

11. Check Fraud

There are several variations of check fraud. The senior may write a check to someone, and that person alters the amount or orders checks with a new address to write fraudulent checks. Blank checks could be stolen and forged for any amount, or scammers could ask the senior for help "clearing" a check because s/he does not have a local bank account but needs the money quickly. The senior deposits the fraudulent check and writes one to the scammer. By the time the check is returned, the scammer and the money are long gone. The scammer may also write checks of larger and larger amounts with the senior until they get the amount they want, and then disappear.

43. Guaranteed Returns in Retirement Savings Plans*

Are They Worth the Cost?

William G. Gale

Several states have recently created state-sponsored retirement savings plans for employees of small businesses, and many other states are considering doing the same.[1] A key element in the design of such plans is the decision whether to provide a minimum level of guaranteed returns to savers. Continued concerns about retirement security—as well as lingering apprehension from the 2007–09 financial crisis, which showed just how quickly assets accumulated over a lifetime can lose their value—are behind the desire for guaranteed returns.

Guarantees are a classic example of the economics dictum that it is impossible to get something for nothing. In principle, rate-of-return guarantees are simple: they protect savers from losses and ensure that they receive a minimum return on their investments. In practice, however, guarantees raise a number of complex issues and are more costly than one might think. First, someone—the saver, the plan sponsor, or the taxpayer—has to pay for the guarantee. When the government pays, it tends to severely underreport the real economic costs of the guarantee in budget documents. Those costs are resources that must be forgone to finance the guaranteed return. Guarantees offered by private insurers reflect their true economic costs more accurately, and they are often quite expensive. Second, the net benefits of rate-of-return guarantees may not be as obvious as they seem, because (a) markets often respond quickly and (b) social security, Medicare, and housing constitute the majority of most people's retirement resources.

Types of Guarantees

A standard rate-of-return guarantee is an insurance policy that ensures that a saver receives at least a minimum return on his or her investments. When those investments earn less than the guarantee during a set time period, the saver receives the difference

---

*Originally published as William G. Gale, "Guaranteed Returns in Retirement Savings Plans: Are They Worth the Cost?," AARP Policy Institute, https://www.aarp.org/ppi/info-2016/guaranteed-returns-in-retirement-savings-plans.html (May 2016). Reprinted with permission of the publisher.

between the actual earnings and the amount promised by the guarantor. If the investments earn more than the guarantee, the investor receives the investment earnings; the insurer (either government or private) does not make a payment. (Guarantees with more complex designs, discussed later, have different payout structures.)

The most common form of guarantee provides a minimum annual rate of return on principal investments (e.g., 3 percent). But guarantees come in many forms. Some insure only the principal. Others adjust the guaranteed return for inflation or cover longer periods. Some base the guarantee on the rate of return on a specific type of government bond, government bond portfolio, or market portfolio.

A number of existing and proposed plans in the United States and in other countries around the world offer minimum rate-of-return guarantees.[2] Several Latin American countries have instituted guarantees, often in conjunction with social security reforms. Denmark, Germany, Japan, Switzerland, and other member countries of the Organisation for Economic Co-operation and Development offer variants of a guaranteed rate of return.

The Teachers Insurance and Annuity Association (TIAA) offers a traditional annuity with a guaranteed minimum rate of return. The guarantee is set annually at the time of contribution and remains valid until distributions for contributions made in that year begin. The rate for new contributions is adjusted each year in conjunction with economic conditions and has recently varied between 1 and 3 percent, adjusted for inflation. The TIAA Board of Trustees may also declare, on a year-to-year basis, additional rates of return for a specific year only, but those rates are not guaranteed for future years. TIAA credited such additional amounts every year from 1948 to 2010.[3]

Cash balance plans are a hybrid form of pension. From the saver's perspective, cash balance plans closely resemble retirement savings plans; in legal terms, however, they are defined benefit plans and are regulated accordingly. Cash balance plans provide their participants notional accounts to which the plans credit an annual return. The plans essentially offer a guaranteed return, with both the minimum and the maximum rate set at the same level.

There have been numerous proposals for minimum guaranteed rates of return in the United States. Martin Feldstein and Andrew Samwick propose private accounts in Social Security with a real principal guarantee (an inflation-adjusted minimum return of zero).[4] Feldstein and Elena Ranguelova propose "accumulated pension collars" (minimum and maximum returns) on private retirement accounts as a way of ensuring that partial privatization of Social Security does not reduce benefits relative to current law.[5] Teresa Ghilarducci proposes retirement savings accounts managed by a government entity with a minimum guaranteed real return of 3 percent. Her proposal would set up a system, similar to the TIAA example, whereby trustees would build and manage a reserve fund and could allocate additional rates of return to savers.[6] The California Secure Choice Retirement Savings Investment Board is investigating the feasibility of providing a minimum guarantee, and the Connecticut Retirement Security Board is considering a state-run automatic Individual Retirement Account program with a minimum guarantee.

Benefits of Guarantees

The benefits of guarantees depend on several factors. These factors include the expected level and variability of savers' retirement wealth, the savers' aversion to risk, and the share of retirement wealth that savers expect their guaranteed accounts to generate. The value of a guarantee also depends on certain psychological factors, including an individual saver's aversion to experiencing a loss if an investment does not produce the expected results or aversion to feelings of regret if a forgone investment would have proved profitable.

Costs of Guarantees

Guarantees are not free. In some cases, savers or plan sponsors pay for the guarantees through insurance premiums. Alternatively, the costs of the guarantees may be implicit. For example, as in the TIAA example, savers may allow the insurer to manage the fund and to pay a minimum return plus any additional amount that trustees deem appropriate. The costs to savers take the form of the lost opportunities for higher returns.

Savers can also pay for guarantees by accepting restrictions on their investments. Restrictions on a saver's portfolio may greatly reduce an insurer's costs, but they impose costs on the saver. For example, if savers are required to invest their contributions in Treasury bonds, a guaranteed minimum return equal to the Treasury bond rate (less an administrative fee) can be insured at virtually no cost to the insurer. But those are precisely the conditions under which the guarantee is worthless to savers, because they can receive the Treasury bond rate anyway if they simply invest in Treasury bonds. A hypothetical guarantee of this type may be inexpensive for insurers, and it might even be a deal savers would be willing to accept, but it would not be costless. In particular, savers would be forgoing the opportunity to earn higher returns.

For example, one study found that if savers placed their entire portfolio in equity, it would cost 3.6 percent of contributions to guarantee a return of principal (a nominal zero return) over 10 years and 16.1 percent of contributions to guarantee a Treasury bond rate. If the saver were required to hold half of the portfolio in bonds and half in equity, these costs would fall to 0.2 percent and 8.1 percent of contributions, respectively. But, of course, the expected return to the saver on the split portfolio would be lower than on the all-equity portfolio.[7]

Another way savers can pay for a minimum guarantee is by selling a portion of their upside potential returns.[8] In this scenario, savers are guaranteed a minimum rate of return, but there is a ceiling on the maximum return they can keep, with any actual return above that ceiling going to the insurer. This setup is usually known as a collar. For example, savers might be guaranteed that their investments will earn no less than 3 percent annually. In exchange, the savers forfeit to the insurer any upside beyond a specific ceiling (e.g., 6 percent annually). Savers' portfolios would thus be collared to generate a 3 to 6 percent annual rate of return. An appropriately designed collar allows savers to receive a guaranteed rate of return and the insurer to be compensated for the risk it is underwriting.

What would happen if the government paid for guarantees? The overall economic costs would still be the same as if a private entity provided the insurance. But the government's budget would show the costs the government incurs, not the economic value of the government's risks. Thus, guarantees offered by the government may look like a good deal, but the true economic costs of those guarantees are not accurately reported in the budget. And this problem is not just a reporting issue; the government (i.e., taxpayers) and the economy still have to bear the costs of the guarantees.

Conclusion

Rate-of-return guarantees for retirement savings plans are getting a lot more attention in the wake of the recent financial crisis, when savers near retirement suffered steep losses. Although guarantees in various forms clearly offer some benefits to savers, those benefits come at a cost. The costs can be paid in many different ways, including insurance premiums, caps on the maximum returns that savers can receive, and portfolio restrictions. The last option may also serve to cap returns and limit savers' potential risk. Government provision of guarantees is not a panacea—it simply hides the economic costs of the policy.

NOTES

1. Pension Rights Center, "State-Based Retirement Plans for the Private Sector" (fact sheet, Pension Rights Center, Washington, DC, 2015).

2. Marie-Eve Lachance, Olivia S. Mitchell, and Kent Smetters, "Guaranteeing Defined Contribution Pensions: The Option to Buy Back a Defined Benefit Promise," *Journal of Risk and Insurance* 70, no. 1 (2003): 1–16, doi:10.1111/1539-6975.00044; John A. Turner and David M. Rajnes, "Retirement Guarantees in Voluntary Defined Contribution Systems," in *The Pension Challenge*, ed. Olivia S. Mitchell and Kent Smetters (New York: Oxford University Press, 2003), 251–67; John A. Turner and David M. Rajnes, "Guarantee Durability: Pension Rate of Return Guarantees in a Market Meltdown" (paper presented at the 10th anniversary conference of the Center for Research on Pensions and Welfare Policies, Collegio Carlo Alberto, Torino, Italy, September 24–25, 2009).

3. John Biggs, "How TIAA-CREF Funded Plans Differ from a Typical 401(k) Plan." *Trends and Issues*, February 2010: TIAA-CREF Institute.

4. Martin Feldstein and Andrew Samwick, "Potential Paths of Social Security Reform," *Tax Policy and the Economy* 16 (2002): 181–224.

5. Martin Feldstein and Elena Ranguelova, "Accumulated Pension Collars: A Market Approach to Reducing the Risk of Investment-Based Social Security Reform," *Tax Policy and the Economy* 15 (2001): 149–65.

6. Teresa Ghilarducci, "Guaranteed Retirement Accounts: Toward Retirement Income Security" (EPI Briefing Paper 204, Economic Policy Institute, 2007). See also Teresa Ghilarducci, Robert Hiltonsmith, and Lauren Schmitz, "State Guaranteed Retirement Accounts: A Low-Cost, Secure Solution to America's Retirement Crisis" (Schwartz Center for Economic Policy Analysis, New School, 2012).

7. Marie-Eve Lachance and Olivia Mitchell, "Understanding Individual Account Guarantees," in *The Pension Challenge: Risk Transfers and Retirement Income Security*, ed. Olivia Mitchell and Kent Smetters (Oxford, UK: Oxford University Press, 2003), 159–186. See also Marie-Eve Lachance and Olivia S. Mitchell, "Guaranteeing Individual Accounts," *American Economic Review* 93, no. 2 (2003): 257–60.

8. Feldstein and Ranguelova, "Accumulated Pension Collars"; Kent Smetters, "Controlling the Cost of Minimum Benefit Guarantees in Public Pension Conversions," *Journal of Pension Economics and Finance* 1, no. 1 (2002): 9–33.

44. Seven Ways to Keep Medical Debt in Check*

Gail Hillebrand

Debt collection is the top complaint that the federal Consumer Financial Protection Bureau has received since September 2013. Out of all debt types, medical collections make up 52 percent of collection accounts on credit reports, far outpacing all other types of debt.

Medical collections are so widespread that an estimated 43 million consumers with an account in collection have medical debt. We analyzed medical collections in our latest report, to explain why medical debt is affecting so many more credit reports than any other type of debt. You can read more about how medical debt hurts your credit report.

Here are steps you can take to keep medical debt in check:

1. Review medical bills carefully: If you don't recognize the provider, check the date of service to see if you had a medical treatment on that day. For more complicated procedures, ask for an itemized bill from the provider in order to check how much you were charged for each service. Some providers who bill you directly may have been associated with a hospital where you were treated, so you may not have known you were receiving services from them at the time you were being treated.

2. Get documentation: Prepare an organized record of all bills. If you need to dispute a bill, send a written notice to the provider and include a copy of all relevant documents, such as records from doctors' offices or credit card statements. Do not send original documents.

3. Check your health insurance policy and make sure your provider has your correct insurance info: You should know what your insurance covers, and what it doesn't—but first your insurance information needs to be up-to-date and accurate! A small mix up can lead to big bills for expenses that your insurance should have covered.

4. Act quickly to resolve or dispute the medical bills that you receive: If you have verified you owe the bill, try to resolve it right away. Verify whether an insurer is paying for all or part of a bill. If you delay the bill and let it end up in collections, it can have a significant impact on your credit score. If you don't owe the bill, act quickly to dispute it.

---

*Originally published as Gail Hillebrand, "Seven Ways to Keep Medical Debt in Check," https://www.consumerfinance.gov/about-us/blog/consumer-advisory-7-ways-to-keep-medical-debt-in-check/ (December 11, 2014).

5. Negotiate your bill: Hospitals may negotiate the amount of the bill with you. The tab may be reduced if you pay the whole amount up front. You can also try asking for the rate that people who have insurance get. The hospital might also offer a plan that enables you to pay off the debt in installments at no interest. It doesn't hurt to ask.

6. Get financial assistance or support: Many hospitals have financial assistance programs, which may be called "charity care," if you are unable to pay your bill. Check the deadlines, which can vary.

7. Don't put medical bills on your credit card, if you can't pay them: If you can't immediately pay off a high debt on your credit card bill, you will be charged high interest, and it will look like regular debt to other creditors. Instead, ask your medical provider for a payment plan with little or no interest.

45. Consumer Advisory[*]

Don't Be Misled by Reverse Mortgage Advertising

NORA DOWD EISENHOWER

You might see enticing images of youthful retirees on the golf course or enjoying other leisure activities in a reverse mortgage advertisement. A reverse mortgage is a special type of loan that allows homeowners 62 and older to borrow against the accrued equity in their homes. The loan must be paid back when the borrower dies, moves, or no longer lives in the home.

Ads for reverse mortgages are found on television, radio, in print, and on the internet, and many ads feature celebrity spokespeople discussing the benefits of reverse mortgages without mentioning risks. The federal Consumer Financial Protection Bureau looked closely at many ads and found incomplete and inaccurate statements used to describe the loans. In addition, most of the important loan requirements were often buried in fine print if they were even mentioned at all. These advertisements may leave older homeowners with the false impression that reverse mortgage loans are a risk-free solution to financial gaps in retirement.

In conducting our study, we met with older homeowners in Washington, D.C., Chicago, and Los Angeles to learn about their thoughts and impressions of reverse mortgage ads. After looking at a variety of ads, many homeowners we spoke to didn't realize reverse mortgage loans need to be repaid. Instead, some thought they could access their equity interest-free, or that the federal government provided the money as a benefit to seniors. Homeowners told us that the most attractive messages in the ads were "you can live in your home as long as you want," and that you "still own your home." Many ads, however, didn't mention that seniors could lose their homes if they don't satisfy the loan requirements, such as paying property taxes or homeowners insurance.

Seniors said the ads made reverse mortgages look like a good way to travel and enjoy retirement while they were still young and active. Yet Americans are living longer, more active lives than ever before. Reverse mortgage borrowers can outlive their loan funds by borrowing without careful planning.

---

[*]Originally published as Nora Dowd Eisenhower, "Consumer Advisory: Don't Be Misled by Reverse Mortgage Advertising," https://www.consumerfinance.gov/about-us/blog/consumer-advisory-dont-be-misled-by-reverse-mortgage-advertising/ (June 4, 2015).

Reverse mortgage ads don't always tell the whole story, so consider these facts when you see advertisements:

A reverse mortgage is a home loan, not a government benefit: Reverse mortgages have fees and compounding interest that must be repaid, just like other home loans. With most reverse mortgages, federal insurance guarantees that borrowers will receive their loan funds if their lender has financial difficulty or if their loan balance exceeds the value of their home. However, borrowers pay for this insurance and it's not a government benefit.

You can lose your home with a reverse mortgage: When a reverse mortgage ad says you'll retain ownership of your home, or that you can live there as long as you want to, don't take these messages at face value. These statements are true only if you continue to meet all requirements of the reverse mortgage. If you fall behind on your property taxes or homeowners' insurance, are absent from your home for longer than six months, or fail to satisfy other requirements, you can trigger a loan default. If you don't take care of the default in time, the lender can foreclose on your home. Sometimes these requirements are listed in fine print, but not always. If you have a question about reverse mortgage requirements, contact a HUD-approved housing counselor near you.

Without a good plan, you could outlive your loan money: After seeing a reverse mortgage ad, you might think that a reverse mortgage guarantees your financial security no matter how long you live. Americans are living longer today than they were just a generation ago. Make sure you have a financial plan in place that accounts for a long life. That way if you need to tap your home equity, you won't do it too early and risk running out of retirement resources later in life.

If you have a problem with your reverse mortgage, check out Ask CFPB to learn more about reverse mortgages. You can also download a printer-friendly version of this information to share with friends or clients. If you're having a problem with your reverse mortgage or having problems getting through to your mortgage servicer, you can submit a complaint to us online or by calling (855) 411-2372 or TTY/TDD (855) 729-2372. We'll forward your complaint to the company and work to get you a response within 15 days.

46. Four Things Older Americans Can Do About Debt Collection Problems[*]

NORA DOWD EISENHOWER

If you're an older American and you're having trouble with debt collectors, you're not alone. Since July 2013, older Americans have submitted approximately 8,700 complaints to the federal Consumer Financial Protection Bureau about debt collection.

The bureau looked at these complaints and described the most common problems that consumers are experiencing in our snapshot of debt collection complaints submitted by older consumers.

People's complaints often express grief, confusion, and frustration regarding the collection of medical debt, debt of deceased family members, and even suspicious calls from individuals who claim to be collectors.

Here's what you or your loved ones can do when experiencing debt collection problems:

Get more information if you don't recognize the debt: Older consumers report that debt collectors may have inaccurate or inadequate information, and sometimes don't provide sufficient information to help them identify the debt. Almost one-third of the older consumers who submitted a complaint couldn't identify the debt being collected.

First things first! Ask the debt collector for the company's name and address. If the debt collector refuses to give you this information, you may be dealing with a fraud. If you think that a caller may be a fake debt collector:

Ask the caller for his or her name, company, street address, telephone number, and professional license number.

If you have the company's name and address but you don't recognize the debt, ask for more information in writing. You can start by using a sample letter (available at https://www.consumerfinance.gov/about-us/blog/four-things-older-americans-can-do-about-debt-collection-problems/). Send this letter as soon as you can—if at all possible, within 30 days of when a debt collector contacts you the first time about a debt.

*Originally published as Nora Dowd Eisenhower, "Four Things Older Americans Can Do About Debt Collection Problems," https://www.consumerfinance.gov/about-us/blog/four-things-older-americans-can-do-about-debt-collection-problems/ (November 5, 2014).

Dispute the debt if it's not yours or if the amount is wrong: You can write a letter disputing the debt or any portion of the debt. It's important to do so as soon as possible after you're first contacted, and to keep copies of any letters you send.

If you dispute a debt (or part of a debt) in writing within 30 days of when you receive the required information from the debt collector, the debt collector cannot call or contact you until after the debt collector has obtained verification of the debt and has provided the verification of the debt in writing to you. You can use this sample letter.

Stop harassing and/or offensive calls: Older consumers told us that debt collectors sometimes refuse to take "No" for an answer, reporting in their complaints that collectors often use offensive language and make threats. To one extreme, we've also heard about collectors making successive calls using profanity or derogatory names.

You don't have to put up with it. You can send a letter to the debt collector telling it to stop contacting you. If you dispute the amount due, or you don't believe that it's your debt, put that in the letter, too. You can use this sample letter.

Telling a debt collector to stop contacting you does not stop the collection, including the filing of a lawsuit against you or reporting negative information to a credit reporting company.

Know your rights—your federal benefits have many protections from garnishment in collection: Many older consumers rely on Social Security or other federal benefits and frequently complained that debt collectors threatened them with garnishment of these benefits. Most federal benefits, such as Social Security, Veterans' (VA) benefits, and Supplemental Security Income (SSI) benefits, are protected in debt collection. There are exceptions for, among other things, money owed in child support, spousal support, federal student loans, or for federal taxes.

When you receive federal benefits by direct deposit to your checking account, your bank or credit union is required automatically to protect up to two months of these benefits that are directly deposited into your account. If you receive your benefits on a government issued prepaid card, they usually are protected too. Some exceptions may exist for debts owed to a federal or state agency.

If you're not sure if your federal benefits are being wrongfully garnished, you should seek legal advice.

Here's how you can find a lawyer:

- Call your local legal aid office, where you may qualify for free legal services
- Call your local senior legal helpline where seniors can get free legal advice and assistance
- Call the attorney referral hotline offered by your state or local bar organization

Learn more about your rights when it comes to debt collection.
You can also:

- Submit a debt collection complaint online or by calling (855) 411-2372. The bureau will forward your issue to the company and work to get you a response, give you a tracking number, and keep you updated on the status of your complaint.

47. Kimochi*

Japanese Self-Help for the Elderly

PAUL MICO *and* WILLIE LEE BRITT

Steve Nakajo, the co-founder and executive director of Kimochi, is of the third-generation Japanese-American Sansei. He was born in Salt Lake City and his formulative years were in Yokohama, Japan. He was raised in San Francisco and called the Japantown neighborhood his home. He grew up being acutely aware of the cultural and language barriers facing the first-generation Japanese-American, the Issei, and the second-generation, the Nisei. He saw these in his own family.

Not only were the elderly prevented by these barriers from utilizing the services they needed, they were devastated by the losses of their civil rights and properties when they were uprooted and incarcerated into remote, barren, concentration camps during World War II. No sooner had they returned after the war and tried to build a new life than they were displaced again during the San Francisco Redevelopment Agency's urban renewal upheaval of Japantown.

In the late 1960s, Mr. Nakajo and a small band of like-minded individuals began to organize to create a force for change to help their people. They shared ideas, sought resources and supporters, and taught themselves the skills of community organization, grantsmanship, and organization development. In 1971 they formed a nonprofit organization and gave it the name Kimochi, which means, "feelings for the older generations." The mission of Kimochi was, and still is, "to provide a continuum of culturally sensitive programs and services to all seniors and their families, with a focus on Japanese-Americans and the Japanese-speaking community."

Today, Kimochi is a cultural-based community-based organization, born of services to Japanese-Americans, though it serves others. It provides care, social services, nutrition, residential respite, and support to more than 3000 seniors and their families throughout the city and county of San Francisco. It has an annual operating budget of $2 million and a staff of fifty employees.

In the beginning, the constituency was Japantown, for all intents and purposes. Then the older first-generation Issei began to die off. It was the second-generation Nisei who began to move up and out, leaving Japantown and tending to relocate in the broader San Francisco city and county geographical area, or farther down the peninsula to the San

---

*Published with permission of the authors.

Mateo area. Kimochi responded initially by opening its services to Southeast Asians in need of the services that Kimochi could provide. In another example of adaptation, Kimochi is in the process of extending its constituency base to the South Bay community in need, Kimochi San Mateo, by building and operating a community care center for seniors there.

Each year, Kimochi takes the time to celebrate the dedication and contribution made by individuals and organizations in support of its mission to provide care to the seniors in the community, fittingly so during the Asia Pacific American Heritage Month. As Kimochi continues to grow and expand its programs and services into the peninsula, it says "we know our success would not be possible without the hard work of our staff and community members, all of whom embody the spirit of Kimochi." Spirit is when the constituency celebrates the accomplishments of its community-based organization. There are annual spirit awards.

Kimochi has a board of directors that supervises the executive director and has access to funding committees and auditor/legal counsel, among others. The executive director is responsible to the board for the command and control of his personnel.

There has been a continuity of leadership. Mr. Nakajo has been the executive director for forty-four years. He is a charismatic figure, a civic leader, and the driving force behind the growth and development of the organization. He is regarded as a quiet leader who leads by example. He "knows everyone" and is well-liked by all. He plans to stay for a forty-fifth year and then step aside. In the beginning, he hand-picked board members based on their roles in the community and how well they would support him and his staff.

The constituency has become so well-developed over the years that he no longer worries about that. He and the board have picked the associate executive director to replace him and they have been grooming him for that eventual responsibility. One way in which they are doing that is by placing him in charge of the program and construction development in the San Mateo Peninsula.

Kimochi offers a range of programs and services for seniors and their families, everything from hot lunches to twenty-four hour residential programs. While Kimochi has its roots in San Francisco's Japantown and many of the programs offer bilingual services, programs and services are open to all San Franciscan seniors. Kimochi:

- Provides care and support for San Francisco Bay Area seniors and their families.
- Offers culturally sensitive, innovative senior services.
- Encourages and helps maintain the autonomy and dignity of seniors.
- Provides support for seniors who must depend on others.
- Operates from a tradition of intergenerational care based on respect and appreciation for elders.
- Seeks to enhance the quality of life both of seniors and the community at large.

The Senior Center:

- Embodies Kimochi's commitment to intergenerational, volunteer-based senior programs by offering a range of exciting activities developed by volunteers and staff specifically for independent, active seniors.
- Activities include ceramics, arts and crafts, exercise, tai chi, overnight Reno trips, day trips, karaoke and group singing.
- Services are offered from two sites in San Francisco's Japantown.

Social Services Program:

- Whether it's a Medicare question or a family crisis, Kimochi's social workers provide personalized, culturally sensitive service to seniors, their families and friends, including Information and Referral, Translation Services, Hospital and Home Visitations, Medical Escorts, Assistance with Government Benefits, Advocacy for the Elderly.
- In-Home Support Services link seniors with providers to assist with household chores and personal care.
- Senior Caregiver Support Groups offer families and friends a place to discuss and share concerns regarding care of seniors.

Transportation:

- Kimochi offers safe and reliable door-to-door van service for individuals and groups.
- Service to Kimochi program sites, medical appointments, shopping trips, recreational outings, church, and cemetery visits.

Congregate Nutrition:

- Hot Japanese-style lunches are prepared and served in San Francisco's Japantown.
- Meals are carefully planned and prepared by the senior center coordinator, nutrition consultant, and kitchen staff.
- Group settings, which are a good place to meet and make friends.
- Educational presentations and information are provided to assist in maintaining health and wellbeing.

Home Delivered Meals:

- Nutrition service provides homebound seniors with a nutritional, well-balanced meal.
- Kimochi delivers over a hundred Japanese-style hot lunches a day to San Francisco residents.
- Each participant is assessed quarterly for any changes in his or her physical and/or mental health needs, and appropriate referrals or information are provided by Kimochi.

Adult Social Day Care:

- A program of a supervised, structured set of daytime social, cultural, and recreational activities for seniors are offered at Kimochi Home.
- Activities include daily exercise, hot lunch, weekly mini-trips, monthly tea parties, singing and art classes, bingo, videos and unique intergenerational, after-school programs.
- Provides respite for caregiver family members. The program assures that loved ones are active and entertained in a safe environment.

Residential/Respite Care:

- Kimochi Home has space for twenty ambulatory seniors for either long-term or short-term stays.

- The Residential Program provides twenty-four hour supervised, non-medical care; three Japanese-style meals a day; recreation, exercise and a host of services; single or shared rooms are available.
- The Respite Program provides temporary senior care during periods of stress, caregiver burnout, or during family vacation, and as a transition point between hospital and home.

Other Factors Affecting Kimochi

Kimochi faces a future of transitioning from a personality-driven organization to a mission-driven one because the executive director plans to retire. The environmental forces which influence the directions Kimochi takes include the rise in the minimum hourly wage, which affects its budget. The shifting constituency-base demonstrates the power of the constituency, causing a splitting of the constituency base from Japantown to the San Mateo Peninsula.

Kimochi employees do not have good pension and retirement plans, which may make it more difficult to attract and retain good staff, and there is no union domain or employee association.

Kimochi uses large numbers of volunteers.

There is a process under way in San Francisco to bring together representatives of community-based organizations to obtain more resources and political support, from local and state resources. Much time is spent in fund-raising, and the high cost of land and construction is forcing Kimochi to borrow funds for the building project.

48. The Pilipino Senior Resource Center, a Glimpse of Our Very Essence[*]

GABBY V. MORALEDA

Servicing the needs of Pilipino seniors and their families is most challenging because it requires cultural sensitivities blended with appropriate caregiving skills encased in a set of relevant interventions. It is in this context that the Pilipino Senior Resource Center (PSRC) has sustained its meaningful existence in the San Francisco Filipino American community since 2006.

The seniors who regularly patronize PSRC are mostly women ages 65 to 98. On Monday and Thursday mornings, attendance is around 15 on a chilly or rainy day, to a high of 30 during sunny, summer days. On special occasions such as a Christmas party, the crowd balloons to 100+ because they invite friends, family and peers. Most prefer to live independently with their partners, if they have one, or with someone they are acquainted with. They reside in socialized housing units within a 3-mile radius of our downtown South of Market (SOMA) office, a district in transition, which is second home to many Filipino families and emerging software and IT companies.

Our center is a bit different from others in that the seniors take extra effort to come to us, not vice versa. We do not own a meeting hall to hold regular forums but are allowed space to use by our tenant, actually a basement hallway we convert for the day as a "classroom," setting up portable tables, chairs and screens. On Thursdays, we hold sessions in an offsite facility made available by WestBay Pilipino Multi Service Center, two blocks away. The seniors walk, ride public transportation or commute to our office on their own. They are prompt—a gauge of how they appreciate and value their time with us. This alone is truly inspiring.

Continually keeping them coming to our events is a week-to-week challenge, something we take seriously, mindful that there are deeply rooted ethnic/regional beliefs, backgrounds, upbringing and differences that differentiate each senior from one another. It is never easy because of set perspectives they have acquired in life—but throughout these years, we have nurtured our seniors to find, learn, discover more of themselves, for purposeful existence. We want to make a difference in their lives.

---

[*]Published with permission of the author.

Health consciousness is at the core of our basic services, such as nutrition, hygiene including breast cancer care. The center has been actively working with mainstream advocates of breast cancer awareness to help navigate Filipina women who would otherwise have fallen through the cracks and not gotten proper treatment had they not come through the open doors of PSRC.

Take the case of Maria (not her real name), who was ushered into PSRC by SFGen/AVON Foundation. She was a 50-year-old certified nursing assistant diagnosed with metastatic stage 4 breast cancer.

Maria, the youngest among her siblings, all of whom are in the Philippines, had lived with her elderly mom, who passed away a few years ago of pneumonia. As expected from most Filipinos in America, she supported her niece and nephew back home with whatever savings she could gather until this dreadful disease hit her. This was when PSRC nurtured and navigated her to get medical care in the first year of treatment. Our staff accompanied her to and from her doctors' appointments and provided housing leads when she was about to lose housing privileges because she no longer qualified to stay in the senior apartment where her mom lived. We were there when she needed to be with someone.

Maria is now a volunteer coordinator in a Christian church where she cooks food for the homeless in the city, something she enjoys doing in spite of her condition. She has had three sets of chemo sessions. She is very proud of what she is doing and grateful for the care and encouragement given by PSRC. When asked if she wanted to take a vacation home, she replied "yes." The center is now looking for sponsors for her trip back to the Philippines. Recently, as she slowly gets her life back, she unselfishly declined what we have budgeted for her because she said there are a lot more women who need it more than her.

In all of these trials, she is thanking her creator for inner strength, finding a way to smile and still sponsoring the education of two low-income students. Undeniably, a story of victory.

Among our partners in this worthwhile cause are To Celebrate Life (TCL), whose battle cry is "No one should should face breast cancer alone" and has been awarded best non-profit of Marin County by the AVON Foundation and the SF Cancer Network. With referrals from San Francisco General Hospital, PSRC's breast cancer program, the only one of its kind among Filipinos in San Francisco, is gaining visibility. It has been the beneficiary of modest private fund-raising projects.

Aside from focusing on seniors, we have steadily worked with the Asia Pacific Islander Family Resource Network (APIFRN) by holding classes among Filipino families in the fields of early child education, parenting and domestic violence. There are a few more areas of cooperation in the pipeline with the Asian Pacific Islander Legal Outreach (APILO) such as teaching English as a second language and citizenship classes. We are proud of these projects because it represents how we have slowly grown in the scope and mix of our services, really a result of our continuous presence in the community and a fitting recognition of our expertise.

In addition, we have been chosen as official contractor of the Mayor's Office for Housing and Community Development (MOHCD) to implement an art and culture project and have been awarded a grant for a capacity building study of our operations. The art project, in collaboration with the Filipino Community Development Center (FCDC), is in its second year. It produced a 2019 calendar picturing fabric painting, mixed media collage, thread art, printmaking, paper sculpture, hand-building clay and silk screening, along with a book focusing on colorful migrant lives in the area, filled with the ups and downs and stories of struggles and victories that can be shared and handed down to younger generations of Filipino Americans. One of them is Nieves (not her real name).

Nieves was born in Pangasinan, a province in the Ilocos region of Northern Luzon. She recalls the humid, hot weather and welcoming the summer precipitation that came with it, recalling how it was refreshing to soak in the rain. She vividly recalls her youthful days, the games she played with friends—jackstones and piko (hopscotch)—and the freshly picked fruits they ate: green mango and kamias, among others.

From her home province, she landed in Manila, where the jobs were. She studied and became a beautician. Fate brought her to San Francisco, where she first worked as a housekeeper. Nieves felt there was more to being a housekeeper and never gave up on her plan to be a beautician in America. She became an apprentice in a salon, endured the low wages and long hours to get the experience and track record, dreaming that one day she would fulfill her lifelong career goal. In 1997 she obtained her cosmetology license. It was one of her proudest moments and in 2011, having saved enough money, she got a business license and opened up her own salon—right in the heart of SOMA. Her tale, like that of many Filipino migrants, is one of struggle and never giving up.

Nieves has a son and a daughter whom she has sent to school through her perseverance and hard work.

In all of these instances we take pride in our humble beginnings and are pleased with the achievements, a result of the work of our staff, a board composed of educators, professionals, caregivers and a representative from the seniors, plus energetic student volunteers from the University of San Francisco (USF) and Golden Gate University (GGU)—adhering to a basic tenet that anything we do must be simple and fun.

Our funders' requirements for us are to conscientiously meet professional and corporate governance standards. In the normal course of doing our business, we have learned our seniors simply need down to earth, creative, practical, participation, including one-on-one coaching. This is what distinguishes PSRC. It defines the very essence of our existence, the nature of our strength in project implementation where our approaches are grounded on basic principles combined with personal touch—simple, creative and above all, fun. Ours is a case of doing more with "less" sophistication to still achieve traction. For, in the final analysis, we believe this is what works.

As a 501c(3) non-profit corporation dependent on private giving and public contracts, funding remains a constant hurdle, a struggle with no ready answers. We get our support through private donations, contracts funded by the city and as a subcontractor of leading non-profit groups. Government-funded projects are secured through competitive bidding. They are quite restrictive, requiring strict compliance with auditing regulations and tricky because they are on a reimbursement basis, meaning one must have cash to start the ball rolling—really a chicken and egg situation of which should come first. Private giving is preferred since it is a bit more flexible and can be programmed accordingly to meet conditions that arise. Building a donor base takes time, energy and effort. In such a confining state, growth becomes elusive, if not distant.

Compounding this is our pressing desire to expand, failing to realize that sudden growth—scaling up too much, too soon, in itself presents an inherent problem. There is a common perception that funding alone will cure everything. But that is not true. Surely, we will accept a surge of donations but with poor visibility it can make us hit a wall, doing us more harm than good in the long run. Scaling our size with crystal clear vision, in the short run, matched with a steady stream of giving and contracts, may yield the best results for the organization, especially for those we serve, not just the Pilipino seniors but also their families.

49. Advocacy for Aging World War II Immigrant Veterans*

Joaquin Jay Gonzalez III

I witnessed an emotional encounter with an elderly veteran who had lived through so much: heavy enemy fire and labor camp as a prisoner of war in his early twenties, and now, in his seventies, he was coping with cancer alone and in a foreign land. Idelfonso "Tatang Floro" Bagasala seemed undaunted by the many challenges he had been through. Smiling, he began his conversation with the audience, saying, "I feel blessed to be with you tonight." Continuing, the 76-year-old Filipino American World War II veteran then proceeded to tell bittersweet life stories which, ironically, were highlighted not by his exploits on the battlefields of Luzon, but instead, the perilous streets of San Francisco's low-income Tenderloin and South of Market neighborhoods.

Tatang Floro told the audience how he earned a living shoulder-to-shoulder with homeless people, pimps, prostitutes, street entertainers, petty thieves, gang members, as well as drug dealers and users. As a former U.S. Commonwealth Army regular, Tatang Floro explained to the attentive crowd, "We were promised U.S. citizenship by General Douglas MacArthur for fighting under his USAFFE [U.S. Armed Forces of the Far East] command." After waiting more than 40 years to be naturalized at the U.S. Embassy in Manila, it became clear that he could no longer count on receiving the veterans' benefits promised to him years earlier. So the aging veteran left his wife, children, and grandchildren in the Philippines to come to the U.S. and earn money to support them. When he arrived in San Francisco, Tatang Floro had no income, so he supplemented his welfare checks doing odd jobs along downtown Market Street.

A few feet away from San Francisco's famous cable cars and trendy shops, he rented out chess tables. "After I was diagnosed with cancer at San Francisco General Hospital, I lay in the hospital begging for an interpreter," he said. The gray-haired Tatang Floro admitted that he did not even understand some of the questions on the forms he was asked to sign, since he barely knew how to read English and did not know how to write. A devout Christian, Tatang Floro credits the power of prayer for what he calls his "miraculous recovery." Having no relatives in the United States, he added that his strong faith in God is what keeps him going from day to day. Many in the dimly lit room became teary-eyed.

The account that Tatang Floro shared with his young audience that evening sums

---

*Published with permission of the author.

up the fate of many aging Filipino World War II veterans (also referred to as the *veteranos*, *manongs*, or elders), as well as their strong faith, which fosters the belief that with the help of the younger generation of Filipino migrants, their pleas would finally be answered in the halls of the U.S. Congress.

Making a Promise: Veterans' Rights and Benefits

Historically, the Filipino military units that would later be called "the Commonwealth Army of the Philippines" were started in the early 1900s at the same time that the United States assumed formal sovereignty over its prized colony. The Philippine Commonwealth Army was formally established through Philippine Commonwealth Act Number 1, approved by the U.S. Congress on December 1935. As Commander-in-Chief of the U.S. Armed Forces, President Franklin Delano Roosevelt issued the Presidential Order (6 Federal Register 3825) that required the Philippine Commonwealth Army to respond to the call to military service of a U.S. President (Meixsel 1995). In addition to these recruitment initiatives, the U.S. Army established many military bases throughout the colony's various islands. These included two of the largest outside of the continental United States—heavyweights Clark Air Base and Subic Naval Base—which gave America a formidable presence in the Asia-Pacific region.

On July 26, 1941, sensing a growing threat from Japan, President Roosevelt ordered the Commonwealth Army of the Philippines—then comprised of U.S. nationals—to serve under General Douglas MacArthur's United States Armed Forces of the Far East (USAFFE). At the time of the USAFFE's formation, the unit consisted of 22,532 troops; 11,972 of these were Philippine Scouts and 10,473 were members of the Philippine Division, which consisted of 2,552 Americans and 7,921 Filipinos. All of the division's enlisted men, with the exception of the 31st Infantry Regiment and various military police and headquarters troops, were Philippine Scouts.

Not long afterwards, imperial Japan began plotting takeovers of nations along the Pacific Rim, supposedly to construct a Greater East Asia Co-Prosperity Sphere—a group of self-sufficient Asian nations that were free of Western powers, and of course, led by the Japanese. One of the nations targeted was the Philippines; after all, the country was America's Pacific buffer and was only a couple of hours from Tokyo by plane. Hence, Japan made plans to cut off America's ties to its Asian outpost. The Japanese military launched a surprise air raid on the U.S. Navy's Fleet stationed at Pearl Harbor, Hawaii, on December 7, 1941, and a subsequent air attack on the following day of key U.S. military targets in the Philippines. Having destroyed parts of Hawaii, Japanese air attacks were conducted against Davao, Baguio and Aparri on the same day in the Philippines, which were all places where American soldiers were stationed. The U.S. and its Asian commonwealth territory had no choice but to defend itself by entering the war against Japan.

President Roosevelt was in desperate need of men and women to serve in the United States military. Fighting a war on both the Asian and European fronts took its toll on the numbers of both active duty and reserve soldiers. To maintain effective air, land, and sea operations, the president and congressional leaders knew that the U.S. Army would need sustained troop replenishments urgently. Understandably, few wanted to enlist during wartime. Since the Philippines was not only an American colony but also under attack by Japan, President Roosevelt turned to Filipinos, who were then U.S. nationals, for help.

The Commonwealth Government of the Philippines complied by drafting Filipino males between the ages of 21 and 50.

Taking the president's cue, the U.S. Congress passed the Second War Powers Act (1942), amending the Nationality Act of 1940. This new legislation essentially liberalized "naturalization requirements for alien servicemen in the United States armed forces outside the territory of the continental United States" and eliminated barriers to naturalization. The drafting of regular and non-traditional Filipino combatants into the U.S. Army helped America's war effort tremendously. Nevertheless, the U.S. lost control of the Philippines in April 1942.

The forced departure of General MacArthur from the Philippines, the surrender of the USAFFE forces to the Japanese Imperial Army in Corregidor, and the consequent Bataan Death March, in which 3,000 Americans and 10,000 Filipinos were killed, fueled the United States' resolve to continue fighting. Surviving Filipino soldiers retreated to the mountains and turned to warfare tactics they had used effectively decades earlier during the Philippine revolution and the Philippine-American War. Welcomed by MacArthur and the USAFFE command, Filipino and American soldiers formed guerrilla and underground units that sabotaged Japanese civil and military activities, hindering Japan's full administrative control of the Philippines. Ultimately, only 12 of 48 provinces fell to Japan's imperial flag. From 1942 to 1946, guerrilla and underground resistance units also passed on critical intelligence to the USAFFE chain of command. In return for their loyalty and gallantry, President Roosevelt and General MacArthur reiterated their promise of citizenship and veterans' benefit to Filipino soldiers fighting under the American flag. Many veterans have also recalled that U.S. government and military officials enticed them to serve by saying "Lay your lives on the line for the American ideals ... and we will make you Americans." As U.S. nationals, the Filipino soldiers recruited in the Philippines—Old and New Philippine Scouts, Philippine Commonwealth Army regulars, and guerrillas—would never forget these promises. But would they ever be fulfilled?

Close to 100,000 Filipino civilians lost their lives during World War II. In September of 1945, Japan was convinced to surrender to the United States after U.S. Air Force planes dropped two atomic bombs on Hiroshima and Nagasaki. Japan's defeat was a proud moment for the U.S. and the Philippines. A month after Japan's surrender, Congress passed the Armed Forces Voluntary Recruitment Act of 1945 (Public Law 79–190), authorizing the recruitment of 50,000 "new" Philippine Scouts. These New Philippine Scouts served under the U.S. Army from October 6, 1945, to June 30, 1947. In gratitude for their heroism in the defense of America and the Philippines, President Roosevelt in a 1945 White House policy speech reiterated his promise that Filipino soldiers—i.e., Scouts, Commonwealth Army and guerrillas—would be granted U.S. citizenship and receive the same benefits as all other U.S. veterans. Roosevelt's policy pronouncement was received by General Omar Bradley, then Administrator of the U.S. Veterans Administration, who began preparing his VA staff to process the inflow of Filipinos as American veterans. After their wartime service, the Filipino World War II veterans waited.

Breaking the Promise: Truman and the Rescission Acts

As it turned out, those Filipino veterans would have to wait for a long time. The emotional fervor of the war and America's promise died with Roosevelt's demise in April

1945. Vice President Harry S. Truman ascended to the presidency to finish the unfinished business of World War II. Germany and Japan were defeated. The year 1946 ushered in three major political events that would become embedded in the national histories of both the United States and Philippines. The first event occurred on July 4: the United States granted full independence to the Philippines after 40 years of colonial rule. Having helped save the Philippines on behalf of the United States, the Filipino World War II veterans anxiously anticipated their promised benefits and pensions. However, two succeeding events in Washington, D.C., would bring the veterans only disappointment and frustration.

Democratic President Truman, assisted by a Democratically controlled Senate and House, disregarded President Roosevelt's promise—but even worse, the Filipino veterans' patriotism and loyalty to America—by signing and executing two Rescission Acts, formally breaking America's promise to them. The initial blow was the First Supplemental Surplus Appropriation Rescission Act, or Public Law 79–301, which authorized a $200 million appropriation to the Commonwealth Army of the Philippines, with the provision that those soldiers be deemed to have never been in the U.S. military. Another blow was delivered through Public Law 79–391, the Second Supplemental Surplus Appropriation Rescission Act, enacted in May, which disenfranchised the Filipinos in the New Philippine Scouts of their U.S. military service. Those who fought in USAFFE guerrilla units were also disowned.

Therefore, only the "old" Philippine Scouts, the First and Second Filipino Infantry Regiments, and others who signed up directly with the Army in the United States were acknowledged as having fought for America in World War II. Ironically, before the passage of the 1946 Rescission Acts, Veterans Administration (VA) officials considered all Filipino military service to have met the statutory requirements for U.S. World War II veteran status. But in 1945, the VA was asked by President Truman to determine how much it cost to provide veterans' benefits to the Filipino soldiers. The VA study estimated that it would cost the U.S. $3.2 billion to award them continuing veterans' benefits. In effect, President Truman and Congress connived to craft legislation that would deny the Filipino World War II soldiers naturalization and privileges because the VA report conceded that these benefits would be very costly. Critics therefore contend that the promises to Filipino recruits of naturalization, benefits, and pensions were also disingenuous.

Fifty Years Later: Citizenship and Welfare Benefits

Congressional justifications for cutting back on Roosevelt's promise did not put a halt to the veterans' fight for justice. Many bilateral talks between the Philippine and the United States governments have involved the problematic Rescission Acts. The veterans took a step closer towards realizing their goal of naturalization in 1990. During that year, President George H. Bush enacted a critical second installment to Roosevelt's promise when he signed the Immigration and Naturalization Act of 1990, or Public Law 101-649. After 40 years of advocacy and litigation, "special provisions" on the naturalization of Filipino veterans were finally introduced by their congressional sympathizers in this comprehensive immigration reform act. Specifically, Section 405 of the law granted U.S. citizenship to Filipino veterans who served honorably in an active duty status under the command of the USAFFE, or within the Philippine Commonwealth Army, the Philippine

Scouts, or recognized Guerrilla Units at any time during the period beginning September 1, 1939, and ending December 31, 1946. Further amendments authorized the Immigration and Naturalization Service to naturalize eligible Filipino veterans at the U.S. Embassy in Manila.

This was definitely a gigantic step in the right direction for the veterans. However, there was still one large problem: although the veterans were allowed to become U.S. citizens, they still did not have the same benefits that U.S. veterans enjoyed. All in all, veterans who had been naturalized found themselves in a situation that was far different than they originally expected. That is, before immigrating, many viewed it as the land of opportunity and open doors. However, those same migrants often find later on that those impressions are not quite accurate. Since President George H. Bush passed the Immigration Act, about 28,000 veterans have moved to the United States from the Philippines and been naturalized. Most of them have settled in various parts of California, but many have also found homes in Hawaii, Nebraska, New Jersey, Illinois, Florida, Texas and New York. Many of these veterans were not able to bring their families with them because they simply could not afford the travel costs. Far from home and separated from their families, these men often suffer from depression, poverty and loneliness. Having no family to turn to, many veterans bond together, creating a community amongst themselves. With little money, they often live under impoverished conditions. Some veterans have told of spending "their first months homeless and destitute, in a chilly storage room basement." Others gathered in "groups of four or more and crowded into cheap, single-room apartments." Their living conditions are often unsanitary, overcrowded and unsafe. Nevertheless, many veterans choose to contend with such conditions as they wait for the government to fulfill its promise to them.

Most of the veterans are in their 70s and 80s and too old to work, but they have discovered sources of money to help them survive. For example, they have learned that the government provides welfare. However, this was not the more generous veterans' welfare that would enable them to support their families; instead, the naturalized veterans were only eligible only for the same, lower welfare payments as non-veterans. Veterans also obtain money from organizations and individuals who support their struggle.

As late life migrants, there was no doubt about it—life is hard in extremely expensive San Francisco. Not having enough money to live on their own, many veterans banded together, sharing expenses and small living spaces. But some who did not, ended up on the streets, homeless and penniless. A residential building that housed many of the veterans at rates they could afford was the Delta Hotel. This former hotel had been converted into tiny apartments to accommodate the high demand for living space, primarily from the Filipino veterans. The areas in which they settled, SoMa and the Tenderloin District, are known as neighborhoods where homelessness, drug problems, gang encounters, vehicle break-ins, petty thefts, street harassment, prostitution, sex shops, and violence abound—these are all things that are particularly frightening to lonely, aging men with very little money and who speak little English. Obviously, jobs are extremely hard to find in these areas, but some have managed to find employment as custodians, janitors, security guards, kitchen helpers, and doormen in various San Francisco businesses—essentially, low-paying, undesirable jobs. To supplement their Social Security income, some of them also provide paid childcare services and elderly company to other migrant families and fellow seniors in the area.

Displaced and impoverished, a group of veterans and their family members experienced further devastation when the residential Delta Hotel burned down on August 11, 1997. The four-alarm fire destroyed the five-story hotel and left many people either dead or homeless. The Red Cross came to the aid of the veterans; to some, the Red Cross cots and the gray blankets brought back memories of the war. The veterans were provided with temporary shelter in a gymnasium. One veteran wryly remarked, "This is like the Army again." A woman—one of the few veterans' wives—tried to put the loss in perspective, adding, "We only lost our means of shelter. We lost everything when we moved here."

Veterans and Youth Advocacy

During the most heated battles with Congress, the aging World War II veterans staged numerous demonstrations and garnered plenty of public support from private individuals and public officials in San Francisco, most especially the youth in high school and college. Veterans like Tatang Floro and San Francisco's youth know that city officials are powerless to change the veterans' situation, since theirs is a federal government issue, but this has not stopped San Francisco politicians from declaring their support of the veterans in official terms. For instance, on May 27, 1999, heavy lobbying from Filipino veterans and students convinced the San Francisco Human Rights Commission (SFHRC) to pass a resolution acknowledging and supporting the battle against the "unjust and inequitable treatment" of Filipino veterans who fought under the American flag in World War II. After all, San Francisco government units, like the Departments of Health and Human Services, will essentially have to care for the veterans, whether or not they get their benefits from Congress and the federal agencies concerned. With Filipino community and church lobbying, the Mayor's office and Board of Supervisors have agreed to budget for social programs that help to fill in the veterans' "equity gap." These include accommodations such as meals, a food bank, and skills enhancement programs to improve their employability. While these programs are helpful, they are ultimately unsatisfying to the veterans and their supporters, as they constitute welfare rather than the well-deserved benefits and pensions they are after.

In Washington, D.C., besides engaging in meditations, prayers and candlelight vigils, Filipino veterans and members of Student Action for Veterans Equity (SAVE) have risked their health and lives by participating in hunger strikes, chaining themselves to the White House fence, and staging fake deaths (or *die-ins*). But this has only gotten them the minor legislative installments mentioned earlier. Nevertheless, they have earned a good amount of publicity, so much that many more people are acknowledging their struggle and joining them in their fight. As I mentioned in the beginning of this chapter, Filipino American youth have joined the Filipino churches and other Filipino community-based organizations in their support of the veterans. As the next generation of activists, listeners, and leaders, this group of youth has proven its commitment and usefulness in demonstrations, marches, parades, and protests for the veterans' cause. SAVE members come from the San Francisco Bay Area's colleges and universities. They have been politicized by information gathered from the internet, newspapers, their peers, documentaries, Filipino American non-profit organizations, and their teachers.

The Results of Intergenerational Advocacy

The aging World War II veterans and their youth group allies prevailed in the end. In 1999, President Bill Clinton signed Public Law 106-169, which expanded income-based Social Security disability benefits to certain World War II veterans, including Filipino veterans of World War II who served in the organized military forces of the Philippines. It gave them the opportunity to return to the Philippines to receive a portion of their Social Security income there. In October 2000, a genuine, i.e., non–welfare-based veteran's benefit law was passed (Public Law 106-377). In it, Congress authorized the VA to provide full-dollar rate compensation payments to veterans of the Commonwealth Army or recognized guerrilla forces residing in the U.S. if they were either U.S. citizens or lawfully admitted permanent resident aliens. Public Law 106-377 also requested the VA to provide care at its clinics for any non-service-related conditions of those same veterans. These Filipino veterans benefit provisions were supplemented by Public Law 106-419, which authorized the payment of burial benefits on behalf of veterans in these groups. Only the New Philippines Scouts remained ineligible for burial allowances.

In 2003, Congress passed Public Law 108-170 (Veterans Health Care, Capital Asset, and Business Improvement Act of 2003) and Public Law 108-183 (Veterans Benefits Act of 2003). Signed into law by President George W. Bush in December of 2003, this legislation expanded compensation and burial benefit payments to the full-dollar rate for New Philippine Scouts residing in the U.S. if they were either U.S. citizens or lawfully admitted permanent resident aliens. It also increased Dependency and Indemnity Compensation benefits to the full-dollar rate for survivors of veterans who served in the New Philippine Scouts, Philippine Commonwealth Army or recognized guerrilla forces, if the survivor resided in the U.S. and was either a U.S. citizen or a legally admitted resident alien. As a result of this legislation, Filipino veterans can now be patients in VA hospitals, clinics and nursing homes. However, these benefits are still not on par with those of other veterans of America's wars. What is still missing? Of the numerous benefits and pensions that require corrective legislation, the most pressing are the death pension and non-service connected disability pension, since most of the veterans are currently in their late 70s. For this reason, the *veteranos* and youth continue to testify in congressional committees to this day.

50. San Francisco and Older Adult LGBTQ Population*

SAN FRANCISCO HUMAN SERVICES AGENCY

San Francisco city and community leaders and California state leaders have celebrated progress implementing programs that serve the unique needs of the older adult LGBTQ population. Older adults are the fastest growing age group in San Francisco, but the specific needs of LGBTQ adults over 60 have often been overlooked. This community's needs were highlighted by the groundbreaking work of the LGBT Aging Policy Task Force, which identified specific recommendations for programs and policies to address the challenges facing older LGBTQ adults and allow them to age within the community. Five years since the report was issued, the task force's recommendations have resulted in the implementation of numerous City programs, services and trainings that have enabled more LGBTQ seniors to age with dignity within their homes and neighborhoods, adding to the vibrancy of San Francisco.

LGBTQ seniors face heightened risk of isolation. This is a significant risk for older adults, particularly in San Francisco, where rates of living alone are higher than the state and nation. According to a 2018 Department of Adult and Aging Services (DAAS) Equity Analysis, 61 percent of LGBTQ senior clients live alone, much higher than 39 percent of the general older adult population. The task force's research also noted that the LGBTQ population is less likely to have biological family for traditional support and many have lost chosen family and close friends to illness, including HIV/AIDS. Fears and experiences of discrimination can cause hesitation in accessing services or seeking out support and many have limited financial means, in some cases the result of unemployment earlier in life while caring for a loved one. LGBTQ seniors of color often experience compounding effects of discrimination based on sexual orientation, gender identity, race, and age.

The 2014 task force report, "LGBT Aging at the Golden Gate: San Francisco Policy Issues and Recommendations," highlighted gaps in serving older LGBTQ adults and outlined 13 recommendations for programs and policies that would enable LGBTQ seniors to age with dignity. As the city agency charged with serving older adults and adults with disabilities, DAAS, in partnership with nonprofit community providers, has undertaken

*Originally published as San Francisco Human Services Agency, "San Francisco and Older Adult LGBTQ Population," https://www.sfhsa.org/about/announcements/city-and-state-leaders-gather-celebrate-progress-lgbtq-aging-issues-allowing (March 9, 2019).

the work of turning the majority of these recommendations into tailored programs and trainings that help LGBTQ older adults obtain needed services and support.

"While there is still more work to be done to ensure that all LGBTQ citizens can age with dignity and support within our community, I want to commend the Department of Aging and Adult Services for their vision and determination in implementing these needed programs," said Mayor London Breed. "As a result, San Francisco is a more inclusive, vibrant and ultimately, a more caring city—one that is closer to ensuring that all of our older adults can age with dignity."

The recommendations have resulted in directly increasing service to the older LGBTQ adult community. In 2017–18, DAAS served 2,039 clients who identified as LGBTQ, a 71 percent increase over enrollment levels four years earlier. This increase is due in part to new programs specifically designed for the LGBTQ senior population recommended by the Task Force; however, this trend also reflects better data gathered about the older adult LGBTQ population. DAAS has provided trainings in gathering demographic data on sexual orientation and gender identity, thereby allowing the city and its nonprofit partners to better align services with the community's needs.

Examples of the policies and programs implemented for LGBTQ older adults include: a new Care Navigation and Isolation Prevention program that utilizes trained staff and peer mentors to help clients access social services and reduce isolation; cultural sensitivity trainings for service providers in working effectively with LGBTQ seniors; a housing subsidy program that is targeted to LGBTQ older adults at risk of eviction; a Financial Literacy empowerment program; and Legal and Life Planning services to ensure their chosen family relationships and end-of-life choices are respected.

"I am incredibly proud of and thankful for the work of the LGBT Aging Policy Taskforce and for San Francisco's leadership in implementing these policies," stated state Senator Scott Wiener. "Our LGBTQ seniors have helped shape the society we live in now and the rights we enjoy. We owe it to these incredible pioneers to ensure they can age with dignity and respect. I am also proud that the work of this task force is influencing state and federal policy so that all of our LGBTQ seniors are protected and uplifted. Work remains, but we must also celebrate and recognize the importance of the progress we've made."

"Thanks to the work of the Task Force and the Department of Aging and Adult Services, San Francisco has made great progress toward ensuring that our LGBTQ seniors are able to age with pride," said Supervisor Rafael Mandelman. "Queer seniors shouldn't be forced back into the closet as they age—they should be celebrated and provided with the resources, housing, and support they need to thrive."

"We are proud of the work our agency and community providers have been able to achieve within five years of the Task Force's report," stated Shireen McSpadden, executive director of DAAS. "Our City is a more inclusive and diverse community as a result of our programs which are enabling more LGBTQ seniors to age within their homes and neighborhoods."

"I am very grateful that the hard work of the Task Force has helped create significant change for aging members of the LGBTQ community," said task force chair Bill Ambrunn. "The Report was a road map for DAAS and other departments to improve the lives of LGBTQ seniors in San Francisco. While there is more work to be done, City officials have delivered impressively on their promise to implement the Task Force recommendations."

Some of the programs DAAS has implemented as a result of the 2014 report:

LGBTQ Care Navigation Program: This partnership between DAAS and nonprofit community provider, Shanti, coordinates care and volunteers to provide emotional and peer support through regular visits with clients. The program also provides pet care resources so that clients can maintain their animal companions, which is important in helping to prevent isolation.

LGBT Dementia Care Project: Led by the Alzheimer's Association with the Family Caregiver Alliance and Openhouse, this program raises awareness and facilitates service providers to assist clients with dementia and connect them to hospitals and community organizations that serve the LGBTQ population.

LGBTQ Financial Literacy Program: The Smart Money Coaching services are tailored to each client's needs and work toward countable outcomes, such as establishing a safe and affordable banking account, decreasing debt by at least 10 percent, and establishing or improving credit score.

Housing Subsidy Program: Administered by the Q Foundation, this program helps stabilize housing in the face of rent hikes or loss of income by providing a housing subsidy payment and access to other supportive services.

Affordable Housing: The city partnered with Openhouse and Mercy Housing to develop LGBTQ-friendly housing developments. These two sites are next to the Bob Ross LGBT Senior Center, which provides social and recreational activities, a communal dining program, case management, and other supportive services.

51. The Intergenerational Imperative*

Irv Katz

Connections between generations have been at the core of community since the emergence of humankind. Yet, life in most developed countries has shifted from parents, children, grandparents, and other relatives living under one roof—or even in the same neighborhood or town.

Industrialization, mobility, prosperity, and other factors made it possible, even desirable, for young adults to move out and start their own lives and then their own families, sometimes in a nearby geographic area but often many, many miles away.

Older adults who cannot or choose not to remain in their homes find a range of housing options, some of them restricted to people over a certain age and without children.

The organization I work for, Generations United, and others in the intergenerational space—researchers, advocates, philanthropies, public officials, business leaders, service providers, journalists, among them—raise the issue of intergenerational connections not out of a sense of nostalgia for the extended family or ideology but because the generations are interdependent and need one another to thrive and survive.

When learning and caring for one another does not occur across generations, people do not fare as well and the additional burdens of learning and caring, particularly among the more vulnerable among us, become costs to society—costs in terms of problems and social needs that now become the responsibility of the public and nonprofit sectors.

In other words, we pay a steep price for generations not being connected and providing at least some of the functions extended families and connected communities once did. Extended families and close communities took in and helped members experiencing rough times; lack of extended family and community leaves those in crisis to depend on government and charities.

Benefits of Connections

Some researchers come at the issue from another vantage point: the effects of intergenerational connections and experiences on children, youth, and older adults. These effects have been found to be positive and beneficial.

---

*Reprinted with permission from "The Intergenerational Imperative," by Irv Katz, ICMA, 2019, March, https://icma.org/articles/pm-magazine/intergenerational-imperative.

There is compelling research on the subject, nationally and internationally. Some of the key conclusions of this research are cited in a 2017 report issued by Generations United and the Eisner Foundation, "I Need You, You Need Me: The Young, the Old, and What We Can Achieve Together" and are listed here with permission. These are among the benefits of intergenerational connections:

For children and youth:

- Social skills. Kids learn to talk and empathize with people they wouldn't otherwise meet.
- Emotional support. Older adults shepherd kids through difficult times and situations.
- School performance. Attendance, behavior, and performance improve. Struggling readers, for example, have made significant gains after being paired with elder tutors.
- Safe and healthy choices. Older adults divert kids from trouble and steer them toward success (https://legacyproject.org/guides/intergenbenefits.html).

For older adults:

- Isolation and loneliness. Older adults who were previously cut off from their communities find connection and companionship.
- Mood and self-esteem. As they help kids, older adults are reminded of their competence and achieve a renewed sense of purpose.
- Skills and knowledge. Kids introduce older adults to new technology and cultural phenomena.
- Exercise. To keep up with kids, older adults need to keep moving, which, in turn, boosts their cognitive, mental, and physical health.
- Practical assistance. Young people help older adults with chores and errands.
- Perceptions of young people. Older adults feel more comfortable around kids and more invested in their well-being.

Demographic Reality

So why should intergenerational connectivity matter to local government managers, and why now?

Children and youth and older adults comprise a significant and collectively growing portion of the U.S. population. Children, age 17 and younger, and older adults, age 65 and above, included 122.8 million people or 38 percent of the population in 2016, according to census estimates.

By 2035, their numbers are projected to rise to 154.4 million; and by 2060, to 174.5 million or 43.3 percent of the population.

While some youth and older adults are wage-earners, including those who delay retirement, the percentage of the rest of the population—those in their primary earning years—declines from 62 percent in 2016 to 56.7 percent in 2060.

In sheer numbers, the young and the old, including those more likely to be dependent and/or require ongoing care, are projected to rise by an astonishing 50+ million between 2016 and 2060.

The situation is more acute in Japan, where the aging of the population, a low birth rate, and relatively low immigration are expected to overwhelm the country's social security system and availability of caregivers for older adults.

Part of the solution in that country is to increase intergenerational connections through programs and activities where young and old get to know one another, so that more young people are willing and able to help care for older family members and neighbors. Increasing immigration is also being discussed.

Fostering connections between young and old and those who care for them is fast becoming a social and economic necessity in Japan and the same is increasingly true for the U.S.

Now is the time for communities to prepare for the looming reality that older adults, children, and youth will represent a growing percentage of the people living in the U.S., not those in their peak-earning and tax-paying years. It is either a looming crisis or an opportunity to redefine how we shape the future.

All social and economic groups within the population can benefit from approaching the future development and well-being of an area through an intergenerational lens. That said, the need for public sector attention will be greater in some parts of a given area than in others—areas with fewer economic resources and where residents have fewer opportunities in life.

Focused intergenerational investment and attention in these areas, integrated with other community revitalization efforts, could help reduce social ills and improve the well-being of all.

Mobilizing Communities

There are "age-friendly communities" or "communities for all ages" in many places across the U.S. Some of them cite intergenerational activities with and for youth but are chiefly about the need for more options and opportunities for older adults.

And while there are coalitions for children and youth in many communities, there is no all-hands-on-deck counterpart of the all-ages and age-friendly movement for children and youth that has achieved the kind of near-critical mass that these communities have. Note: UNICEF has launched a Youth-Friendly Communities Initiative, but it is young and has not taken hold in the U.S. in a significant way at this writing.

On the intergenerational community building front, Matthew Kaplan of Penn State University, Mildred Warner of Cornell University, Nancy Henkin, formerly of Temple University, now of Generations United, and others write extensively and compellingly on the subject.

Communities for All Ages mobilizations is an approach to intergenerational community building developed by Nancy Henkin while head of the Intergenerational Center at Temple University. It is an approach that Generations United and Dr. Henkin continue to promote.

Here are elements that either occur alone, in groupings, or as a total community strategy in communities aspiring to be intergenerational:

Intergenerational shared sites. Settings that house programs and activities for older adults and for children and youth with planned and informal interaction between the two. This concept goes beyond children trooping through older adult housing at holiday time and instead embraces, for example, a child-care center housed in an independent living complex in which older adults and children interact regularly.

Attention to grandfamilies. Programs, services, and advocacy intended to help grandparents (and other relatives) with the challenges of raising grandchildren, one of the key issues being that relative caregivers seldom access the same benefits and supports as unrelated foster parents.

Intergenerational housing. Bridge Meadows in Portland, Oregon, is a flagship for this fledgling movement. The concept is housing that is inclusive of older adults and households with children, including grandfamilies and those headed by older adults, with accessibility for all (i.e., universal design), and design that encourages interaction between young and old.

Intergenerational community events. Community convenings or rallies to educate and excite people about the value and practices of intergenerational action, for example a "future fair" demonstrating intergenerational programs and activities that young and old can enjoy together.

Intergenerational community building. Structured mobilization of young and old for young and old and the community, typically starting with a community assessment and leading to a plan of action and implementation of action strategies.

Intergenerational planning. Generations United and the American Planning Association are developing this concept, responsive to the demographic imperative this chapter cites.

The kind of planning envisioned seeks to weave population cohorts, particularly young and old and connections among them, into planning by local authorities, potentially leading to an enhanced standard of practice for community planning going forward.

Viewing communities through an intergenerational lens is not an option; it is a necessity and not in some far-off future, but right now. Beyond employing a lens is action, specific to each community, and that requires planning.

City and county managers are ideally suited to be adopters of approaching community as an intergenerational entity, where connecting generations leverages the best we can achieve for people and the communities where they live.

How to Unite Young and Old in Big Cities

No American metropolitan area has done more to unite the generations than San Diego County, where the local government considers age integration a core community value.

The county employs five "intergenerational coordinators": one in the department of aging services, one in the department of child welfare, and one in each of three geographical regions. The coordinators work together, with their colleagues throughout county government, and with leaders in the nonprofit and business sectors to create opportunities for the young and the old to serve one another and the broader community.

The county library department, for example, recently asked the coordinators for help designing intergenerational programs at its branches, and the county parks department wants guidance on uniting the patrons of one of its teen centers with the elder patrons of a nearby community center. The coordinators are helping both departments create surveys to assess what sort of programs might succeed; later, they'll help launch, advertise, and implement the programs.

The coordinators also oversee two "intergenerational councils," one in the northern part of the county and one in the eastern, that give officials from the public and private sectors a chance to strategize together. The councils meet every other month.

REFERENCES

American Planning Association (R.A. Ghazaleh, Esther Greenhouse, George Homsy, Mildred Warner). "Using Smart Growth and Universal Design to Link the Needs of Children and the Aging Population." https://www.planning.org/publications/document/9148235.
Brown, Corita, and Henkin, Nancy. "Building Communities for All Ages: Lessons Learned from an Intergenerational Community-Building Initiative." https://onlinelibrary.wiley.com/doi/pdf/10.1002/casp.2172.
Brown, Corita, and Henkin, Nancy. "Communities for All Ages. Intergenerational Community Building: Resource Guide." *Journal of Intergenerational Relationships*, https://www.tandfonline.com/doi/abs/10.1080/15350770.2015.1058317?journalCode=wjir20.
Generations United, The Eisner Foundation. "I Need You, You Need Me: The Young, the Old, and What We Can Achieve Together." https://www.gu.org/resources/i-need-you-you-need-me-the-young-the-old-and-what-we-can-achieve-together/.
Generations United, MetLife Foundation. "Creating an Age-Advantaged Community: A Toolkit for Building Intergenerational Communities that Recognize, Engage and Support All Ages." https://www.gu.org/resources/creating-an-age-advantaged-community.
Generations United, MetLife Foundation. "Best Intergenerational Communities Awards." https://www.gu.org/what-we-do/programs/best-intergenerational-communities-awards/.
Kaplan, Matthew, Sanchez, Mariano, and Hoffman, Jaco. "Intergenerational Pathways to a Sustainable Society." https://www.springer.com/us/book/9783319470177.
Warner, M.E. "Multigenerational Planning: Theory and Practice," 2017. http://cms.mildredwarner.org/p/282.

52. Intergenerational Outreach[*]

Yueqing (Queenie) Lin

The University of San Francisco encompasses a holistic approach to education, including a mandatory community service-learning course as an opportunity for students to engage in activities that "address human and community needs while promoting personal development." This core requirement is at the center of USF's vision to educate leaders who will fashion a more humane and just world. As part of my requirement, I had chosen POL 390, "Filipino Politics and Justice," a course taught by professor-practitioner Jay Gonzalez which focuses on the connections of the Philippines and their global immigrant communities.

Growing up in Hawaii, I was always surrounded by an assortment of cultures. The melting pot of ethnic groups in Hawaii consists of 38.6 percent Asian, 24.7 percent white, 10 percent native Hawaiian or other Pacific Islanders, 8.9 percent Hispanic, 1.6 percent black or African American, and 0.3 percent American Indian and Alaska Native, with the provision that 23.6 percent of all Hawaii residents are of multi-ethnic background (two or more races) (https://www.to-hawaii.com/ethnicity.php). During my junior and senior years of high school, I volunteered at the Kuakini Medical Center's Therapeutic Recreational Team, where I would engage in hourlong conversations, lead arts and crafts activities, or participate in karaoke with seniors living in the Kuakini Care Home. Volunteering at the local hospital had helped me gain a newfound respect for my volunteering work, and the concept of limited lifespan became more apparent following my grandfather's passing.

Thus, I wanted to continue my volunteering experience with seniors at the Pilipino Senior Resource Center (PSRC), a community outreach program for seniors of 60 and older, to embrace their positivity and respectfully accept their knowledge, as well as display acts of kindness. PSRC executive director Gabby Moraleda, the onsite volunteer coordinator, was extremely helpful and made the necessary arrangements with the volunteering experience. Through a number of phone calls and email exchanges, we decided on the topic of introducing the seniors to different methods of telecommunication such as Facebook Messenger, Viber, and FaceTime that they can utilize to make free calls to their families in the Philippines.

Moreover, I believe that the integration of generations and closing of generational gap will create a bridge that connects the seniors at PSRC to other resources. By 2050,

---

*Published with permission of the author.

223

there will be 92 million seniors over the age of 65. This presents a huge potential for designers to engage the growing number of Americans with technology, which will make technology even more accessible for all seniors. We need to engage the seniors with social media because it serves to connect people and resources together. We also need to utilize technology, primarily the social media aspect, to show the community, the sponsors, and more that PSRC is a great resource. The website should be updated so it reflects recent events and can also serve as a memory capsule for the seniors, containing relevant information about the organization and the service it provides in the SOMA (South of Market neighborhood) community.

I began preparing for my PSRC workshop by researching ways to engage the seniors in technology—to make learning the subject manner simple, practical, and enjoyable. I assembled a simple, practical PowerPoint presentation that included statistics on the growing population of seniors that are using technology, proceeded with the basics of WiFi and the app store, then provided step-by-step instructions on how to use their new social media accounts.

On April 25, 2019, I was met with a friendly and enthusiastic crowd of about fifteen seniors, ages 74 to 92, some of whom arrived early to mingle, while others trickled in after they finished grocery shopping. I started the presentation with a pitch—"How many of you like free things?" and "Do you remember when you had to buy international phone cards?"—then proceeded to go through my PowerPoint. However, I discovered that more than half of the seniors already utilized one form or another of Facebook Messenger, Viber, and FaceTime, so what began as a lecture type workshop evolved into a conversation about cheaper Xfinify packages they can use to watch Filipino telenovelas. At the end of presentation, I offered to help them with any personal problems they have with their phones and was able to provide some IT support on the spot.

I was truly impressed by the open-mindedness and adaptability of these individuals. Aunty Tia (name changed to protect identity) mentioned that she attended this workshop not because she didn't know how to make free long distance calls, but because she wanted to take the opportunity to see if there were new trends among the younger population (and gossip with her friends, of course). Others agreed, noting that the PSRC allows for them to have human connections and engage in conversations, which ultimately stimulate their mental state. We also covered topics ranging from Social Security in the U.S. to the lifting of the one child policy in China. These seniors are very well versed and knowledgeable.

By opening this gateway of technology, we are integrating the generations and closing the generational gap, which will allow people to interact and stay together as a community. Being comfortable with technology also includes a better daily experience for those with mobility or memory issues, such as using a device to track medication dispensing, or solutions that are able to detect falls and other medical alerts on a real-time basis. For the seniors at PSRC, this could even mean learning how to use Uber or Lyft for the convenience and safety of a trip to the doctor's office. It also means building a stronger *kasamahan* network between the Filipino-American and Filipino population.

With the large number of volunteers that come in from both the University of San Francisco and Golden Gate University contributing to the betterment of the Pilipino Senior Resource Center, the future of PSRC is promising. Jay Gonzalez, president of the organization, has plans on implementing future training sessions for these seniors. My tips for other GenZers who wish to partake in intergenerational outreach is be patient, be kind, and be understanding. It may seem like a long task to bridge this generation gap, but every step is a small victory that can be celebrated, because it could mean someone reconnecting with a long-lost friend. These seniors have a lifetime of wisdom and stories they want to share that go beyond the scope of what you can teach them within an hour. Yet, they're curious about new technology and trends, as well as experiencing the world through a younger perspective. This learning opportunity was morally rewarding to me, and I hope that other GenZers can take initiative to do the same.

53. Belichick Versus McVay*

An Age-Old Question of Leadership

Megan Gerhardt

Super Bowl LIII would pit the Los Angeles Rams against the New England Patriots, but the sidelines would be the setting for another kind of matchup: youth versus experience.

In 2017, Sean McVay, at 30, was the youngest head coach to be hired in NFL history. In his second season, he had to face off against Bill Belichick, the league's longest tenured head coach.

As a leadership professor, I study how leaders of all ages navigate generational differences, including how to motivate those that might be on the other side of the generation gap.

For Belichick and McVay, the challenges might seem particularly acute. Most of Belichick's players hadn't even been born when Belichick secured his first coaching gig. And while McVay can probably talk about social media with his players in a way Belichick can't, he's in charge of a coaching staff that includes septuagenarians.

But it doesn't matter if you're the greenest of leaders or a grizzled veteran: With some insight into generational dynamics, your age can become irrelevant.

Bridging the Generational Divide

Having a leader at one end of the age spectrum can lead to all kinds of assumptions.

Research has shown that older leaders are expected to be stable, dependable and interested in upholding the status quo. Younger leaders are thought to be natural change agents and innovators.

There seems to be a basis for these assumptions. Studies have found older leaders do tend to take a more measured approach and lead in ways that are described as structured and conservative. Younger leaders, in contrast, are more energetic and have what employees describe as a "take charge" approach.

*Originally published as Megan Gerhardt, "Belichick Versus Mcvay: An Age-Old Question of Leadership," *The Conversation*, https://theconversation.com/belichick-versus-mcvay-an-age-old-question-of-leadership-110563 (February 1, 2019). Reprinted with permission of the publisher.

But one approach isn't necessarily better than the other. Instead, what matters is the ability of a leader, young or old, to do two things.

First, they must reflect certain leadership qualities. Research shows that people want leaders who they see as inspiring, competent, forward-looking and honest.

Second, a good leader must also understand the needs and perspectives of team members—specifically, the different kinds of support younger and older employees require from their leaders. Navigating these generational differences requires what I call "gentelligence."

For example, a young employee and an older employee might interpret the same action differently. While boomers tend to interpret a lack of feedback as a sign that everything is going well, millennials may assume the opposite. Studies show that they expect a steady stream of feedback and mentoring.

We also know that millennials place a lot of weight on how well a leader communicates and connects with them on a personal level, which makes them feel valued. Boomers also want to feel valued, but asking them what they did over the weekend isn't the way to do it. Instead, a boss could ask them to offer advice or input.

The Yang to McVay's Yin

The Rams aren't the only organization giving the keys to a young leader: Across many industries, the number of millennial bosses is rising. Those born between 1981 and 1996 now make up 20 percent of organizational leadership roles. Baby boomers like the 66-year-old Bill Belichick hold just 18 percent of these roles.

Baby boomers may appreciate the energy and communication skills of younger leaders. But in order to gain the trust of older employees, young leaders often need to be willing to openly acknowledge what they don't know yet and ask others for input.

McVay appears eager to do just this. When asked what it means to have the older, more experienced Wade Phillips as his defensive coordinator, McVay described it as a "yin and yang" dynamic.

"It allows you to have a sounding board from someone who has been through a whole lot more than you have, have somebody to bounce things off of," he told NBC Sports' Mike Tirico. "It's all about the people you're around," he later added, "and not being afraid to say, 'Hey, help me figure this out.'"

Sean McVay, who admits he can be too "wired" at times, values the wisdom of his levelheaded assistant, Wade Phillips.

Belichick Never Rests on His Laurels

Older leaders need to grapple with a different set of challenges when engaging younger members of their team. Established leaders such as Belichick grew up in an age when holding positions of leadership meant unquestioned respect. But younger generations are less inclined to listen to someone simply because they hold a title.

Nonetheless, older leaders are still well positioned to connect with younger employees who are eager for guidance, and their years of experience make them effective mentors. They also tend to bring a calm and consensus-building approach.

Just as important is an older leader's openness to the ideas of their young employees. It signals that they're confident enough in their own experience and track record to empower those beneath them.

According to his coaching staff, what makes Belichick such an effective leader is his willingness to listen to and trust his staff.

As former defensive coordinator Matt Patricia explained, "We go to him with new ideas all the time—or what we think are new ideas."

"He wants you to disagree," receivers coach Chad O'Shea added. "He respects that. He listens. He trusts us and demonstrates that by letting us go out and make decisions."

Success, whether in the boardroom or on the field, depends on the talent of a leader to understand and navigate the expectations and needs of all their team members—no matter their age.

For a leader in today's 21st-century workplace, that may be the most important playbook of all.

54. Seniors and Lifelong Learning*

ALAN R. ROPER

Why Should Seasoned Adults Consider Lifelong Learning?

Lifelong learning is broadly defined as any learning activity undertaken throughout life. The idea of seniors participating in any formal type of learning is not new but has been gaining renewed popularity in recent years. The field of neuroscience has produced new research that shows the benefits of lifelong learning for adults ages 50 and older on both mental and physical health. Seniors who frequently read, play mentally challenging games, or engage in other intellectually stimulating activities are 2.5 times less likely to develop different types of cognitive impairment like memory loss, dementia and Alzheimer's. When older adults learn something new or apply what they already know in a new way, the brain grows new cells and builds new connections. Engaging in learning activities has proven benefits for problem-solving and memory skills. By participating in learning activities with others, seniors can help build social connections and ward off isolation.

Learning is a vital function of the human experience which begins in at the earliest stages of development and continues throughout a person's life. Learning begins with sensory experience, which is unique to each individual. Learning at every age can be both an individual and social experience. The concept of social learning begins through imitation and an early natural inclination toward conformity. Childhood social learning helps an individual conform to basic societal norms, which provide a basis for thriving within a social context. As people age, seeking out learning opportunities, especially those involving social learning are beneficial to both cognitive and physical health. One study (Gidicsin, et al., 2015) out of Massachusetts General Hospital and Harvard Medical School found that seniors who were involved in higher levels of intellectual stimulation throughout their lifetime had a significant marked delay in the onset of memory issues and Alzheimer's symptoms. An interesting part of these findings is that these seniors reported a delay of Alzheimer's symptoms and issues, despite not actually having lower amounts of Amyloid Beta protein plaques in their brains (the protein which clogs memory and destroys synapse connections). Another study conducted by neuroscientists at the

---

*Published with permission of the author.

University of Texas at Dallas, found that when seniors took on a new mentally challenging hobby they saw a lasting increase in their memory skills (Park, Lodi-Smith, & Drew 2013).

Paul Nussbaum, Ph.D., director of the Aging Research and Education Center in Pittsburgh (2005), explains: "Every time your heart beats, 25% of that blood goes right to the brain. But while exercise is critical, it may be education that is more important. In the 21st century, education and information may become for the brain what exercise is for the heart." In the same way the cardiovascular system requires aerobic exercises like walking, jogging, running, swimming, and bicycling, the brain also needs to be exercised. Lifelong learning may be comparable to going to a health club for the mind as people age. Researchers David Cutler and Adriana Lleras-Muney (2006) reported on the beneficial relationship between education and health. The findings of their study explain that the more educated a person is, the lower the likelihood of anxiety and depression, as rates of common chronic diseases, like heart disease, stroke, hypertension, high cholesterol, emphysema, diabetes, asthma, and ulcer (Cutler & Lleras-Muney 2006).

A study conducted by cognitive neuropsychologists (Lewis, 2009) at the University of Sussex in England found that reading for as little as six minutes can lower stress levels. The participants in the study experienced a slower heart rate and an easing in muscle tension. Cognitive neuropsychologist Dr. David Lewis (2009) explains: "Reading can reduce stress levels by 68 per cent, listening to music reduced the levels by 61 percent." Research has also demonstrated the benefits of social interaction for seniors. A study by Cynthia Meyer (2018) reveals that a person's sense of purpose and belonging can be greatly impacted by daily social interaction. Participation in life-long learning programs can produce more friendships through increased social interaction. "Positive indicators of social well-being may be associated with lower levels of interleukin-6 in otherwise healthy people. Interleukin-6 is an inflammatory factor implicated in age-related disorders such as Alzheimer's disease, osteoporosis, rheumatoid arthritis, cardiovascular disease, and some forms of cancer" (NIA, 2017).

Lifelong Learning Programs

Colleges, universities, community centers and libraries across the country recognize the value of offering senior members of society educational opportunities and as such offer reduced fees, tax credits, scholarships and in some cases even free classes for seniors. Seniors committed to an active intellectual life can find new and innovative options to participate in learning, both in-person and online. Programs have been initiated and expanded during the last two decades, but this idea dates to the beginning of the 20th century. In 1904, Boston University introduced evening and Saturday courses for teachers. They have recently opened a new division that extends lifelong learning called Division of Extended Education (EXTED) which offers noncredit cultural and lifestyle programs for people 60+ years (Fitzgerald, 2001). The College for Lifelong Learning (CLL) from the University System of New Hampshire, established in 1972, has specialized in teaching adults, serving over 4000 adults yearly. As their website states: "Once you get to know us, you'll find that everything we do, every program we have developed, and every course we offer is designed with you, the adult learner, in mind" (www.cll.edu). South Florida has a large population of seniors, as well as a significant number of opportunities for lifelong learning. Some examples are Learning in Retirement at Nova Southeastern University; the University of Miami's Institute for Retired Professionals; Broward Community College (BCC)'s Institute for Active Adults 50 Plus; Florida Atlantic University's Lifelong Learning Society; Palm Beach Atlantic University's College for Seniors; and Florida Memorial College's Entrepreneurial Institute among others (Werne, 2003).

The city of San Francisco, California, is home to an estimated 864,816 people. San Francisco's age distribution shows that the average age is 38.5 years, and that 13.6 percent of its population are 65 or older. This means that an estimated 117,615 residents of San Francisco are in the 65 years or older age group. San Francisco offers many opportunities for learning and social interaction for seniors, including the following programs offered by the two largest universities that reside in the City of San Francisco. Some older adults enroll in university degree programs or classes they always wanted to take but didn't have time for due to the demands of their jobs and families. Some older adult learners participate in classes at community centers and adult schools to become proficient using current technology.

The Fromm Institute for Lifelong Learning at the University of San Francisco offers daytime courses for retired adults over 50 years of age, offering intellectual stimulation by introducing members to a wide range of college level learning opportunities with full access to the facilities and services at the university. The Institute employs a model in which older students learn within a peer setting taught by emeritus professors of their own age. Courses are offered in popular subject areas such as psychology, literature, philosophy, science, theology, history, art, music, politics and creative writing. The Fromm Institute even has a Student Association with elected officers who handle a social agenda and plan special events. The Fromm Institute welcomes all people regardless of previous academic achievement or the ability to pay a modest membership fee. This program serves hundreds of older students each day and includes thousands of people among its lifelong learning student body and alumni.

The Bernard Osher Foundation makes grants and endowment gifts to colleges, universities, and other non-profit organizations for lifelong learning institutes for seasoned adults. The Osher Lifelong Learning Institute (OLLI) at San Francisco State University is an active community of peers age 50 and up engaged in learning through classes, interest groups, and events at the San Francisco State downtown and main campuses. Stimulating and provocative six-week courses provide personal and social enrichment, taught by current and retired SF State professors and other experts.

Considerations for Teaching Lifelong Learning

Differences exist between older and younger learners which are important to keep in mind for older adult learning activities. One study that found some learning-style preference differences as people aged revealed that many older adults preferred auditory to visual learning, and active rather than passive learning (Van Wynan, 1997, 2001). When Kuznar and associates (1991) compared learning styles of older and younger women, they found that the older adults had higher motivation, preferred to learn alone and learn earlier in the day. Additionally, older adults wanted a personal and humanized presentation that allowed for interaction, as opposed to video or computer. Also, it is important to recognize the differences between lifelong learning and lifelong education. Where lifelong learning is a personal process, lifelong education may involve formal and/or institutional participation (Searle, 1995). Lifelong learning is something that occurs all of the time as individuals think and act.

An older adult's learning capacity typically remains at an efficient level well into their 80s. One way doctors and neuroscientists determine subclinical disease process in an aging person is when they detect an inability to absorb new information. The instructor facilitating a learning event with older adults should be aware that incremental assessment can help detect any disconnect between the instruction and learning. This also provides an on-going analysis of the effectiveness of instruction, or the delivery method. Instructors should be aware that as people age, there is a corresponding normal decline in sensory function, including vision, hearing, and touch. Two-thirds of seniors over the age of 70 have vision and hearing deficits. Many educators who work with older adults find that education is most effective when it can be individualized to fit the needs and lifestyle of the older learner. This may include a process of having the senior learner(s) participate actively in goal setting or planning the sequence of learning.

Conclusion

A National Institutes of Health study of 2800 adults over the age of 65 who underwent memory training found that 26 percent "significantly" benefited (Morrison, 2003). Older adults have a variety of different programs for all interests and levels. These are available at universities, adult schools, senior centers, and many other locations. Participating in lifelong learning activities can enrich the lives of older adults no matter what their health status is. Educators, and other health professionals involved in teaching older adults can provide age-related accommodations and make changes in the instructional methods when planning lifelong learning activities. Learning new and different things provides both cognitive and physical benefits for older adults that extend beyond the acquisition of new knowledge. Participating in lifelong learning activities and learning new subjects will benefit older adults by providing new, novel experiences which will exercise the mind and will improve the quality of daily life as well as their memory (Fielding, 1999).

REFERENCES

Billett, S. (2009). "Conceptualising Learning Experiences: Contributions and Mediations of the Social, Personal and Brute." *Mind, Culture and Activity*, 16(1), 32–47. doi:https://doi.org/10.1080/10749030802477317.

Cutler, D., Lleras-Muney, A. (2006). "Education and Health: Evaluating Theories and Evidence," prepared for the conference on the Health Effects of Non-Health Policies, organized by the National Poverty Center. Working Paper 12352, http://www.nber.org/papers/w12352.

Edleson, H. (2016, Jan. 1). "Older Students Learn for the Sake of Learning." *New York Times*.

Fielding, Betty. (1999). *The Memory Manual: 10 Simple Things You Can Do to Improve Your Memory After 50.* Clovis, CA: Quill Driver/Word Dancer.

Fitzgerald, B. (2001). "New Division Extends Lifelong Learning." *Bostonia*, Fall, 41.

Gidicsin, C., Gidicsin, J., Locascio, J., Pepin, L., Philiossaint, M., Becker, J., Younger, A., Dekhtyar M., Amariglio, R., Marshall, G, Rentz, D., Hedden, T., Sperling, R., & Johnson, K. (2015). "Cognitive Activity Relates to Cognitive Performance but Not to Alzheimer Disease Biomarkers." *Neurology*, June 10, 2015, DOI: https://doi.org/10.1212/WNL.0000000000001704.

Jarvis, P. (2012) *Adult Education and Lifelong Learning: Theory and Practice*, 4th ed. Abingdon-on-Thames, UK: Routledge.

Kolb, D. A. (1984). *Experiential Learning: Experience as the Source of Learning and Development.* Englewood Cliffs, NJ: Prentice-Hall.

Lewis, D. (2009). "Reading 'Can Help Reduce Stress.'" *The Telegraph*, retrieved from https://www.telegraph.co.uk/news/health/news/5070874/Reading-can-help-reduce-stress.html.

Meyer, C. (2018) "The Importance of Social Interaction for Seniors, Second Wind Movement." Retrieved from http://secondwindmovement.com/social-interaction-for-seniors/.

Morrison, Jim. (2003). "Aerobicize the Mind." *American Way*, 74–77.

National Institute on Aging (2017). "Research Suggests a Positive Correlation between Social Interaction and Health." National Institute on Aging, U.S. Department of Health and Human Services. Retrieved from https://www.nia.nih.gov/about/living-long-well-21st-century-strategic-directions-research-aging/research-suggests-positive.

Nordstrom, N. (2010) "Lifelong Learning—Encourage Elders to Exercise Mind, Body, and Spirit." *Aging Well*, vol. 3 no. 2, p. 27.

Nussbaum, P. (2005), "Ten Tips for Maintaining Brain Health: Research Shows Impact of Environmental Factors on Brain Function." Retrieved from http://www.paulnussbaum.com/tentips2.html.

Park, D., Lodi-Smith, J., & Drew, L. (2103, Nov. 8). "The Impact of Sustained Engagement on Cognitive Function in Older Adults: The Synapse Project." *Psychological Science*, https://doi.org/10.1177/0956797613499592.

Ruholl, L. (2003). "Tips for Teaching the Elderly." *RN* 66 (5), 48–52.

Searle, J. R. (1995). *The Construction of Social Reality*. London: Penguin.

Weinstein, L. (2008). "Lifelong Learning Benefits Older Adults." *Activities, Adaptation & Aging*, 28:4, 1–12, DOI: 10.1300/J016v28n04_01.

Werne, J. (2003). "Eager to Learn at Any Age." *Miami Herald*, 30–32.

55. Participating in the Arts Creates Paths to Healthy Aging[*]

NATIONAL INSTITUTE ON AGING

We all know to eat right, exercise, and get a good night's sleep to stay healthy. But can flexing our creative muscles help us thrive as we age? Ongoing research looking at singing group programs, theater training, and visual arts for older adults suggest that participating in the arts may improve the health, well-being, and independence of older adults.

"Researchers are highly interested in examining if and how participating in arts activities may be linked to improving cognitive function and memory and improving self-esteem and well-being. Scientists are also interested in studying how music can be used to reduce behavioral symptoms of dementia, such as stress, aggression, agitation, and apathy, as well as promoting social interaction, which has multiple psychosocial benefits," said Lisa Onken, Ph.D., of NIA's Division of Behavioral and Social Research.

Lifting Their Voices for Healthy Aging

"There's a pressing need to develop novel, sustainable, and cost-effective approaches to improve the lives of older adults," said Julene K. Johnson, Ph.D., of the University of California, San Francisco School of Nursing. "Singing in a community choir may be a unique approach to promote the health of diverse older adults by helping them remain active and engaged. It may even reduce health disparities."

Dr. Johnson tested this approach, leading Community of Voices, the largest randomized clinical trial to test the impact of participating in a community choir on the health and well-being of nearly 400 culturally diverse adults, age 60 and older, from 12 senior centers in San Francisco. The centers were randomly chosen to conduct the choir program immediately (six intervention groups) or six months later (six control groups). Outcome measures were collected at baseline (prior to starting the intervention), six months (end of randomization phase), and 12 months (one year after enrollment). Each

[*]Originally published as National Institute on Aging, "Participating in the Arts Creates Paths to Healthy Aging," https://www.nia.nih.gov/news/participating-arts-creates-paths-healthy-aging (February 15, 2019).

choir met once a week in 90-minute sessions for 44 weeks and performed in several informal concerts.

At weekly rehearsals, professional choral directors from the San Francisco Community Music Center trained in the intervention led activities to promote health and well-being. Researchers assessed participants' cognition, physical function, and psychosocial function, as well as their use and cost of healthcare services, before they started the choir program and again after 6 and 12 months.

A unique aspect of the study was its use of community partners to engage, enroll, and retain a large group of racially and ethnically diverse and low-income older adults. Participants were recruited and completed all choir activities and assessments at the senior centers, which made it more convenient for them to join and continue in the study. Participating in the community choir showed positive results within six months. In particular, it reduced feelings of loneliness and increased interest in life. However, cognitive and physical outcomes and healthcare costs did not change significantly. Dr. Johnson attributed the improvements to the choir providing a meaningful, regular opportunity to meet new people, build social support, and increase a sense of belonging.

"The study showed increased interest in life because singing in the choir provided a regular, structured activity for participants," she said. "Access to regular activities in diverse, low-income communities is vital for older adults to remain active and engaged in their community."

Dr. Onken noted, "By examining the mechanisms through which arts participation may provide benefits to health and well-being, and by studying arts participation with scientific rigor, we hope to establish a firm basis on which to develop programs to improve the health and well-being of older people. As these studies continue, we expect the results to show us how we can implement cost-effective, community-based programs that benefit older people."

Theater Improvising to Cope with Dementia

Northwestern University is looking to another art form, theater improvisation, to help older adults with early stage dementia be social and improve their quality of life. "'The Memory Ensemble' is for people newly diagnosed with Alzheimer's disease and other types of dementia who are looking for opportunities to engage in programs that fit their needs," said Darby Morhardt, Ph.D., Outreach, Recruitment and Education Core Leader at Northwestern's Mesulam Center for Cognitive Neurology and Alzheimer's Disease.

The Memory Ensemble's 69 participants learn how to use their instincts, creativity, and spontaneity to explore and create improvisational theater. The program, developed in 2010 by Northwestern and the Lookingglass Theatre Company in Chicago, seeks to improve the quality of life for people living with Alzheimer's and related disorders and to transfer these benefits to other communities.

As part of the eight-week program, groups of 10 to 15 participants, age 50 to 90, attend 90-minute sessions that are purposely repetitive and follow a specific pattern. Two facilitators—a clinical social worker and a master teaching artist in theater and improvisational techniques—guide participants through various activities.

Many Memory Ensemble exercises involve practicing observation, listening, and then using one's imagination to find creative solutions. Here are some examples:

- Participants' moods are assessed at check-in with "smiley faces."
- A metaphor exercise: "If my feelings could be a color, they would be…"
- A gentle warmup of stretching and breathing.
- A skill-building exercise in which participants imagine a character in a challenging situation or pretend to turn an object into something else.
- The "checkout" activity, another smiley face assessment

"We wanted participants to be in a safe but challenging environment," said the program's co-founder, Christine Mary Dunford, Ph.D., of Lookingglass Theater Company. "We're putting them in situations where they may feel anxiety. But our motto is, 'When I feel anxious or uncertain, I can stop, breathe, observe, and turn to my imagination, and an answer will come.' As a result, we've found they feel more successful and empowered."

The program does not aim to slow decline or improve cognition, but to help people with dementia enjoy their lives, according to Dr. Morhardt. "There are limits to medical treatments for people with dementia," she said. "Patients and families are looking for ways to continue to engage. For participants in the program, it's about being in the moment and using their imagination. We enhance their remaining skills and mood. As the condition progresses, it can become challenging to communicate with words, so we really focus on nonverbal means of expression."

Preliminary results show participation in the Memory Ensemble improves mood, decreases anxiety, and increases a sense of belonging, normalcy, and destigmatization, said Dr. Dunford. Participants also report feelings of achievement, empowerment, and self-discovery.

Plans include developing an evidence-based curriculum for researchers, arts therapists, and theater professionals to replicate the program in other communities and a theater intervention program for caregivers.

Making the Connection Between Music and the Brain

To explore the connections between music and wellness at all ages, the National Institutes of Health (NIH) and the John F. Kennedy Center for the Performing Arts in Washington, D.C., in collaboration with the National Endowment for the Arts (NEA), launched Sound Health in 2017. The goal is to expand knowledge about how music affects the brain.

At a January 2017 NIH workshop on this topic, a panel of medical experts, scientists, music therapists, performers, and arts professionals discussed research on how the brain processes music and how this research is applied in clinical settings. The workshop generated recommendations to further this area of research.

Later in 2017 and again in 2018, the program hosted a series of performances, lectures, and hands-on workshops at the Kennedy Center that brought together leading researchers and performers to explore the intersection of music and science.

NIH established a working group to follow up on outcomes and recommendations from the workshops. The group plans to develop and implement basic and applied research initiatives, methodological improvements, and an infrastructure to support additional large-scale studies.

NIH has issued funding opportunity announcements for additional research on how music can affect brain development, improve treatment for people with certain health conditions, and enhance quality of life for people as they age.

Learn more about the Sound Health initiative—for example, how music can help people with Parkinson's disease walk, protect adults from hearing loss as they age, and other scientific findings see "Sound Health: Music Gets You Moving and More" at https://newsinhealth.nih.gov/2018/01/sound-health.

Research on music, theater, dance, creative writing, and other participatory arts shows promise for improving older adults' quality of life and well-being, from better cognitive function, memory, and self-esteem to reduced stress and increased social interaction. NIA is addressing the need for more rigorous research, including new or alternative research designs and measurements that can demonstrate the efficacy and cost advantage of arts interventions.

REFERENCES

Cheever, T., Taylor, A., Finkelstein, R., et al. "NIH/Kennedy Center Workshop on Music and the Brain: Finding Harmony.: *Neuron* 2018; 97(6):1214–1218.

Dunford, C.M., Yoshizaki-Gibbons, H.M., Morhardt, D. "The Memory Ensemble: Improvising Connections among Performance, Disability, and Aging." *Research in Drama Education* 2017; 22(3):420–426.

Johnson, J.K., Stewart, A.L., Acree, M., et al. "A Community Choir Intervention to Promote Well-Being among Diverse Older Adults: Results from the Community of Voices Trial." *Journals of Gerontology: Series B,* Nov. 9, 2018.

National Endowment for the Arts. "The Arts and Aging: Building the Science. (PDF, 2.3M) Summary of a National Academies workshop, 'Research gaps and opportunities for exploring the relationship of the arts to health and well-being in older adults.'" February 2013.

56. Public Service Delivery for Aging Populations[*]

Using Social Media to Support Seniors

JEFFREY ZIMMERMAN

Governments at all levels are charged to deliver services to all the inhabitants of their respective jurisdictions, and, 17 years into this millennium, technology affords society the ability to provide these services in a more efficient manner. However, with advancements in technology come levels of understanding about using this technology properly. This is a question many governments find themselves attempting to answer regarding using or implementing social media to support society but specifically to the senior citizen population. What social media platforms should government officials use to disseminate information to the senior citizens? What information about which services should be disseminated via social media platforms? The advancements in technology have overwhelmed society with countless social media platforms.

By conducting a simple search using Google search engine and typing in "social media sites" I could see a list of the most popular sites in 2016. Here are the top ten:

Facebook
Twitter
LinkedIn
Google+
YouTube
Pinterest
Instagram
Tumblr
Flickr
Reddit

I am not advocating any government agency hire a full-time social media team to manage their social media messaging. They would likely have to hire a few full-time

---

*Originally published as Jeffrey Zimmerman, "Public Service Delivery for Aging Populations: Using Social Media to Support Seniors," *PA Times*, https://patimes.org/public-service-delivery-aging-populations-social-media-support-seniors/ (January 27, 2017). Reprinted with permission of the publisher.

individuals to manage just the above ten sites, not to mention the dozens of other sites not listed here, to ensure their agency's message was disseminated on as many sites as possible. So, then the question becomes which social media sites should governments use to either disseminate crucial information (such as weather alerts or traffic conditions) or even general information? Which sites should governments use to provide other public services? These are questions our leaders both elected or hired must answer to provide public services in the most efficient manner possible. In North Carolina, where I work and reside, the two most popular social media sites the governments use to disseminate information on a variety of topics and issues are Facebook and Twitter. I am sure governments use other social media sites to disseminate information and provide services but I am not up to date with those sites or agencies.

C.J. Hutto and colleagues in a 2015 Web Intelligence article titled "Social Media Gerontology: Understanding Social Media Usage Among Older Adults" assert the percentage of older adults using social media has increased substantially in recent years, yet little research has been done to understand the foundations underlying social media technology usage by older adults. Such an understanding is useful for developing intelligent user modeling and personalization techniques specific to this growing community. Governments that can understand these foundations of underlying social media usage by senior citizens will be better able to determine which services or messages can be disseminated to the population on the specific social media platforms the senior citizens are using. Governments have several tools to assist them with gaining a better understanding of these foundations at their disposal, the first tool that immediately comes to thought is conducting a survey. Governments can conduct surveys in several different ways: dissemination of survey on multiple social media sites, telephone surveys, mailed surveys and possibly door-to-door surveys. The goal of this survey is to attempt to ascertain the number of senior citizens using social media and which sites they are using as well as their frequency of usage.

Collecting and analyzing this information will better assist government leaders in determining the type of information that can be disseminated on the appropriate social media sites that will be the most benefit to the senior citizens. Hutto and colleagues further assert that social media technology has the potential to facilitate social connectedness among older adults who otherwise might be physically or geographically isolated from family and friends. Governments can reach a larger portion of the population by using social media to disseminate information. Social media is much more convenient and faster than newspapers, radio or even news stations as most senior citizens have smart phones now and subsequently they are using social media for a variety of reasons. Social media is an opportunity for governments to reach a larger audience with their information and services being provided than in decades previously and it opens more opportunities for future growth in providing services and communication with the senior citizen population. Governments can be more transparent by using social media with the senior citizen population and can continue building and strengthening the relationship between government and the senior citizen community.

57. The Use of Social Media Platforms to Support Seniors[*]

Andrew Vaz

Now, I wouldn't be honest if I compiled this piece without stating that social media is not a domain strictly for the younger population for our world. The elderly are frequent users of Facebook, Twitter, Instagram and many others platforms. My parents, computer novices whom are a part of this community, are frequent users of Facebook—I actually created their account for them and they often visit my page and make comments on my posts. Yes, social media and the elders are no longer considered mutually exclusive.

The only item that should be addressed regarding the use of social media by other elders is how to make our favorite platforms such as Facebook more user-friendly for seniors.

Health Benefits of Social Media Use for Seniors

Making social media platforms more user-friendly for seniors helps with social isolation and the feeling of loneliness. To be clear, social isolation and loneliness are not the same thing: for example, someone may be surrounded by many people but still feel alone. Other people may isolate themselves because they prefer to be alone. The effect on longevity, however, is much the same for those two scenarios.

Thus, the lack of positive relationships where there is communication can be debilitating to seniors who do not have regular contact with other people. Social media, for seniors, can help to mitigate the effects of loneliness by helping them to feel more connected to friends and family.

Social media can serve as an outlet for building groups devoted to health issues, such as dementia. Doctors and other professionals have keyed into this demographic and set up social media pages to take advantage of this customer and patient outlet. Groups for the elderly experiencing specific ailments as well as groups directed at their caregivers are all set up for those elderly who are increasingly availing themselves of this supportive network.

*Originally published as Andrew Vaz, "The Use of Social Media Platforms to Support Seniors," *PA Times*, https://patimes.org/social-media-platforms-support-seniors/ (March 17, 2017). Reprinted with permission of the publisher.

Finding Employment for Seniors on Social Media

Seniors are turning to social media to look for employment: platforms such as LinkedIn are available to seniors looking for work or volunteering opportunities. Plenty of job resources have moved to online posting that older people looking for work need to go online just to find good opportunities. Seniors increasingly use social media to join support groups and search out volunteer opportunities.

AARP estimates more than 3 million workers age 50-plus are looking for full-time employment. Unfortunately, there's also a rise in reports of discrimination against older adults in the workplace. This is terrible as older workers present years of experience and discipline for any employer. According to an AARP study, healthcare workers over the age of 55 had the highest level of employee engagement, which greatly correlates with employer loyalty, performing well with little supervision and motivation to do their very best.

LinkedIn has caught on to the idea of getting the elderly to use social media to connect with potential employers. In today's current employment environment, 65 is no longer the retirement age and seniors want to work longer and earn more savings.

Improving Technology Education for Seniors

To improve social media interaction for seniors, we must improve technology education. Research shows the Internet has become an important way to exercise the minds of seniors: when the elderly are trained in the use of social media as well as Skype and email, they perform better cognitively and experience improved health. Computer classes at senior centers are growing in popularity. Classes on computer basics as well as instruction in using email and other social media platforms such as Facebook have become more common.

My parents are also interested in research and adore searching on Google and enquiring on topics of their interests. Seniors can use social media tools to learn more about topics that interest them. In some cases it can lead them to cultivate hobbies and business ideas, and in other cases, such as with all the inaccurate health information available, it can be a confusing mix of resources.

The importance of improving technology education will lead to more seniors becoming involved in social media as through the evidence based on research, the elder are becoming more active with these platforms and it is helping to improve their health and their relationships with family and friends.

Conclusion

In the coming decades, social media platforms will take towards the elderly as the current population of young people age. It is pleasant to know the generations of seniors in the future will be more computer proficient than the generations of the past.

58. Emerging Technologies to Support an Aging Population*

TASK FORCE ON RESEARCH AND DEVELOPMENT
FOR TECHNOLOGY TO SUPPORT AGING ADULTS

The Task Force on Research and Development for Technology to Support Aging Adults was established under the National Science and Technology Council's Committee on Technology to examine the potential of technology to maximize the independence of aging Americans by increasing opportunities for social engagement and connectivity as well as reducing the impact of any cognitive and physical limitations.

The task force report identifies a range of emerging technologies that have significant potential to assist older adults with successfully aging in place, each categorized by their role in supporting a set of primary capabilities. It identifies a number of focus areas that could support each capability and provides recommendations for research and development (R&D) that are required to develop key technology solutions over the coming decade. Cross-cutting topics that affect multiple capabilities are also discussed. These recommendations are offered as a guide for both public and private sector R&D. The overall goal is to improve the quality of life, enhance individual choice, reduce the financial and emotional burden of care to individuals and families, and reduce the burden of providing care on the American healthcare infrastructure.

The number of Americans aged 65 or older is growing rapidly—increasing by 40 percent between 2000 and 2016 to approximately 50 million people, over 15 percent of the total population—and is expected to grow to nearly a quarter of the population by 2060. For older Americans living outside of a nursing home, 25 percent of those aged 65 to 74 and 50 percent of those aged 75 and older have reported some kind of disability, such as problems with vision, hearing, or mobility. The combination of the projected growth of this segment of the population and the desire of many older Americans to live independently in their homes and communities makes it critical that the federal government proactively develop strategies, tools, and recommendations to enable older Americans to live healthy, independent lives for as long as possible.

---

*Originally published as Task Force on Research and Development for Technology to Support Aging Adults, "Emerging Technologies to Support an Aging Population: Introduction," https://www.white house.gov/wp-content/uploads/2019/03/Emerging-Tech-to-Support-Aging-2019.pdf (March 2019); this is the Introduction to the report.

President Donald J. Trump says, "We're on the verge of new technological revolutions that could improve virtually every aspect of our lives, create vast new wealth for American workers and families, and open up bold, new frontiers in science, medicine, and communication."

The Trump Administration has made finding solutions for an aging population a research and development (R&D) priority. The overarching goals of this R&D should be to enhance the functional independence and continued safety, well-being, and health of older Americans, while reducing overall economic costs and the stress on the Nation's healthcare infrastructure.

Achieving these goals will:

- improve the quality of life and continued contributions of active and independent individuals to the greater community and the economy;
- enhance individual choice with respect to living arrangements;
- reduce the financial and emotional stress on informal and unpaid family caregivers; and
- reduce the cost to the American healthcare system, including not only hospital and nursing home expenses, but also expenses related to long-term care services and support.

While the primary purpose of this report is to broadly identify for both public and private sector stakeholders the R&D that is needed to create technology to support an aging population, the capabilities enabled by such technology also hold promise to improve and enrich the lives of all Americans with challenges common in older adults, such as mobility, social connection, cognitive changes, and general health and nutrition. The development of technology to assist older adults is a large and rapidly growing industry that could be accelerated by R&D in areas highlighted in this report.

Scope and Organization of This Report

In preparing this report, the Task Force first identified the primary capabilities that older adults must maintain to continue to live independently (e.g., the ability to perform the Key Activities of Independent Living), as well as more focused areas deemed key to those capabilities and most likely to benefit from advances in technology (e.g., hygiene, nutrition). It then reviewed a diverse spectrum of emerging technologies and systems designed or with the potential to maintain those capabilities within each area. Based on this review and a subsequent gap analysis, the Task Force identified functional needs (e.g., maintain oral health) that could potentially be met by new technological advances (e.g., develop systems to support personalized dental regimens) and the R&D required to develop those technology solutions over the next five to ten years. This report and the technologies discussed herein do not represent a comprehensive review of the current state of each field but are intended to highlight a range of promising and/or key technologies in each of the focus areas of the report.

In addition to scientific and engineering research needed to further the development of the technology itself, the report includes recommendations for research necessary to inform the development of standards and policies. In addition, the report notes a number of social and behavioral science factors that will impact acceptance and implementation of new technologies. Achieving all of these advances will require partnerships between the public and private sectors for both R&D and implementation, with the private sector leading the way in product development and deployment.

The Task Force recognizes that the abilities of individuals and their needs for technology will vary significantly—both within the population and for individuals over time. Age-related changes in cognitive and physical abilities are not static and, in some cases, may be either transient (e.g., movement limitations following joint replacement) or time-variable (e.g., sundowning phenomenon of dementia). Therefore, the ability to monitor and assess the needs of aging individuals over time, and to identify appropriate technologies or adapt technologies to these changing needs, will be key to each of these areas of technology R&D and implementation. In addition, the needs of older adults living at home are expected to differ from the general population, and research targeted at identifying these unique factors is recommended such that appropriate and optimized solutions can be developed.

This report identifies a range of emerging technologies that have significant potential to assist older adults, and it is offered as a guide for both public and private sector research and development (R&D) to improve the quality of life, enhance individual choice, reduce caregiver stress, and cut healthcare costs. The task force identified six primary functional capabilities as being critical to individuals who wish to maintain their independence as they age and for which technology may have a positive impact.

1. Key Activities of Independent Living. Living independently requires the ability to perform a range of activities that impact our daily lives. Many of these activities can be assisted through technology, including those that support good nutrition, hygiene, and medication management.

2. Cognition. Cognitive changes are common during aging, with increasing prevalence at older ages—varying in severity and impact. These changes can affect the ability to live independently as well as personal safety. Technology holds the promise to help older adults monitor changes in their cognition, provide mental training to reduce the impact of these changes, and create systems that assist individuals and families to maintain financial security.

3. Communication and Social Connectivity. Older adults may face communication challenges as the result of hearing loss, social isolation, and loneliness, especially in economically distressed and rural communities. Technology can improve hearing and strengthen connections to larger communities.

4. Personal Mobility. Mobility is a key factor in successful aging. To live independently, an individual must have the ability to comfortably and safely move around the home and throughout the larger community. Technology can assist older adults in staying mobile and able to safely perform key activities necessary for day-to-day life as well as interact with their communities.

5. Transportation. True independence requires mobility outside of the home and neighborhood. Transportation needs and limitations are dictated to an extent by the changes to individual physical and cognitive abilities that come with age. While some older adults remain completely independent and continue to drive without assistance, others may be able to drive but require vehicle modification and/or advanced technologies to assist them while operating a vehicle. New technologies could also help older adults more safely and easily use public transportation.

6. Access to Healthcare. Access to healthcare plays a critical role in helping older adults stay active and independent as they age. Activities and strategies that support the maintenance of function and independence with age are multifaceted. Alignment and coordination of these efforts through technology can increase the effectiveness and efficiency of these services.

In the process of identifying primary capabilities and focus areas in which technological advances can have a positive impact in enabling older adults to age in place, several areas emerged that are associated with a number of technological solutions and were therefore not specific to individual R&D recommendations. These areas are included in the final section of the report, Cross-Cutting Themes.

PART III

The Future

59. Keep Age Out of It[*]

Ageism Has No Place in Hiring Practices

ROBERT SHAPIRO

I found my job at the Village of Friendship Heights, Maryland, in the obituary section of *The Washington Post*. The former village manager had just passed away. Since I had been looking for a job at the time, with little success, I took a chance and called the village mayor whom I knew while living in the village 20 years earlier.

I was told the village was in the final stages of interviewing for both a manager and an assistant manager, and the mayor invited me to come in for what I was sure was a courtesy interview. Long story short, I have been with the village, first as assistant manager, then as assistant village manager/finance director for nearly 23 years.

Up until that time I had not seen a lot of courtesy in my job search. There had been a time in my career when sending a resume almost guaranteed an interview and often led to an offer.

That was no longer my experience. Of the piles of resumes I had sent out, each with a customized cover letter, the response had been about 50–50. Half the time I was rejected without an interview; the other half of the time I didn't get a response at all.

I was 50 years old when I was hired by Friendship Heights. My new boss, the manager, was 29. He had been there for six years, starting as the assistant to the manager. I am sure he had his concerns when the mayor at the time wanted to hire the "old guy," but he was willing to give it a shot.

Nearly all other employees were also older than he was. Fortunately, I had some experience being a young boss and knew it could be challenging.

We were both willing to teach and learn from each other, which is a recipe for success. We have enjoyed working together all of these years, and we have also accomplished quite a bit.

---

*Reprinted with permission from "Keep Age Out of It: Ageism Has No Place in Hiring Practices," by Robert Shapiro, ICMA, 2019, April, https://icma.org/articles/pm-magazine/commentary-keep-age-out-it.

Rampant Prejudice

Ageism, in my opinion, is the last frontier of "acceptable" illegal discrimination, and I believe it is rampant in today's world. I attended a workshop where the topic was discrimination in hiring. The moderator was talking about things to avoid when advertising a position that might be interpreted as discriminatory.

I asked about including such wording in job advertisements as three to five years of experience or five to 10 years. I could understand setting a minimum standard for the position but thought stating a maximum was equivalent to putting in a maximum age. The workshop instructor saw no problem with the maximum wording.

My wife was recently told at a consulting firm that they were looking for someone "less seasoned." She knew exactly what that meant. A few years ago, I saw this language in a brochure I received from a recruiter concerning a position in Florida: "Finally, the council is looking for someone who will commit to the city for the long term. They are not looking for someone who views this position as a steppingstone to the next position or to retirement (unless retirement is a long way off). The city manager's position in [location] is a destination in and of itself."

I contacted the company advertising the position, noting that this sounded like blatant age discrimination and asked them what, given this wording, was the maximum age for the position. This was the response: "Thank you for (the) comment, but I disagree. The city wants someone who will stay five to 10 years and preferably the latter. Hence, they do not want someone who will be moving on after two or three years—whether it is because they will be looking for the next, better position or someone who plans to hang it up in two or three years.

"We will consider anyone who is willing to make a five- or 10-year commitment. As I am sure you are aware, some people retire at 40 and others, like my father, retire in their 80s or later. The point, again, is the city wants someone who will stay five to 10 years."

If these are the facts, then I think the job advertisement should say that. Two years ago, I received a brochure from the same company with this wording: "The assistant city manager needs to be someone who does not settle for second best because this community is one where the best is merely adequate and something to be exceeded. This job is not a retirement job. Only the serious and vigorous will be successful."

Maybe I am just too sensitive.

Birth Dates and Such

When I first joined ICMA, I received a printed directory each year. The member listings included birth dates and a resume of experience. I contacted ICMA and requested that my birth date be removed, and my experience be limited to my local government experience. The person I spoke with complied but thought this was fraud. By understating my experience? The only thing I was obfuscating, possibly, was my age.

I asked the purpose of including anyone's age in bio information and was told it was so people of similar ages could network. Kind of like at the assistant's lunches at the ICMA conferences. Interestingly, my ICMA profile still lists my college graduation date, another hint employers use to determine age.

A few times since working for the village of Friendship Heights I have tested the waters for other jobs. I admit it. Twice I applied to larger Washington area jurisdictions. I didn't get an interview either time.

As it turned out, the same person was hired for both jobs. Twenty years my junior. And no longer in either position. Both of the people I sent my application to have also moved on.

Once, I sent a resume for a town manager position in Florida. I didn't get an interview. When I saw the announcement for the person hired I looked up the name in my trusty ICMA directory. Very similar background in local government to mine. I just had 20 years of additional experience.

Attitudes Are Important

There are concerns, of course, when hiring someone older, especially for a position for which they might be considered "overqualified" (I've also heard that one a few times) or where they will be working for people younger and possibly less experienced.

One thing I accepted when I joined the Friendship Heights staff is that I was now the assistant manager of the village. Who I might have been before, professionally, was part of me but not the role I was playing at this time. That let me not only do the job, but ultimately grow while in the job. It also left me free to learn. My boss had a lot to teach me.

He also realized that giving me a long leash often came back to benefit him. We all need to remember that what we now herald as "diversity" used to be considered reasons why a potential hire would not "fit in."

I was fortunate that my courtesy interview was indeed courteous. We discussed the village and discussed my background. I didn't offer my previous salary, and I wasn't asked. I did, however, explain that salary was not a key issue for me.

There are other situations where I would have been dismissed as the dreaded "overqualified." Ironically, when I started my new job I found that the village didn't even have the cash flow to pay my reduced compensation.

Over the years, that has been fixed. Cash flow is no longer a problem, and fortunately, all staff salaries have risen considerably.

Am I responsible for this? Of course not. There were a lot of factors coming together. Did my presence and perhaps age help? I like to think so.

A Unique Community

Friendship Heights is a unique place. The village is a 32-acre enclave of high-rise buildings, housing some 4,500 people, just over the Maryland line from Washington, D.C. We have the second largest concentration of people over the age of 65 in Montgomery County, Maryland. Second only to Leisure World, an age-restricted community.

There are also a nearly equal number of residents under 35. We have a central community center catering to all residents, but with many programs aimed at older people. The village council's goal has been to help keep people independent, in their homes, for as long as possible.

The 11-member village staff reflects the uniqueness. We range in age from 49 to 97. Some employees were hired in their 20s and just stayed. Others were hired when they were much older and with other careers behind them. It certainly works for us.

In my opinion it is time for ICMA to step to the forefront of opposing ageism in hiring. Simply by natural demographics, the membership will age with the boomers. I believe that there is much ICMA and its members can do to both identify factors in age discrimination and to assist members in dealing with them.

60. Seniors Increasingly Getting High, Study Shows*

Carmen Heredia Rodriguez

Baby boomers are getting high in increasing numbers, reflecting growing acceptance of marijuana as treatment for various medical conditions, according to a study published in the journal *Addiction*.

The findings reveal overall use among the 50-and-older study group increased "significantly" from 2006 to 2013. Marijuana users peaked between ages 50 to 64, then declined among the 65-and-over crowd.

Men used marijuana more frequently than women, the study showed, but marital status and educational levels were not major factors in determining users.

The study by researchers at New York University School of Medicine suggests more data is needed about the long-term health impact of marijuana use among seniors. Study participants said they did not perceive the drug as dangerous, a sign of changing attitudes.

The study was based on 47,140 responses collected from the National Survey on Drug Use and Health.

Joseph Palamar, a professor at the NYU medical school and a co-author of the study, said the findings reinforce the need for research and a call for providers to screen the elderly for drug use. "They shouldn't just assume that someone is not a drug user because they're older," Palamar said.

Growing use of the drug among the 50-and-older crowd reflects the national trend toward pushing cannabis into mainstream culture. Over 22 million people used the drug in 2015, according to the Substance Abuse and Mental Health Services Administration.

Eight states have legalized the drug for recreational use as well as medicinal use, according to Marijuana Policy Project, a non-profit advocacy group dedicated to enacting non-punitive marijuana policies across the United States. The drug has also proved to be a financial boon for state economies, generating over $19 million in September 2016 in Colorado.

---

*Originally published as Carmen Heredia Rodriguez, "Seniors Increasingly Getting High, Study Shows," *Kaiser Health News*, https://khn.org/news/seniors-increasingly-getting-high-study-shows/ (December 6, 2016). *Kaiser Health News* is a nonprofit news service covering health issues. It is an editorially independent program of the Kaiser Family Foundation that is not affiliated with Kaiser Permanente. KHN's coverage of end-of-life and serious illness issues is supported by The Gordon and Betty Moore Foundation.

Researchers also uncovered an increasing diversity in marijuana users. Past-year use doubled among married couples and those earning less than $20,000 per year.

More people living with medical conditions also sought out marijuana. The study showed the number of individuals living with two or more chronic conditions who used the drug over the past year more than doubled. Among those living with depression, the rate also doubled to 11.4 percent.

Palamar says the increase among the sick could be attributed to more individuals seeking to self-medicate. Historically, the plant was difficult to research due to the government crackdown on the substance. The Drug Enforcement Administration classifies the plant as a Schedule I substance, "defined as drugs with no currently accepted medical use and a high potential for abuse."

Benjamin Han, assistant professor at the New York University School of Medicine and the study's lead author, fears that marijuana used with prescription drugs could make the elderly more vulnerable to adverse health outcomes, particularly to falls and cognitive impairment.

"While there may be benefits to using marijuana such as [relief of] chronic pain," he said, "there may be risks that we don't know about."

The push and pull between state and federal governments has resulted in varying degrees of legality across the United States. Palamar says this variation places populations at risk of unknowingly breaking the law and getting arrested for drug possession. The issue poses one of the biggest public health concerns associated with marijuana, Palamar says.

But unlike the marijuana of their youth, seniors living in states that legalized marijuana for medicinal use now can access a drug that has been tested for quality and purity, said Paul Armentano, deputy director of NORML, a non-profit group advocating for marijuana legalization. Additionally, the plant is prescribed to manage diseases that usually strike in older age, pointing to an increasing desire to take a medication that has lesser side effects than traditional prescription drugs.

The study found over half of the users picked up the habit before turning 18, and over 90 percent of them before age 36.

"We are coming to a point where state lawmakers are responding to the rapidly emerging consensus—both public consensus and a scientific consensus—that marijuana is not an agent that possesses risks that qualifies it as a legally prohibited substance," he said.

61. Day-Tripping to the Dispensary*

Seniors in Pain Hop Aboard the Canna-Bus

STEPHANIE O'NEILL

Shirley Avedon, 90, had never been a cannabis user. But carpal tunnel syndrome that sends shooting pains into both of her hands and an aversion to conventional steroid and surgical treatments is prompting her to consider some new options.

"It's very painful, sometimes I can't even open my hand," Avedon said.

So for the second time in two months, she's climbed on board a bus that provides seniors at the Laguna Woods Village retirement community in Orange County, Calif., with a free shuttle to a nearby marijuana dispensary.

The retired manager of an oncology office says she's seeking the same relief she saw cancer patients get from smoking marijuana 25 years ago.

"At that time [marijuana] wasn't legal, so they used to get it off their children," she said with a laugh. "It was fantastic what it did for them."

Avedon, who doesn't want to get high from anything she uses, picked up a topical cream on her first trip that was sold as a pain reliever. It contained cannabidiol, or CBD, but was formulated without THC, or tetrahydrocannabinol, marijuana's psychoactive ingredient.

"It helped a little," she said. "Now I'm going back for the second time hoping they have something better."

As more states legalize marijuana for medical or recreational use—30 states plus the District of Columbia to date—the cannabis industry is booming. Among the fastest growing group of users: people over 50, with especially steep increases among those 65 and older. And some dispensaries are tailoring their pitches to seniors like Avedon who are seeking alternative treatments for their aches, pains and other medical conditions.

On this particular morning, about 35 seniors climb on board the free shuttle—paid

*Originally published as Stephanie O'Neill, "Day-Tripping to The Dispensary: Seniors in Pain Hop Aboard the Canna-Bus," *Kaiser Health News*, https://khn.org/news/day-tripping-to-the-dispensary-seniors-in-pain-hop-aboard-the-canna-bus/ (September 18, 2018). Jenny Gold and Mara Gordon contributed to this report. This story is part of a partnership that includes NPR and *Kaiser Health News*. *KHN*'s coverage of these topics is supported by the John A. Hartford Foundation and the SCAN Foundation. *Kaiser Health News* is a nonprofit news service covering health issues. It is an editorially independent program of the Kaiser Family Foundation that is not affiliated with Kaiser Permanente.

for by Bud and Bloom, a licensed cannabis dispensary in Santa Ana. After about a half-hour drive, the large white bus pulls up to the parking lot of the dispensary.

About half of the seniors on board today are repeat customers; the other half are cannabis newbies who've never tried it before, said Kandice Hawes, director of community outreach for Bud and Bloom. "Not everybody is coming to be a customer," Hawes said. "A lot are just coming to be educated."

Among them, Layla Sabet, 72, a first-timer seeking relief from back pain that keeps her awake at night, she said. "I'm taking so much medication to sleep and still I can't sleep," she said. "So I'm trying it for the back pain and the sleep."

Hawes invited the seniors into a large room with chairs and a table set up with free sandwiches and drinks. As they ate, she gave a presentation focused on the potential benefits of cannabis as a reliever of anxiety, insomnia and chronic pain and the various ways people can consume it.

Several vendors on site took turns speaking to the group about the goods they sell. Then, the seniors entered the dispensary for the chance to buy everything from old-school rolled joints and high-tech vaporizer pens to liquid sublingual tinctures, topical creams and an assortment of sweet, cannabis-infused edibles.

Jim Lebowitz, 75, is a return customer who suffers pain from back surgery two years ago. He prefers to eat his cannabis, he said. "I got chocolate and I got gummies," he told a visitor. "Never had the chocolate before, but I've had the gummies and they worked pretty good."

"Gummies" are cannabis-infused chewy candies. His contain both the CBD and THC, two active ingredients in marijuana.

Derek Tauchman rings up sales at one of several Bud and Bloom registers in the dispensary. Fear of getting high is the biggest concern expressed by senior consumers, who make up the bulk of the dispensary's new business, he said. "What they don't realize is there's so many different ways to medicate now that you don't have to actually get high to relieve all your aches and pains," he said.

But despite such enthusiasm, marijuana isn't well researched, said Dr. David Reuben, the Archstone Foundation professor of medicine and geriatrics at UCLA's David Geffen School of Medicine. While cannabis is legal both medically and recreationally in California, it remains a Schedule 1 substance—meaning it's illegal under federal law. And that makes it harder to study.

The limited research that exists suggests that marijuana may be helpful in treating pain and nausea, according to a research overview published last year by the National Academies of Sciences, Engineering and Medicine. Less conclusive research points to it helping with sleep problems and anxiety.

Reuben said he sees a growing number of patients interested in using it for things like anxiety, chronic pain and depression. "I am, in general, fairly supportive of this because these are conditions [for which] there aren't good alternatives," he said.

But Reuben cautions his patients that products bought at marijuana dispensaries aren't FDA-regulated, as are prescription drugs. That means dose and consistency can vary. "There's still so much left to learn about how to package, how to ensure quality and standards," he said. "So the question is how to make sure the people are getting high-quality product and then testing its effectiveness."

And there are risks associated with cannabis use too, said Dr. Elinore McCance-Katz, who directs the Substance Abuse and Mental Health Services Administration.

"When you have an industry that does nothing but blanket our society with messages about the medicinal value of marijuana, people get the idea this is a safe substance to use. And that's not true," she said.

Side effects can include increased heart rate, nausea and vomiting, and with long-term use, there's a potential for addiction, some studies say. Research suggests that between 9 and 30 percent of those who use marijuana may develop some degree of marijuana use disorder.

Still, Reuben said, if it gets patients off more addictive and potentially dangerous prescription drugs—like opioids—all the better.

Jim Levy, 71, suffers a pinched nerve that shoots pain down both his legs. He uses a topical cream and ingests cannabis gelatin capsules and lozenges. "I have no way to measure, but I'd say it gets rid of 90 percent of the pain," said Levy, who—like other seniors here—pays for these products out-of-pocket, as Medicare doesn't cover cannabis.

"I got something they say is wonderful and I hope it works," said Shirley Avedon. "It's a cream."

The price tag: $90. Avedon said if it helps ease the carpal tunnel pain she suffers, it'll be worth it.

"It's better than having surgery," she said.

Precautions to Keep in Mind

Though marijuana use remains illegal under federal law, it's legal in some form in 30 states and the District of Columbia. And a growing number of Americans are considering trying it for health reasons. For people who are, doctors advise the following cautions.

Talk to your doctor. Tell your doctor you're thinking about trying medical marijuana. Although he or she may have some concerns, most doctors won't judge you for seeking out alternative treatments.

Make sure your prescriber is aware of all the medications you take. Marijuana might have dangerous interactions with prescription medications, particularly medicines that can be sedating, said Dr. Benjamin Han, a geriatrician at New York University School of Medicine who studies marijuana use in the elderly.

Watch out for dosing. Older adults metabolize drugs differently than young people. If your doctor gives you the go-ahead, try the lowest possible dose first to avoid feeling intoxicated. And be especially careful with edibles. They can have very concentrated doses that don't take effect right away.

Elderly people are also more sensitive to side effects. If you start to feel unwell, talk to your doctor right away. "When you're older, you're more vulnerable to the side effects of everything," Han said. "I'm cautious about everything."

Look for licensed providers. In some states like California, licensed dispensaries must test for contaminants. Be especially careful with marijuana bought illegally. "If you're just buying marijuana down the street … you don't really know what's in that," said Dr. Joshua Briscoe, a palliative care doctor at Duke University School of Medicine who has studied the use of marijuana for pain and nausea in older patients. "Buyer, beware."

Bottom line: The research on medical marijuana is limited. There's even less we know about marijuana use in older people. Proceed with caution.

62. Lethal Plans*

When Seniors Turn to Suicide in Long-Term Care

Melissa Bailey *and* JoNel Aleccia

When Larry Anders moved into the Bay at Burlington nursing home in late 2017, he wasn't supposed to be there long. At 77, the stoic Wisconsin machinist had just endured the death of his wife of 51 years and a grim new diagnosis: throat cancer, stage 4.

His son and daughter expected him to stay two weeks, tops, before going home to begin chemotherapy. From the start, they were alarmed by the lack of care at the center, where, they said, staff seemed indifferent, if not incompetent—failing to check on him promptly, handing pills to a man who couldn't swallow.

Anders never mentioned suicide to his children, who camped out day and night by his bedside to monitor his care.

But two days after Christmas, alone in his nursing home room, Anders killed himself. He didn't leave a note.

The act stunned his family. His daughter, Lorie Juno, 50, was so distressed that, a year later, she still refused to learn the details of her father's death. The official cause was asphyxiation.

"It's sad he was feeling in such a desperate place in the end," Juno said.

In a nation where suicide continues to climb, claiming more than 47,000 lives in 2017, such deaths among older adults—including the 2.2 million who live in long-term care settings—are often overlooked. A six-month investigation by *Kaiser Health News* and *PBS NewsHour* finds that older Americans are quietly killing themselves in nursing homes, assisted living centers and adult care homes.

Poor documentation makes it difficult to tell exactly how often such deaths occur. But a *KHN* analysis of new data from the University of Michigan suggests that hundreds of suicides by older adults each year—nearly one per day—are related to long-term care. Thousands more people may be at risk in those settings, where up to a third of residents report suicidal thoughts, research shows.

---

*Originally published as Melissa Bailey and JoNel Aleccia, "Lethal Plans: When Seniors Turn to Suicide in Long-Term Care," *Kaiser Health News*, https://khn.org/news/suicide-seniors-long-term-care-nursing-homes/ (April 9, 2019). *Kaiser Health News* is a nonprofit news service covering health issues. It is an editorially independent program of the Kaiser Family Foundation that is not affiliated with Kaiser Permanente.

Each suicide results from a unique blend of factors, of course. But the fact that frail older Americans are managing to kill themselves in what are supposed to be safe, supervised havens raises questions about whether these facilities pay enough attention to risk factors like mental health, physical decline and disconnectedness—and events such as losing a spouse or leaving one's home. More controversial is whether older adults in those settings should be able to take their lives through what some fiercely defend as "rational suicide."

Tracking suicides in long-term care is difficult. No federal regulations require reporting of such deaths and most states either don't count—or won't divulge—how many people end their own lives in those settings.

Briana Mezuk, an associate professor of epidemiology at the University of Michigan, found in 2015 that the rate of suicide in older adults in nursing homes in Virginia was nearly the same as the rate in the general population, despite the greater supervision the facilities provide.

In research they presented at the 2018 Gerontological Society of America annual meeting, Mezuk's team looked at nearly 50,000 suicides among people 55 and older in the National Violent Death Reporting System (NVDRS) from 2003 to 2015 in 27 states. They found that 2.2 percent of those suicides were related to long-term care. The people who died were either people living in or transitioning to long-term care, or caregivers of people in those circumstances.

KHN extrapolated the finding to the entire U.S., where 16,500 suicides were reported among people 55 and older in 2017, according to federal figures. That suggests that at least 364 suicides a year occur among people living in or moving to long-term care settings, or among their caregivers. The numbers are likely higher, Mezuk said, since the NVDRS data did not include such states as California and Florida, which have large populations of elders living in long-term care sites.

But representatives of the long-term care industry point out that by any measure, such suicides are rare.

The deaths are "horrifically tragic" when they occur, said Dr. David Gifford, of the American Health Care Association. But, he added, the facilities offer "a very supervised environment," and settings that receive Medicare or Medicaid funding are required to assess and monitor patients for suicidal behavior.

"I think the industry is pretty attuned to it and paying attention to it," Gifford said, noting that mental health issues among older adults in general must be addressed. "I don't see this data as pointing to a problem in the facilities."

KHN examined over 500 attempted and completed suicides in long-term care settings from 2012 to 2017 by analyzing thousands of death records, medical examiner reports, state inspections, court cases and incident reports.

Even in supervised settings, records show, older people find ways to end their own lives. Many used guns, sometimes in places where firearms weren't allowed or should have been securely stored. Others hanged themselves, jumped from windows, overdosed on pills or suffocated themselves with plastic bags. (The analysis did not examine medical aid-in-dying, a rare and restricted method by which people who are terminally ill and mentally competent can get a doctor's prescription for lethal drugs. That is legal only in seven states and the District of Columbia.)

Descriptions *KHN* unearthed in public records shed light on residents' despair: Some told nursing home staff they were depressed or lonely; some felt that their families had abandoned them or that they had nothing to live for. Others said they had just lived long enough: "I am too old to still be living," one patient told staff. In some cases, state inspectors found nursing homes to blame for failing to heed suicidal warning signs or evicting patients who tried to kill themselves.

A better understanding is crucial: Experts agree that late-life suicide is an under-recognized problem that is poised to grow.

By 2030, all baby boomers will be older than 65 and one in five U.S. residents will be of retirement age, according to census data. Of those who reach 65, two-thirds can expect to need some type of long-term care. And, for poorly understood reasons, that generation has had higher rates of suicide at every stage, said Dr. Yeates Conwell, director of the Office for Aging Research and Health Services at the University of Rochester.

"The rise in rates in people in middle age is going to be carried with them into older adulthood," he said.

Long-term care settings could be a critical place to intervene to avert suicide—and to help people find meaning, purpose and quality of life, Mezuk argued: "There's so much more that can be done. It would be hard for us to be doing less."

"In a Desperate Place"

In Wisconsin, Larry Anders' children chose to speak publicly because they felt the nursing home failed their father.

Anders, a taciturn Army veteran, lived a low-key retirement in Waukesha, outside of Milwaukee. He grew asparagus, watched *Wheel of Fortune* with his wife, Lorna, in matching blue recliners and played the slot machines at a Chinese restaurant.

Following the November 2017 death of his wife, and his throat cancer diagnosis, he initially refused treatment, but then agreed to give it a try.

Anders landed at the Bay at Burlington, 40 minutes from his home, the closest facility his Medicare Advantage plan would cover. The first day, Lorie Juno grew worried when no one came to greet her father after the ambulance crew wheeled him to his room. The room had no hand sanitizer and the sink had no hot water.

In his week in the Burlington, Wis., center, Anders wrestled with anxiety and insomnia. Anders, who rarely complained, called his daughter in a panic around 2 a.m. one day, saying that he couldn't sleep and that "they don't know what the hell they're doing here," according to Juno. When she called, staff assured her that Anders had just had a "snack," which she knew wasn't true because he ate only through a feeding tube.

His children scrambled to transfer him elsewhere, but they ran out of time. On December 27, Mike Anders, 48, woke up in an armchair next to his father's bed after spending the night. He left for his job as a machinist between 5 and 6 a.m. At 6:40 a.m., Larry Anders was found dead in his room.

"I firmly believe that had he had better care, it would've been a different ending," Mike Anders said.

Research shows events like losing a spouse and a new cancer diagnosis put people at higher risk of suicide, but close monitoring requires resources that many facilities don't have.

Nursing homes already struggle to provide enough staffing for basic care. Assisted living centers that promote independence and autonomy can miss warning signs of suicide risk, experts warn.

In the weeks before and after Anders' death, state inspectors found a litany of problems at the facility, including staffing shortages. When inspectors found a patient lying on the floor, they couldn't locate any staff in the unit to help.

Champion Care, the New York firm that runs the Bay at Burlington and other Wisconsin nursing homes, noted that neither police nor state health officials found staff at fault in Anders' death.

Merely having a suicide on-site does not mean a nursing home broke federal rules. But in some suicides KHN reviewed, nursing homes were penalized for failing to meet requirements for federally funded facilities, such as maintaining residents' well-being, preventing avoidable accidents and telling a patient's doctor and family if they are at risk of harm.

For example:

- An 81-year-old architect fatally shot himself while his roommate was nearby in their shared room in a Massachusetts nursing home in 2016. The facility was fined $66,705.
- A 95-year-old World War II pilot hanged himself in an Ohio nursing home in 2016, six months after a previous attempt in the same location. The facility was fined $42,575.
- An 82-year-old former aircraft mechanic, who had a history of suicidal ideation, suffocated himself with a plastic bag in a Connecticut nursing home in 2015. The facility was fined $1,020.

Prevention needs to start long before these deaths occur, with thorough screenings upon entry to the facilities and ongoing monitoring, Conwell said. The main risk factors for senior suicide are what he calls "the four D's": depression, debility, access to deadly means and disconnectedness.

"Pretty much all of the factors that we associate with completed suicide risk are going to be concentrated in long-term care," Conwell said.

Most seniors who choose to end their lives don't talk about it in advance, and they often die on the first attempt, he said.

"I Choose This 'Shortcut'"

That was the case for the Rev. Milton P. Andrews Jr., a former Seattle pastor, who "gave no hint" he wanted to end his life six years ago at a Wesley Homes retirement center in nearby Des Moines, Wash. Neither his son, Paul Andrews, nor the staff at the center had any suspicions, they said.

"My father was an infinitely deliberate person," said Paul Andrews, 69, a retired Seattle journalist. "There's no way once he decided his own fate that he was going to give a clue about it, since that would have defeated the whole plan."

At 90, the Methodist minister and human rights activist had a long history of making what he saw as unpopular but morally necessary decisions. He drew controversy in the pulpit in the 1950s for inviting African Americans into his Seattle sanctuary. He opposed the Vietnam War and was arrested for protesting nuclear armament. His daughter was once called a "pinko" because Andrews demanded equal time on a local radio station to rebut a conservative broadcaster.

In 2013, facing a possible second bout of congestive heart failure and the decline of his beloved wife, Ruth, who had dementia, Andrews made his final decision. On Valentine's Day, he took a handful of sleeping pills, pulled a plastic bag over his head and died.

Milton Andrews wrote a goodbye note on the cover of his laptop computer in bold, black marker.

"Fare-well! I am ready to die! I choose this 'shortcut,'" it read in part. "I love you all, and do not wish a long, protracted death—with my loved ones waiting for me to die."

Christine Tremain, a spokeswoman for Wesley Homes, said Andrews' death has been the only suicide reported in her 18 years at the center. "Elder suicide is an issue that we take seriously and work to prevent through the formal and informal support systems that we have in place," she said.

At first, Paul Andrews said he was shocked, devastated and even angry about his dad's death. Now, he just misses him. "I always feel like he was gone too soon, even though I don't think he felt like that at all," he said.

Andrews has come to believe that elderly people should be able to decide when they're ready to die. "I think it's a human right," he said. "If you go out when you're still functioning and still have the ability to choose, that may be the best way to do it and not leave it to other people to decide."

That's a view shared by Dena Davis, 72, a bioethics professor at Lehigh University in Pennsylvania. Suicide "could be a rational choice for anyone of any age if they feel that the benefits of their continued life are no longer worth it," she said.

"The older you get, the more of your life you've already lived—hopefully, enjoyed—the less of it there is to look forward to," said Davis, who has publicly discussed her desire to end her own life rather than die of dementia, as her mother did.

But Conwell, a leading geriatric psychiatrist, finds the idea of rational suicide by older Americans "really troublesome." "We have this ageist society, and it's awfully easy to hand over the message that they're all doing us a favor," he said.

"So Preventable"

When older adults struggle with mental illness, families often turn to long-term care to keep them safe.

A jovial social worker who loved to dance, Ellen Karpas fell into a catatonic depression after losing her job at age 74 and was diagnosed with bipolar disorder. Concerned that she was "dwindling away" at home, losing weight and skipping medications, her children persuaded her to move to an assisted living facility in Minneapolis in 2017.

Karpas enjoyed watching the sunset from the large, fourth-story window of her room at Ebenezer Loren on Park. But she had trouble adjusting to the sterile environment, according to son Timothy Schultz, 52. "I do not want to live here for the rest of my life," she told him.

On October 4, 2017, less than a month after she moved in, Karpas was unusually irritable during a visit, her daughter, Sandy Pahlen, 54, recalled. Pahlen and her husband left the room briefly. When they returned, Karpas was gone. Pahlen looked out an open window and saw her mother on the ground below. Karpas, 79, was declared dead at the scene.

Schultz said he thinks the death was premeditated, because his mother took off her eyeglasses and pulled a stool next to the window. Escaping was easy: She just had to retract a screen that rolled up like a roller blind and open the window with a hand crank.

Pahlen said she believes medication mismanagement—the staff's failure to give Karpas her regular mood stabilizer pills—contributed to her suicide. But a state health department investigation found staffers were not at fault in the death. Eric Schubert, a spokesman for Fairview Health Services, which owns the facility, called Karpas' death "very tragic" but said he could not comment further because the family has hired a lawyer. Their lawyer, Joel Smith, said the family plans to sue the facility and may pursue state legislation to make windows suicide-proof at similar places. "Where do I even begin to heal from something that is so painful, because it was so preventable?" said Raven Baker, Karpas' 26-year-old granddaughter.

Nationwide, about half of people who die by suicide had a known mental health condition, according to the Centers for Disease Control and Prevention. Mental health is a significant concern in U.S. nursing homes: Nearly half of residents are diagnosed with depression, according to a 2013 CDC report.

That often leads caregivers, families and patients themselves to believe that depression is inevitable, so they dismiss or ignore signs of suicide risk, said Conwell. "Older adulthood is not a time when it's normal to feel depressed. It's not a time when it's normal to feel as if your life has no meaning," he said. "If those things are coming across, that should send up a red flag."

Solutions

Still, not everyone with depression is suicidal, and some who are suicidal don't appear depressed, said Julie Rickard, a psychologist in Wenatchee, Wash., who founded a regional suicide prevention coalition in 2012. She's launching one of the nation's few pilot projects to train staff and engage fellow residents to address suicides in long-term care.

In the past 18 months, three suicides occurred at assisted living centers in the rural central Washington community of 50,000 people. That included Roland K. Tiedemann, 89, who jumped from the fourth-story window of a local center on January 22, 2018. "He was very methodical. He had it planned out," Rickard said. "Had the staff been trained, they would have been able to prevent it. Because none of them had been trained, they missed all the signs."

Tiedemann, known as "Dutch," lived there with his wife, Mary, who has dementia. The couple had nearly exhausted resources to pay for their care and faced moving to a new center, said their daughter, Jane Davis, 45, of Steamboat Springs, Colo. Transitions into or out of long-term care can be a key time for suicide risk, data shows.

After Tiedemann's death, Davis moved her mother to a different facility in a nearby city. Mary Tiedemann, whose dementia is worse, doesn't understand that her husband died, Davis said. "At first I would tell her. And I was telling her over and over," she said. "Now I just tell her he's hiking."

At the facility where Tiedemann died, Rickard met with the residents, including many who reported thoughts of suicide. "The room was filled with people who wanted to die," she said. "These people came to me to say: 'Tell me why I should still live.'"

Most suicide prevention funding targets young or middle-aged people, in part because those groups have so many years ahead of them. But it's also because of ageist attitudes that suggest such investments and interventions are not as necessary for older adults, said Jerry Reed, a nationally recognized suicide expert with the nonprofit Education Development Center. "Life at 80 is just as possible as life at 18," Reed said. "Our suicide prevention strategies need to evolve. If they don't, we're going to be losing people we don't need to lose."

Even when there are clear indications of risk, there's no consensus on the most effective way to respond. The most common responses—checking patients every 15 minutes, close observation, referring patients to psychiatric hospitals—may not be effective and may even be harmful, research shows.

But intervening can make a difference, said Eleanor Feldman Barbera, a New York psychologist who works in long-term care settings.

She recalled a 98-year-old woman who entered a local nursing home last year after suffering several falls. The transition from the home she shared with her elderly brother was difficult. When the woman developed a urinary tract infection, her condition worsened. Anxious and depressed, she told an aide she wanted to hurt herself with a knife. She was referred for psychological services and improved. Weeks later, after a transfer to a new unit, she was found in her room with the cord of a call bell around her neck.

After a brief hospitalization, she returned to the nursing home and was surrounded by increased care: a referral to a psychiatrist, extra oversight by aides and social workers, regular calls from her brother. During weekly counseling sessions, the woman now reports she feels better. Barbera considers it a victory. "She enjoys the music. She hangs out with peers. She watches what's going on," Barbera said. "She's 99 now—and she's looking toward 100."

63. Does a Year in Space Make You Older or Younger?*

SUSAN BAILEY

Daily life aboard the International Space Station moves fast. Really fast. Traveling at approximately 17,000 miles per hour, 300 miles above the Earth, astronauts watch 16 sunrises and sunsets every "day" while floating around in a box with a handful of people they depend on for survival.

One need look no further than Hollywood blockbusters like *The Martian*, *Gravity* and *Interstellar* for futuristic visions of life beyond Earth as we venture longer and deeper into outer space. But what about the human body's response to real-life spaceflight—what are the health effects? Will space travelers age at different rates than those of us on Earth? Just how adaptable to the space environment are we?

Certainly, these are concerns for NASA. How space travel and long-duration missions might change the human body, and whether those changes are permanent or reversible once astronauts return to Earth, is largely unknown. The opportunity to explore these intriguing questions arose with identical twin astronauts Scott and Mark Kelly.

In November of 2012, NASA selected astronaut Scott Kelly for its first one-year mission. At a press conference not long thereafter, it was Scott who hinted that this mission might provide the chance to compare the impact of space living on his body with his Earth-dwelling identical twin brother, Mark Kelly, who had also been an astronaut and former Navy test pilot.

Remarkably, the Kelly twins were individuals of similar "nature (genetics) and nurture (environment)," and so the perfect space experiment was conceived—featuring "space twin and Earth twin" as the stars. Scott would spend a year in space aboard the International Space Station, while his identical twin brother, Mark, would remain on Earth.

The NASA Twins Study represents the most comprehensive view of the human body's response to space flight ever conducted. Results will guide future studies and personalized approaches for evaluating health effects of individual astronauts for years to come.

As a cancer biologist at Colorado State University I study the impact of radiation

*Originally published as Susan Bailey, "Does a Year in Space Make You Older or Younger?," *The Conversation*, https://theconversation.com/does-a-year-in-space-make-you-older-or-younger-111812 (April 11, 2019). Reprinted with permission of the publisher.

exposure on human cells. As part of the Twins Study, I was particularly interested in evaluating how the ends of the chromosomes, called telomeres, were altered by a year in space.

Teasing Apart Health Effects of Space Living

NASA put out a call and selected 10 peer-reviewed investigations from around the country for the Twins Study. Studies included molecular, physiological and behavioral measures, and for the first time ever in astronauts, "omics"-based studies. Some teams evaluated the impact of space on the genome—the entire complement of DNA in a cell (genomics). Other teams examined which genes were turned on and producing a molecule called mRNA (transcriptomics). Some studies focused on how chemical modifications—which do not alter the DNA code—affected the regulation of the genes (epigenomics). Some researchers explored the proteins produced in the cells (proteomics), whereas others scrutinized the products of metabolism (metabolomics).

There were also studies examining how the space environment might alter the microbiome—the collection of bacteria, viruses and fungi that live in and on our bodies. One investigation examined the immune response to the flu vaccine. Other teams searched Scott's biological samples for biomarkers of atherosclerosis and upward fluid shifts in the body due to microgravity, which can affect vision and cause headaches. Cognitive performance was also evaluated using computer-run cognition tests specifically designed for astronauts.

More than 300 biological samples—stool, urine and blood—were collected from the twins at multiple times before, during and after the one-year mission.

The Kelly twins are without a doubt one of the most profiled pairs—on or off our planet. They are also one of the most interviewed. One question often asked is whether Scott will return from space younger than Mark—a situation reminiscent of *Interstellar* or Einstein's so-called twin paradox. However, because the ISS is not traveling anywhere near the speed of light relative to us, time dilation—or the slowing of time due to motion—is very minimal. So any age difference between the brothers would only be a few milliseconds.

Even so, the question of spaceflight-associated aging and the accompanying risk of developing age-related diseases like dementia, cardiovascular disease and cancer—during or after a mission—is an important one, and one that we aimed to address directly with our study of telomere length.

Telomeres are the ends of chromosomes that protect them from damage and from "fraying"—much like the end of a shoestring. Telomeres are critical for maintaining chromosome and genome stability. However, telomeres naturally shorten as our cells divide, and so also as we age. The rate at which telomeres shorten over time is influenced by many factors, including oxidative stress and inflammation, nutrition, physical activity, psychological stresses and environmental exposures like air pollution, UV rays and ionizing radiation. Thus, telomere length reflects an individual's genetics, experiences and exposures, and so are informative indicators of general health and aging.

Telomeres and Aging

Our study proposed that the unique stresses and out-of-this-world exposures the astronauts experience during spaceflight—things like isolation, microgravity, high carbon dioxide levels and galactic cosmic rays—would accelerate telomere shortening and aging. To test this, we evaluated telomere length in blood samples received from both twins before, during and after the one-year mission.

Scott and Mark started the study with relatively similar telomere lengths, which is consistent with a strong genetic component. Also as expected, the length of Earth-bound Mark's telomeres was relatively stable over the course of the study. But much to our surprise, Scott's telomeres were significantly longer at every time point and in every sample tested during spaceflight. That was exactly the opposite of what we expected.

Furthermore, upon Scott's return to Earth, telomere length shortened rapidly, then stabilized during the following months to near pre-flight averages. However, from the perspective of aging and risk of disease, he had many more short telomeres after spaceflight than he did before. Our challenge now is to figure out how and why such spaceflight specific shifts in telomere length dynamics are occurring.

Our findings will have relevance to earthlings as well, since we all grow old and develop age-related conditions. These Twins Study results may provide new clues into the processes involved, and thereby improve our understanding of what we might do to avoid them or extend health span.

The long-term health effects of long duration spaceflight are yet to be determined, but the Twins Study represents a landmark step in humankind's journey to the moon, Mars and beyond ... and to making science fiction science fact.

64. NASA Twins Study Reveals Health Effects of Space Flight[*]

NATIONAL INSTITUTE ON AGING

Sending one identical twin into space while the other stays behind on Earth might sound like the plot of a sci-fi thriller. But it's actually a setup for some truly fascinating scientific research.

As part of NASA's landmark Twins Study, Scott Kelly became the first U.S. astronaut to spend nearly a year in "weightless" microgravity conditions aboard the International Space Station.

Meanwhile, his identical twin, retired astronaut Mark Kelly, remained earthbound. Researchers put both men—who like all identical twins shared the same genetic makeup at birth—through the same battery of biomedical tests to gauge how the human body responds to life in space. The good news for the future of space travel is that the results indicated that health is "mostly sustained" during a prolonged stay in space.

Reporting in the journal *Science*, the Twins Study team, which included several NIH-funded researchers, detailed many thousands of differences between the Kelly twins at the molecular, cellular, and physiological levels during the 340-day observation period. However, most of Scott's measures returned to near pre-flight levels within six months of rejoining Mark on Earth.

Over the past nearly 60 years, 559 people have flown in space. While weightless conditions are known to speed various processes associated with aging, few astronauts have remained in space for more than a few months at a time. With up to three-year missions to the moon or Mars planned for the future, researchers want to get a better sense of how the human body will hold up under microgravity conditions for longer periods.

To get a more holistic answer, researchers collected a variety of biological samples from the Kelly twins before, during, and after Scott's spaceflight. All told, more than 300 samples were collected over the course of 27 months.

Multiple labs around the country used state-of-the art tools to examine those samples in essentially every way they could think of doing. Those analyses offer a remarkably detailed view of changes in an astronaut's biology and health while in space.

---

*Originally published as National Institute on Aging, "NASA Twins Study Reveals Health Effects of Space Flight," https://www.nia.nih.gov/news/nasa-twins-study-reveals-health-effects-space-flight (May 3, 2019).

With so much data, there were lots of interesting findings to report, including many changes in the expression of Scott's genes that weren't observed in his twin. While most of these changes returned to preflight levels within six months of Scott's return to Earth, about 7 percent of his genes continued to be expressed at different levels. These included some related to DNA repair and the immune system.

Despite those changes in immunity-related gene expression, his immune system appeared to remain fully functional. His body responded to the flu vaccine administered in space just as would be expected back home on Earth.

Scott also had some measurable changes in telomeres—complexes of specialized DNA sequences, RNA, and protein that protect the tips of our chromosomes. These generally shorten a bit each time cells divide. But during the time in space, the telomeres in Scott's white blood cells measured out at somewhat greater length.

Potentially, this is because some of his stem cells, which are younger and haven't gone through as many cell divisions, were being released into the blood. Back on Earth, his telomere lengths returned to an average length within six months of his return. Over the course of the study, the earthbound telomeres of his twin brother Mark remained stable.

Researchers also uncovered small but significant changes to Scott's gut microbiome, the collection of microbes that play important roles in digestion and the immune system. More specifically, there was a shift in the ratio of two major groups of bacteria. Once back on Earth, his microbiome quickly shifted back to its original preflight state.

The data also provided some metabolic evidence suggesting that Scott's mitochondria, the cellular powerhouses that supply the body with energy, weren't functioning at full capacity in space. While further study is needed, the NIH-funded team led by Kumar Sharma, University of Texas Health Science Center, San Antonio, suggests that changes in the mitochondria might underlie changes often seen in space to the human cardiovascular system, kidneys, and eyes.

Of course, such a small, two-person study makes it hard to draw any general conclusions about human health in space. But the comparisons certainly help to point us in the right direction. They provide a framework for understanding how the human body responds on a molecular and cellular level to microgravity over time. They also may hold important lessons for understanding human health and precision medicine down here on Earth.

I look forward to future space missions and their contributions to biomedical research. I'm also happy to report, it will be a short wait.

In 2018, I highlighted the Tissue Chips in Space Initiative. It's a unique collaboration between NIH and NASA in which dozens of human tissue chips—tiny, 3D devices bioengineered to model different tissues and organs—will be sent to the International Space Station to study the accelerated aging that occurs in space.

The first tissue chips were sent to the International Space Station last December 2018. And I'm pleased to report that more will be aboard the SpaceX Dragon cargo spacecraft, now rescheduled to lift off no earlier than May 3, 2018, from Cape Canaveral Air Force Station in Florida. The spacecraft will be on a resupply run to the International Space Station, and the astronauts there will offload miniaturized tissue chips of the lungs, bone marrow, and kidneys, enabling more truly unique science in low gravity that couldn't be performed down here on Earth.

Reference

Garrett-Bakelman, F.E., Darshi, M., Green, S.J., Gur, R.C., Lin, L., Macias, B.R., et al. "The NASA Twins Study: A Multidimensional Analysis of a Year-Long Human Spaceflight." *Science* 2019 Apr 12; 364(6436).

65. State Revenues and the Aging Population[*]

KATHERINE BARRETT *and* RICHARD GREENE

A few years ago, *The State*, a South Carolina newspaper, ran an article titled, "SC Bracing for Cost of Aging Population." It would be reasonably easy to find similar commentary for almost all 50 states, as governors and legislators recognize that healthcare costs—notably from an aging inmate population in state prisons—are growing higher and higher. Indeed, the over-85 population is one of the fastest growing segments of society.

What set this article apart from most was that it recognized that the aging population hits states' finances from two directions at once. Not only are older people likely to need more services, especially healthcare; they also are inclined to bring in smaller amounts of revenue dollars, largely because their earned incomes tend to decline. Equally important, many states have tax laws that do not fully cover income from Social Security or pensions. This issue is growing in significance as the makeup of the population shifts. The number of U.S. residents over 65 is anticipated to grow by one-third over the next 15 years, according to the Census Bureau.

While we were doing research for the Council of State Governments, Susan Brower, state demographer from Minnesota, told us, "I don't think that people think about the revenue side of aging very often. But, it's an issue that's straightforward in terms of what we can expect. And, it is politically charged." One reason this phenomenon often goes unnoticed is that few states calculate their budgets for more than one or two years out; the impact on revenues of aging does not make itself clear as it is a long-term proposition.

As *The State* article pointed out, "Residents age 85 and older, for example, are exempt from one cent on the dollar of the state's sales tax. In addition, taxpayers age 65 and older can exempt $15,000 from state income taxes."

The impact does not just come from exemptions, but from the simple fact that older people spend less. Alison Felix, vice president of the Federal Reserve Bank in Kansas City's Denver Branch, co-wrote a paper that explained: "On average, spending by those

*Originally published as Katherine Barrett and Richard Greene, "State Revenues and the Aging Population," *PA Times*, https://patimes.org/state-revenues-aging-population/ (June 13, 2017). Reprinted with permission of the publisher.

younger than 25 and those older than 75 was slightly more than half of that of middle-aged consumers." If the U.S. population in 2011 already had the age composition projected for 2030, the total of state tax revenues would have been lower by $8.1 billion, according to Felix's calculations.

Of course, the underlying statutes that create tax-free income for older Americans vary from state to state. A few examples from the National Conference of State Legislatures' summary of state personal income taxes on retirement income in tax year 2014 are as follows:

In Missouri, residents age 62 and older get a 100 percent exclusion on income that comes from state and local pension plans. The first $6,000 of private pensions are not taxed. Some income limits apply and the amount free from taxation is capped at $36,442 per spouse.

Regardless of whether the income comes from pensions or Social Security, Virginia "provides individual taxpayers age 75 or older a deduction of up to $12,000 ($24,000 for married couples filing jointly). For taxpayers age 65–74, the $12,000 deduction is reduced and phased out at higher income levels, beginning at $50,000 for single taxpayers."

A rather extreme example to be sure, Mississippi provides a full exemption for money that comes in from Social Security and from almost all pension plans.

Other factors are at play, too. It is well documented that some states are leaning ever more steadily on so-called "sin taxes" to balance their budgets. But older Americans tend to smoke, drink and gamble less than their younger counterparts. So, as the older population grows, the revenues from these sources will shrink.

Of course, states that tax the majority of income from pensions and Social Security may be wary of initiating new exemptions. One example is Minnesota, a state that has provided minimal exemptions. Yet the pressure to cut taxes thus far has seemed to outweigh the pressure to raise taxes on pensions, particularly military ones.

What are states supposed to do when their budgets are tight and millions of dollars in potential revenues are forgone? The simple, honest answer: very little. Older citizens tend to vote. Even a gradual increase in the taxes they pay on Social Security or pensions is the kind of thing that tends to upset people when it is time for election day.

Appendices

A. Glossary of Senior Care and Services*

ALAN R. ROPER

Accelerated death benefits: Pre-death benefits from a life insurance company to a terminally ill policy holder

Activities of daily living: Activities normally associated with the day-to-day personal care, such as personal hygiene, using a toilet/continence, dressing, cooking, eating and taking one's medication.

Administration on Aging (AoA): The AoA is a division of the Department of Health and Human Services. This Federal agency is dedicated to promoting matters of interest for older people and their caregivers. The AoA works under the auspices of the Aging Services Network to develop the most effective system of home and community-based long-term care, drawing on locally based service providers.

Adult day care: A daytime program for functionally impaired adults that provides a variety of social and related support services in a protective setting.

Adult day health care: A daytime program for functionally impaired adults that provides a variety of social, medical and related support services in a protective setting.

Advance directive (AD): There are various forms of an advance directive, though the two most common forms are (1) a living will and (2) a durable power of attorney for health care.

Aging in place: Aging in place refers to the senior continuing to age in the home of their choice versus taking up residence in a senior health care facility. This choice indicates that they can have all their needs met, through a blend of their own efforts and those of caregivers, professional and/or nonprofessional.

Aid & Attendance: A type of pension program for wartime veterans

Alzheimer's Disease: There is much confusion among those both inside as well as outside the scientific community concerning the precise distinction between Alzheimer's and dementia. However, though the two terms are often used interchangeably, Alzheimer's is a specific form of or cause of dementia but, unlike certain forms of dementia, is not curable. The chief symptoms of Alzheimer's involve its effects on the parts of the brain that control thought, memory, and language.

Americans with Disabilities Act (ADA): Passed by Congress in 1980, this law

---

*Published with permission of the author.

275

establishes a clear and comprehensive prohibition of discrimination on the basis of disability. Resources: Wikipedia: Americans with Disabilities Act.

Assisted living: A supportive housing facility designed for those who need extra help in their day-to-day lives but who do not require the 24-hour skilled nursing care found in traditional nursing homes.

At home care: Medical care provided to seniors in their place of residence other than in an assisted living or skilled nursing facility. A level of care in which the patient has healthcare issues but, with the assistance of a family member or friend or some other trusted person (i.e., a person who does not need professional training) can manage daily activities such as ensuring medications are taken, meals eaten, etc.

BID (meaning two times per day): As seen on a prescription bottle, BID (alternatively b.i.d. or bid) is an abbreviation of the Latin "bis in die" meaning "two times a day," referring to the number of doses the patient should be given of that medication per day.

Care Allowance Plan: A type of long-term care insurance benefit in which the insurance company pays out a set dollar amount for care on a daily, monthly or annual basis instead of paying for the actual cost of care.

Cash surrender value: The cash value of a life insurance policy were the policy holder to terminate the contract and resell the agreement to the insurance company.

CHAMPVA: Civilian Health and Medical Program of the Department of Veterans Affairs, a medical insurance programs for veterans' families.

CHAMPVA for Life: An extension of CHAMPVA benefits for individuals over 65.

Companion living: Companion living, within an assisted living facility, involves two unrelated people of the same sex sharing a suite, whether in independent living, assisted living, or memory care. This option is meant to encourage socialization, increase the sense of personal security, and to contribute to happier and healthier residents, while also allowing these residents to save money by sharing expenses.

Conservator: A conservator is the legally appointed representative of an individual (a conservatee) who has been deemed incapable of managing their own financial affairs and, in some cases, their own personal affairs as well. By personal affairs is meant the issues of day-to-day living including healthcare and living arrangements. The process of appointment begins with a petition, produced by a friend or relative of the individual in question, to the local superior court.

Continuing care contract: Is a continuing care retirement communities contract that restricts the total number of days one can receive care. Should the senior require additional care, it can be purchased at the time for a discounted rate.

Continuing care retirement communities: A community that provides a continuum of care, from private residences to assisted living and skilled nursing care. These are designed for individuals that want to remain in a single location for senior years and for seniors with declining conditions.

Continuum of care: A full spectrum of care available at continuing care retirement communities which may include independent living, assisted living, nursing care, home health, home care, and home and community based services.

Custodial care: Care primarily for meeting personal needs such as assistance in bathing, dressing, eating or taking medicine which can be provided by someone without medical training.

Death benefit loans: A loan from a life insurance company to a policy holder that is secured by the death benefits.

Dementia: While frequently confused with Alzheimer's (even by doctors), dementia is a general term for a range of mental impairments that can be caused by numerous ailments including Alzheimer's, Huntington's Disease, Parkinson's Disease, and Creutzfeldt-Jakob disease.

DME (durable medical equipment): DME refers to equipment or devices that would be used by seniors (as well as others) who are still able to reside in their homes but require medical aids to do so. Medicare, or one's insurance policy, will cover, all or in part, many such items. Among the dozens of items that may be covered are: Air cleaners, air conditioners, bathtub lifts and/or seats, blood glucose monitors, continuous passive motion devices, disposable sheets and bags, electric hospital beds, grab bars, nebulizers, portable room heaters, rolling chairs, respirators. Check with your insurance provider to see what they would cover.

DNR (do not resuscitate order): A legal directive stating that no attempt to revive the patient should be attempted. Ideally, the patient created this document at the same time as their will. If the patient enters the hospital before creating such a directive, s/he can ask the attending physician to write such a document and attach it to that patient's chart. If the patient fails to do this and then becomes incapable of providing direction, then a spokesperson that the patient appointed or, failing that, a family friend or a relative may be allowed to agree to a DNR for that patient.

Doll therapy: A form of Alzheimer's therapy where patients can use dolls that symbolize people.

Durable power of attorney: Designates any proficient adult(s) to see to an individual's affairs should they become either mentally or physically incapacitated. It is imperative to keep good, clear records of such agreements and recommended that you have a lawyer draft any durable power of attorney.

The Eden Alternative: This international non-profit 501(c)3 organization was founded by Dr. William Thomas in the early 1990s. The goal was to take existing assisted living facilities and nursing homes and make them over into a positive new type of senior housing that generates, encourages, and then maintains the highest quality of life for elders, and in which elders are treated as still-valuable people.

Elimination period: The number of days an individual must hold a long-term care policy before benefits can begin.

Emergency medical services (EMS): (aka paramedic services or ambulance services). All these terms refer to the emergency medical treatment (by paramedics) and, when necessary, the transport (by ambulance service professionals) applied to those who have experienced a possibly life-threatening health situation following events like a car accident or an explosion.

Extended congregate care (ECC): ECC is a relatively recent development in the realm of assisted living facilities. When independent living is no longer an option, but full-fledged assisted living would be excessive, residents can select this transitional level, which allows them to continue to reside in their own homes/separate living quarters, while also sharing one or more meals a day in a communal setting, and to benefit from services and activities similar to those found in assisted living.

Fannie Mae home keeper: A type of reverse mortgage that is now obsolete.

Fee-for-service contract: A continuing care retirement communities contract that requires residents to pay separately for their residential and medical costs.

Front wheeled walker: A four-legged walker with the two rear legs having rubber-capped feet while the two front legs each have a wheel. The wheels result in improved stability, allowing the person using it to move more smoothly and easily, over even or rough terrain. Like other four-legged walkers, this can include a seat, permitting the user to either stand and push the walker or propel it forward while seated.

Full Code (FC): The term refers to the permission given to the attending physician to do whatever is required to prolong the life of a given patient, a patient who is no longer able to make decisions for himself.

Geriatric: Can either refer to an elderly person, or anything related to the elderly, in particular healthcare for the elderly.

Geriatric assessment: A comprehensive assessment of an older person's health, social and financial needs with the goal of improving the overall quality of life.

Geriatric care manager: A healthcare professional who helps an elderly individual and his or her family members identify the individuals physical and mental needs and finds way to meet those needs. Learn more about geriatric care managers here.

Geriatric research studies: Scientific studies that examine issues related to aging and the elderly. Learn more about the Abramson Center's geriatric research studies here.

HCBS (Home and Community Based Services): assistance provided to persons in their homes or communities instead of in nursing homes. Term is commonly used by Medicaid programs.

HMO (health maintenance organization): While there are several types of health care plans, one of the most popular is the prepaid HMO. Basically, HMO coverage applies only when a subscriber agrees to use the specified doctors and facilities the HMO includes. These doctors agree to charge a reduced fee to the subscribers of the HMO in exchange for their best medical care.

Home equity sharing programs: An agreement in which a homeowner receives a cash payment today in exchange for some percentage of their home equity in the future.

Home health aide: A healthcare professional who provides in-home care to those with issues such as chronic illnesses or age-related problems.

Hospice: A care program that alleviates the symptoms but does not cure the underlying cause provided to dying persons and their families, in the form of physical, psychological, social and spiritual care.

Hospice care: The support given to terminally ill patients who wish to, and can (with adequate support), remain in their homes versus entering a hospital, though a hospital- or clinic-stay may be required to treat a specific condition.

Housebound: A type of pension program for wartime veterans.

Improved pension program: A type of pension program for wartime veterans

In home care: A level of care in which the patient has health care issues but, with the assistance of a family member or friend or some other trusted person (i.e., a person who does not need professional training) to assist with daily activities and ensure medications are taken, meals eaten, etc., the patient can continue to reside safely in their own home.

Income cap trust: A legal document required by some state governments when a Medicaid applicant has more than the maximum amount of qualifying income (as of 2017 $2,205 per month).

IND (independent care, congregate housing, or retirement living): Suitable for seniors who are active, mentally and physically, able to care for themselves, and who want to have their own home but as part of a community.

Independent living: Communities, typically of single-family homes or townhomes for self-sufficient seniors that want the security and social activities of a community living environment.

Instrumental activities of daily living (IADL): ADLs relate to basic abilities like dressing one's self and performing basic hygiene. IADLs refers to more advanced and complicated tasks like balancing a checkbook, grocery shopping, meal preparation, driving, or taking public transportation.

Intermediate care facility (ICF): A health care facility catering to those with mental or physical issues that require constant care. Not considered a medical facility by the government, the payment source falls under Medicaid and private pay rather than Medicare. While state regulations do vary, federal regulations do require that each ICF have a registered nurse as the director of nursing, with a licensed nurse on duty at least eight hours of each day.

Jumbo reverse mortgage: A type of reverse mortgage for high value homes.

Life care contract: A type of continuing care retirement communities contract in which all long-term care costs are covered with no additional fees.

Life settlement: The sale, by the policyholder, of his life insurance to a third party in exchange for a lump sum of cash.

Living will: A written, legal document that states the wishes of an individual regarding life saving devices and procedures in the event of a terminal illness or injury and is no longer competent and able to make decisions on their own.

LMH (limited mental health): LMH refers to the certification required for all staff, including administrators and managers, who work in a facility that houses at least three mental health patients, and that applies to those staff members who will have contact with any or all of those patients. The certification process varies from state to state, but generally involves a minimum of three hours of training, with continuing education required every two years.

Long-term care insurance: LTC insurance may be helpful in defraying the costs of long-term health care, but may not be a worthwhile purchase unless the applicant has assets with a net worth greater than $150,000. Those with assets valued at less than $150,000 will generally be able to rely on Medicaid once funds are depleted to pay the balance due on their long-term care and thus avoid paying the high premiums required for LTC. If you have any doubts or questions about this issue, contact Medicaid or an eldercare attorney.

Look back penalty: In an attempt to gain eligibility, some seniors transfer their financial assets to other family members. To discourage this activity, Medicaid considers "lookback" asset transfers as far as five years previous.

Managed care: "Managed" is the key term, as in being thoroughly organized. This approach to health care is predicated on the coordination of the actions of all caregivers (whether professional or nonprofessional) involved in the care of a given senior.

Medicaid: Created in 1965, Medicaid is a U.S.-based social health care program providing low to no-cost health care, as well as long-term care, to families and individuals, regardless of age, with limited income and resources. It is funded by both the federal government and the states, but it is left up to each state to create its own regulations as to eligibility and appropriate benefits.

Medicaid gap: If a senior's assets are greater than the Medicaid eligibility requirement, but are less than the monthly cost of long term care, the senior falls into this category.

Medical director: A physician who operates as, in effect, chief of the medical staff in a hospital. This person's responsibilities include overseeing all matters both medical and administrative, and possibly acting as liaison for the medical staff with top management.

Medicare: Created in 1965 by President Lyndon Johnson, Medicare is a health insurance program funded strictly by the federal government (not, like Medicaid, also by the states). Medicare covers people who are 65 or older, some younger people with disabilities, and people with End-Stage Renal Disease (permanent kidney failure requiring dialysis or a transplant, sometimes called ESRD).

Medicare saving program: A series of programs designed to help financially needy seniors who are not eligible for Medicaid with the cost of co-pays, premiums and care.

Medicare supplemental insurance: Sometimes referred to as Medigap plans, this insurance may extend Medicare benefits.

Medication management, aka medication administration: These terms both apply to the method employed (whether by a professional nurse, a nonprofessional caregiver, or the patient himself, in either senior housing or the patient's home) to ensure that everyone involved knows which medications (whether prescription, over-the-counter, or herbal supplements) are to be taken by the patient, and that each is taken at the prescribed time and in the correct amount.

Military retiree: A "retired" member of the military is someone who has 20 years of service. All military retirees are veterans but not all veterans are military retirees.

Mortgage insurance premium: A special type of insurance required for reverse mortgages borrowers that provides additional consumer protections.

NOC (nocturnal, at night or needing night care): Meaning nocturnal, the term NOC is used in a variety of ways. A NOC nurse would be the nurse who is on shift at night. You will see this term most often in charting and physician orders.

Occupational therapy (OT): Occupational therapy involves the assessment of an individual's physical state and capabilities. The goal is to maintain the patient's maximum degree of independence, given that person's current limitations.

Older Americans Act of 1965: Enacted by Lyndon B. Johnson on July 14, 1965, this was the first ever U.S. federal-level initiative geared to protect the interests of seniors by creating the National Aging Network. The NAN is comprised of a three-tier network of agencies: (1) the federal Administration on Aging, (2) state units on aging, and (3) local level agencies on aging.

Ombudsman: An ombudsman (from a Scandinavian term meaning "representative") is an impartial individual who investigates complaints and then resolves disputes between two parties. For the purposes of this glossary, we will consider, specifically, eldercare, or long-term care, ombudsmen. The Older Americans Act requires each state to support an ombudsmen program. If a resident of a board-and-care home, a nursing home, or an assisted living facility raises a complaint with the management of their home but fails to achieve resolution, they, or whoever advocates for them, can go online, typing in the term "eldercare ombudsman" followed by the name of the state in which the facility is located.

Origination fee: A fee charged by a lender in loan transaction that covers the lender's expenses and margin.

PACE (Program of All Inclusive Care for the Elderly): a comprehensive care program offered by Medicare.

Palliative care: A care program that alleviates the symptoms but does not cure the underlying cause, usually provided to dying patients.

PCP (primary care provider): This term refers to the doctor who oversees a patient's everyday healthcare needs. If required by the patient's Medicare insurance plan, the PCP must be consulted by the patient for a referral before that patient can make an appointment with another doctor or specialist. If the PCP denies the validity of the request, should the patient make an appointment with that other doctor or specialist, Medicare disavows all responsibility for the resulting charges, meaning the patient is solely responsible for the resulting charges.

PERS (personal emergency response system): An alarm system a private person can purchase and install in his home. More commonly marketed as a medical alert system (as seen in the "I've fallen and I can't get up!" television commercials), these systems can be adapted to both landline (preferred, for overall reliability and clarity of information transmission) and cell phone.

Personal care aides: Individuals that provide custodial care, or non-medical care, in a senior's place of residence.

Personal care services: The services performed by health care workers in assisting their patients in basic, everyday activities which the patient can no longer accomplish alone. Such services would include, but are not limited to, meal preparation, bathing, dressing, getting to and from appointments, and shopping.

Physical therapy/therapist (PT): While anyone of any age could theoretically benefit from the attentions of a PT, seniors specifically require the skills of a PT to recover from injuries or surgeries or following a stroke. The PT, likely advised by an occupational therapist (see OT), will assist their patient in the prescribed exercises, coach them in proper use of equipment and provide other advice so that the patient may improve, possibly even regaining their former physical abilities.

PPO (preferred provider organization): A popular form of membership-based health insurance, this type of healthcare (aka participating provider organization or preferred provider option) employs financial incentives to encourage the insured to use a specific network of doctors, laboratories, and hospitals medical staff. Though the premiums for PPO coverage are often higher than those of an HMO (heath maintenance organization) and the insured is somewhat restricted in his medical choices, it may result in more flexibility for the insured. (See HMO, above.)

Priority group: One of eight groups into which all veterans are assigned based on disabilities, assets and other factors. These are major determining factors in what health benefits the veteran receives.

Progressive neurological condition: Any of a number of conditions in which the patient has progressively advancing symptoms such as Alzheimer's or dementia.

q.h. (every hour): As seen on a prescription bottle, q.h. is derived from the Latin quaque (every) and hora (hour). E.g., if the prescription reads, "2 caps q3h" that means the patient is to take two capsules every three hours.

QID (meaning four times per day): As seen on a prescription bottle, QID (alternatively q.i.d. or qid) is an abbreviation of the Latin "quater in die" meaning "four times a day," referring to the number of doses the patient should be given of that medication per day.

Qualified Disabled & Working Individuals (QDWI): One of several programs designed to help financially needy seniors who are not eligible for Medicaid with the cost of co-pays, premiums and care.

Qualified Medicare Beneficiary (QMB): one of several programs designed to help financially needy seniors who are not eligible for Medicaid with the cost of co-pays, premiums and care.

Qualifying Individual (QI): one of several programs designed to help financially needy seniors who are not eligible for Medicaid with the cost of co-pays, premiums and care.

Reminiscence therapy: This therapy has proven effective in engendering a sense of comforting security, belonging, and empowerment to those suffering Alzheimer's or dementia. Stimulating memories of positive episodes and happier times from times past can be achieved through various mediums including those of sight, sound, smell, and taste.

Residential care facility (RCF): A facility that provides custodial, but not medical, care to persons who, because of physical, mental, or emotional disorders, are not able to live independently. RCFs can be known by other names. For instance, if there are 16 or more beds onsite, the facility may be termed an assisted care facility. If there are only four to six beds onsite, it could be termed "board and care."

Respiratory therapy (RT): The first step in RT is the identification of the causes and effects of a patient's breathing issues so as to arrive at the most effective treatments for that patient. The recommendations could include, among other things, smoking cessation, prescribed exercises, advice as to inhalers, nebulizers, oxygen, or CPAP and BIPAP (both non-invasive forms of advanced ventilation therapy).

Respite care: Respite care is designed to provide temporary relief for those who have the responsibility of caring for a senior family member. It is known that providing such care may result in increasing the caregiver's fatigue and anxiety, impairing the caregiver's ability to function effectively. Respite care, whether in-home or in a social day group, adult day care facility, or in the form of emergency respite care, can improve the quality of life for all involved.

Reverse Mortgage: A loan with high levels of consumer protection for seniors, secured by their home equity, in which the lender makes payments to the homeowner.

Section 8 rental certificates: A type of government assisted housing.

Section 202 housing: A type of government assisted housing.

Senior apartment: A form of senior housing for those still able to live independently and (at least generally) do not require food or transportation services. It involves a multi-unit housing situation with individual apartments for the residents.

Senior move manager: Should one eventually decide it is better to leave one's home and move into senior housing (whether assisted living, a nursing home, or one of the many alternatives), one should consider hiring an objective but sympathetic and trained senior move manager to plan and execute the move. A senior move manager would be responsible for everything from coordinating with the senior (or someone acting for the senior), assisting in downsizing decisions, fully choreographing the move, and helping to set up and decorate the new home.

Service-connected disability: A disability incurred by a veteran that was in some way connected to his time in service.

Short-term stay: A stay in an assisted living facility or nursing home may be advisable when a loved one is recovering from an accident or surgery, or as a form of respite care.

Skilled care: Care ordered by a physician that requires the medical knowledge or technical training of a licensed healthcare professional, or both.

Skilled nursing facilities: A residential home for seniors in which care is provided by licensed healthcare professionals.

Specified low-income Medicare beneficiary: One of several programs designed to help financially needy seniors who are not eligible for Medicaid with the cost of co-pays, premiums and care.

Speech therapy (ST): Therapy applied to those suffering from speech or communication impediments, the specific mode of treatment dependent on that patient's needs. In the case of a senior, this could refer to their need for assistance to regain or refine their power of speech following a stroke, a head injury following a fall, or while dealing with dementia.

Spend down: The process by which a senior will deplete all his assets on care until the assets are depleted sufficiently to qualify for Medicaid.

Telehealth: An innovative approach to healthcare intended to streamline the healthcare process, making it more efficient, cost-effective, and more effective overall while reducing stress for the patient, caregivers, family and friends.

Telemedicine: A remote (vs. in the doctor's office or in a hospital setting) method of delivering medical care using the latest technology including landlines, cell phones, and the internet. (See also Telehealth.)

TID: As seen on a prescription bottle, TID (alternatively t.i.d. or tid) is an abbreviation of the Latin "ter in die" meaning "three times a day," referring to the number of doses the patient should be given of that medication per day.

TMC (transitional memory care): TMC is a relatively new level of care within assisted living facilities and is meant to ease a senior's journey from assisted living into a memory care unit, a move that many seniors have found painful, causing them, as well as their loved ones, enormous stress. TMC is recommended, then, for those seniors have begun to exhibit indications of possible early stage dementias or Alzheimer's. TMC not only makes the shift easier but delays it as long as possible. The TMC staff offers appropriate support, activities and opportunities to socialize. Along those lines, it is common for management to match this resident up with a carefully chosen roommate, the two of them offering support and friendship to each other.

TRICARE: A medical insurance program for military retirees and their families.

TRICARE for Life: An extension of the TRICARE program for individuals over 65.

University-based retirement community (UBRC): A relatively new form of senior housing that is rapidly expanding in popularity, this alternative to traditional independent or assisted living facilities provides the retiree with easy access to educational and cultural opportunities as well as to a generally stimulating living situation. It has been shown that both retirees and college students benefit from sharing such an arrangement.

Viatical settlement: The sale, by a terminally ill policyholder, of their life insurance to a third party in exchange for a lump sum of cash.

Wartime Veterans: Veterans who served at least 90 days at least one of which was during the wartime dates below, but not necessarily in combat.

World War II: Dec 7, 1941—Dec 31, 1946
Korean War: Jun 27, 1950–Jan 31, 1955
Vietnam War: Aug 5, 1964–May 7, 1975
Gulf War: Aug 2, 1990–Undetermined

B. Older Americans Month[*]

Profile America Facts for Features

U.S. Census Bureau

Older Americans Month: May 2017

After a meeting with the National Council of Senior Citizens, President John F. Kennedy encouraged all Americans to pay tribute to older people across the country by designating May 1963 as Senior Citizens Month. Every president since has issued a formal proclamation during or before the month of May in support of older Americans. In 1980, President Jimmy Carter issued a proclamation changing the name of this observance to Older Americans Month. This month continues to be a time to celebrate the age 65 and older population through ceremonies, events and public recognition.

Population

47.8 million: The number of people age 65 and older in the United States on July 1, 2015. This group accounted for 14.9 percent of the total population. The age 65 and older population grew 1.6 million from 2014. Source: Vintage 2015 Population Estimates (ww.factfinder.census.gov/faces/tableservices/jsf/pages/productview.xhtml?pid=PEP_2015_PEPAGESEX&prodType=table).

98.2 million: The projected population of people age 65 and older in 2060. People in this age group will comprise nearly one in four U.S. residents. Of this number, 19.7 million will be age 85 or older. Source: 2014 National Population Projections, Table 3 (www.census.gov/population/projections/data/national/2014/summarytables.html).

Income and Poverty

$38,515: The median income of households with householders age 65 and older in 2015. Source: Income and Poverty in the United States: 2015, Table 1 (www.census.gov/content/dam/Census/library/publications/2016/demo/p60–256.pdf).

---

*Originally published as U.S. Census Bureau, "Older Americans Month: Profile America Facts for Features," https://www.census.gov/content/dam/Census/newsroom/facts-for-features/2017/cb17-ff08.pdf (March 27, 2017).

8.8 percent: The percentage of people age 65 and older in poverty in 2015, down from 10.0 percent in 2014. Source: Income and Poverty in the United States: 2015, Table 3 (www.census.gov/content/dam/Census/library/publications/2016/demo/p60–256.pdf).

$170,516: The median net worth for householders age 65 and older in 2011. Source: Survey of Income and Program Participation, Net Worth and Asset Ownership of Households: 2011 (www.census.gov/people/wealth).

13.7 percent: The supplemental poverty rate for those age 65 or older, equating to 6.5 million people in 2015. Excluding Social Security from income would more than triple the poverty rate for this group. Source: The Supplemental Poverty Measure: 2015, Table 2 (www.census.gov/library/publications/2016/demo/p60–258.html).

Serving Our Nation

9.3 million: The estimated number of U.S. veterans age 65 and older in 2015. Source: 2015 American Community Survey, Table B21001 (www.factfinder.census.gov/faces/tableservices/jsf/pages/productview.xhtml?pid=ACS_15_1YR_B21001).

Jobs

4.6 million: The number of men age 65 and older in the labor force in 2015. There were 3.7 million women age 65 and older in the labor force in 2015. Source: 2015 American Community Survey, Table B23001 (www.factfinder.census.gov/faces/tableservices/jsf/pages/productview.xhtml?pid=ACS_15_1YR_B23001&prodType=table).

5.3 million: The number of full-time, year-round workers age 65 and older with earnings in 2015. Source: Current Population Survey, Historical Income Tables: People, Table P-32 (www.census.gov/data/tables /time-series/demo/income-poverty/historical-income-people.html).

Business Owners

15.6 percent: The estimated percentage of business owners in respondent firms with and without paid employees in 2012 who were age 65 and older. Source: 2012 Survey of Business Owners, Table SB1200CSCBO08 (www.factfinder.census.gov/faces/tableservices/jsf/pages/productview.xhtml?pid=SBO_2012_00CSCBO08&prodType=table).

13.2 percent: The estimated percentage of women business owners in respondent firms with and without paid employees in 2012 who were age 65 and older. Source: 2012 Survey of Business Owners, Table SB1200CSCBO08 (www.factfinder.census.gov/faces/tableservices/jsf/pages/productview.xhtml?pid=SBO_2012_00CSCBO08&prodType=table).

Education

82.8 percent: The percentage of the population age 65 and older in 2015 who had completed high school or higher education. Source: 2015 American Community Survey, Table S1501 (www.factfinder.census.gov/bkmk/table/1.0/en/ACS/15_1YR/S1501).

25.8 percent: The percentage of the population age 65 and older in 2015 who had earned a bachelor's degree or higher. Source: 2015 American Community Survey, Table S1501 (www.factfinder.census.gov/bkmk/table/1.0/en/ACS/15_1YR/S1501).

Marital Status and Living Arrangements

57.8 percent: The percentage of the population age 65 and older in 2016 who are married. Source: Families and Living Arrangements: 2016, Table A1 (www.census.gov/hhes/families/data/cps2016A.html).

24 percent: The percentage of the population age 65 and older in 2016 who are widowed. Source: Families and Living Arrangements: 2016, Table A1 (www.census.gov/hhes/families/data/cps2016A.html).

Computer and Internet Use

35.3 million: The number of responders age 65 and older who reported living in homes with computers in 2015. This is an increase from 2014 (32.9 million). Additionally, 30.9 million accessed the internet through a high-speed internet connection in 2015, up from 28.8 million in 2014. Source: 2015 American Community Survey, Table B28005 (www.factfinder.census.gov/faces/tableservices/jsf/pages/productview.xhtml?pid=ACS_15_1YR_B28005&prodType=table).

Voting

59.4 percent: The percentage of citizens age 65 and older who reported casting a ballot in the 2014 elections. Source: Voting and Registration in the Election of November 2014, Table 2 (www2.census.gov/programs-surveys/cps/tables/p20/577/table02_1.xls).

Homeownership

79.5 percent: The percentage of householders age 65 and older who owned their homes as of fourth quarter 2016. Source: Current Population Survey/Housing Vacancy Survey, Historical Table 19 (www.census.gov/housing/hvs/data/histtabs.html).

Services for the Older Population

4,815: The number of continuing care retirement communities in 2012. These businesses employed 423,627 people and generated $27.6 billion in revenues. In 2007, there were 5,373 such establishments, employing 416,402 people and generating $24.7 billion in revenues. These establishments provide a range of residential and personal care services with on-site nursing care facilities for the elderly and other people who are unable to care for themselves, and the elderly and other people who do not desire to live independently. Individuals live in a variety of residential settings with meals, housekeeping, social, leisure and other services available to assist residents in daily living. Source: 2012 Economic Census Geographic Area Series, Table EC1200CCOMP1 (www.factfinder.census.gov/faces/tableservices/jsf/pages/productview.xhtml?pid=ECN_2012_U.S._00CCOMP1&prodType=table).

25,964: The number of business establishments providing services for the elderly and people with disabilities in 2012. These businesses employed 901,359 people and generated $34.1 billion in revenues. In 2007, there were 20,433 such establishments, employing 621,545 people and generating $25.3 billion in revenues. These establishments provide nonresidential social assistance services to improve the quality of life for the elderly, persons diagnosed with intellectual and developmental disabilities, or persons with disabilities. Senior citizens centers are among the establishments in this industry. Source: 2012 Economic Census Geographic Area Series, Table EC1200CCOMP1 (www.factfinder. census.gov/faces/tableservices/jsf/pages/productview.xhtml?pid=ECN_2012_U.S._00 CCOMP1&prodType=table).

Geography

19.4 percent: The percentage of Florida's population age 65 and older in 2015, followed by Maine (18.8 percent). Alaska had the lowest percentage (9.9 percent) followed by Utah (10.3 percent). Source: Vintage 2015 Population Estimates (www.census.gov/ newsroom/press-releases/2016/cb16–107.html).

54.8 percent: The percentage of the population in Sumter, Fla., age 65 and older in 2015, which led all of the nation's counties. Source: Vintage 2015 Population Estimates (www.census.gov/newsroom/press-releases/2016/cb16–107.html).

118,891: The estimated population of The Villages, Fla., metro area on July 1, 2015. The Villages, a metro area located to the west of the Orlando metro area, was the nation's fastest-growing metro area between July 1, 2014, and July 1, 2015, with its population increasing by 4.3 percent. The metro area is home to one of the largest age-restricted retirement communities in the world. Source: Vintage 2015 Population Estimates (www. census.gov/newsroom/press-releases/2016/cb16-43.html, www.factfinder.census.gov/ faces/tableservices/jsf/pages/productview.xhtml?src=bkmk).

Centenarians

53,364: The number of people age 100 and older counted by the 2010 Census. In 2010, over half (62.5 percent) of the 53,364 centenarians were age 100 or 101. Source: Centenarians: 2010, Figure 1 (www.census.gov/prod/cen2010/reports/c2010sr-03.pdf).

20.7: The number of centenarian men in 2010 for every 100 centenarian women. Source: Centenarians: 2010, Page 3 (www.census.gov/prod/cen2010/reports/c2010sr-03. pdf).

43.5 percent: The percentage of centenarian men who lived with others in a household in 2010, the most common living arrangement for this group. For their female counterparts, the most common living arrangement was residing in a nursing home (35.2 percent). Source: Centenarians: 2010, Figure 4 (www.census.gov/prod/cen2010/reports/ c2010sr-03.pdf).

3.3: The number of centenarians per 10,000 people in North Dakota in 2010. North Dakota was the only state with more than three centenarians per 10,000 people. Source: Centenarians: 2010, Table 2 (www.census.gov/prod/cen2010/reports/c2010sr-03.pdf).

C. Senior Citizens Services Act

State of Washington: Chapter 74.38 RCW

Sections

74.38.010 Legislative recognition—Public policy.
74.38.020 Definitions.
74.38.030 Administration of community-based services program—Area plans—Annual state plan—Determination of low-income eligible persons.
74.38.040 Scope and extent of community based services program.
74.38.050 Availability of services for persons other than those of low income—Utilization of volunteers and public assistance recipients—Private agencies—Well-adult clinics—Fee schedule, exceptions.
74.38.060 Expansion of federal programs authorized.
74.38.061 Expansion of federal programs authorized.
74.38.070 Reduced utility rates for low-income senior citizens and other low-income citizens.
74.38.900 Short title.

74.38.010

Legislative recognition—Public policy.

The legislature recognizes the need for the development and expansion of alternative services and forms of care for senior citizens. Such services should be designed to restore individuals to, or maintain them at, the level of independent living they are capable of attaining. These alternative services and forms of care should be designed to both complement the present forms of institutional care and create a system whereby appropriate services can be rendered according to the care needs of an individual. The provision of service should continue until the client is able to function independently, moves to an institution, moves from the state, dies, or withdraws from the program.

Therefore, it shall be the policy of this state to develop, expand, or maintain those programs which provide an alternative to institutional care when that form of care is premature, unnecessary, or inappropriate.

[1977 ex.s. c 321 § 1; 1975–'76 2nd ex.s. c 131 § 1.]

74.38.020

Definitions.

As used in this chapter, the following words and phrases shall have the following meaning unless the content clearly requires otherwise:

(1) "Area agency" means an agency, other than a state agency, designated by the department to carry out programs or services approved by the department in a designated geographical area of the state.

(2) "Area plan" means the document submitted annually by an area agency to the department for approval which sets forth (a) goals and measurable objectives, (b) review of past expenditures and accounting of revenue for the previous year, (c) estimated revenue and expenditures for the ensuing year, and (d) the planning, coordination, administration, social services, and evaluation activities to be undertaken to carry out the purposes of the Older Americans Act of 1965 (42 U.S.C. Sec. 3024 et seq.), as now or hereafter amended.

(3) "Department" means the department of social and health services.

(4) "Office" shall mean the office on aging which is the organizational unit within the department responsible for coordinating and administering aging problems.

(5) "Eligible persons" means senior citizens who are:

    (a) Sixty-five years of age or more; or

    (b) Sixty years of age or more and are either (i) nonemployed, or (ii) employed for twenty hours per week or less; and

    (c) In need of services to enable them to remain in their customary homes because of physical, mental, or other debilitating impairments.

(6) "Low income" means initial resources or subsequent income at or below forty percent of the state median income as promulgated by the secretary of the United States department of health, education and welfare for Title XX of the Social Security Act, or, in the alternative, a level determined by the department and approved by the legislature.

(7) "Income" shall have the same meaning as in chapter **74.04** RCW, as now or hereafter amended; except, that money received from RCW **74.38.060** shall be excluded from this definition.

(8) "Resource" shall have the same meaning as in chapter **74.04** RCW, as now or hereafter amended.

(9) "Need" shall have the same meaning as in chapter **74.04** RCW, as now or hereafter amended.

[**1989 1st ex.s. c 9 § 817; 1977 ex.s. c 321 § 2;** 1975-'76 2nd ex.s. c 131 § 2.]

NOTES:

    Effective date—Severability—1989 1st ex.s. c 9: See RCW **43.70.910** and **43.70.920.**

74.38.030

Administration of community-based services program—Area plans—Annual state plan—Determination of low-income eligible persons.

(1) The program of community-based services authorized under this chapter shall

be administered by the department. Such services may be provided by the department or through purchase of service contracts, vendor payments or direct client grants.

The department shall, under stipend or grant programs provided under RCW 74.38.060, utilize, to the maximum staffing level possible, eligible persons in its administration, supervision, and operation.

(2) The department shall be responsible for planning, coordination, monitoring and evaluation of services provided under this chapter but shall avoid duplication of services.

(3) The department may designate area agencies in cities of not less than twenty thousand population or in regional areas within the state. These agencies shall submit area plans, as required by the department. For area plans prepared for submission in 2009, and thereafter, the area agencies may include the findings and recommendations of area-wide planning initiatives that they may undertake with appropriate local and regional partners regarding the changing age demographics of their area and the implications of this demographic change for public policies and public services. They shall also submit, in the manner prescribed by the department, such other program or fiscal data as may be required.

(4) The department shall develop an annual state plan pursuant to the Older Americans Act of 1965, as now or hereafter amended. This plan shall include, but not be limited to:

(a) Area agencies' programs and services approved by the department;

(b) Other programs and services authorized by the department; and

(c) Coordination of all programs and services.

(5) The department shall establish rules and regulations for the determination of low-income eligible persons. Such determination shall be related to need based on the initial resources and subsequent income of the person entering into a program or service. This determination shall not prevent the eligible person from utilizing a program or service provided by the department or area agency. However, if the determination is that such eligible person is nonlow income, the provision of RCW 74.38.050 shall be applied as of the date of such determination.

[2008 c 146 § 5; 1975-'76 2nd ex.s. c 131 § 3.]

NOTES:

Findings—Intent—Severability—2008 c 146: See notes following RCW 74.41.040.

74.38.040

Scope and extent of community based services program.

The community based services for low-income eligible persons provided by the department or the respective area agencies may include:

(1) Access services designed to provide identification of eligible persons, assessment of individual needs, reference to the appropriate service, and follow-up service where required. These services shall include information and referral, outreach, transportation, and counseling;

(2) Day care offered on a regular, recurrent basis. General nursing, rehabilitation,

personal care, nutritional services, social casework, mental health as provided pursuant to chapter **71.24** RCW, and/or limited transportation services may be made available within this program;

(3) In-home care for persons, including basic health care; performance of various household tasks and other necessary chores, or, a combination of these services;

(4) Counseling on death for the terminally ill and care and attendance at the time of death; except, that this is not to include reimbursement for the use of life-sustaining mechanisms;

(5) Health services which will identify health needs and which are designed to avoid institutionalization; assist in securing admission to medical institutions or other health related facilities when required; and, assist in obtaining health services from public or private agencies or providers of health services. These services shall include health screening and evaluation, in-home services, health education, and such health appliances which will further the independence and well-being of the person;

(6) The provision of low-cost, nutritionally sound meals in central locations or in the person's home in the instance of incapacity. Also, supportive services may be provided in nutritional education, shopping assistance, diet counseling, and other services to sustain the nutritional well-being of these persons;

(7) The provisions of services to maintain a person's home in a state of adequate repair, insofar as is possible, for their safety and comfort. These services shall be limited, but may include housing counseling, minor repair and maintenance, and moving assistance when such repair will not attain standards of health and safety, as determined by the department;

(8) Civil legal services, as limited by RCW **2.50.100**, for counseling and representation in the areas of housing, consumer protection, public entitlements, property, and related fields of law;

(9) Long-term care ombuds programs for residents of all long-term care facilities.
[**2013 c 23 § 225; 1983 c 290 § 14; 1977 ex.s. c 321 § 3;** 1975–'76 2nd ex.s. c 131 § 4.]

74.38.050

Availability of services for persons other than those of low income—Utilization of volunteers and public assistance recipients—Private agencies—Well-adult clinics— Fee schedule, exceptions.

The services provided in RCW **74.38.040** may be provided to nonlow-income eligible persons: PROVIDED, That the department and the area agencies on aging shall utilize volunteer workers and public assistant recipients to the maximum extent possible to provide the services provided in RCW **74.38.040**: PROVIDED, FURTHER, That the department and the area agencies shall utilize the bid procedure pursuant to chapter **43.19** RCW for providing such services to low-income and nonlow-income persons whenever the services to be provided are available through private agencies at a cost savings to the department. The department shall establish a fee schedule based on the ability to pay and graduated to full recovery of the cost of the service provided; except, that nutritional services, health screening, services under the long-term care ombuds program under chapter **43.190** RCW, and access services provided in RCW **74.38.040** shall not be based on need and no fee shall be charged; except further, notwithstanding any other provision of this chapter, that well-adult clinic services may be provided in lieu of health screening services if such clinics use the fee schedule established by this section.

[2013 c 23 § 226; 1983 c 290 § 15; 1979 ex.s. c 147 § 1; 1977 ex.s. c 321 § 4; 1975–'76 2nd ex.s. c 131 § 5.]

NOTES:
Effective date—1979 ex.s. c 147: "This act is necessary for the immediate preservation of the public peace, health, and safety, the support of the state government and its existing public institutions, and shall take effect July 1, 1979." [1979 ex.s. c 147 § 4.]

74.38.060

Expansion of federal programs authorized.
The department may expand the foster grandparent, senior companion and retired senior volunteer programs funded under the Federal Volunteer Agency (ACTION) (P.L. 93–113 Title II), or its successor agency, which provide senior citizens with volunteer stipends, out-of-pocket expenses, or wages to perform services in the community.

[1975–'76 2nd ex.s. c 131 § 6.]

NOTES:
RSVP funding: RCW 43.63A.275.

74.38.061

Expansion of federal programs authorized.
The department may expand the foster grandparent, senior companion, and retired senior volunteer programs funded under the Federal Volunteer Agency (ACTION) (P.L. 93–113 Title II), or its successor agency, which provide senior citizens with volunteer stipends, out-of-pocket expenses, or wages to perform services in the community.

[1977 ex.s. c 321 § 5.]

74.38.070

Reduced utility rates for low-income senior citizens and other low-income citizens.
Notwithstanding any other provision of law, any county, city, town, public utility district or other municipal corporation, or quasi municipal corporation providing utility services may provide such services at reduced rates for low-income senior citizens or other low-income citizens: PROVIDED, That, for the purposes of this section, "low-income senior citizen" or "other low-income citizen" shall be defined by appropriate ordi-

nance or resolution adopted by the governing body of the county, city, town, public utility district or other municipal corporation, or quasi municipal corporation providing the utility services. Any reduction in rates granted in whatever manner to low-income senior citizens or other low-income citizens in one part of a service area shall be uniformly extended to low-income senior citizens or other low-income citizens in all other parts of the service area.

[2002 c 270 § 1; 1998 c 300 § 8; 1990 c 164 § 1; 1988 c 44 § 1; 1980 c 160 § 1; 1979 c 116 § 1.]

NOTES:
   Findings—Intent—1998 c 300: See RCW 19.29A.005.
   Construction—1998 c 300: See RCW 19.29A.900.

74.38.900

Short title.
Sections 1 through 6 of this act shall be known and may be cited as the "Senior Citizens Services Act."

[1975–'76 2nd ex.s. c 131 § 7.]

About the Contributors

Jean **Accius** is the vice president of the Long-Term Services & Supports and Livable Communities Group within the AARP Public Policy Institute.

Administration for Community Living is part of the U.S. Department of Health and Human Services and was created around the fundamental principle that older adults and people of all ages with disabilities should be able to live where they choose, with the people they choose, and with the ability to participate fully in their communities.

JoNel **Aleccia** is a senior correspondent focused on aging and end-of-life issues on the *Kaiser Health News* enterprise team.

Melissa **Bailey** is a contributing columnist with *Kaiser Health News*.

Susan **Bailey** is a professor of radiation cancer biology and oncology, Colorado State University.

Katherine **Barrett** is a senior advisor to the Pew Charitable Trusts' government performance unit, senior fellow with the Council of State Governments and fellow in the National Academy of Public Administration.

Flora G. **Becket** is a graduate of Golden Gate University's Executive Master of Public Administration Program.

Basia **Belza** is the Aljoya Endowed Professor of Aging, director of the de Tornyay Center for Healthy Aging, University of Washington.

Benefits.gov (formerly GovBenefits.gov) was one of the earliest "E-Government" initiatives to launch in 2002 as part of the President's Management Agenda and was established as the official benefits website of the U.S. government.

Willie Lee **Britt** is a distinguished adjunct professor of public administration at Golden Gate University, vice president of the Pilipino Senior Resource Center, and business manager of Makati Chiropractic Center, USA.

Stacy **Canan** is the assistant director for the Office for Older Americans, U.S. Consumer Financial Protection Bureau.

DeKalb County Office of Aging (OOA) is committed to providing exceptional resources and information to DeKalb County Seniors.

Nora Dowd **Eisenhower** is the assistant director for the Office of Older Americans at the U.S. Consumer Financial Protection Bureau.

Lynn Friss **Feinberg** is a senior strategic policy advisor for the AARP Public Policy Institute.

Brendan **Flinn** is a policy research senior analyst at AARP Public Policy Institute's LTSS & Livable Communities team.

Rachel L. **Fontenot**, a graduate of Golden Gate University's EMPA program, has worked in the field of aging for over 25 years and works for the State of California.

William G. **Gale** is the Arjay and Frances Miller Chair in Federal Economic Policy and a senior fellow in the Economic Studies Program at the Brookings Institution.

Megan **Gerhardt** is a professor of management, Farmer School of Business, Miami University.

Joaquin Jay **Gonzalez** III is Mayor George Christopher Professor of Public Administration at the Edward S. Ageno School of Business of Golden Gate University and president of the Pilipino Senior Resource Center of San Francisco, California.

Judith **Graham** is a *Kaiser Health News* contributing columnist.

Richard **Greene** is a senior advisor to the Pew Charitable Trusts' government performance unit, senior fellow with the Council of State Governments and fellow in the National Academy of Public Administration.

Shannon **Guzman** is a policy research senior analyst with the AARP Public Policy Institute.

Elisha **Harig-Blaine** is a manager for veterans and special needs, Center for City Solutions, National League of Cities.

Gail **Hillebrand** is the associate director, Consumer Education & Engagement, Consumer Financial Protection Bureau.

Bruce **Horovitz** is a free-lance journalist writing for the *New York Times*, *Washington Post*, AARP, and *Kaiser Health News*.

International City/County Management Association is the leading organization of local government professionals dedicated to creating and sustaining thriving communities throughout the world.

Irv **Katz** is a senior fellow, Generations United, Washington, D.C.

Jeanine R. **Kelada** is an analyst at Sutter Health, Sacramento California.

Roger L. **Kemp** is a distinguished adjunct professor of public administration at the Department of Public Administration of Golden Gate University.

Yueqing (Queenie) **Lin,** a 2019 graduate of the University of San Francisco, has volunteered with senior programs in Hawaii and California.

Mickey P. **McGee** is an associate professor of public administration at the Edward S. Ageno School of Business of Golden Gate University.

Medicare.gov is the official government website for Medicare, the U.S. national health insurance program.

Paul **Mico** was a private first class, 29th Infantry Division, U.S. Army on Omaha Beach on June 6, 1944, and was a doctor of public administration graduate of Golden Gate University.

Gabby V. **Moraleda** is the executive director, Pilipino Senior Resource Center, San Francisco, California.

National Institute on Aging is one of the 27 institutes and centers of the National Institutes of Health, leading scientific efforts to understand the nature of aging and to extend the healthy, active years of life.

Joshua **Odetunde** is the consulting director at Community Housing Market Support Network Inc., Louisville, Kentucky.

Sunday Akin **Olukoju** is the president of Canadian Center for Global Studies, a non-profit organization and teaches at Athabasca University in Alberta, Canada.

Stephanie **O'Neill** is an award-winning healthcare journalist with the National Public Radio/*Kaiser Health News* Collaboration.

Hector **Ortiz** is a policy analyst, U.S. Consumer Financial Protection Bureau.

Marcia G. **Ory** is a friend of the Conversation and Regents and a distinguished professor and associate vice president for Strategic Partnerships and Initiatives, Texas A&M University.

Norman A. **Paradis** is a professor of medicine, Dartmouth College.

Irina **Reykhel** earned a master's of public administration degree at Golden Gate University, San Francisco, California.

Carmen Heredia **Rodriguez** is a reporter for *Kaiser Health News*.

Alan R. **Roper** is a senior adjunct professor at Golden Gate University and instructional designer/curriculum developer for the University of California, Office of the President.

Claire M. **Rygg** is with the Colton Hall Museum in the City of Monterey and is a graduate of Golden Gate University's Executive Master of Public Administration Program.

Emily **Salomon** was formerly with the National Housing Conference.

Ruth Astle **Samas** is a retired State of California administrative law judge and senior adjunct professor of public administration at Golden Gate University.

Warren **Sanderson** is a professor of economics, Stony Brook University (The State University of New York).

San Francisco Human Services Agency promotes well-being and self-sufficiency among individuals, families and communities in San Francisco, including delivering a safety net of protective services and public benefits that are designed to meet the unique needs of low-income individuals, children and families, older adults, and adults with disabilities.

San Francisco Department of Aging and Adult Services is part of the San Francisco Human Services Agency and provides services for older adults, veterans, people with disabilities and their caregivers to maximize their safety, health, and independence.

Sergei **Scherbov** is the director of the International Laboratory of Demography and Human Capital, Russian Presidential Academy of National Economy and Public Administration.

Ellen **Schneider** is a research scientist, University of North Carolina at Chapel Hill.

Robert **Shapiro** is the assistant village manager/finance director, Village of Friendship Heights, Maryland.

Alison **Shelton** is a senior strategic policy advisor with the AARP Public Policy Institute Economics Team.

Tiffany **Shubert** is an adjunct assistant professor, public health, University of North Carolina at Chapel Hill.

Matthew Lee **Smith** is the co-director of the Texas A&M Center for Population Health and Aging, Texas A&M University.

Task Force on Research and Development for Technology to Support Aging Adults was established to examine the potential of technology to maximize the independence of aging Americans by increasing opportunities for social engagement and connectivity as well as reducing the impact of any cognitive and physical limitations.

Marisa **Taylor** is a senior correspondent at *Kaiser Health News*.

U.S. Census Bureau is a principal agency of the Federal Statistical System, responsible for producing data about the American people and economy.

U.S. Consumer Financial Protection Bureau is a government agency that makes sure banks, lenders, and other financial companies treat you fairly.

Andrew **Vaz** is a doctoral student in public policy and administration program at Walden University.

Janet **Viveiros** is a program and policy analyst at Nemours, Washington, D.C.

White House Conference on Aging brings together older Americans and their families, caregivers, and advocates at the White House every year to identify and advance actions to improve the quality of life of older Americans.

Jeffrey **Zimmerman** serves as the director of processing services within the North Carolina Division of Motor Vehicles.

Index

Administration for Community Living 57–62, 161–163
Administration on Aging (AoA) 13, 39, 53
Administration on Intelligence and Developmental Disabilities (AIDD) 161
adult and aging services 29–32
advertising, mortgage 196–197
advisory, consumer 196–197
Affordable Care Act 2, 45–50, 57, 66, 70, 150
Age Discrimination Act (ADA) 42
Age Friendly Cities and Communities Program (AFCCP) 146
Age-Friendly Initiative 169–171
ageism, hiring practices and 249–252
aging: and adult services 29–32; fighting it 111–113; and housing 144–151; in place 13–18; population and emerging technologies 242–248; population and social media 238–239, 240–241; population and state revenues 265–267, 268–270; and space flights 265–267, 268–270;tools 108–110; in the 21st century 108–110
Aging and Disability Resource Center (ADRC) 31
Aging in Place 144–145
Aging Services Network (ASN) 41
Aging with Dignity 8
Albert Einstein College of Medicine 113
Alliance on Aging 10, 11
Alzheimer's Disease 3, 96–98, 99–101
American Association of Retired Persons (AARP) 7, 9, 55, 70, 121, 145, 241
American Cancer Society (ACS) 27
American Geriatrics Society (AGS) 84
American Health Care Act 67, 68
American Health Care Association (AHCA) 85
American Home Care Association (AHCA) 259

American Medical Association (AMA) 45–46
American Planning Association (APA) 221
American Psychologist 127
Americans with Disabilities Act (ADA) 127, 165–166, 168, 172–174
Area Agencies on Aging (AAA) 10, 12, 82, 121
arts and healthy aging 234–237
Atlanta, Georgia 15, 21, 22, 25, 27
Atlanta Regional Commission (ARC) 15
Atlantic University 231

Behavioral & Social Sciences Librarian 127
Belichick Versus McVay 226–228
Bernard Osher Foundation 231
Boston, Massachusetts 54, 148
Boston University 230
brain disorder 99–101
Brigham Young University 136
Brown University 85
Budget Control Act (BCA) 11
Burlington, Wisconsin 260
bus services to dispensary 255–257

California Courts, senior housing and 172–179
Cambridge University 115
Canadian Journal of Aging 127
Canadian Medical Association (CMA) 126
Cape Canaveral, Florida 269
care, long-term 128–131
caregiving 120–143
Center for Innovative Care and Aging (CICA) 124
Centers for Disease Control and Prevention 263
Cherokee County, Georgia 27
Chicago, Illinois 116, 134, 196, 238
Children's Health Insurance Program (CHIP) 48
City and County of San Francisco, California 29–32, 63
Civil Service Retirement Act (CSRA) 41
Clayton County, Georgia 27

Cleveland, Ohio 54
Cobb County, Georgia 15, 27
Colorado State University 265–266
Colton Hall 164–168
Columbia University 135
Commission on Aging (COA) 42–44
Community Living Assistance Services and Support Program (CLASS) 131
Community Services Care Program (CSCP) 23
Congressional Budget Office 67
consumer advisory 196–197
Consumer Financial Protection Bureau (CFPB) 194–198
Contra Costa County, California 175–177
Cornell University 220
Council of State Governments (COSG) 271

Dallas, Texas 37, 133–134
dangerous events, senior citizens and 80–82
debt collections problems 198–199
debt, medical 194–195
Decatur, Georgia 21
DeKalb County, Georgia 2, 19–28
Department of Aging and Adult Services, San Francisco, California 29–32
Department of Treasury 2
Depression 1
Disaster Recovery for Older Americans (DROA) 51
dispensary, bus services to 255–257
Drug Enforcement Administration 254
drugs, prescription 111–113
Duke University 257

Eisner Foundation 219
Elder Justice Act 2, 57–62, 127
Elder Justice Innovation Grants Program (EJIGP) 57
elder orphans 132–134
elder scams 186–189

emerging technologies, senior citizens and 242–248
Empowerment of the Aging 33–38
end-of-life planning 87–95
European Society for Clinical Nutrition and Metabolism 78–79

Fair Housing Act (FHA) 147
Family Caregivers Act (FCA) 121
Farm and Rural Housing Program 42
Fearless Fallback Plan 132–134
Federal Caregiving Advisory Council (FCAC) 121
Federal Council on Aging (FCA) 41–42
Federal Financial Participation (FFP) 40
Federal Security Agency (FSA) 41
fighting aging 111–113
Financial Crimes Enforcement Network (FCEN) 186
Financial Review 117
Fort Worth, Texas 37
Fountain of Youth Pill 114–119
frail seniors 123–125
Friendship Heights, Maryland 249–252
Fromm Institute 231
Fulton County, Georgia 27

Galveston, Texas 79
Gerontological Society of America (GSA) 259
getting high, senior citizens 253–254
Golden Gate University 206, 224
Government Information Quarterly 127
Great Recession 149

Harvard University 114, 117–119, 159, 229
Health Aging Research Network (HARN) 102
Health and Wellness 63–101
healthy: aging 102–104; aging and the arts 234–237; homes 152–157
Heritage Foundation 50
hiring practices and senior citizens 249–252
hospitalization and recovery 83–86
Housing and Accommodations 144–179
housing: and accessibility 164–168; California Courts 172–179; by non-profit organizations 158–160; policies 144–151
Human Nutrition Research Center on Aging 77

immigrant veterans, World War II 208–214
immigrants, minorities and LGBTQ 200–217

inclusion and integration 161–163
independent living 123–125, 161–163
integration and inclusion 161–163
intergenerational issues 218–222, 223–225
Intergenerational Lifelong Learning and Technology 218–248
Internal Revenue Service (IRS) 189
International City/County Management Association (ICMA) 13–18, 169–171, 250–252
International Labor Organization (ILO) 109
International Space Station (ISS) 265–266
International Year of Older Persons (IYOP) 44
issues, intergenerational 218–222, 223–225

Japanese self-help programs 200–203
Johns Hopkins University 124–125

Kaiser Health News 112,258
Kansas City, Missouri 271

leadership and senior citizens 226–228
Lehigh University 262
lethal plans 258–264
Lexington, Kentucky 100
LGBTQ population 1–3, 31, 32, 215–217
life begins again at 65 7–9
life expectations 102–104
lifelong learning and senior citizens 229–233
Little Havana Activities 11
living independently 123–125, 161–163
loneliness in older adults 135–138, 139–143
long-term care 128–131; and suicide 258–264
Long-Term Care Ombudsman Program (LTCOP) 39
longevity 102–119
Los Angeles, California 196, 226

Marijuana Policy Project (MPP) 253–254
Marin County, California 205
Massachusetts Institute of Technology (MIT) 114, 119
mayor, housing issues 169–171
The McCarrran-Ferguson Act 66
McMaster University 78
McVay Versus Belichick 226–228
measuring 21st century aging 108–110
media, social 238–239, 240–241
Medicaid Programs, facts about 2, 23, 24, 25, 40, 49, 51, 54–55, 64–67, 70–73, 74–76, 83–84, 91, 124–125, 127

medical debt 194–195
Medicare Programs, facts about 7, 34, 35, 42, 44, 46, 49, 51–52, 64–67, 70–73, 74–76, 83–84, 91, 124–125, 127
Miami, Florida 10
Miami Gardens, Florida 10
Milwaukee, Wisconsin 260
Monterey, California 164–168
Montgomery County, Maryland 251
mortgage advertising 196–197

National Adult Maltreatment Reporting System (NAMRS) 57
National Aeronautics and Space Administration (NASA) 265–266, 268–279
National Affordable Housing Act (NAHA) 43
National Aging and Disability Transportation Center (NADTC) 41
National Center for Health Housing (NCHH) 152
National Conference of State Legislatures (NCSL) 272
National Conference on Aging (NCA) 41
National Council on Aging (NCA) 7, 127
National Endowment for the Arts (NEA) 236
National Family Caregiver Support Program (NFCSP) 44, 120–122
National Institute of Aging (NIA) 42, 89, 99–101, 112, 115, 123, 139–143, 234–237, 268–270
National Institute of Health (NIH) 99, 115, 232, 236
National Occurring Retirement Communities (NORC) 17
National Preservation Act (NPA) 168
National Primary Caregiver Support Program (NPCSP) 40
National Science and Technology Council (NSTC) 242–245
National Survey on Drug Use and Health (NSDUH) 253–254
National Violent Death Reporting System (NVDRS) 259
Nationality Act (NA) 210
Network of Age-Friendly Communities (NAFC) 145–146
New England 226–229
New Westminster, British Columbia, Canada 15
New York, New York 84, 134
New York University 253–254, 257
Non-Profit Sector Institutions (NPSI) 158–160
Norfolk, Virginia 69
Northwestern University 235
Nursing Home Reform Act (NHRA) 42

Obama Administration 66, 67
Office of Aging, DeKalb County, Georgia 19–28
Old Age Assistance 41
old age is getting younger 105–107
Old Age Survivors Insurance 41
older adults: and debt collection 198–199; and the LGBTQ population 214–217; and loneliness 135–138, 143–148; and protein 77–79; and San Francisco 251–217; and social media 238–239, 240–241
Older Americans Act (OAA) 2, 10, 11, 39–44, 54, 120–122, 127
Older Americans Month 3, 284–287
Orange County, California 255
Oxford University 115

PA Times 158
Patient Protection and Affordable Care Act (PPACA) 48, 130
PBS NewsHour 258
Pearl Harbor, Hawaii 209
Pennsylvania State University 220
Phoenix, Arizona 54
Pilipino Senior Resource Center 204–207
Pill, Fountain of Youth 114–119
planning, end-of-life 87–95
plans: lethal 258–264; retirement savings 190–193
policies, housing 144–151
population and new technologies, aging 242–248
Port Hueneme, California 113
Portland, Oregon 134, 221
practices and senior citizens, hiring 249–252
prescription drugs 111–113
problems, debt collection 198–199
protein and older adults 77–79
Public Policy Institute 70
Purdue University 78

Quality Home Care (QHC) 11
Queens, New York 111

Railroad Retirement Act (RRA) 41
recovery after hospitalization 83–86
Retirement Savings Plans 180–183
revenues and state services to seniors 271–272
Rutgers University 170

safe homes 152–157
Salt Lake City, Utah 45, 200
San Diego, California 134
San Francisco, California 152–156, 200–201, 204–208, 212, 215–217, 223, 234
San Francisco Bay Area 2, 37, 128–131
San Francisco Human Services Agency 215–217

San Jose, California 33, 34
Santa Ana, California 256
Santa Clara County, California 33, 37
Santa Clara Valley, California 33
Santa Cruz, California 148
scams, elder 186–189
Seattle, Washington 54, 134, 261
self-help programs, Japanese 200–203
senior citizen services: Alzheimer's Disease 96–98, 99–101; brain disorder 99–101; City and County of San Francisco, California 29–32; and dangerous events 80–82; DeKalb County, Georgia 19–28; elder scams 186–189; and emerging technologies 242–248; end-of-life planning 87–95; Fearless Fallback Plan 132–134; frail support services 123–125; health care 63–69; hospitalization and recovery 83–86; housing 158–160, 172–179; life expectations 102–104; lifelong learning 229–233; loneliness, understanding it 135–138, 139–143; long-term care 128–131; policies and programs in local California communities 33–38; senior citizens 51–53, 126–127; social isolation 139–143; Social Security 180–183, 184–185; and state revenues 271–272; suicide and long-term care 258–264
senior citizens: and getting high 253–254; and hiring practices 249–252; and leadership 226–228; and scams 186–189; services and state revenues 271–272; and social media 238–239, 240–241; and suicide 258–264
Senior Citizens Services Act 3, 288–294
Senior Resource Center, Pilipino 204–207
seniors and the U. S. Government 39–62
seniors helping seniors 126–127
silver tsunami 10–12
Smart Growth 13–18
social isolation 139–143
social media and senior citizens 238–239, 240–241
Social Security 2, 8, 34, 41–42, 44–45, 51–52, 75, 180–185, 191, 199, 271–272; and finance 180–199
solutions to housing problems 144–151
Southeastern University 231
space flights and aging 265–267, 268–270
Stanford University 125, 136
State Aging and Disability Resource Center (SADRC) 40
state revenues and senior services 271–272
Steamboat Springs, Colorado 263

study on senior getting high 253–254
suicide and senior citizens 258–264

Tampa, Florida 54
Task Force on Research and Development 242–248
Teaneck, New Jersey 169
technologies and senior citizens, emerging 242–248
Temple University 220
TRICARE 75

United Home Care (UHC) 11
United Hospital Fund (UHF) 8
U.S. Administration on Aging 126
U.S. Air Force 210
U.S. Army 209
U.S. Bureau of Labor Statistics 107
U.S. Census Bureau 271
U.S. Congress 209–210
U.S. Consumer Financial Protection Bureau 186–189
U.S. Department of Agriculture 52, 55
U.S. Department of Health and Human Services 44–45, 53, 121–122, 138–139, 161, 213
U.S. Department of Housing and Urban Development 55, 197
U.S. Department of Labor 53, 55
U.S. Department of State 69
U.S. Department of Treasury 51–52
U.S. Food and Drug Administration 98
U.S. Healthcare 45–50
U.S. House of Representatives 66
U.S. Housing Act 160
U.S. Navy 10, 209
U.S. Social Security Act 108–109
U.S. Supreme Court 66, 162
U.S. Veterans Administration 210
University of California, Los Angeles 140, 256
University of California, San Francisco 125, 137, 142, 206, 223, 230, 234
University of Illinois 116
University of Kentucky 100
University of Michigan 85, 115, 135, 258–259
University of Pennsylvania 83–84
University of Rochester 260
University of Texas 78–79, 230
University of Washington 112
University of Wisconsin 118
USA Today 8–9

Ventura County, California 175–176
Veterans Administration 24
Veterans Affairs Medical Center (VAMC) 11

Veterans Benefits Act (VBA) 214
veterans, World War II immigrants 208–214
Vietnam War 10

The Wall Street Journal 116
Washington, D.C. 52, 54–55, 57,

149, 196, 211–213, 236, 251, 255,
   257, 259
The Washington Post 249
Waukesha, Wisconsin 260
Wenatchee, Washington 263
White House Conference on
   Aging 2, 41–43, 54–56

World War II 33, 208–211, 214,
   261; immigrant veterans 208–
   214

www.ingramcontent.com/pod-product-compliance
Lightning Source LLC
Chambersburg PA
CBHW080549270326
41929CB00019B/3246